HARMLESS WRONGDOING

The MORAL LIMITS

VOLUME FOUR

NEW YORK OXFORD

of the CRIMINAL LAW

Harmless
Wrongdoing

JOEL FEINBERG

OXFORD UNIVERSITY PRESS   1988

Oxford University Press

Oxford New York Toronto
Delhi Bombay Calcutta Madras Karachi
Petaling Jaya Singapore Hong Kong Tokyo
Nairobi Dar es Salaam Cape Town
Melbourne Auckland

and associated companies in
Berlin Ibadan

Copyright © 1988 by Oxford University Press, Inc.

Published by Oxford University Press, Inc.,
200 Madison Avenue, New York, New York 10016

Oxford is a registered trademark of Oxford University Press

Library of Congress Cataloging-in-Publication Data
(Revised for vol. 4)
Feinberg, Joel, 1926–
The moral limits of the criminal law.
Includes bibliographies and indexes.
Contents: v. 1. Harm to others—v. 2. Offense to others—
v. 3. Harm to self—v. 4. Harmless wrongdoing.
1. Criminal law—Philosophy. 2. Criminal law—Moral and ethical aspects.
3. Crimes without victims. I. Title.
K5018.F44 1984   83-13431
ISBN 0-19-504253-0

9 8 7 6 5 4 3 2 1

Printed in the United States of America
on acid-free paper

For Betty one more time

About the Longer Work

Harmless Wrongdoing is the final volume in a four-volume work, *The Moral Limits of the Criminal Law*. The volumes have been published separately at short intervals, the later ones each containing a synopsis of the earlier ones. Volume one, *Harm to Others*, discusses the concept of harm, its relation to interests, wants, hurts, offenses, rights, and consent; hard cases for the application of the concept of harm, like "moral harm," "vicarious harm," and "posthumous harm"; the status of failures to prevent harms; and problems involved in assessing, comparing, and imputing harms. Volume two, *Offense to Others*, discusses the modes and meanings of "offense" as a state distinct from harm; offensive nuisances, profoundly offensive conduct (like mistreatment of dead bodies, desecration of sacred symbols, and the public brandishing of odious political emblems like swastikas and K.K.K. garments); pornography, obscenity, and "dirty words." Volume three, *Harm to Self*, discusses legal paternalism, the view that the state may legitimately deprive persons of their liberty "for their own good." In developing its argument, Volume three gives an analysis of personal autonomy, and considers the riddle of voluntary slavery, other irrevocable commitments, dangerous drugs, laws requiring protective helmets, the concepts of voluntariness and consent, the main families of "voluntariness-reducing factors"—coercion, defective belief, and incapacity—and finally the problem of appraising the voluntariness of death requests from depressed patients.

Synopsis of Volumes One, Two, and Three

The basic question of the longer work that Volume one introduces is a deceptively simple one: What sorts of conduct may the state rightly make criminal? Philosophers have attempted to answer this question by proposing what I call "liberty-limiting principles" (or equivalently, "coercion-legitimizing principles") which state that a given type of consideration is always a morally relevant reason in support of penal legislation even if other reasons may in the circumstances outweigh it. Each volume of *The Moral Limits of the Criminal Law* corresponds to a leading liberty-limiting principle (but see the longer list, with definitions, of ten such principles at the end of this synopsis). The principle that the need to prevent harm to persons other than the actor is always a morally relevant reason in support of proposed state coercion I call *the harm to others principle* ("the harm principle" for short). At least in that vague formulation it is accepted as valid by nearly all writers. Controversy arises when we consider whether it is the *only* valid liberty-limiting principle, as John Stuart Mill declared.

Three other coercion-legitimizing principles, in particular, have won widespread support. It has been held (but not always by the same person) that it is always a good and relevant reason in support of penal legislation that (1) it is necessary to prevent hurt or offense (as opposed to injury or harm) to others (*the offense principle*); (2) it is necessary to prevent harm to the very person it prohibits from acting, as opposed to "others" (*legal paternalism*); (3) it is necessary to prevent inherently immoral conduct whether or not such conduct is harmful or offensive to anyone (*legal moralism*). I defined "liberalism" in respect to the subject matter of this book as the view that the harm and offense principles, duly clarified and qualified, between them exhaust the class of morally relevant reasons for criminal prohibitions. ("Extreme liberalism" rejects the offense principle too, holding that only the harm principle states an acceptable reason.) I then candidly expressed my own liberal predilections.

The liberal program of this work is twofold. Volumes one and two propose interpretations and qualifications of the liberal liberty-limiting principles that are necessary if those two principles are to warrant our endorsement (assuming from the start that they do warrant endorsement). Assuming that the harm and offense principles are correct, we ask, how must those principles be understood? What are we to mean by the key terms "harm" and "offense," and how are these vague principles to be applied to the complex problems that actually arise in legislatures? Volumes one and two attempt to define, interpret, qualify, and buttress liberalism in such ways that in the end we can say that the refined product is what liberalism must be to have its strongest claim to plausibility, and to do this without departing *drastically* from the traditional usage of the liberal label or from the motivating spirit of past liberal writers, notably John Stuart Mill. The second part of the liberal program, to which Volumes three and four are devoted, is to argue against the non-liberal principles (especially paternalism and moralism) that many writers claim must supplement the liberal principles in any adequate theory.

Volume one then proceeds to ask what is the sense of "harm" in the harm principle as we shall understand it in this work. I distinguish at the outset a non-normative sense of "harm" as setback to interest, and a normative sense of "harm" as a *wrong*, that is a violation of a person's rights. Examples are given of rare "non-harmful wrongs," that is wrongs that do not set back the wronged party's interests, and more common "non-wrongful harms," that is setbacks to interest, like those to which the "harmed party" consented, that do not violate his rights. Neither of these will count as "harms" in the sense of the harm principle. Rather, that sense will represent the overlap of the other two senses, and apply only to setbacks of interests that are also wrongs, and only to wrongs that are also setbacks to interests. Chapters 1 and 2 are devoted to problems about harm that stem from its character as a setback to interest, while Chapter 3 discusses in more detail the features of harmful acts that stem from their character as violations of rights.

Chapter 2 discusses hard cases for the application of the concept of harm: Does it make sense to speak of "moral harm," "vicarious harm," "posthumous harm," or "prenatal harm"? First, can we harm a person by making him a worse person than he was before? Plato insisted that "moral harm" *is* harm (and severe harm) even when it does not set back interests. But our analysis of harm denies Platonism. A person does not necessarily become "worse off" when he becomes "worse"; he is "morally harmed" only if he had an anteced-ent interest in having a good character. Second, can we harm one person by harming another? This question I answer in the affirmative. *A* causes "vicari-ous harm" to *B* when *B* has an interest in *C*'s welfare or in *C*'s character, and *A* then directly harms or corrupts *C*. Third, can a person be harmed by his own death or by events that occur after his death? These questions raise extremely subtle problems that defy brief summary. My conclusion, how-ever, is that death can be a harm to the person who dies, in virtue of the interests he had ante-mortem that are totally and irrevocably defeated by his death. Posthumous harm too can occur, when a "surviving interest" of the deceased is thwarted after his death. The subject of a surviving interest, and of the harm or benefit that can accrue to it after a person's death, is the living person ante-mortem whose interest it was. Events after death do not retroac-tively produce effects at an earlier time (as this account may at first suggest), but their occurrence can lead us to revise our estimates of an earlier person's well-being, and correct the record before closing the book on his life.

As for prenatal harms, I argue that fetuses (even if they are not yet persons) can be harmed in the womb, but only on the assumption that they will eventually be born to suffer the harmful consequences of their prenatal in-juries. People can also be harmed by wrongful actions that occurred before they were even conceived, when the wrongdoer deliberately or negligently initiated a causal sequence that he might have known would injure a real person months or years later. I even conceded that in certain unusual circum-stances a person might be harmed by the act of being given birth when that was avoidable. I denied, however, that a person can be harmed by the very act of sexual congress that brings him into existence unless he is doomed thereby to be born in a handicapped condition so severe that he would be "better off dead." If a child was wrongfully conceived by parents who knew or ought to have known that he would be born in a handicapped condition less severe than *that*, then he cannot later complain that he was wronged, for the only alternative to the wrongful conception was for him never to have come into existence at all, and he would not have preferred that. If parents are to be legally punished for wrongfully bringing other persons into exis-tence in an initially handicapped condition, but one that is preferable to nonexistence, it will have to be under the principle of legal moralism. The harm principle won't stretch that far.

Another difficult analytic question, discussed in Chapter 4, is whether the harm principle will stretch to cover blamable failures to prevent harm. I consider the standard arguments in the common law tradition against so-called "bad samaritan statutes" that require persons to undertake "easy res-cues" under threat of legal punishment for failure to do so. I reject all of these arguments on the grounds either that they systematically confuse active aid with gratuitous benefit, or that they take far too seriously the problem of drawing a non-arbitrary line between reasonably easy and unreasonably difficult rescues. (Similar line-drawing problems exist throughout the law, and most have been found manageable.) I conclude then that requiring people to help prevent harms is sometimes as reasonable a legal policy as preventing people, by threat of punishment, from actively causing harms. The more difficult question is whether this conclusion marks a departure from the harm principle as previously defined. I argued that it does not, partly on the ground that omissions, under some circumstances, can themselves be the cause of harms. To defend *that* contention, I must rebut powerful arguments on the other side, and in the final section of Chapter 4 I attempt to do so.

The final two chapters (5 and 6) of Volume one attempt to formulate "mediating maxims" to guide the legislature in applying the harm principle to certain especially complicated kinds of factual situations. Its formulation, up to that point, is so vague that without further guidance there may be no way in principle to determine how it applies to merely minor harms, moderately probable harms, harms to some interests preventable only at the cost of harms to other interests irreconcilable with them, structured competitive harms, imitative harms, aggregative harms, accumulative harms, and so on. I argue for various supplementary criteria to govern the application of the harm principle to these difficult problems, thus giving its bare bones some normative flesh and blood. These supplementary guides take a variety of forms. Some are themselves independent moral principles or rules of fairness. Others apply rules of probability or risk assessment. Others are common-sense maxims such as the legal *de minimis* rule for minor harms. Others distinguish dimensions of interests to be used in comparing the relative "importance" of conflicting harms in interest-balancing, or for putting the "interest in liberty" itself on the scales. Others are practical rules of institutional regulation to avoid the extremes of blanket permission and blanket prohibition in the case of aggregative and accumulative harms. As a consequence of these and other mediating maxims, the harm principle begins to lose its character as a merely vacuous ideal, but it also loses all semblance of factual simplicity and normative neutrality.

Volume two opens with a discussion of the meaning of "offense." Like the word "harm," "offense" has both a general and a specifically normative sense, the former including in its reference any or all of a miscellany of disliked mental states, and the latter referring to those states only when caused by the wrongful (right-violating) conduct of others. Only the latter sense—wrongful offense—is intended in the offense principle. The question raised by Chapter 7 is whether there are any human experiences that are harmless in themselves yet so unpleasant that we can rightly demand legal protection from them even at a cost to other persons' liberties. The affirmative answer to this question, though not subject to proof, is supported by hypothetical examples ("A ride on the bus") of offensive conduct to which the reader is asked to imagine himself an unwilling witness.

Chapter 8 uses the model of nuisance law, borrowed mainly from the law of torts, to suggest how the offense principle should be mediated in its application to repugnant but harmless conduct. Inevitably, balancing tests must be devised for weighing the seriousness of the inconvenience caused to the offended party against the reasonableness of the offending party's conduct. The seriousness of the offensiveness must be determined by (1) the intensity and durability of the repugnance produced, and the extent to which repugnance could be anticipated to be the general reaction to the conduct that produced it; (2) the ease with which unwilling witnesses can avoid the offensive display; and (3) whether or not the witnesses have assumed the risk themselves of being offended. These factors must be weighed as a group against the reasonableness of the offending party's conduct as determined by (1) its personal importance to the actor himself and its social value generally; (2) the availability of alternative times and places where the conduct would cause less offense; and (3) the extent, if any, to which the offense is caused by spiteful motives. There is no simple formula for reading the balance when the reasonableness of conduct, as so measured, is weighed against the seriousness of the offense in its various dimensions. There are some easy cases that fall clearly under one or another standard in such a way as to leave no doubt how they must be decided. One cannot be *wrongly* offended by that to which one fully consents, for example, so the *Volenti* standard ("one cannot be wronged by that to which one consents") preempts all the rest when it clearly applies. In some cases, even though no one standard is preemptive, all the applicable standards pull together toward one inevitable decision. In genuinely hard cases, however, when standards conflict and none apply in a preemptive way, when for example a given kind of conduct is offensive to a moderate degree and only moderately unreasonable, there will be no automatic way of coming to a clearly correct decision, and no substitute for judgment.

Chapter 9 begins by acknowledging that nuisance law is an inadequate model for understanding what it calls "profound offenses." These mental states have a different felt "tone" from mere nuisances, best approximated by saying that they are deep, profound, shattering, or serious, and even when one does not perceive the offending conduct directly, one can be offended at the very idea of that sort of thing happening even in private. Moreover, profound offense offends because the conduct that occasions it is believed to be wrong; that conduct is not believed to be wrong simply and entirely

because it offends someone. Profound offenses are usually experienced, therefore, as entirely impersonal. The offended party does not think of *himself* as
the victim in unwitnessed flag defacings, corpse mutilations, or religious icon
desecrations, and he does not therefore feel aggrieved (wronged) on his own
behalf. Chapter 9 then continues by raising the famous "bare knowledge
problem" for liberalism. Can liberal principles support a criminal prohibition
of private (unwitnessed) and harmless conduct on the ground that some
persons need protection from the profound offense attendant on the bare
knowledge that such conduct is, or might be for all we know, occuring
somewhere behind drawn blinds? I concede that the offense principle mediated by the balancing tests does not give the liberal all the reassurance he
needs. I observe, however, that in the case of profound offense from unwitnessed acts it is not the offended party himself who needs "protection." His
grievance is not a personal one made in his own behalf. He feels outraged at
what he takes to be wrongful behavior, but is not himself wronged by it.
(This is part of what is meant by classifying his offense as "profound.") The
offensive conduct is wrongful *and* it is a cause of a severely offended mental
state. But that is not yet sufficient for it to be a "wrongful offense" in the
sense intended in a truly liberal offense principle. The offense-causing action
must be more than wrong; it must be *a wrong* to the offended party, in short a
violation of *his* rights. If his impersonal moral outrage is to be the ground for
legal coercion and punishment of the offending party, it must be by virtue of
the principle of legal moralism to which the liberal is adamantly opposed. It is
likely then that there is no argument open to a liberal that legitimizes punishing private harmless behavior in order to prevent bare-knowledge offense.

Chapter 10 turns to the concept to the obscene, a form of acute offensiveness which, unlike "profound offensiveness," is inseparable from direct perception. The chapter is devoted to the "judgmental sense" of "obscene," that
in which the word serves to express an adverse judgment on that to which it is
applied. Discussion of the two other primary senses of "obscene" is undertaken in the following chapters. (These two nonjudgmental senses of "obscene" are that in which it is simply a synonym of "pornographic," as in
prevailing American legal usage, and that in which it is a conventional label
for a certain class of impolite words.) To call something obscene in the
standard judgmental uses of that term is to condemn that thing as shockingly
vulgar or blatantly disgusting, for the word "obscene," like the word
"funny," is used to claim that a given response (in this case repugnance, in the
other amusement) is likely to be the general one and/or to endorse that
response as appropriate. The term "pornographic," on the other hand, is a
purely descriptive word referring to sexually explicit writing and pictures
designed entirely and plausibly to induce sexual excitement in the reader or

observer. To use the terms "obscene" and "pornographic" interchangeably then, as if they necessarily referred to precisely the same things, is to beg the essentially controversial question of whether any or all (or only) pornographic materials really are obscene.

Chapter 11, "Obscenity as Pornography," contrasts pornographic writing with literary and dramatic art, grudgingly acknowledges the possibility of pornographic pictorial art, poetry, and (with difficulty) program music, explains why sex (of all things) can be obscene, and then concludes in an extended examination of "the feminist case" against pornography. Unlike more traditional arguments against pornography, especially those enshrined in law, which tacitly appeal to legal moralism and moralistic paternalism, recent feminist arguments either make a plausible appeal to empirical data in applying the harm principle, or else invoke the offense principle, not in order to prevent mere "nuisances," but to prevent profound offense analogous to that caused to the Jews of Skokie by the American Nazis, or to the blacks in a town where the K.K.K. rallies. The two traditional legal categories involved in the harm-principle arguments are defamation and incitement (to rape). I find the defamation argument ("Pornography degrades women") defective. I treat the incitement argument with respect, leaving the door open to criminal prohibitions of pornography legitimized on liberal (harm principle) grounds should better empirical evidence accumulate, while expressing skepticism over simple causal explanations of male sexual violence. The argument from profound offense is the more interesting, and the closest to acceptability even on present evidence, but in the end I decline to endorse it because of subtle but telling differences between pornography and other models of profound offense relied upon in the argument. I conclude that "wherever a line is drawn between permission and prohibition, there will be cases close to the line on both sides of it."

Chapter 12 returns to more traditional ways of discussing the moral and legal status of pornography from the period before people thought of treating its more egregious forms primarily under the headings of affront and danger to women. In particular, a leading alternative to the liberal way of treating the problem is considered in detail, namely that which has prevailed in the American courts in so-called obscenity cases. After a thorough criticism of decisions from *Hicklin* to *Roth*, and from *Roth* to *Paris Adult Theatre*, the chapter concludes: "Where pornography is not a nuisance, and (we must now add) not a threat to the safety of women, it can be none of the state's proper business."

The final four chapters (13 to 16) deal with obscene language—the so-called "dirty words." The primary function of these words, I suggested, is simply to offend, but by virtue of that basic function, obscene words have a number of highly useful derivative functions that would make their disappearance from the language regrettable. These words have an immediate offensive impact almost entirely because they violate taboos against uttering certain sounds or writing certain marks. In defying the taboos against the very utterance of the proscribed sounds, we underline, emphasize, call attention to ourselves and what we are doing or saying, express disrespectful attitudes either toward the norms themselves, or toward our listeners or the subject of our discourse. That in turn enables us, depending on other contextual features, to achieve such derivative purposes as deep expression, counter-evocation, suppression of pain and conquest of fear, the disowning of assumed pieties, effective badinage, emphatic insult, challenge, provocation, and even the triggering of waggish or ribald laughter. The "paradox of obscenity" grows out of this assertion that the primary and immediate job of obscenities is to violate the general taboos against their own use. Looked at in a utilitarian light, it is as if the main point of having the taboos in the first place is to make their violation possible so that certain "derivative" purposes can be achieved. What seems paradoxical is that if we all understood the rationale of the rules in this way, then none of us would take them very seriously as independently grounded norms and their "magic" would disappear; they could no longer achieve their useful derivative purposes. In Chapter 15, "Obscene Words and Social Policy," I try to resolve, or at least soften, this paradox, in the course of arguing against those who would attempt to rid the language of obscene words either through encouraging the use of euphemism or through deliberate overuse. In Chapter 16, "Obscene Words and the Law," I distinguish among "bare utterance and instant offense," offensive nuisance, and harassment. Applying the standards of earlier chapters, I conclude that the offense principle, properly mediated, cannot justify the criminal prohibition of the bare utterance of obscenities in public places even when they are used intentionally to cause offense. Offensive nuisance through the constant bombardment of obscenities can properly be prohibited, but only when the words are used in such a way as to constitute harassment. This chapter concludes by endorsing a liberal case against the regulation of indecent language on radio and television, rejecting the majority arguments in *F.C.C. v. Pacifica Foundation*.

The main purposes of Volume two are to endorse the offense principle, to show why it is plausible to affirm that the prevention of harmless offenses is among the legitimate purposes of the criminal law, and to propose a set of mediating maxims and balancing tests for applying the offense principle to difficult social problems, while minimizing the possibility of its abuse.

Chapter 17 opens Volume three with a definition of legal paternalism, a liberty-limiting principle the liberal is bound to reject: "It is always a good and relevant (though not necessarily decisive) reason in support of a criminal prohibition that it will prevent harm (physical, psychological, or economic) to the actor himself." A distinction is then drawn between "hard paternalism," which justifies interference with self-regarding dangerous behavior even when it is wholly voluntary, and "soft paternalism," which but for prevailing custom we would call "soft anti-paternalism," which is, properly speaking, no kind of paternalism at all. The latter principle warrants state interference with dangerous self-regarding behavior when but only when that behavior is substantially nonvoluntary, or when temporary intervention is necessary to establish whether it is voluntary or not.

Presumptive cases can be made both for and against hard legal paternalism. In favor of the principle is the fact that there are many laws now on the books that *seem* to have hard paternalism as an essential part of their implicit ratio-nales, and that some of these, at least, seem to most of us to be sensible and legitimate restrictions. Moreover, if the reduction of harms to interest from *all* sources is the moral basis underlying the harm to others principle, why should it not have application as well to self-caused harm, which need be no less injurious for being self-caused? On the other side, one can argue that a consistent application of (hard) legal paternalism would lead to the creation of new crimes that call for general punishment of risk-takers, the enforcement of prudence, and interference with selfless saints and heroes. Moreover, all paternalistic interference is offensive morally because it invades the realm of personal autonomy where each competent, responsible, adult human being should reign supreme. The most promising antipaternalist strategy would be to construct a convincing conception of personal autonomy that can explain how that notion is a moral trump card, and then to consider the most impres-sive examples of apparently reasonable paternalistic legislation, and argue, case by case, either that they are not reasonable or that they are not (hard) paternalistic. The latter project led me to defend "soft paternalism" as an alternative, essentially liberal, rationale for what seems reasonable in appar-ently paternalistic restrictions.

Chapter 18 offers a comprehensive analysis of the concept of autonomy in its senses of capacity for self-government, *de facto* condition of self-government, an ideal of character associated with that condition, and most importantly, *de jure* self-government interpreted on the analogy to a political state, as sovereign authority to govern oneself that is absolute within one's own moral boundaries. Chapter 19 then addresses the question of how the moral boundaries of per-sonal sovereignty are to be drawn. Legal paternalism, I argue, provides an inadequate conception of those boundaries, or at least one that is demeaning to personal sovereignty, in that it subordinates a person's *right* of self-determination to the person's own *good*. Whether an autonomous person's liberty is intefered with in the name of his own good, his health, his wealth, or even his future open options (his liberty)—which are themselves constituents of his well-being—it is still a violation of his personal sovereignty. How then can the state justify its ban on such obviously unacceptable arrangements as "voluntary slavery"? True respect for autonomy, interpreted as personal sovereignty, would permit unlimited forfeitures of life, liberty, and *pace* Mill, even of autonomy itself, provided only that they are fully voluntary. Why then refuse to enforce slavery contracts? One line of liberal argument is that for total and irrevocable transactions even of a wholly self-regarding kind, the highest standards for testing voluntariness are required, and these would necessitate the use of cumbersome and highly fallible tests. Given the uncertain quality of evidence on these matters, and (in the case of slavery) the strong general presumption of nonvoluntariness, the state might be justified in presuming nonvoluntariness conclusively in every case as the least risky course. Other rationales for the anti-slavery policy are also open to the soft paternalist, including the "public charge" argument, which employs only the harm to others principle in arguing that third parties need protection when they are forced either to attempt to liberate unwilling slaves at great cost or turn their backs on intolerable misery.

Chapter 20, "Voluntariness and Assumptions of Risk," undertakes a more thorough development and illustration of the soft paternalist strategy. It attempts to show that there is a rationale for protective interference with some self-endangering risk-taking that gives decisive significance, after all, to respect for *de jure* autonomy. In these cases, the reasonableness of the restriction consists in the protection it provides the actor from dangerous choices that are not truly his own. The strategy makes critical use of the concept of a voluntary choice, which is such a difficult notion that in effect the remainder of the book is devoted to its elucidation and application to a great variety of legislative problems. I treat voluntariness as a "variable concept," determined by varying standards depending on the nature of the circumstances, the interests at stake, and the moral or legal purposes to be served. The political/legal purpose to which primary attention is paid in this book, that of determining when self-regarding dangerous choices are "voluntary enough" to be immune from restriction, is only one of many such purposes, all of which require us to decide when partially voluntary behavior is "voluntary enough," e.g. voluntary enough for a criminal to be punished, for a will to be valid, for consent to be effective, and so on.

The remainder of *Harm to Self* is absorbed with the various riddles of voluntariness, both as part of its soft paternalist strategy and as a means to understand the concept generally. It examines the various "voluntariness-reducing factors"—coercion (Chapters 23, 24), mistake (Chapter 25), and incapacity (Chapter 26), as these apply both to the single-party case (Chapter 21) and to two-party cases involving "consent or its counterfeits" in Chapters 23–27. (The analysis of consent is undertaken in Chapter 22).

Chapter 27, "The Choice of Death," examines from a special perspective the problem of voluntary euthanasia. In particular it considers the effects on voluntariness of "understandable depression," and concludes that depression need not vitiate the voluntariness even of a choice of death, provided certain other conditions are met, and that only a kind of defective reasoning—the "catch 22 arguments"—can seem to show the contrary. On the larger question of the moral permissibility of active euthanasia generally, after considering the role of living wills and durable power of attorney, the chapter concludes that the only possible reason for maintaining the present absolute prohibition is that it is necessary to prevent mistakes and abuse. If there is no such necessity then there is no morally respectable reason to interfere with the liberty of an autonomous person to dispose of his own lot in life, even if his choice is for death.

Definitions of Liberty-limiting Principles

1. *The Harm Principle:* It is always a good reason in support of penal legislation that it would be effective in preventing (eliminating, reducing) harm to persons other than the actor (the one prohibited from acting) *and* there is no other means that is equally effective at no greater cost to other values.*

2. *The Offense Principle:* It is always a good reason in support of a proposed criminal prohibition that it is necessary to prevent serious offense to persons other than the actor and would be an effective means to that end if enacted.†

3. *The Liberal Position* (on the moral limits of the criminal law): The harm and offense principles, duly clarified and qualified, between them exhaust the class of good reasons for criminal prohibitions. ("The extreme liberal position" is that only the harm principle states a good reason . . .)

4. *Legal Paternalism* (a view excluded by the liberal position): It is always a good reason in support of a prohibition that it is necessary to prevent harm (physical, psychological, or economic) to the actor himself.

5. *Legal Moralism* (in the usual narrow sense): It can be morally legitimate to

---

*The clause following "and" is abbreviated in the subsequent definitions as "it is necessary for . . . ," or "the need to . . ." Note also that part of a conjunctive reason ("effective *and* necessary") is itself a "reason," that is, itself has some relevance in support of the legislation.

†The clause following "and" goes without saying in the subsequent definitions, but it is understood. All the definitions have a common form: X is necessary to achieve Y (as spelled out in definition 1) and is an effective means for producing Y (as stated explicitly in definitions 1 and 2).

prohibit conduct on the ground that it is inherently immoral, even though it causes neither harm nor offense to the actor or to others.*

6. *Moralistic Legal Paternalism* (where paternalism and moralism overlap *via* the dubious notion of a "moral harm"): It is always a good reason in support of a proposed prohibition that it is necessary to prevent *moral harm* (as opposed to physical, psychological, or economic harm) to the actor himself. (Moral harm is "harm to one's character," "becoming a worse person," as opposed to harm to one's body, psyche, or purse.)

7. *Legal Moralism* (in the broad sense): It can be morally legitimate for the state to prohibit certain types of action that cause neither harm nor offense to anyone, on the grounds that such actions constitute or cause evils of other ("free-floating") kinds.*

8. *The Benefit-to-Others Principle:* It is always a morally relevant reason in support of a proposed prohibition that it is necessary for the production of some *benefit* for persons other than the person who is prohibited.

9. *Benefit-Conferring Legal Paternalism:* It is always a morally relevant reason in support of a criminal prohibition that it is necessary to *benefit* the very person who is prohibited.

10. *Perfectionism* (Moral Benefit Theories): It is always a good reason in support of a proposed prohibition that it is necessary for the improvement (elevation, perfection) of the character—
    a. of citizens generally, or certain citizens other than the person whose liberty is limited (*The Moralistic Benefit-to-Others Principle*), or
    b. of the very person whose liberty is limited (*Moralistic Benefit-Conferring Legal Paternalism*).

Principles 8, 9, and 10b are the strong analogues of the harm principle, legal paternalism, and moralistic legal paternalism, respectively, that result when "production of benefit" is substituted for "prevention of harm."

*This definition will be revised on p. 324 *infra.*

Acknowledgments

Various parts of this volume, from small passages to the major sections of whole chapters, have already been published in independent articles. I am grateful to the publishers for permission to republish these copyrighted materials here. Sections 6 and 7 of Chapter 28 and section 1 of Chapter 29 incorporate parts of my article "Legal Moralism and Free-floating Evils," *Pacific Philosophical Quarterly*, vol. 61, nos. 1&2 (1980), pp. 130–163. This article was reprinted in *The Philosopher's Annual*, vol. 4 (Ridgeview Publishing Co., 1981). Section 8 of Chapter 28 is from my "Wrongful Life and the Counterfactual Element in Harming," *Social Philosophy and Policy*, vol. 4 (1986), pp. 145–178. (This article, incidentally, makes a substantial improvement in the analysis of harm in Vol. I, Chap. 1 of *Harm to Others*, and in the treatment of "Birth and Prenatal Harms" in Chap. 2, §8 of *Harm to Others*.) Chapter 29 expands my earlier paper, "Protecting a Way of Life," in *Absolute Values and the Search for the Peace of Mankind*, Vol. I (New York: The International Cultural Foundations Press, 1981), pp. 185–201. The major portion of Chapter 29A was published as "Liberalism, Community, and Tradition" in the proceedings of the Kyoto American Studies Summer Seminar, Specialists' Conference, Kyoto, Japan, 1987, pp. 165–229. An abridged version of that paper appeared in *Tikkun*, May/June, 1988. (Chapter 29A was an afterthought in my plan for this volume which had to be numbered in this special fashion to preserve the correctness of prior references to later chapters already printed in the earlier volumes. This chapter can be considered an "appendix" to Chapter 29.) Sections 5–7 of Chapter 30 were published as

"Some Unswept Debris from the Hart-Devlin Debate" in *Synthese*, August 1987, pp. 249–275. Chapter 31 is a revision of my article "Noncoercive Exploitation," originally published in *Paternalism*, edited by Rolf Sartorius (Minneapolis: University of Minnesota Press, 1983), pp. 201–235. Sections 5 and 6 of Chapter 32 were presented to the Twelfth International Wittgenstein Symposium, August 9, 1987, in Kirchberg am Wechsel, Austria, and published both in the official proceedings of that conference and in the journal *Ratio Juris*, vol. I (1988), under the title "The Paradox of Blackmail."

The manuscript for this volume profited greatly from detailed critical discussions in my graduate seminar in the philosophy of law at the University of Arizona in 1986. I am grateful to all of the talented students in that class for their contributions, but I must single out for special acknowledgement David Gill and Tom Senor whose comments actually led me to make last minute changes in the manuscript. Others whose comments have substantially influenced my writing of this volume include Keith Burgess-Jackson, Robert Schopp, and Eugene Schlossberger. Most of all I want to thank Allan Buchanan who has given me valuable philosophical criticism and support throughout the period of final preparation of the four volumes. My thanks are due also to Lois Day who typed the manuscripts for the second, third, and fourth volumes. She showed me that if there is anything better than a good word processor, it is a good secretary with a good word processor. The help of my wife, Betty Feinberg, with the proofreading for all four volumes was invaluable. She examined every letter of every word in over 1400 pages while I read aloud from the typescript. Susan Meigs of Oxford University Press did an exceptionally helpful job of copy editing Volumes two through four, and prevented the manuscript from being even wordier than it now is. Finally, I must mention Professor Josiah Carberry, word of whose death has just reached me. *De mortuis nil nisi bonum*. On his behalf it must be said, in all fairness, that his actions were rarely as bad as his intentions.

Contents

Explanation of the Title
and Caution to the Reader

In order to understand the title of this volume and the subject matter to which it calls attention, the reader must understand the special way in which the treacherous word "harm" has been used throughout this four-volume work. Chapter 1 of Volume one acknowledged that the word "harm" is both vague and ambiguous, and entangled with other concepts, like "wrong," in ordinary usage. In the first place there is the common ordinary sense in which to harm a person is to set back or otherwise adversely affect his interest. The harm a person suffers in this sense is precisely the state of adversely affected interest caused by the other party. Whether we are using the verb "to harm" or the noun "a harm" in the present sense, then, we are referring to a way in which actions or omissions have an impact on interests. There is also a closely related broader sense of "harm" in which that word refers to *any* state of adversely affected interest, whatever its cause. In that broader sense, people are often harmed by microbes, unforeseeable eruptions of nature, innocent actions of other persons, and actions of other persons to which they have freely consented. These are all examples of nonwrongful setbacks to, or adverse effects on, interest which we might naturally describe as "harms that are not wrongs" to the one who suffers them.

When we use the word "harm" in the ways summarized in the preceding paragraph, as we often do, we could, for purposes of clarity, attach the subscript numeral 1 to it, and say, for example, "*B* suffered a harm$_1$ that was not a wrong," or "*A* (innocently) harmed$_1$ *B* but did not wrong him," or "*A* harmed$_1$ *B* and in so doing wronged *B* as well." In all such examples, a harm$_1$

is a state of adversely affected interest whatever its cause, and even when the cause is another's action or omission, we determine whether a harm$_1$ has occurred, not by examining the action for some further identifying marks, but by looking exclusively at the affected interest.

In Chapter 1 of Volume one, I described the concept of a suffered wrong, or violated right, as another "sense of harm," but perhaps there has already been too great a proliferation of senses, and it would better serve clarity if we simply contrasted the first (interest-connected) sense of "harm" with the distinct but often intertwined concept of a wrong. Very frequently harms$_1$ inflicted by one person upon another are also wrongs to the person who suffers them; they are inflicted without justification or excuse, and they violate the other party's rights. Thus, they both harm$_1$ and wrong him. But there are many "wrongless harms$_1$" too, as for example when A harms$_1$ B by doing something to which B consented, or when B freely assumed the risk of being harmed$_1$, or when the harm$_1$ occurred in a fair competition. B cannot complain in these cases that his rights have been violated, but the harm$_1$ to his interests is real enough.

There are also examples, though less common ones, of wrongs that are not harms$_1$, or, to use the verbal forms, of a person being wronged without being harmed$_1$, that is without having his interests affected adversely. Perhaps a wrongly broken promise that redounds by a fluke to the promisee's advantage is one kind of example. Trespassing on another's land (a violation of his property right) while actually improving his property (advancing his interests) may be another. (See Vol. I, Chap. 1, pp. 34–36.)

There are two ways in which an action can be morally wrongful. On the one hand, we might say that A did the wrong thing, or that what he did was wrong, precisely because in doing it he wronged B (violated B's rights). In this case, we can say that B is A's *victim*. On the other hand, we may be inclined to condemn A's action as wrong even though we admit that it had no wronged victim. It *may* be wrong (though this is controversial among moral philosophers) for some reason other than that it wronged anyone. Again examples are difficult to construct, but some might claim that discreet homosexual behavior between fully consenting adults is wrong because it disobeys a biblical injunction, yet not such that anyone can complain that his rights have been violated by it. In any case, if the morally illicit act in question does not adversely affect anyone's *interests*, then (assuming it is wrong anyway, for whatever reason) it would be an example of *harmless$_1$ wrongdoing*. If, furthermore, it is wrong without wronging any victim, then it is both harmless$_1$ and (how shall we say it?) nonwronging wrongdoing.

Throughout this volume I have also used the word "harm" in a special technical sense—the sense it must bear, I have assumed, in the formulation of the harm principle if that principle is to have any plausibility. This second sense of "harming," to which we can attach the subscript 2, is the overlap of harming₁ and wronging (one particular way of acting wrongly). A harms₂ B in this second sense when he both harms₁ him *and* in so doing also wrongs him. Thus harming₂ includes all harming₁ that is also wronging, and all wronging that is also harming₁. More precisely,

"A harms₁ B" means "A adversely affects B's interest."

"A harms₂ B" means "A adversely affects B's interest and in so doing wrongs B (violates B's right)."

Thus there are two ways in which an act can be an instance of harmless wrongdoing. It can be a wrongful act that adversely affects no one else's interest, or it can be a wrongful act that does adversely affect the interest of another person but does so without wronging that person, for example because of the latter's prior consent to the risk.

I should also point out two further terminological consequences of these definitions. First, there can be wrongless harmdoing₁, but there cannot be wrongless harmdoing₂, for if an act does not wrong another, it cannot be a case of harmdoing₂, but is at most harmdoing₁. Second, corresponding to the technical term harm₂ is a special sense of "victim" designed to go exclusively with it. In this sense B is A's victim if and only if A harms₂ him, that is, both sets back his interests and wrongs him.

In this volume, as in the others, I will not use subscripts to distinguish the contrasting senses of "harm," "harming," "harmless," and "harmdoing." Instead, I shall continue to rely on the context to indicate the sense intended and, where the context is ambiguous, to explicitly stipulate the sense I intend. Throughout I shall invite the reader to consider the main questions of this volume: whether the state can rightfully criminalize on the ground of its moral wrongfulness conduct that harms₁ no one, or, if it does harm₁ others, does so without wronging them, that is without harming₂ them.

HARMLESS WRONGDOING

28

Legal Moralism and Non-grievance Evils

1. Broad and narrow (strict) conceptions of legal moralism

In restricting the list of valid liberty-limiting principles to the harm and offense principles, liberalism, as we have seen, denies that the need to protect a free, informed, and competent actor from the harmful consequences of his own voluntary conduct is ever a good reason for restricting his liberty. That is to say that "liberalism," as I am using the term, rejects the legitimizing principle called "legal paternalism." But the liberal view also denies that the need and opportunity to prevent any class of evils other than harms and offenses can ever be a good reason for criminal prohibitions. An alternative to the liberal view, then, can be put in the following very general way: "It can be morally legitimate for the state, by means of the criminal law, to prohibit certain types of action that cause neither harm nor offense to anyone, on the grounds that such actions constitute or cause evils of other kinds." This straightforward but vague denial of liberalism we can call "legal moralism in the broad sense."

Conceived in this broad way, legal moralism permits any of a large miscellany of reasons having no reference to harm or offense to anyone to have relevance and cogency in support of criminal legislation. The reasons most commonly advanced, however, are the need (1) to preserve a traditional way of life, (2) to enforce morality, (3) to prevent wrongful gain, and (4) to elevate or perfect human character. All these reasons are said to have weight even in

the absence of threats to interest or sensibility of the kind required by the
harm and offense principles.

More commonly, "legal moralism" is defined in a much narrower way,
referring only to one subclass of the larger genus of impersonal reasons
accepted by legal moralism in the broad sense, namely the enforcement of
morality. According to this narrower principle, which we can call "legal
moralism in the strict sense" the class of evils other than harms and offenses
that can warrant preventive interference by the state are those "immoralities"
or "sins" that can be committed not only in publicly harmful and offensive
ways, but also discreetly by consenting and hence unharmed parties, in
private or before consenting (hence unharmed and unoffended) audiences. "It
can be morally legitimate," according to legal moralism in this strict and
narrow sense, "to prohibit conduct on the ground that it is inherently immoral, even though it causes neither harm nor offense to the actor or to
others." Harmless and inoffensive (indeed unobserved) actions that are nevertheless immoral (if there be such) would be a subclass of the wider genus of
acts that produce certain "evils" other than harms and offenses. I will try to
show that this wider class of impersonal or free-floating evils contains a
variety of specimens (drastic social change, consented-to exploitation, and
degraded taste are only the more obvious examples), some of which, at least,
are as theoretically interesting and important as the "harmless immoralities"
themselves. For that reason, unless otherwise specified (mainly in Chapter
30), I shall be referring to the broader conception when I use the phrase "legal
moralism" throughout this discussion.

How might a liberal argue against legal moralism? Most liberals are content
to put legal moralism on the defensive.[1] That is, they examine the writings of
philosophers in the other camp to find out what arguments they give for legal
moralism and then find flaws in those arguments. That of course does not
prove the liberal's case, but the liberal can say that the burden of proof is on
the shoulders of whoever advocates legal coercion. The notion of a "burden of
proof," however, is a vague idea when employed outside rule-governed foren-
sic contests, debates, trials, and the like. Outside of such contexts, the expression usually suggests only that there exists a set of "background considerations" that tend to support, or are reasons in favor of, or make a case for, one
side or the other, not a case that is known in advance to be conclusive, but
rather one that is in principle rebuttable. After a certain number of unsuccess-
ful efforts at rebuttal we can think of the presumptive case as greatly strengthened, and even tentatively endorse it as correct until or unless it is overturned. So when we agree that a burden of proof is on he who advocates legal
prohibition we are probably making reference to the standing *prima facie* case

for liberty. That a given law would diminish liberty is a reason against having the law.

But maybe there is a similar, equally plausible, presumptive case on the other side. That would shift the burden the other way without of course settling the matter conclusively one way or the other. (All of this is like deciding what score a "handicapped" baseball game is to have at the moment it begins, as well as which team is to bat first.) What would such a case look like? Let me suggest that it would take as its general principle that it is always right, other things being equal, to prevent evils; that the need to prevent evils of any description is a good kind of reason in support of a legal prohibition. That appears at first sight to be as plausible a principle as that which makes the need to prevent one particular kind of evil, namely the loss of liberty, a presumptively good reason against legal coercion. If we then add to the legal moralist's case the proposition that there are kinds of evils that are neither harms in themselves nor the causes of harm or offense, his presumptive case is complete, and "the score of the game before it starts" is even, unless or until it can be shown that one of the conflicting presumptive cases is a great deal stronger than the other.

In conceding, however grudgingly, that there is a standing presumptive case for moralistic legislation, the liberal abandons his opposition to legal moralism as we have defined it in these volumes. If legal moralism is the principle that it is always a *relevant reason* of at least minimal cogency in support of penal legislation that it will prevent genuine evils other than harm and offense, *and* if the prevention of evils, any evils at all, is a point in favor of any course of action however preponderant the reasons against it, then it follows logically that legal moralism so defined is correct. Although the word "evil" is vague, it seems plausible to claim that it is better that evils not exist; that their existence is always to be regretted; and that their eradication and prevention are always reasons for action. Even the liberal, then, must acknowledge that legal moralism is, in principle, a valid liberty-limiting principle. What then is left of the liberal position? I think the liberal can salvage almost everything he originally meant to protect by insisting that while the prevention of evils as such is a reason, nevertheless as reasons go it is not much of one, typically putting only a modest weight on the balancing scales, rarely if ever enough to offset the presumptive case for liberty. The liberal then will have to argue this afresh for each main category of nonharmful evils posited by the moralist, and he must be prepared to admit that some of the moralist's evils may be weightier than others, even though few of them amount to very much as reasons for coercion. Many liberals will deny that there are any genuine evils at all other than harm and offense, but these liberals, if they follow the tack I suggest, will insist that even if there are (or were) such evils, they would have very little weight, as a class, when compared with harms and (even) offenses. In specific cases of proposed legislation then, liberals, despite their grudging concession, can nearly always oppose moralistic statutes.

To the reader who has followed the argument from personal sovereignty in Volume three, however, it will understandably appear that I grant a concession here to legal moralism that I have arbitrarily withheld from legal paternalism. After all, voluntarily consented-to risks that result in injury to the risk-taker, while not causes of harm in the strict sense employed by the harm principle (since in virtue of the consent they do not *wrong* those who suffer them), nevertheless cause serious setbacks to interests, and those setbacks may themselves be thought of as evils even though they are not right-violating harms. Why not say then that the prevention of these "welfare-connected non-grievance evils" (see §8 below), is also always a relevant reason, though a relatively slight one, for criminal prohibitions? Then we would be obliged to acknowledge that legal paternalism also becomes true by definition, even though paternalistic reasons are rarely, if ever, weighty enough to legitimize penal legislation. That would be to restore a kind of parity to the two nonliberal liberty-limiting principles, and thus to treat similar principles in similar ways. That would not be *much* of a concession to paternalism after all, if we adhere to our liberal resolution that paternalistic reasons can *never* outweigh personal sovereignty when the two are clearly and entirely in conflict, and it would be only in a trivial sense that legal paternalism (like legal moralism) is conceded to be "true."

There may, nonetheless, be a point in distinguishing between legal moralism and legal paternalism in the present respect, though it need not be insisted upon here. In the case in which paternalistic interference is ruled out by liberal principles, the voluntarily risked injury, when or if it comes about, is treated by the liberal *as if* it were no evil at all. That is because as an evil it would have to be weighed against personal sovereignty on the other side of the scale, and in comparison to the absolute trumping effect of sovereignty, it would have no "weight" at all. Actually, sovereignty is not the kind of value that *can* be "weighed" against particular evils on a common scale. (See Vol. III, pp. 93–94.) Its "weight" in such a comparison would always tip the balance its way. In particular, no set of dangers to the actor himself could outweigh his right to determine his own lot within the proper boundaries of his sovereign domain.

But isn't sovereignty equally violated by state interference when the evils to be prevented are nonharmful ones from the legal moralist's miscellaneous list? Do we not invade an individual's personal sovereignty when we restrict her liberty in order to prevent the gradual erosion of a traditional way of life, for example, or to prevent her from harmlessly violating a taboo, or committing some other harmless infraction of morality (if there are such things)? (See below, §§7 and 8.) The problem is that there is no way of determining whether the production of these evils falls within or without the boundaries of a person's sovereignty so long as our sole determinant of those boundaries is the vague distinction between self- and other-regarding activity. When A's act threatens harm to B it is clearly "other-regarding," and when it threatens to set back A's own interest it is clearly "self-regarding." When it endangers the interests both of A and B, then it is both self- and other-regarding. But what are we to say when it threatens *no one's* interests but does seem likely to produce an evil of a genuine but impersonal kind? Two interpretations seem possible. We might say that whatever voluntary actions do not directly affect (harm) the interests or sensibilities of other people are within the actor's own self-regarding sphere by definition, and hence squarely within his inviolable sovereign domain. In that case the various "harmless evils" that trouble the legal moralists are protected by the actor's sovereignty just as his "harms to self" are, and thus harmless evils are "as if weightless" on the scales when balanced against sovereignty. We need not concede, in that case, that moralistic considerations, any more than paternalistic ones, are ever reasons in support of criminal prohibitions. That would restore parity between the two nonliberal principles and make it possible for the liberal completely to reject them both after all.

There is, on the other hand, a second way of interpreting the self- and other-regarding distinction. We might say that voluntary actions that directly harm neither the interests of other parties nor the interests of the actor, but instead produce some intermediate evil that harms no one, are *not* within the actor's exclusively self-regarding zone (and not within anyone else's either). On that second interpretation, such actions are not protected by the actor's sovereignty, and the fact that they produce nonharmful evils *can* be treated as a reason (of a relatively slight kind) for criminalization. On this view it demeans a sovereign person when he is told that he must be coerced from acting as he chooses "for his own good," but not when he is told that he may be interfered with to prevent the production of a harmless evil. "My own good," he might say, "is my own business except insofar as it directly affects the interests of others. But what is 'inherently immoral' is not uniquely *my* 'own business' in the same way." This second interpretation is the tack we have taken in this section, and to reaffirm it here is once more to destroy the parity between the two nonliberal principles by requiring us to say that moralistic considerations can, but paternalistic considerations cannot, be reasons for criminal prohibitions. The issue is hard to settle, but it is hardly

momentous, since the person of staunch liberal sentiment will not acknowledge much weight to moralistic reasons in any case.[2]

2. Pure and impure legal moralism

Whatever the evil cited in the legal moralist's case for criminalization, if it is
taken to be an evil in itself, quite apart from its causal relations to harm and
offense, then its proponent's case for it is *purely* moralistic. He will argue that
prohibiting conduct that tends to produce the evil can be legitimate simply
because of that preventive effect, everything else being equal. The pure legal
moralist does not have to argue that the evil he wishes to prevent by means of
criminal prohibition is properly preventable only because it is linked to still
other evils of other kinds. He makes no argumentative appeal beyond the
inherent character of the evil itself. On the other hand, some writers are
called legal moralists even though the basic appeal in their arguments is to the
private or public harm principles or to the offense principle. For example,
Patrick Devlin's social disintegration thesis (see Chap. 30, §3) cites as his
basic reason for "enforcing morality" the harm he expects would otherwise
come to the public interest in social cohesion. The argument, therefore,
appeals ultimately to the harm principle, and for that reason we can characterize Devlin's approach as "impure moralism." Similarly, the claims that pornography causes a rise in sex crimes, and that the proliferation of "topless
bars," "adult bookstores," "porno flicks," "message parlors," and streetwalk-
ers damages the ambience of neighborhoods, are both basically liberal appeals, invoking the harm and offense principles when they appear in arguments for legal prohibitions. These positions too are instances of "impure
legal moralism." They can be contrasted with the purely moralistic arguments of James Fitzjames Stephen, William Buckley, and Irving Kristol
(discussed in Chap. 30, §2) that such evils as "sexual depravity," even when
harmless and unoffending, must be prohibited, since being inherently immoral, they are socially intolerable.

The distinctions between pure and impure moralism and between moralism in the strict and broad senses cut across one another, generating four
categories. The *pure legal moralist in the strict sense* demands that the law
prevent and/or punish inherent immoralities even when they are harmless
(because voluntary or consented to) and unoffending (because not forced on
the attention of unwilling observers). He rests his entire case on the desirability of eliminating and preventing states of affairs whose evil, even though
free-floating,[3] is intuitively manifest and extreme. This is moralism in the
strict sense because the evil it cites is inherently immoral, as opposed to a free-

floating evil of some other kind, like drastic social change, wrongful gain, or degraded taste. It is *pure* moralism because the evil it wishes to prevent is thought to be evil in itself, and there is no argumentative appeal to social harm or offense.

Pure moralism in the broad sense certifies as a reason for criminalization the need to prevent a free-floating evil other than objective immorality as such. It is pure when its ultimate argument appeals to this evil, rather than (covertly) to the evil of social or individual harm, or the evil of offended mental states. The view that we shall call (in Chap. 29) "moral conservatism" falls into this category when it argues that drastic social change is an evil in itself even when it occurs in such a way or at such a pace that no one is harmed and few are offended by it. But moral conservatism is impurely moralistic when it appeals to fairness, claiming that a majority of traditionalists is *wronged* ("harmed" in the appropriate sense) in being made into a minority, or that given individuals in its ranks will be deeply offended by the changing moral scene when, as members of a shrinking minority, they will be subjected to the flaunting of new ways when they have lost the protection of a plausibly mediated offense principle. Similarly the moralistic view that could be called "moral environmentalism" is "pure" when it states that it is an end in itself that the moral as well as the physical environment not be "polluted," and that moral pollution would be an inherent evil even if human beings became so hardened to it that it would no longer cause harm or offense. On the other hand, moral environmentalism is "impure" when it rests its case on the evil of offending captive observers of sordid scenes.

Impure moralism in the strict sense argues for criminal legislation against "inherent immoralities," not as free-floating evils but as events or states of affairs which in virtue of their coarsening effect on those who participate in or observe them, or their power of suggestion to others, will produce—albeit indirectly—immense harm over the long run. Even though the acts that produce these evils may not be directly harmful, their overall effects show that they are not "victimless crimes." This kind of legal moralism is narrow (strict) because the conduct whose criminalization it advocates is said to be inherently immoral, but it is impure because the reason given for prohibiting it is not *that*, but rather one acceptable to the liberal—its indirect harmfulness.

Finally, *impure moralism in the broad sense* argues for intervention by the criminal law to prevent a free-floating evil other than inherent immorality, but gives as its ultimate legitimizing reason the need to prevent the harm or offense incidentally associated with or produced by that evil. For example, the legal perfectionist (see Chap. 33) who worries about the greater social harm expectable from people with deficient characters, or who takes the decline of public taste to be a threat to his own interests (say in the dissemina-

tion of great art, music, and literature) or to a public interest in the flourishing of the arts, may be a legal moralist in the broad sense if he urges legal
coercion, but is a moralist of an impure kind since he appeals ultimately to the
harm principle.

3. Moralism and harm to others

Before we begin to examine the allegedly free-floating evils that impress the
pure legal moralist, we need to be very clear about what it is we are inquiring
into. In particular we must be sure that the liberty-limiting principles already
discussed in this book cannot encompass the evils the legal moralist wants to
eliminate, so that legal moralism would be a redundant principle. From the
other direction it is often argued that legal moralism is logically presupposed
in the very formulation of one of the other liberty-limiting principles. In
either case, the distinction between free-floating moral evils and harm (or
offense) would be conceptually indistinct. The impure legal moralist might
argue that the causal linkage between immorality (or any of the other allegedly free-floating evils) and harm is strong and virtually invariant, so that if
one has accepted the harm principle one can argue for criminalization of any
true immorality (or any true evil) on that ground alone. There is a stronger
skeptical claim, however, which, if true, would make the connection between
moral evils and harms utterly impossible to disentangle. That is the claim
that moral evil is not (or not merely) causally tied, but *conceptually* linked to
harm, since the former is part of the very conception of the latter. There are a
number of grounds for making this stronger claim, at least four of which
deserve our careful consideration.

The first way of challenging the distinction between harm and (other)
moral evil is by means of a theory of "social rights" rendered forever disreputable by J.S. Mill in *On Liberty*. As lampooned by Mill, the theory is reduced
to the claim that ". . . it is the absolute social right of every individual that
every other individual shall act in every respect exactly as he ought; that
whosoever fails thereof in the smallest particular violates my social right and
entitles me to demand from the legislature the removal of the grievance."[4] If it
were true, *pace* Mill, that any citizen's failure to do what is morally right
violates the moral right (and interest) of every other citizen, then we are all
"victims" of the solitary wrongdoer even in the absence of causal effect on any
of our other interests, even without our observation or knowledge of what has
been done. In that case the private tippler, or masturbator, or evil-thinker
wrongs all of us (by violating our right that he behave himself) and each of us
has a *grievance* against him. In virtue of our "social right" all immorality is
harm to others, and there can be no "free-floating evil" in wrongdoing, no

"harmless immoralities." It is plainly absurd, however, to suppose that everyone has the "social right" in question since hardly anybody ever claims such a
right, and hardly anybody[5] can plausibly claim to have the corresponding
interest. In the sense of "harm" as set-back interest, no one is harmed to any
extent, much less harmed on balance, by the unknown peccadillos of neighbors or strangers. There would seem to be no ground, therefore, for claiming
the corresponding right.

A second way of undermining the conceptual distinction between moral
evil and harm to others is far more plausible.[6] Some versions of the utilitarian
theory of the standard of right conduct hold not merely that there is a *de facto*
or contingent coincidence between immorality and harm to others so that the
latter is a reliable sign of the former, but rather that the connection is a
necessary one, because harm to others is the very ground of immorality, the
"wrong-making characteristic." Plausible as this theory is at first sight, however, it is threatened by various standard counterexamples. Some paternalistic invasions of autonomy are immoral as such even when their consequences
turn out to be beneficial for all concerned. Similarly, breaking "desert island
promises" after the promisee has died, or giving a student a better grade than
he deserves in order to make him happy, are subject to moral censure on
grounds other than their harmfulness. The utilitarian has well known replies
to such objections, however, and there is no need here for us to get embroiled
in these ancient controversies. Their resolution would affect at most the fate
of legal moralism narrowly conceived (in terms of immoral but harmless
conduct) but not legal moralism in the wider sense that permits criminalization to prevent other free-floating evils (like evil thoughts, consented-to ineq-
uities, cultural extinction, or debased taste). Utilitarianism attacks the view
that there are morally wrong acts that do no harm, but it is not a serious
threat to the simple contention that there are evils (other than actions) that are
distinct from harms.

A third reason sometimes presented for denying that legal moralism and the
harm principle can be disentangled is that the concept of harm itself is "morally
loaded and essentially contested."[7] Neil MacCormick and Ernest Nagel,[8] who
are among the leading exponents of this position, argue, I think, from quite
unassailable premises. They point out that before any adequate notion of harm
can be applied, an avoidably controversial moral decision must be made about
which interests to protect. Some interests are unavoidably in conflict and
cannot be protected except by suppressing the interests with which they con-
tend. Deciding which, if either, should be protected, is a moral decision made
on grounds of greater relative worthiness or importance. Judgments of moral
priority, however, must bring into play genuine moral considerations like
rights and deserts; they are essentially contestable on moral grounds and are in

fact made in different ways in different societies. The harm principle calls for
the protection of possessory interests from theft, but, as Nagel shrewdly
observes, we can always ask in the case of alleged theft "whether the article
taken from a person 'really' belonged to him,"[9] a question of law settled by
appeals to the rules of property, which in turn represent moral decisions about
which possessory interests are worth protecting on moral grounds, decisions
made in different ways in societies with different moral commitments. "The
harm principle," MacCormick concludes, "would be vacuous without some
such conception of legitimate interests."[10]

All of this must be admitted. The same points, in fact, are made with equal
emphasis and in greater detail in Volume one, the main purpose of which is
to supply normative substance to the otherwise vacuous and merely formal
concept of harm. Nevertheless it seems clear that one need not be committed
to the untenable notion of harm as a morally neutral concept to insist that the
contrast between the harm principle (as incorporating one kind of morality)
and legal moralism (as incorporating another) can be preserved. The harm
principle mediated by the *Volenti* maxim protects personal autonomy and the
moral value of "respect for persons" that is associated with it; it incorporates
nonarbitrary interest-ranking principles and principles of fairness regulating
competitions; it "enforces" the moral principles that protect individual projects that are necessary for human fulfillment. But there are other moral
principles, other normative judgments, other ideals, other values—some
well-founded, some not—that the harm principle does not enforce, since its
aim is only to respect personal autonomy and protect human rights, not to
vindicate correct evaluative judgments of any and all kinds.

We are thus strongly tempted to conclude at this point that "the laws
authorized by the harm principle only coincide or overlap with moral requirements, but do not actually enforce moral values as such. What the state
authorities are properly concerned with is the harmfulness of harmful behavior not its [admittedly] immoral character. . ."[11] After all, it *is* immoral intentionally to cause others harm, to invade their moral rights without justification or excuse. So the harm principle does "enforce" *that* part of the public
morality, but not (we are tempted to say) because it is morality, but rather
simply to protect rights and prevent harm. The temptation, however, should
be resisted. MacCormick's arguments are persuasive that even a penal code
based exclusively on the harm principle (and any penal code will be *largely*
based on that principle) is meant to do more than merely prevent harm. In so
protecting people, it also means to vindicate the morality of preventing harm
and respecting autonomy. That is why its sanctions are *punishments* expressing public reprobation and moral censure of the harm-causing wrongdoer.
Indeed, *any* liberty-limiting principle, in the sense we have assigned that

term, is a principle for enforcing some segment of some morality. That is because the very apparatus of the criminal law, with its characteristic symbolic and expressive functions, is a means of giving the seal of authoritative moral judgment to its verdicts and punishments. The criminal law can even be understood as an instrument for *creating* and reenforcing moral consensus. As MacCormick puts it, "precisely because of its symbolic force as the public morality of the state, the criminal law with its public drama and symbolism of trials and punishment can be to some extent *constitutive* of a common morality for the body of citizens as such."[12]

Like the other proposed coercion-legitimizing principles then, the harm principle *is*, obviously, a kind of moralistic principle, aimed at determining the moral values that may properly be enforced by the morality-shaping apparatus of the criminal law. But it still does not follow that the harm principle permits the criminal law to proscribe any and all kinds of wrongdoing, or any and all kinds of evil. By definition, that principle remains substantially narrower than the (other) moralistic principles, and can be coherently contrasted with them. The question before us is *which* judgments on behavior may rightly receive the stamp of moral certification from the criminal law, *not* whether in applying that stamp the criminal law is enforcing some moral judgments or other. I discuss the connections between the harm principle and the enforcement of morality more fully in Chapter 30 below.

A fourth threat to the distinction between harm and other moral evils is posed by admitted evils that are difficult, if not impossible, to classify. I have in mind, in particular, "exploitative injustices" which may not harm their victims, either because the exploitees' interests are not set back, or because the exploitees have freely consented to them, thus satisfying the conditions of the *Volenti* maxim. Some of these borderline cases are actions which *if general* would be harmful, and whose prohibition is justified on that ground alone by the harm principle, but which nonetheless can be perfectly harmless in some instances. "Freeloading" and similar examples of cheating are cases in point. In a familiar sense these examples are all instances of exploitative injustices, even when they injure the interests of no one. In various cooperative undertakings, each person must do his own share if all are to gain, but it is possible for a person to cheat, not do his share, and thus take his benefit as "free" only because the others are doing their shares. By cheating, the freeloader exploits the others' cooperativeness to his own benefit. He "takes advantage of them," as we say. If many of his partners did the same, then the result would be harm to the interests of everyone in the group. But when no others do the same, the harmful effects of one free-rider may be so trivial and diluted as to count for nothing. When one rider (only) avoids paying his train fare, the others' shares of the costs of the railroad, reflected in the owner's adjusted prices, may go up only a tiny fraction of a penny because of his nonpayment. But the others have voluntarily foregone the benefits he got in expectation that he would forgo them too. Their grievance is not that their interests were harmed, and surely not that they were morally offended by what he did. (They were offended because of the perceived wrong done them; the basis of the wrong was not simply that they were offended.) Their grievance is simply that he took unfair advantage of their trust and profited only because of their forbearance.

And so we must add another category of legally recognizable evils (in addition to harms and offenses) to our general classification, namely those exploitative injustices that consist of benefits gained without causing harm to others when those gains are made possible only because others have voluntarily refrained from seeking the same gains for themselves. (See Vol. I, Chap. 6, §3.) This new category, however, does not require a new ("moralistic") legislative principle. Since the wrongful conduct would be harmful if very widely practiced, and since there is no reason to exempt free-riders from the general duties of participants in the cooperative scheme, the harm principle will justify prohibitions of actions that can produce this third kind of evil.

There are other forms of advantage-taking, however, whose coverage by the harm principle is more problematic, if only because the projected consequences of their general practice is more difficult to gauge. Professor Zeno Vendler once recounted an experience he had as a motorist in a pea-soup fog on the Palisades Parkway in New Jersey. Visibility was reduced to a dangerous point, and Vendler drove very slowly, peering intently into the scattered beams from his headlights. Suddenly he noticed a flash of light in his rearview mirror. Another motorist had apparently pulled off the road to wait in the darkness for a car to pass by, and had then turned his headlights back on, pulled back on to the road, and made his way through the fog by keeping Vendler's red taillights in view. This is a perfect example of parasitic exploitation. Vendler was doing the hard and anxious work for both of them, while the parasite's progress was relatively effortless. The parasitic driver's practice offends the sense of justice; yet he did not harm Vendler's interests in any way. Vendler's plight was made no worse than it would have been had the parasite not appeared behind him. I find it difficult to decide whether or not this parasitic form of advantage-taking would be socially harmful if it were more generally practiced, but whether or not its prohibition would be legitimized by the harm principle, it does seem in the particular case to be a piece of harmless behavior that is nonetheless to some degree morally blameworthy, hence an "evil." More persuasive examples of exploitation not covered by the harm principle (because they are freely consented to by the exploitee) will be considered in Chapter 31.

4. Moralism and offense to others

It has also been argued frequently, and with *prima facie* plausibility, that it is impossible to separate moral judgments from the offense some behavior causes to those who must observe it or who simply learn about it after the fact. The cases that occasion this judgment are those in which the conduct in question offends the *moral sensibility* (see Vol. II, Chap. 7, §4, Chap. 9, §2, and p. 115). We say in these cases that we are morally offended even at the "bare thought" that conduct of the kind in question occurred. As Ernest Nagel points out,[13] it is a mistake to claim in these instances that the conduct is prohibitable because of the moral offense it causes, as if it were the unhappy state of mind of offended parties rather than the immorality they attribute to the offending behavior that is the ground of the prohibition. That is no way to save liberalism from resorting to legal moralism. The fact is that the behavior offends precisely because it is judged to be immoral; it is not judged to be immoral because it causes the nuisance of offended mental states in those who learn about it.

H.L.A. Hart once suggested that the nuisance (offense) principle might supply the rationale for criminal statutes against bigamy which are "accepted as an attempt to protect religious feelings from offense by a public act desecrating the [marriage] ceremony." On this interpretation, he points out, "the bigamist is punished neither as irreligious nor as immoral but as a nuisance. For the law is then concerned with the offensiveness to others of his public conduct, not with the immorality of his private conduct."[14] A bigamous marriage, however, as Patrick Devlin was quick to point out,[15] could be performed in the privacy of a magistrate's office or a clergyman's study, but that would make it no less illegal. Building on Devlin's observation, Nagel accuses Hart of "begging the question if he assumes that to judge an action to be a nuisance (or offense) to others, is *always* independent of any judgment of its morality."[16] He then draws exactly the right conclusion: ". . . some conduct is regarded as a nuisance to others, just because those others regard the conduct as immoral. Accordingly, if bigamy is a crime because it is a nuisance to others, it does not follow without further argument that the bigamist is not punished because he is judged by society to be immoral, but for some other reason."[17]

It is Nagel, however, who is begging the question if he assumes that to judge an action to be a nuisance is *never* independent of any judgment of its morality. If public nudity, public defecation, or public married intercourse are judged immoral by most people, it is obviously not because they are thought to be inherently wicked wherever and whenever they occur, but rather precisely because they offend those who witness them. In these cases

the actions are immoral (better "indecent") because they offend; they do not
offend because they are judged to be, in their essential nature, immoral. Thus
one can urge their prohibition entirely on the liberal ground of the offense
principle, without recourse to legal moralism at all. These examples belie the
claim that the offense principle in its very formulation presupposes legal
moralism and cannot be disentangled from it. As for the bigamy example, the
liberal can with consistency agree with Devlin and Nagel that its only intelligible rationale is provided by legal moralism, while rejecting moralism, and
therefore opposing the criminalization of bigamy. That in fact is the stand
taken in our own discussion of bigamy (Vol. III, Chap. 24, §7).

5. Moralism and harm to self

Moralism has even been said to be presupposed by legal paternalism, and the
concept of protecting the actor from self-imposed harm to be inextricably
connected with the concept of enforcing the moral law. Again, the Hart–
Devlin debate is the source of this piece of conceptual assimilation. Hart had
admitted (inadvisedly, I believe) that a certain amount of physical paternalism could be tolerated by the twentieth-century liberal. He had no objection,
he wrote, to laws designed to protect persons from inflicting (inadvertently?)
physical harm on themselves, and indeed, he suggests, "the rules excluding
the victim's consent as a defense to charges of murder or assault"[18] may have
this paternalistic purpose. At this point Devlin places Hart's view on the
brink of a slippery slope and gives it a push. First, he draws a distinction
between "physical paternalism" and "moral paternalism." (The latter corresponds to the liberty-limiting principle I have called "moralistic legal paternalism," and I shall refer to it here simply as "moralistic paternalism.") The
former view legitimizes criminal prohibitions designed to protect an actor
from physical injury; the latter endorses the legitimacy of restrictions designed to protect him from "moral harm." Devlin can see no consistent way
in which the physical paternalist can avoid commitment to moralistic paternalism: "If society has an interest which permits it to legislate in the one case,
why not in the other? If, on the other hand, we are grown up enough to look
after our own morals, why not after our own bodies?"[19] Once we have arrived
at moralistic paternalism, we are already half way down the bumpy slope to
legal moralism, for

> If it is difficult to draw a line between moral and physical paternalism, it is
> impossible to draw one of any significance between moral paternalism and the
> enforcement of the moral law. A moral law, that is a public morality, is a
> necessity for [moralistic] paternalism, otherwise it would be impossible to arrive
> at a common judgment about what would be for a man's moral good. If then

society compels a man to act for his own moral good, society is enforcing the moral law; and it is a distinction without a difference to say that society is acting for a man's own good and not for the enforcement of the [moral] law.[20]

This is a clever argument, and one that might well have made Hart rue his original paternalistic concession. Its weak point is its uncritical acceptance of a concept of moral harm that is "harm" in the same sense as that in which physical injury is harm, except that the object of the latter is one's body and the object of the former is one's character. (See Vol. I, Chap. 2, §1.) Physical injury, however, is a setback to the welfare interest all normal persons are presumed to have in the efficient functioning of their bodies. In almost every case, a person would be handicapped in his pursuit of his own good, whatever that might be, if his body no longer functioned properly. Harm to character, on the other hand, need not be a setback to one's interests (although it often is, if the person does not have a certain compensatory guile), and when it is not, it cannot be a harm in the primary sense unless the person has a prior interest (and again he need not) in the excellence of his character. Harm to a person's character when it does not set back the interests of the person is harm only in the "derivative sense" distinguished in Vol. I, Chap. 1, §1. It is like harm to one of his possessions when he has withdrawn his investment of interest in it; and that "harm" is no harm to *him*.

6. A taxonomy of evils

We can now resume our discussion of the sorts of evils the criminal law might be designed to eliminate or prevent, depending on the liberty-limiting principles legislators might adopt. Three classes of evils that we have already discussed—harms, offenses, and exploitative injustices—can be grouped in one category. The exploitative injustices, as we have seen, are in many cases covered by the harm principle in virtue of the harmful consequences we could expect if they were to become general. But even when (or if) they are not plausibly judged to be harmful, they can be grouped with the harm and offense evils in virtue of one very important characteristic they share in common with them. All three types of evil are grounds of personal grievances. People may sometimes understandably protest that they have been *wronged* (taken advantage of) even while admitting that their interests have not been set back. The question we must now raise is whether there are still other classes of evils that wrong no one in particular and thus cannot be [considered] grievances. Insofar as they are detached from individual needs, interests, deserts, claims, and rights, such evils can be characterized as "free-floating." What, then, do we mean by calling them "evils?"

Let us mean by an evil, in the most generic sense, any occurrence or state of affairs that is rather seriously to be regretted. To say of such an event or condition that it is an evil is to say that it would be better (in some objective sense) if it did not exist or had never come to exist, that the universe would be a better place without it. This *summum genus* can then be divided exhaustively into two subordinate genera, which we can label "Legislative Evils" (or evils of legislative interest) and "Theological Evils" (or evils of theological interest) respectively. The former class contains all the evils that are reasonably foreseeable or preventable consequences of human beings' actions or omissions. The latter class contains the natural disasters that law books have traditionally called "Acts of God" and other regrettable occurrences and circumstances, such as the existence of killer diseases despite reasonable and even heroic human efforts to stamp them out, that are not imputable to human misconduct, indifference, or error. Such things of course are evils in the generic sense. Some of them help create "the problem of evil" in natural theology. Our concern here, however, is with the evil people do, for only that kind of evil could be the concern of rational coercive (criminal) legislation.

The legislative evils subdivide further into two species, the "Grievance Evils" and the "Non-grievance Evils." The former, which contains the familiar harms, offensive nuisances, and exploitative unfairness, consists of all the legislative evils that can be grounds of personal grievances. The latter are evils that are imputable to human beings, but which do not give rise to personal grievances.

Bernard Gert has defended a thesis that would undermine the above classification. He has claimed that "evil" and "harm" are virtual synonyms, so that it is impossible to think of a harm that is not an evil or an evil that is not a harm. He may well have been led to this hasty identification by his concentration on evils that can be inflicted upon persons, for example as punishments.[21] As we shall see, however, there are other putative evils that could not in any usual sense be "inflicted" upon individual persons. To give Gert his due, most generic evils, or the most important generic evils, may well be harms, and indeed all harms, as such, are evils, at least to some degree "to be regretted." But if (as appears to be the case) there are non-grievance evils, then not all evils are harms, and indeed some genuine evils are neither harms, offensive nuisances, nor exploitative injustices.

It will be useful to divide the non-grievance category into two subspecies, the *welfare-connected non-grievance evils* and the genuinely *free-floating evils*. (See Diagram 28-1.) For the time being, we can leave open the question of whether these subclasses are empty or not, or, if not empty, what the typical specimens of each might be. A welfare-connected non-grievance evil is an evil in the generic sense which cannot be the ground of any particular person's

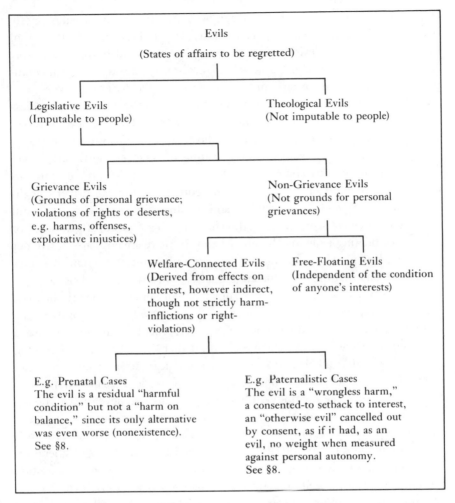

Diagram 28-1. A taxonomy of evils.

grievance, yet it is a state or event whose evil character consists entirely in its adverse impact[22] on human interests. The most familiar examples are probably those that legal paternalists wish to prevent—setbacks to interest that are consented to and therefore not violations of the "victim's" rights—but there are other types of examples as well. Infants who come into existence already impaired as a consequence of parental negligence in permitting them to be conceived, but who are not so badly impaired that their nonexistence would be rationally preferable to existence with the impairment, appear to have no grievance against anyone. (See Vol. I, Chap. 2, §8.) They have been avoidably brought into existence in a harmful condition, but they have not been "harmed on balance." That harmful condition nevertheless is an evil precisely because of its deleterious impact on interests; it does not "float free" of intersts, needs, and desires. Similar examples are found frequently in tort suits when the wrongful act of a defendant directly causes a harmful condition in a plaintiff but in circumstances in which that harm or a worse one would soon have occurred anyway. On the way to the airport the reckless driving of a taxi driver causes a collision with a truck. Its passenger, severely injured, is rushed in an ambulance to a hospital, and thus misses his plane. The plane, however, develops engine trouble and crashes shortly after take-off, killing all the passengers. The taxi passenger, therefore, despite his injuries, is better off on balance as a consequence of the cab driver's negligence than he would be otherwise, and yet his injuries remain a harmful condition, a welfare-connected evil, whether the ground of a grievance or not.[23] Free-floating evils, on the other hand, (if there are any) are clearly not the ground of plausible grievances and are evil in their inherent character despite the fact that they have no adverse effects on anyone's well-being.

Liberalism, as we have defined it thus far, will not allow the criminal law to prohibit *any* merely non-grievance evil, and *certainly not* the free-floating evils. We have seen in section 1 above, however, that liberalism must make a grudging concession to moralism and admit that the prevention of an evil, any kind of evil at all, is *a* reason for criminal legislation, though it is not much of a reason when the evil in question is a non-grievance one. In particular, evils of the free-floating kind, the liberal insists, never have enough weight to counterbalance the standing case for liberty, though perhaps our unfettered philosophical imaginations can conceive, just barely, of some such evils coming close to tipping the balance. (See Chap. 29, §4.) But liberalism may, in the most extreme cases, have to weaken its opposition to legislation designed to prevent welfare-connected evils even when those evils are not plausible grounds of grievances or violations of rights. We will consider one such extreme case—prenatal injury—in section 8.

7. Candidates for free-floating evils

Not everyone will agree that all or even most of the items on the following list are genuine evils.[24] I do not even make that claim myself, but I submit (a) that most readers will acknowledge that at least one of them is plausibly held to be an evil in the legislative genus, and (b) that it will be very difficult to claim sincerely of any given item so acknowledged to be an evil that it is also a personal harm, offense, or exploitative injustice.

1. *Violations of taboos.* It has been said that all known human societies, primitive and advanced, have incest rules. In characterizing these rules as

taboos, anthropologists mean that they are absolutely unconditional prohibitions applying without exception, whose violation not only cannot be justified, but cannot be excused either by any of the normal exculpating appeals (mistake, duress, etc.). A taboo is a prohibition whose form "puts the demand for reason out of place"[25]; it is thought to be inviolate and sacrosanct, and such that anyone who feels bound by it will think of it as underived from reasons, in any usual way, but rather something as basic and underivative as the process of giving reasons itself. Not that a given taboo cannot be supported by reasons. An isolated instance of brother-sister incest could lead to genetic abnormalities; isolated instances of parent-child incest would be clear cases of the sexual abuse of children and likely to cause severe emotional damage to the victim; widespread violation of the rules would undermine, for better or worse, traditional social institutions like the nuclear family. But the incest rules do not function simply to prevent injustices or inutilities. They have a powerful grip on us even when such reasons do not apply. After all, contraceptives and sterilization can prevent genetic disasters; intercourse in private can prevent offense and contagious example; and incestuous relations between consenting adults might be exempt from the objection based on child abuse. In the words of Graham Hughes: "It is hard to see what reason there is to declare it a heinous crime for a thirty-five-year-old man and his thirty-year-old sister to decide to go to bed together."[26] One reason why Hughes is right about this (though it is not his reason) is that criminal sanctions are hardly necessary to enforce a genuine taboo; crime statistics do not show a rash of brother-sister incest crimes. But leaving the question of criminal enforcement aside, how many of us can calmly consider, without flinching, the example of a contraceptively protected, privately performed, and genuinely consensual sexual act between a thirty-eight-year-old father and a twenty-year-old daughter, or (even more unthinkable to many) a thirty-eight-year-old mother and a twenty-year-old son? If such discreet and private acts are "evils," it cannot be simply because they harm or offend.

2. *Conventional "immoralities" when discreet and harmless.* I have in mind here the usual list of so-called morals offenses when performed in private between consenting adults. They include all extramarital and homosexual intercourse, and perhaps solitary masturbation as well. Not many sophisticated persons will regard all these forms of conduct as "evils," but it is worth pointing out nonetheless that if they are evils they are often harmless and (since unobserved) inoffensive ones. It is more difficult to think of examples under this heading that do not pertain to sexual conduct, but the following contrived one might do. Imagine that a death in a family occasions not the usual public funeral and period of mourning but rather a secret family banquet at which the body of the deceased, hacked into pieces and backed in a garlic and

mushroom sauce, is consumed by the survivors, having earlier secured the consent of the deceased while he was still alive. Our prevailing morality would certainly condemn such conduct, even though no interests were harmed or endangered by it, and no sensibilities offended.

3. *Religiously tabooed practices*. Other dietary restrictions tend to be ascribed to religious codes instead of moral ones, or if to the moral ones, then only on the grounds that they are religiously forbidden. Similarly, religious rules enforcing sabbatarian abstentions or prescribing somber modes of dress do not make violators (at least in our pluralistic society) "immoral"; violators cannot be "good Hasidic Jews" or "good Mennonite Christians," or the like, but they can be good people, for all that. Even the religiously loyal subjects of the rules are likely to think of them as forbidding conduct that is *malum prohibitum* rather than *malum in se*. But then any kind of genuine *malum* is an evil. I have in mind under this heading not widespread and public deviance, which could be thought to be a threat to the norm itself or to the religious way of life it helps define, but rather isolated and private violations—wolfing down an illicit pork chop in the privacy of one's chambers, or sipping the fermented juice of the grape in one's desert tent. It is interesting to note in passing that we think of such conduct as evil (when or if we do) only because it violates religious norms, whereas the sexual prohibitions are thought to be moral rules quite independently of religious sanction.

4. *Moral corruption of another (or of oneself)*. It is surely an evil to make a person a worse person than he would otherwise be, to change his virtues into flaws, to encourage his follies, and play to his weaknesses. Usually to corrupt a person is indirectly to harm his interests, since most moral virtues are useful possessions which, by contributing to one's popularity and reputation for trustworthiness, help one to make one's way in the world. Even if it should not harm the person who is made worse by the evil actions of another, his corrupted character is likely to produce more harm in the long run for those he deals with. It is at least conceivable, however, that circumstances nullify these indirect sources of harm, so that the corrupt person prospers from his moral flaws and others are largely unaffected by them. (See Vol. I, Chap. 2, §1.) In that case the evil acts of his corruptor cause harm only to his character; it becomes a worse character than it would otherwise have been. But unless a person has an interest in having a good character, *he* is not harmed by the "harm" done to it, and his character itself is "harmed" only in the transferred sense, discussed and dismissed earlier (Vol. I, Chap. 1, §1). You do not harm me by "harming" my bicycle after I have thrown it away and abandoned all interest in it. And if *nobody* has an interest in the bicycle, you cause no genuine harm at all even if you smash it to bits. In the primary sense of harm, only beings with interests can be harmed, and that account excludes mere

things, artifacts, lower animals, and even such valuable possessions as one's body, one's reputation, or one's character. Nevertheless, it seems obvious that a bad or worsened character is, in itself, an evil thing.

5. *Evil thoughts.* We are all proud of the Anglo-American law for its traditional reluctance to punish evil thoughts, but legal commentators themselves, when explaining this reluctance, eagerly pass the whole subject off to the moralists, who have always attached great importance to it. *Evil intentions*, in particular, have long been thought to be the primary thing for which persons can be blamed, so that a person can be thought to be evil just insofar as his intentions are evil, even though those intentions, through lack of opportunity or change of mind, never issue in action, or because of lack of control, issue in actions more benign than those envisaged by the actor when he undertook them. Abelard identified sinning with evil intending and insisted that sin consists not merely in having evil desires but in consenting to them, that is resolving to act on them.[27] That may well be a plausible account of sin, but it won't do for what I have called "evil in the generic sense." Surely an evil desire is itself an evil state of affairs, and so are evil attitudes and emotional responses. The presence of an intention is hardly necessary to the evil of other kinds of mental states. Imagine, for example, a person of impeccable rectitude, who would never ever intend to do anything but her duty as she and Immanuel Kant understand it, yet whose "empirical nature" is so corrupt that she welcomes and celebrates harm to others though she would never intend to cause it—the wife of an invalid, for instance, who does her duty to the end but then kicks up her heels and dances with malicious joy at the thought of her husband's agonizing death.

6. *Impure thoughts.* Moralists who use this expression have in mind lust mainly, or the entertaining of sexual fantasies. Abelard found nothing sinful in these thoughts as such, provided they remained idle and ungeared either to specific evil intention or to the kind of desiring he called "covetousness."[28] Still, other things being equal, I suppose he would think it a bad thing that such fantasies occur at all, even though no one is to blame for them. Moralists have been preoccupied with sexual impurity, but surely there is no conceptual reason why any type of forbidden conduct should not have its own corresponding type of "impure thought." One might classify under this heading, for example, the newly converted Moslem, "lusting" in his fantasies after pork or wine, or the pious youth dreaming of playing baseball on the sabbath.

7. *False beliefs.* Consider beliefs we have, for example, about the distant past: about the conduct of the Peloponnesian War or about the character of Emperor Nero. Some of these beliefs (of course I know not which of them) are probably dead wrong, the result of early errors of observation or transmission, now beyond all correction. It would seem an evil state of affairs for *all* of

us to believe something about an ancient figure that is in fact not only untrue of him but unfair to him as well. All the more so for that false belief to be enshrined in the history books as the official record of our civilization. The universe would be a better place (in that quaint phrase of the English intuitionists) if only beliefs that are at least approximately true and just were so certified. The point has a certain vividness when confined to beliefs about actual persons and their works, though a purist might well insist that "the universe would also be a better place" without false beliefs about continental drift, or the origins of planets, or the existence of God.

8. *The wanton, capricious squashing of a beetle (frog, worm, spider, wild flower) in the wild.* Small wriggling creatures often cause harm and/or offense to people who find them in city homes and apartments, but in the wilderness they bother no one. Still, while it might be harmful indirectly to many other animals, including human beings, to slaughter beetles by the thousands, no one, surely, will be harmed by the loss of just one. Perhaps the beetle itself is harmed by the taking of its life. Human beings and some of the higher animals do have an interest in staying alive which is harmed by their premature deaths. If a beetle has any interests at all, as opposed to mere instinctual urges and propensities, then no doubt an interest in staying alive is one of them, but it is implausible, I think, to ascribe desires, goals, projects, or aspirations to a creature whose cognitive capacities (if any at all) are so primitive. So I doubt whether one harms such a being by painlessly killing it. Still the blotting out of any vital force, however rudimentary, when done for no reason at all, might strike many of us as an evil, much to be regretted.[29]

9. *The extinction of a species.* A few years ago, there were only forty odd whooping cranes left, and our government, with the full support of the people, has poured thousands of dollars into an effort to increase their numbers and allay the specter of extinction. Perhaps the effort is meant to prevent indirect harm to human interests, since the loss of any species is likely to have profound effects on the whole ecosystem of which we are a dependent part. But that cannot be the whole of the evil we perceive in such a loss, and environmental harm does not follow necessarily when a species disappears anyway. Consider the Colorado cave fish who have existed almost unchanged for millions of years in the dark isolation of their shallow cavern pools. The tiny ecosystem of which they are a part has no known effect on the rest of nature; yet the courts have recently prohibited engineering projects that would cause their extinction. In any case, to return to the whooping cranes, the serious environmental harm caused by their decline must have been caused by the reduction of their numbers, in only a few decades, from (say) four hundred thousand to forty. Compared to that, the further reduction from forty to zero would be a trifle. Those of us who

would be crushed in disappointment by the loss of the final forty, if we examined the grounds of our feelings, would find that we believe that the world would somehow be diminished in value by the loss of the whooping cranes, that the human beings who allow it to happen under their steward-ship after all these millions of years of natural evolution would be (collec-tively) as wasteful and wanton as the squasher of the beetle, indeed much more so, for the avoidable loss of a whole species is a greater evil in "the eyes of the universe" than the loss of any single animal, indeed an evil of a different order of magnitude.[30]

If there are acceptable examples of free-floating evils, either from the above list (which is to be continued in Chap. 29) or elsewhere, then legal moralism begins to assume a plausible shape, for an evil is something we are well rid of, and if criminal prohibitions seem both necessary and effective means of eliminating it, that would seem to be a reason, of at least some weight, in favor of them. When that evil is something other than harm or offense (more exactly when it is not in the "grievance" category), then it follows that there is a kind of minimal case for legal moralism. That case is simple, but not obviously simplistic. It is not conceptually muddled, nor defeated in its own formulation. Neither does legal moralism (in its "pure" versions) have to ride on the coattails of one or more of the other liberty-limiting principles. So we must give at least this much of a grudging nod to its credentials. The question now is whether the minimal case for legal moralism, even in principle, is strong enough to give any but minuscule support to proposals for criminaliza-tion. How much weight, at a maximum, are non-grievance evils capable of putting on the scales to be weighed against liberty? To settle that question we must look more closely at the leading non-grievance evils cited in the argu-ments of the legal moralists.

8. Welfare-connected non-grievance evils

Before resuming our survey of supposed free-floating evils, let us consider the other, admittedly weightier, subclass of non-grievance evils, those that are welfare-connected. These too are a motley assortment. They include, first of all, the setbacks to interest that are voluntarily suffered or risked which we examined in Volume three in our discussion of paternalism. The person who suffers such setbacks is not wronged by them; hence they do not constitute "harms" in the sense of that term employed by the harm principle. The strict liberal, therefore, would not permit the criminal law to be used to prevent them. But very often, at least, the voluntary setbacks (which would be harms proper if only they were not consented to) are much to be regretted; they are evils, though of a non-grievance sort. For this reason, one would think, the liberal must admit that their prevention would be a reason of *some* weight, however minuscule, in support of paternalistic restrictions. As we have reconstructed the liberal argument against paternalism (see Vol. III, Chap. 1, §6), however, the trumping effect of the principle of personal autonomy is absolute, and the legislator must treat appeals to the evil of consented-to setbacks as if they were no reasons at all.

Another class of welfare-connected non-grievance evils must command more respect even from the most stubborn liberal. These are states of adversely affected interests (harmful states) that are not the consequences of acts of harming only because the culpable actions that produced them did not satisfy what might be called "the counterfactual test for harming." We can mean by the phrase *harmful condition* a state in which a person is handicapped or impaired, a condition that has adverse effects on his whole network of interests. By a *harmed condition*, on the other hand, we can mean a harmful condition that is the product of an act of harming.[31] The "counterfactual test" is one of the conditions commonly held to be necessary for an act to be an act of harming in the sense that is of interest to the law.[32] In that sense, A harms B if and only if:

1. A acts (in a sense wide enough to include omissions and extended sequences of activity)
2. in a manner which is defective or faulty in respect to the risks it creates to B, that is, either with the intention of producing the consequences for B that follow, or similarly adverse ones, or with negligence or recklessness in respect to those consequences; and
3. A's acting in that manner is indefensible, that is, neither excusable nor justifiable; and
4. A's action is the cause of an adverse effect on B's self-interest (a "harmful condition"), which is also
5. a violation of B's right; and
6. B's personal interest is in a worse condition than it would have been had A not acted as he did.

The sixth condition is "the counterfactual test." Because it is not satisfied in certain puzzling cases, we must say in those cases that a wrongdoer (A) did not harm another party (B) by putting him into a harmful condition. While it is true in those cases that A wrongly produced a harmful condition in B, B is not in a worse condition than he would have been had A not acted as he did, for in that event, B would have been worse off still, on balance. One set of examples are the causal overdetermination cases, like that of the taxi passenger whose accident prevented him from being in a plane crash.[33] The examples I shall use here, however, are cases of wrongfully conceiving a child when there is an unreasonable risk that it will be born in a seriously harmful condition. For this purpose, we must turn once more to an ingenious example of Derek Parfit's[34] (see Vol. I, p. 103).

In Parfit's story, to repeat, a woman is warned that if she becomes pregnant while she suffers from some temporary illness, her baby will be born in a defective condition. Nonetheless, whether through intentional perversity or reckless impulsiveness, she heeds not her physician's warning and gets pregnant at the dangerous time. If her child were so defective that his life was not worth living, then he would have a strong case for wrongful life damages against the mother. He would surely have a *moral* grievance against her. "But for your wrongful conduct," he might say (or his laywer might say for him), "I would never have been conceived, much less born, and nonexistence would surely be preferable to my miserable state." By the counterfactual test, reformulated for wrongful life cases, this wretched infant has indeed been harmed: he is in a condition so bad that even nonexistence would have been preferable to it. Moreover, his birthright has been violated from the moment he came into existence, since the conditions for a minimally decent life had already been destroyed. His interests have been adversely affected and he has been wronged, so it follows that he has been harmed in the full sense, and his impaired state can be understood as a harmed state, i.e. a state of harm that is the product of a prior act of harming.

In Parfit's example, however, the inherited defect is *not* so severe as to render the child's life not worth living. The child never regrets that he was born, but only that he was born (say) with a withered arm—a serious handicap but surely not such that nonexistence would be preferable to it. Therefore, when we apply the counterfactual test as reformulated for wrongful life situations, it turns out that the mother did not harm her child. She had only two options in respect to his birth. One was to do what she did, which led to his being born with the withered arm. The other was to obey the doctor, which would have led to his never having existed at all, which even the child acknowledges was the worse fate. Hence, she picked the option which had the best total consequences for the child that eventually emerged. Hence, her act did not harm that child (at least by the revised counterfactual test). Thus the child's impaired condition is not a *harmed condition*, that is not a state of harm that is the product of a prior act of harming. It clearly is nevertheless a state of harm, however we characterize its causal antecedents, since it does have adverse effects on the child's interests. I prefer to call it, therefore, a *harmful condition* rather than a harmed condition.

Did the mother *wrong* the child by causing him to come into existence in a harmful (handicapped) condition? I don't think the child can establish a grievance against her so long as he concedes that his handicapped existence is far preferable to no existence at all. For if he were to claim that she wronged him by doing what she did, that would commit him to the judgment that her duty to him had been to refrain from doing what she did; but if she had refrained that would have led to his never having been born, an even worse result from his point of view. There is no doubt that the mother did act wrongly, but it does not follow that her wrongdoing wronged any particular person, or had any particular victim. She must be blamed for wantonly introducing a certain evil into the world, not for harming, or for violating the rights of, a person.

If I am right about this, no criminal statute based on the harm principle and the interpretation of "harming" proposed here could apply to the negligent mother of Parfit's example. When the harmful condition has been wrongfully caused and is so bad that the counterfactual test would be satisfied, that is, so bad that even nonexistence (the result if the wrongdoer had done otherwise) would be rationally preferable to it,[35] then the harm principle as we have interpreted it could legitimize criminal liability. Imagine an evil scientist who does genetic research on fetuses and newborns in the hope of creating a super-race, or, alternatively, a slave-race. He creates test-tube embryos through *in vitro* fertilization from chemically altered sperm and ova. Then he reimplants them in the natural womb of a willing subject. The emergent infants have horrible afflictions and no opportunity of ever having normal lives, but the scientist respects their "right to life" and keeps them under observation until their lives mercifully sputter out. Perhaps there is a crime with some familiar name that is already applicable to this sort of behavior, but, if not, a bill of legislation carefully defining "criminal wrongful life" might well be in order. At present, fortunately, there seems no need for it.

The harm principle will not legitimize "criminal wrongful life," however, when the permanently impaired condition of the newborn is *not* so bad that his life on balance is not worth living. The evils such legislation would be designed to prevent would be non-grievance evils, hence outside the scope of the liberal's legitimizing principles. Such a statute would create a victimless crime and could be justified only on the grounds that wrongdoing deserves punishment even when it harms no one (on balance) and violates no one's rights (the illiberal doctrine of "strict legal moralism.")

The evil of severe birth defects can be so closely connected with human well-being and happiness, however, that the liberal, whose respect for liberty generally is only limited by his humanitarianism, cannot help but feel a strain in his principles. If "negligent conception" (as we might call it) were more common, and impaired infants began to appear in increased numbers, it might not seem unjust even to a liberal's conscience to create a class of "victimless crimes." In an example of Gerald Dworkin's, we are asked to suppose that when the barometer falls to X, any baby conceived under those meteorological conditions will be born with some serious impairment, much worse than cleft palates, club feet, or withered arms, but not so severe that his life will not be worth living. Imagine that nearly every bedroom has a barometer on the nightstand, and that all radio and television stations broadcast warnings when the barometric pressure reaches the dangerous point. A criminal statute forbidding unprotected intercourse at such times would seem, at least at first sight, to create a victimless crime, since babies born with these handicaps, severe as they are, would not be wronged/ harmed by their negligent or self-indulgent parents. And yet, in the example, a certain amount of avoidable misery might be introduced into the world if we do not pass the statute. Surely, one might argue (on grounds that *resemble* the liberal's), that the prevention of unnecessary suffering is a legitimate reason for a criminal prohibition. Still, we can imagine a child born with the handicap in question who feels positively lucky that his parents negligently conceived *him* (of all people) against huge odds. He does not rejoice in his handicaps, but since he does not regret having been born, handicaps notwithstanding, he does not *feel* like a "victim," and he might resent the injustice of treating his parents as criminals.

We can strengthen the case for the legitimacy in principle of criminal legislation, by imagining hypothetical examples of "wrongful conception" that are not merely negligent, but deliberate, malicious, and sadistic. In conducting this experient in the imagination it is important to notice that there is a great conceptual, though perhaps not as great a moral, difference between the case in which a woman takes a drug *after* she is pregnant, causing her fetus to be born later in a harmed condition, and the case in which she takes drugs first and then, *after* she is herself in a condition that would be perilous for a fetus, she has intercourse and becomes pregnant. If a woman takes thalidymide while already pregnant, knowing its well-publicized effects, then the child that is born months later is her victim. The counterfactual test for harming yields a clear and unequivocal judgment in his case. He is much worse off than he would have been had his mother not taken the dangerous drug. This case is perfectly parallel to that of the negligent motorist who runs over a pregnant woman, causing her child, months later, to be born in an impaired condition. Since it is criminal liability we are considering, however, let us imagine that the mother's fault is much more serious than mere negligence. Suppose she deliberately damages her fetus because she wants the experience later of mothering a child that will be more completely dependent on her, and for a longer period than a normal child would, or, even worse, she wishes to glory sadistically in a child's frustrations and

sufferings. Now we have a picture of a parent who is morally indistinguishable from a serious criminal. Criminal liability for her, given her culpability
and her real victim, does not seem illegitimate.

But now change the example in only one small respect. Suppose the
mother has already been taking some dangerous drug for a long time when
she chooses to become pregnant. Suppose she is, as a consequence, in a
bodily condition such that any fetus conceived while she is in that condition
will develop deformities. Knowing full well the dangers, she deliberately
becomes pregnant, precisely in order to have a dependent child whose
sufferings she can enjoy. She is just as culpable morally as the woman in the
other version of the story, but she doesn't harm her child, since had she
behaved otherwise her child would never have existed, and since the deformities are preferable to nonexistence, the counterfactual test for harming is not
satisfied, and there is no proper victim. The advocate of criminalization
might argue that so trivial a difference between the two cases as the order in
which the pill-taking and the act of conception took place cannot support so
crucial a moral difference as that between criminal liability and no criminal
liability. If criminal prohibition would be legitimate in the one case, he might
conclude, then it must be equally legitimate in the other, victim or not.

Of course, there are powerful reasons against criminalizing the behavior in
the highly artificial examples we have been driven to in this section. Criminalization would not be necessary in the barometric pressure example, because people can be presumed to have more than enough incentive to avoid
producing impaired infants, quite without gratuitous threats from the state.
And deliberate conception of handicapped infants for selfish or sadistic reasons would be so rare and extraordinary that surely more economical means
of dealing with it could be used than the cumbersome apparatus of the
criminal justice system. But these rejoinders miss the point. The examples do
not show that there are some imaginable circumstances in which criminal
legislation would be justified as good public policy. Rather these examples,
contrived and unlikely though they might be, are designed to show that there
are conceivable circumstances in which criminalization even without a victim
would be *legitimate in principle*, even if unjustifiable, for practical reasons, on
balance.

One might attempt to rescue strict liberalism from the embarrassment of
its apparent refusal on principle to endorse criminalization of non-grievance
evils in the hypothetical prenatal cases we have imagined by insisting that the
extreme evils of the type that Parfit discusses are grievance evils after all. The
liberal might insist that there *is* a victim in these cases whose right has been
violated and who therefore has a genuine moral grievance against the wrong-

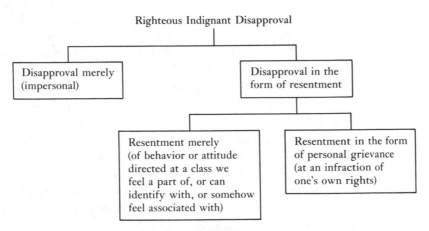

Diagram 28-2. The subvarieties of disapproval.

doer. I think we can grant this kind of liberal part of his point but not all of it. The impaired person is indeed in a special moral relation to the wrongdoer that makes a certain kind of negative attitude toward her appropriate and understandable. I think the best word for that attitude is "resentment." The specific type of righteous moral indignation that stems from an awareness that one has been personally wronged by another is not quite the same thing as generic resentment, since it is closely linked with a perceived right-infraction, and resentment need not be. Neither must resentment imply the imputation of guilt, charges or claims, or other such legalistic postures. "Having a grievance" is a vague phrase that might conceal the difference between resentment and the feeling that one has been personally wronged. To be sure, there is something personal in the disapproving sort of ill-will we call "resentment." We do not resent everything that we disapprove of. But it is sufficient for resentment that the attitudes or behavior we disapprove of were directed at a class we feel part of, or can identify with, or somehow feel associated with. (See Diagram 28-2.)

The handicapped child in the hypothetical stories we are considering may come in time to resent his biological parent, not for violating his right by an act that made him worse off on balance than he would otherwise be but, rather, for being the sort of scoundrel he or she is, a person who has manifested an indifference to the possibility of human suffering and who is prepared to bring people into existence with harmful impairments for no morally respectable reason. The child recognizes that he is a member of a class of possible persons, those that might have come into being through the parent's wrong act, toward whom the parent's hateful unconcern was directed. Only in that way is there anything "personal" in his resentment. He is in a position similar to that of a black in the presence of an honorable bigot who never violates the rights of blacks, but shows by his behavior that he always prefers the well-being of whites to blacks, other things being equal. He always roots for the white boxer, for example, when watching televised matches between a white and a black, and he gives generously to worthy white charities but not at all to worthy black ones. (It is possible to have that sort of bigoted character while also being a resolute Kantian determined never to violate anyone's rights.) The white person's attitude does not by itself give the black person a personal grievance in the absence of any right-infractions, but the black person's resentment, as a member of a group whose welfare is valued less than others', is well grounded and understandable.

In summary, then, it is beyond question that the severe handicaps of wrongfully conceived children (even when the wrongful conceiving follows rather than precedes the event that causes the impairment) constitutes a great evil. I have argued moreover, that this evil, unless so widespread as to be a public harm, is a "non-grievance evil," lacking determinate victims who can complain that their rights have been violated. As non-grievance evils go, however, this one carries a great deal of moral weight, enough to command even the liberal's respect. The evil is not the basis of anyone's legitimate personal grievance, but it is not an evil that is unassociated with human interests and well-being. A criminal statute designed to prevent such evils would be a departure from strict liberal legitimizing standards, but it would not be contrary to the animating humane spirit of the liberal's harm principle. Outside of the criminal-legislative context, at any rate, the liberal can be expected to combat *harmful* conditions of other human beings even when they are not *harmed* conditions. Such conditions may be non-grievance evils, but their connection to human suffering puts them in a special category of non-grievance evils, having much greater moral weight, for example, than consensual taboo infractions, "unnatural" matings, beetle squashings, defamations of the ancient dead, evil thoughts, even inconsequential extinctions of species. They have as much weight, in fact, as it is possible for a non-grievance evil to have in the legislative scales, and for some liberals that might even be enough, *ceteris paribus*, to warrant criminal legislation. I do not think that such liberals can be charged with making an *ad hoc* exception (in the illicit sense) to liberalism. The case is an exception, but on the other hand the circumstances truly are special and not likely to recur indiscriminately. For those who suffer congenital defects, the evil of their condition does not "float free" of their interests, even though it has not set back their interests on balance nor violated their rights. I can concede then that non-grievance evils do have *some* weight, simply as evils, but no other non-grievance evil has as much weight as this one, derived from avoidable nonconsensual suffering. Liberalism must bend to permit an exception in this special kind of case. I think it can bend without breaking.

9. A note on public and collective harms

The distinction between grievance and non-grievance evils must be drawn tighter if we are plausibly to classify various "public harms" (see Vol. I, pp. 63–64 and 221–25) such as tax fraud, perjury, or contempt of court. It would be absurd to deny the legitimacy of criminal statutes forbidding these harms, yet the liberal is committed to just that if he restricts legitimate criminalization to the prevention of grievance evils and cannot show the personal grievance in merely public harms. Moreover, it is not immediately evident that anybody can claim that his own rights have been violated each time a person causes a public harm. It would appear on the face of it implausible for *me* to complain that *I* was wronged by some stranger who committed perjury in a case unrelated to me, or tax fraud, or littering in some distant place. His act may have had no direct effect on my interests or on any other individual either. We say that it was "the public" at large that was harmed, as if "the public" were a large super-person with super-interests of his own. But of course there is no such super-person. Rather the public is composed of a multitude of individuals with independent and convergent interests in (among other things) the efficient operation of their institutions. The publicly harmful acts set back, or rather *threaten* to set back, those convergent interests. It seems then that some personal grievances must be voiced in the first person plural. When public harms are committed, *we* are wronged, and the public grievance is *our* grievance. I have a grievance as an individual because *we* have a grievance as a group, and my share of that collective complaint is only fractional. Yet the harm may be a serious grievance-evil nevertheless, since a wrong has been done to real individuals collectively that is more serious than the wrong any single individual suffers for his own part.

It would be easy to fall into an error at this point. If a public institution has been impaired in its functioning only to a minor extent, or only weakly threatened with impairment, by some given wrongful act, we should not say that while this citizen has been harmed only a tiny bit, and that citizen only a tiny bit, etc., nontheless all the tiny harms add up to a major harm to *us* (the group). Public harms are not additive in that way. Neither are they diluted by their wide distribution. If the actual or threatened impairment is minor, the public harm is minor too, and if it is major then the public harm is major too, no matter how widely distributed. The two factors that are relevant vary independently: (1) the extent of the actual or threatened impairment to an institution's function, and (2) the strength or importance of each individual's interest in the institution's health, and the seriousness of the resultant harm when that interest is set back. If the widely shared interest is an important one to the sharing individuals, but the impairment is only trivial, then the socially shared harm is minor. If the impairment is great and the shared interest important, then the social harm is also great, indeed even great enough, in extreme cases, to render it natural for most individuals to address their grievances in the first person singular. If the shared interest is only a weak one in most individuals (like, say, the interest in richly stocked public libraries) and the degree of impairment done or threatened by a wrongful act also is minor, then the public harm is relatively minor too. Finally, if the shared interest is weak but the impairment severe (e.g. widespread arson of public libraries) then the public harm is serious, even though it would be natural for most individuals to voice their grievances only in the first person plural. In no case is the degree of public harm multiplied or divided simply because it is publicly shared. It is important to emphasize that if not much damage is done or threatened to the object of a widespread interest then not much harm has been done to the possessors of that interest, no matter how many there are.

In some instances of public harms, of course, single individuals are more directly affected. Your littering may destroy the attractiveness of just that area that I had planned to picnic in. Your perjury may cast suspicion unjustly on me. Your tax evasion (if you are rich) may render impossible (because too expensive) some public service that would directly benefit me. In other cases, there may be individual grievances without any direct harm if the criminal act unjustly exploited the trustworthiness and self-restraint of other individuals, as for example, when you profit by cheating on your taxes only because I and many others with the same opportunity and temptation to cheat do not. But the public harm remains even when these individual wrongs are not directly inflicted. The harm is to *us*, and *we* (collectively) have the right to complain, though every individual's share of the wrong, as determined by the degree of impairment and the importance of the shared interest, is small. It may well be that only when we speak collectively through a public spokesman is our grievance at all impressive. But the grievance is real even when it cannot appropriately be expressed by any individual in his own name and for his own part.

The public interest, in examples like those discussed above, is in a sense constructed out of individual shares, even though individuals cannot impressively or even appropriately complain about their shares of the total harm. One can have a personal grievance that it would not be appropriate in most circumstances to give expression to, e.g. my grievance as a taxpayer when negligence causes the loss of a billion dollar shuttle and seven human lives. I dare not suggest that *I* was the primary wronged party when others have been so directly injured. But I may have a grievance anyway as one of millions of taxpayers whose money has been wasted. Another example is the way women other than the rape victim are wronged every time a woman is raped, because it is all the more difficult for them to move about freely in safety, and is thus a violation of their rights. Yet it would be insensitive for any one of them to express their personal grievance in the aftermath of serious injuries to the direct victim. In these cases there are setbacks to shared interests that constitute real and impressive shared grievances, though no one of the sharing parties can voice the grievance on her own part without suggesting misleadingly that she is the exclusive or primary victim.

There are other "collective evils," however, which, as Gerald Postema has convincingly demonstrated,[36] are unlike the "public harms" discussed above, in that they are in no comparable way derivative from independently defined individual interests, but rather have a certain logical priority to them. Corresponding to these evils are "collective goods," the chief features of which Postema lists as follows:

> 1. They express and depend essentially upon shared meanings, understandings, and valuings which are not just convergent, but common and *interdependent*. [Key word; emphasis added]
> 2. They concern matters of value and a way of life which are not *mine* or *yours* but *ours*.
> 3. They are not constructed out of (or instrumental to) private goods or interests, but rather the private good or 'stake' in achievement of collective goods *presupposes* them. . .
> 4. To say that they concern matters of *our* way of life also means that I regard these values as *mine* insofar as I regard myself as a member of the group, as *one of us*.[37]

In a perfect community, no individual's good is defined entirely apart from the common good, but instead is in large degree derived from that common good, and each setback to the interests shared collectively is, vicariously, harm to each sharing individual. Each person has some important interests of his own precisely because, and only because, they are also thought to be the interests of all the others. Every community member defines his collective interests in the same way, each interdependent on the others. Among the examples of collective goods given by Postema are the preservation of the wilderness, our whole cultural heritage, and a distinctive city ambience of parks and monuments. The interests in these goods, as held by many persons, can be contrasted with the interests most people share in some of the

"public goods" mentioned earlier, like the interest we have in important
public institutions such as courts and other governmental agencies. These
institutions are "*means* to the satisfaction of many of the [independently exis-
tent] varied interests of the members of the [public]."[38] On the other hand,
"collective goods" (in Postema's sense) can serve prior private interests too,
but, in the typical case, each person also has an interest that is derived from
his perception of a like interest of all the others.

The distinction between a public (and its "public goods") and a community
(with its "collective goods") can be summarized as follows. The public is a *de
facto* assemblage of persons whose interests happen to converge on the same
objects or instrumentalities. The objects of these public interests are valued
as means to protect or promote each person's own varied private interests, but
the latter exists antecedently and independently of the public instrumentalities that serve them. A community (see Chap. 29A, below) is an assemblage
of individuals with interdependent interests in the preservation and enhance-
ment of their common "possessions" taken as an end in itself, a component of
each person's good that could not exist prior to and independently of its
object. Collective interests define a *vicarious* good in the value systems of each
individual in the community (see Vol. I, Chap. 2, §2), a state of affairs in
which each individual has invested his or her own good, so that none of them
can flourish unless it does. Their collective interests make the community
members into a community, but it is equally true that it is community
membership that gives rise to collective interests. A corollary of this point is
that striving for a collective good, itself a form of cooperative undertaking, is
not felt as a cost so much as "akin to the good sought, and perhaps even as an
important *component* of it. For the cooperative striving is itself an expression of
a common aim and manifestation of a solidarity that already exists."[39] There
is no reason why a given group cannot be, in respect to some of its interests,
both a public and a community, or why some valuable institutions (e.g. the
national parks) cannot be the objects both of public and collective interests of
the same people. Other institutions (e.g. the post office) might be public
goods, in the present sense, but not collective ones. And members of the
same publics and communities may differ to some extent in how they value
given common possessions.

Who then is harmed when someone causes a "collective harm"? The victim
is not some entity existing apart from particular flesh and blood individuals.
Rather, Postema suggests, the harm is suffered by "individuals considering
questions of how *they together* wished to live and what they wished to be and
stand for as a community." He continues: "Thus we can say that *individuals*
have a *direct personal stake* in the avoidance of collective evils just insofar as
they are active self-identified participants in its traditions and practices, that

is, just insofar as they regard themselves as members of the community."[40] An individual who fits Postema's description, then, might claim that *he* was wronged/ harmed by another party's act that led to a neglect of a community tradition, or a tarnishing of a community symbol or monument, or a destruction of a city's (*our* city's) distinctive architectural ambience. If the wrongdoer challenges him by asking "What is that to you? I haven't directly harmed *you*," he can reply that he has a personal stake in the preservation of his ("our") community traditions, a vicarious stake analogous[41] to that which one person, e.g. a mother, can have in the well-being of another, e.g. her grown child, so that when the other is harmed, *ipso facto* she is also.

To be sure, Postema must admit that it is odd (or inappropriate or unimpressive) for a person to complain that *he* has been wronged by the creation of a "collective harm," but such a complaint is appropriate, he insists, when and only when it comes from a person claiming to speak for the community as a whole (in the first person plural). There must be no suggestion that "such a person is in some sense especially or exclusively entitled to complain or entitled to compensation."[42] For all their differences, collective harms are in the same boat as public harms (e.g. to government agencies) in this respect. In both cases, most individuals can voice personal grievances only to the extent that they claim also to represent the interests of a wider collectivity . The difference between them may make the collective-harm protester's grievance seem, if anything, the more impressive, since he claims that he has an other-regarding vicarious interest in the collective good, that the good of the community as defined by the interdependent collective interests of its members is a component of, not merely a means to, his own personal good.

The acknowledgment of collective harms, as Postema analyzes them, does not threaten the traditional liberal with the forced abandonment of his exclusive commitment to the harm and offense principles. It does not make him any friendlier to legal moralism in the strict and narrow sense. But it does threaten to permit the reintroduction of many of the legal moralist's favorite causes "dressed in harm principle clothes."[43] That is to say that by enlarging our conception of what can count as "harm" and what can count as "wrong," the acknowledgment of collective harms may render respectable some versions of "impure legal moralism in the broad sense" that the liberal, given his respect for autonomy, has every motive to exclude.

10. Summary and transition

There is a bare minimal case for legal moralism which proves that that liberty-limiting principle, as we have defined it, is correct. Since evils are, by definition, something to be regretted and prevented when possible, it seems to follow that the prevention of an evil, *any* evil, is always *a reason* of some relevance, however slight, in support of a criminal prohibition. If, as seems likely, there are some genuine evils that are neither harms nor offenses, then the prevention of *these* evils would be a relevant reason, however weak, in support of criminal prohibitions. The game, however, is not completely lost for the liberal. He can grant that this shows that legal moralism is technically correct, or correct in the abstract, but insist that, in fact, non-grievance evils can never (or hardly ever) have enough weight to justify the invasion of personal autonomy. This fallback position is congruent with the motive and animating spirit of liberalism, even while departing from its letter.

This chapter's taxonomy of evils, however, creates pressures for the revision of liberalism in several directions. The liberal in certain extreme cases (e.g. the wrongful conception of infants likely to be born in an impaired condition) may be forced to concede the legitimacy of criminal legislation designed to prevent non-grievance evils in the welfare-connected category, but he can remain resolute in his opposition to criminal prohibitions against merely free-floating evils, if there should be such. Second, the liberal will have to acknowledge that in certain other cases (e.g. collective harms) there can be genuine personal interests that would be protected by legislation forbidding what might otherwise seem to be non-grievance, even free-floating, evils. Thus, he must seriously address arguments invoking his own harm principle for an "impure legal moralism in the broad sense" that would otherwise be odious to him. We have also left open the door, in the third place, to the possibility that even free-floating evils of some descriptions might provide reasons of more than mere minimal weight for criminalization. The questions of how much weight that can be, and whether that weight can ever decisively tell for criminalization, awaits our further survey of the non-grievance evils commonly cited by legal moralists.

In the next chapter I shall extend the list of putative free-floating evils into the category of evils that one type of legal moralism, which I shall call "moral conservatism," holds to be sufficiently evil to warrant criminal prohibition, namely the inherent evils in radical social change. In later chapters we shall turn our attention to the evil of "harmless immoralities," wrongful gain achieved without causing another party a wrongful loss, and the corruption of character.

29

Moral Conservatism: Preserving a Way of Life

1. Focus on free-floating social-change evils

A form of pure legal moralism implicit in the arguments of many "conserva-tive" persons who would use the criminal law to prevent deviant or eccentric conduct whether or not it is harmful or offensive can be called "moral conser-vatism."[1] I shall attach this label to the liberty-limiting principle which en-dorses legal coercion that appears likely to prevent drastic change in a group's way of life. Drastic or "essential" social change, to the pure moral conserva-tive, is an evil in itself, whatever its effect on personal interests and sensibili-ties, and an evil of such magnitude that it is morally legitimate to use criminal penalties to prevent it.

It is surprising how often it is fear of change rather than commitment to an objectively true morality that motivates partisans of coercive laws in debates over "morals offenses," censorship, and the like. Often moral conservatism is the principle invoked quite explicitly in such debates. Even the Ayatollah Khomeini (who might well be expected to appeal to more absolutist grounds) refers repeatedly to the need to preserve the traditional customs of Islamic culture by stern and vigilant enforcement of criminal laws. His aim is to prevent the "corruption" of the traditional ways that comes from the distract-ing example of alternative Western life-styles.[2] And yet Khomeini would not advocate that Western nations introduce similarly draconian laws against drinking stimulants, dancing, or women exposing their necks in public. "*We* have the right to enforce our customs [he seems to say] and *you* have the right to enforce yours." The moral conservative would add that in neither case should the appeal be to what is the true morality or the most natural or rational prototype of a way of life, but only to the need to protect the way of life that is actually established. The morality of a group deserves protection because it is the group's morality, not (necessarily) because it is the true morality binding on all peoples.

It often seems as if the model for the social-change evils that trouble the conservative is the extinction of a biological species. (See number 9 in the list of free-floating evils in Chap. 28, §7.) Cultural changes too seem to him to lead, sometimes, to an equally regrettable kind of "extinction." Let us continue our list of purported free-floating evils, focusing now on those that involve drastic social changes.

10. *The extinction of a national or cultural group.* One way of destroying an ethnic group is to commit mass murder or genocide, to destroy the group by killing all of its members, the method, in fact, by which human beings have destroyed whole biological species. That would be to cause enormous harm, directly to the victims and indirectly to many others, so it is not a good example of a "harmless evil." A more humane mechanism is that of cultural assimilation. In the first millennium A.D. the Jewish community of China was "killed by kindness." Welcomed by their Chinese hosts with warmth and friendliness and treated with unaccustomed equality, the Chinese Jews intermarried and disappeared with hardly a trace. The assimilative process sometimes takes place in a spontaneous, almost "voluntary" way, as a group neglects its ancestral language and customs, adopts those of its neighbors, and gradually ceases to be the group it once was, even though no individuals are directly harmed in the process. The Sumerians, Carthaginians, and Incas were conquered by force and then suffered the imposition of an alien language, religion, and culture, but the Welsh, the Bretons, and the Louisiana Cajuns might yet leave the stage of history in a quieter, less "harmful" manner. It is not only the present members of those groups who think of that possibility as an evil to be averted.

It is important to contrast the "evils" of cultural assimilation (if that's what they are) with the evils of cultural disintegration of which Lord Patrick Devlin has warned us. (See *infra,* Chap. 30, §§3 and 4.) Devlin apparently has in mind the actual scattering of a group as the communal bonds among the individuals break, or their military conquest by foreign powers, made possible by the weakening of their moral fiber and group loyalty, or "the breakdown of law and order, something approaching anarchy"[3] as individuals, having come to doubt parts of their seamless morality, quickly chuck all the rest of it. These kinds of disintegration are of course extremely harmful to the individuals who are violently torn away from one another, but the extinction of cultural identity through a kind of accelerated evolution need harm no one at all.

11. *Drastic change in the moral and aesthetic climate, or in the prevailing style or "way of life."* Changes in habits, customs, and practices, in the way businesses concentrate or disperse in neighborhoods, in the way buildings are decorated and maintained, in the way people dress, speak, joke, find their entertainment, express their feelings, observe or ignore their religions, engage in courtship rituals and childbearing practices—these and other cultural changes occur constantly and rapidly in twentieth-century societies unless strongly braked by moral and legal constraints. When they proceed too rapidly, the older members of a community sometimes come to feel like strangers in their own neighborhoods, aliens in their own country, isolated, lonely, out of the mainstream. The general social environment, the ambience of day to day living, the "tone" of social life, can change so drastically in one generation that individuals may think of their community as essentially different from what it once was, as a pair of blue cotton socks constantly darned with red wool patches may eventually become a different pair of socks, made of a different kind of stuff and showing a very different color. This too is a kind of cultural extinction.

More commonly people think of their communities as being unchanged in their essential identity although what is vaguely called their "way of life" is radically transformed. The New England Protestant community still exists, but the law against blasphemy is no longer enforced, and profanity is in the very air that everyone breathes, originally no doubt a stench in the nostrils of the pious, but now hardly noticed. Miscegenation is no longer a crime in the South, and interracial couples can now be seen in public throughout the land. Here and there coercive laws have been advocated or adopted to "preserve the traditional Welsh Sunday,"[4] to ban hog-raising or nonkosher food; to slow down the trend toward nudity which in the 1960s moved from Bermuda shorts to bikinis to see-through blouses; even to ban modern dancing, modern art, and jazz.[5] The Equal Rights Amendment ran into strong resistance, in Bible Belt states especially, from those who rightly sensed that changing sex roles presage wholesale and widespread changes in the prevailing way of life. What is called a "moral code" is only a small part of a way of life, but it too is subject to the same forces of cultural change, as when premarital liaisons, for example, become common and eventually even accepted by prevailing standards. Not all changes in a way of life are to be regretted by any means, and indeed a case can be made that most changes respond to genuine personal and interpersonal needs. But it would be sanguine, I think, to suppose that all such changes must be for the better; when they are for the worse, we can think of them as evils even before we know whether they harm anyone or not.

12. *Lower standards of manners and the spread of morally graceless conduct.* Every world traveler knows that standards of public manners vary widely from country to country. New York, London, and Tokyo are dynamic crowded centers of comparable size, but citizens of London and Tokyo, in their quite different ways, are elaborately polite and apologetic in their public encounters, whereas equally good-hearted New Yorkers tend to be more aggressive and gruffly blunt. There should be room for a great deal of relativity in the judgments we make about the customary responses of people in different cultures. Rules of manners are a great deal like rules of the road. The important thing is that there *be* rules and that they be understood and followed in similar ways by everyone. There is no reason why widely different sorts of standard manners might not work equally well in different places. The Londoner may find New York to be a jungle, but the New Yorker, knowing what to expect from his fellows, get along just fine. It is possible, moreover, for a society to be too well-mannered. A certain natural bluntness is often to be preferred to highly ritualized circumlocutions. Perhaps that too is, in large degree, a matter of taste. But when relativity has been paid its due, it must be acknowledged that certain critical judgments about standards of manners have the ring of truth to them. A society that respects its aged, for example, is much to be preferred to one in which the infirmities of old age are objects of mockery (even though there may be no more suffering on balance in the latter because the attitudes in question are traditional and expected). And there might well be some golden mean—or at least some acceptable range— between overly mannered and overly aggressive styles. It is possible, I think, to imagine gradual changes in our standards of manners in objectively undesirable directions—changes that threaten to take the grace and civility out of our encounters with strangers. If such changes were little noted nor long regretted, people would take them in stride, and develop immunity to any harm from them. Nevertheless, the change might be regrettable.

13. *General ugliness, depressing drabness, and the like.* How pleasing things look may be a matter of taste, but tastes too are sometimes subject to objective standards of criticism. Negative judgments about the look of the south Bronx are not like expressions of dislike for brussels sprouts. The "tone" or "ambience" of a neighborhood is not only a function of the design, decoration, and condition of its buildings, but also of such factors as the cleanliness of its streets, the freshness of its air, its spaciousness or crowdedness, its coherence or jumbledness, its smells and noises, the visible character of the people on its streets and their conspicuous enterprises, its signs and symbols, its color, verve, and mood. Some communities, blessed with a pleasing look and tone, protect the attractiveness of their neighborhoods with zoning restrictions: only buildings in the traditional style can be constructed in Nantucket. If the

pleasing look of that lovely isle were to be replaced by the familiar commercial tawdriness of most tourist heavens, that might be a "loss," even if it were no one's loss in particular.

2. The conservative thesis

It will repay our attention to examine the purportedly free-floating social-change evils more carefully, for when legal moralists rests their case (as they do surprisingly often) on the need to prevent these evils, they are defending what H.L.A. Hart calls "the conservative thesis,"[6] a quite special variant of the general moralistic position that has perhaps the greatest intuitive plausibility. We can define it here as the equivalent of what we have called "moral conservatism," the thesis that it can be morally legitimate to preserve a society's traditional way of life from radical or essential change by means of legal coercion. That leaves open the question of whether the grounds of the alleged legitimacy is the inherent evil of those changes themselves (their free-floating character) or some incidental evil consequences. Often the conservative thesis is itself derived from, or at least reenforced by, one of the other liberty-limiting principles, and to that extent its defense is "impure."

Frequently the conservative thesis is confused, even by its advocates, with appeals to other grounds for "enforcing morality," grounds that do not include an independent need to arrest social change. The *psychic aggression thesis* and the *social disintegration thesis*, for example, when applied to the enforcement of moral codes (rather than to whole ways of life) appeal to certain indirectly harmful consequences of tolerating otherwise harmless conventional immoralities. The former rests on the dubious empirical premise that deviations from conventional morality even in private are threats to the mental health of others; the latter rests on the even more dubious sociological premise that conventional immoralities threaten every individual with the disintegration of his society and ensuing anarchy. Psychic wounds of sufficient severity are personal harms, and so are conditions of anarchy, so any liberal who accepts the empirical premises stating that such harm follows indirectly from private immoralities can respectfully consider the claim that the immoralities ought to be forbidden by the criminal law.

A third indirect way of arguing for the legal enforcement of a society's customary moral expectations is to invoke explicitly or tacitly the *offense principle*, and argue against legal impunity for discreetly private immoralities on the ground that they would come to be directly offensive anyway, their original privacy notwithstanding. (The conclusion supported by this mode of argument, of course, is just as "impurely moralistic" as that supported by appeals to the harm principle.) As the "immoralities" spread, it is claimed, their presence will inevitably be felt in subtle but pervasive ways that shock or disgust the ordinary person. If 10% of the population is homosexual, allowing homosexual behavior even in private (and only in private) would be like sweeping so much dirt under the rug that large crinkles and bulges would show, which would be as offensive to the unwilling observer as the dirt itself (or almost so). There are empirical presuppositions behind this version of the argument, too, which if true would require the liberal to admit at least the relevance of the reasoning.

A fourth way of arguing for the enforcement of morality is even easier to confuse with pure moral conservatism, since like pure conservatism it does not depend on an appeal to the harm or offense principles. I refer to that "pure legal moralism in the strict sense" which will be discussed in Chapter 30. According to this way of arguing, certain types of genuine immoralities, even when private and harmless, are such evident and odious evils that they should be forbidden on that ground alone. The argument has a perfect simplicity: single premise and single conclusion. James Fitzjames Stephen gave the most eloquent expression of this kind of pure moralism when he wrote his much quoted line: "There are acts of wickedness so gross and outrageous that. . .[protection of others apart], they must be prevented at any cost to the offender and punished if they occur with exemplary severity."[7] Stephen's view is easy to confuse with the "conservative thesis" but it is really quite distinct from it. He argues that such and such activities are inherently immoral; ergo they should be prohibited even when private and harmless to individuals. But according to the conservative, it is drastic social change, not immorality as such, that is the relevant free-floating evil, and it is a common "way of life," not the interests and sensibilities of individual citizens, that requires protection by the criminal law.

It bears repetition that a group's moral code is only part of its "way of life," and by no means the only part that the conservative wishes to preserve. The conservative argument would apply just as well to whatever other elements are central to a way of life. It might seem that no other elements could be as central as the shared moral convictions of a group and that the priority of a moral code is true almost by definition, or at least that its truth follows from a clear understanding of what the morality of a group is. This objection can be forestalled, I think, by a distinction Hart made between a "moral minimum," namely "those restraints and prohibitions that are essential to the existence of any society of human beings whatever"[8] and rules that are not essential to all societies but are distinctive of the society in question. The moral minimum includes rules against violence, homicide, mendacity, and fraud, and it goes without question that these rules are central to *any* group's way of life. The moral minimum rules, however, are all derived from the harm principle, and no one has ever seriously suggested that they do not warrant legal enforcement. Controversy arises only over the moral residuum, those rules that hold their place in a society's moral code whether or not they are thought to prevent individual harms.

Another distinction, one in terms of "centrality," can be made among the rules of the moral residuum itself. Some of these are, and some are not, part of a society's "central core of rules or principles which constitute its pervasive and distinctive style of life."[9] These rules, Hart adds, "do not include every jot and tittle" of a society's code. Among rules in our "central core" that need not even be in the code of every conceivable society are the rules defining and protecting the institution of monogamous marriage which, according to Hart, "is at the heart of our conception of family life" and whose "disappearance would carry with it vast changes throughout society so that without exaggeration we might say that it had changed its essential character."[10] No doubt the moral rules Hart has in mind, including perhaps the prohibition of polygamy, polyandry, and adultery, are indeed among the central parts of the moral code of our society, but they are probably joined in that central core by prohibitions of sexual conduct that cannot be thought to threaten monogamous marriage at all, for example bestiality, masturbation (until recently), and nonpromiscuous cohabitation as a kind of trial marriage. There are, moreover, rules, standards, and ideals in the central core that cannot be thought of as "moral" at all: standards of dress and decorum, religious rites, rituals, and festivals, use of a particular common language, patriotic observances, and the like. "Way of life" is a vague notion in the extreme, but it was once thought precise enough to include baseball and apple pie near the top of the list of what constituted the "American way of life."

Such conservative writers as Walter Berns[11] and Alexander Bickel[12] argue for the legal enforcement of moral norms not because they think that sin should be punished and immorality diminished as ends in themselves (à la Stephen), but because they think legal force is needed to counter threats to the "moral environment" for our traditional way of life. Their targets are such things as dirty words, pornographic books, and live sex shows to consenting audiences. But the form of their arguments is that which has been used in the past to argue for the prohibition of alcoholic beverages, gambling, soft drugs, even modern dancing and modern art. The temperance movement that succeeded in imposing Prohibition on the country was only partly concerned to prevent the harms caused by excessive drinking, and the forms of its arguments were not typically paternalistic. One of its primary targets was the spreading influence of life-styles that deviated from the traditional norms the movement represented, on the one hand the freewheeling style of the sophisticated cocktail-swigging urban or suburban middle classes, on the

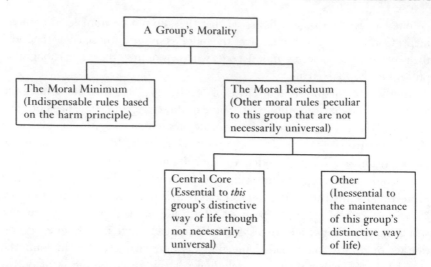

Diagram 29-1. Subdivisions of group morality.

other the ethnic customs of immigrant workers of Catholic and Lutheran backgrounds in which the social drinking of whiskey or beer played a large role. Joseph Gusfield writes that

> the issue of drinking . . . became a politically significant focus for the conflicts between Protestant and Catholic, rural and urban, native and immigrant, middle and lower class. . . . The demand for prohibition laws arises when drinkers have social and political powers as a group, and in their customary habits and beliefs deny the validity of [the] abstinence norms [that form a central part of the way of life of the earlier dominant majority]. By the 1840's the tavern and beer parlor had a leading [and unquestioned] place in the leisure of Germans and Irish. . . . There was no tradition [among them] of temperance norms to appeal effectively to a sense of sin. By the 1850's the issue of drinking reflected a general clash over cultural values and the temperance movement found political allies among the nativist movements. . . . Prohibition came as the culmination of the movement to reform the immigrant cultures and at the height of the immigrant influx into the U.S. . . . *The process of deviance designation in drinking must be seen in terms of the cultural dominance rather than as reflecting necessities of social control* [emphasis added].[13]

It may be thought that the norm against drinking in Bible Belt communities was a *moral* norm, and I confess that I sometimes find the distinction between moral and nonmoral norms very difficult to grasp, especially when the norms in question are at most part of the moral residuum. (Within the class of norms constituting the "moral minimum" there is no difficulty.

"Thou shalt not kill" and "Thou shalt not cheat" are prototypically moral rules.) But if the norm against drinking is borderline "moral," many of the other norms for which the Prohibitionists sought legal sanction were not: "During the 1920's the prohibition organizations included . . . among other non-alcohol problems to which they gave attention, . . . obscene literature, modern dancing, and jazz."[14] And who has not heard fulminations against neighborhood crap games, interracial courtships, sabbatarian violations, rhythm and blues (what used to be called "racial music"), and more, the advocacy of coercive legislation against them in order to prevent cultural erosion and similar evils?

Moral and nonmoral norms that do not prevent harms so much as preserve a traditional way of life are not themselves threatened by every kind of nonconforming action. Gusfield tells us that the repentant deviant who never doubts the legitimacy of the norm but breaks it in a morally weak moment is no threat to the existence of the norm he violates. Nor is the so-called sick deviant who is thought to be unable to help himself. Even the cynical deviant who is self-seeking, amoral, and unrepentant is no real threat to the norm. He doesn't denounce the norms he violates and brandish alternative ones which he deems superior. On the contrary, he owes allegiance to no norms but self-serving ones, and he is an unappealing model for imitation. The real threat to the norm itself, according to Gusfield, is the "enemy deviant": "He accepts his own behavior as proper and derogates the public norm as illegitimate. Such an attitude is particularly apparent in instances of 'business crimes'— gambling, prostitution, drug use—where the very acceptance of such action as legitimate supports the presence of buyers on an economic market."[15] Middle-class housewives who hear from their cleaning women about winnings and losses in the numbers game will learn that betting is as much a part of distinctive black subculture, and as natural and accepted by its members, as gospel singing and soul food. And one is not likely to encounter much guilt about marijuana smoking in the subculture where it prevails. When deviant conduct becomes respectable in this way it is perceived as a real threat to the existence of the norm itself and not merely a deviation from it. Cultural conflict is in the offing and the traditional norm might lose, and with its loss will come drastic change in a way of life. That is the point at which the demand for legal enforcement becomes most insistent.

Despite the familiarity of the conservative style of argument and its common appearance in editorials, sermons, and "letters to the editor," both its friends and enemies among academic writers tend to get it not quite right when they paraphrase it in their learned articles. A case in point: Ronald Dworkin attributes to Lord Devlin the view that the enforcement of morals

(that is, the prohibition of "immoral acts" even when harmless and private)
derives its justification from "the majority's right to follow its own moral
convictions in defending its social environment from changes it opposes."[16]
He then argues effectively that the opinions held by the majority about
certain deviant sexual practices, most notably homosexuality, are not genuine
moral convictions at all, but only prejudices, emotional allergies, feeble rationalizations, mere parrotings of alleged moral authorities, and the like. If they
were genuine moral convictions based on reasons and consistent with widely
shared general principles, then Dworkin suggests that he would have little
objection to their legal enforcement even when unnecessary to prevent harm
and offense. "What is shocking and wrong is not Devlin's idea that the
community's morality counts, but his idea of what counts as the community's
morality."[17] Dworkin himself then is in theory a kind of legal moralist: that
an act is of a sort deemed wrong by the consensus of genuine moral conviction in a community is itself a good and relevant reason, on his view, for
banning it, even when it is harmless and inoffensive. The occurrence even in
private of such acts (if there are any) would, on Dworkin's view, be a kind of
free-floating evil that the state is entitled to prevent. This view resembles
pure moralism in the strict sense more than it resembles the conservative
thesis, but unlike Stephen's view that an act's objective wickedness is a
sufficient ground for prohibiting it, Dworkin requires only that there be a
consensus of sincere and genuinely moral conviction that it is wicked, a
condition that might be somewhat easier to satisfy.

But, in any case, neither Dworkin's position nor the one he ascribes to
Devlin are forms of the conservative thesis as commonly defended. The
conservative is not directly affronted by what he cannot see, nor does he
believe that anyone is wronged by private consensual acts between adults.
But he insists that deviant conduct changes "his" society in essential ways and
makes him an alien in his own community. The people with whom he comes
in contact every day may, for all he knows, have different attitudes and
opinions from those he used to be able to count on. Now he cannot be as free
and easy with them as before. They may in turn suspect that he is not really
one of them, and either turn a cold shoulder or be resentful or patronizing. In
any case, one will have to be more careful than before when there is no
knowing whether one's associates are discreet homosexuals or sexual "perverts," or (even worse) respecters and defenders of such deviants. There may
be no garish public displays of their deviance if the law employs an offense
principle, but still one can see them pouring out of theaters whose marquees
advertise (discreetly of course) x-rated films, and one can notice the proliferation of books with sexual themes in bookstores and libraries.

Inevitably there is a concomitant change in the way people—especially young people—talk. Offensive words lose their offensiveness to most of one's fellow citizens, and subjects rarely talked about in public are now routine topics of general conversation. The air one breathes is a different air, and one is impelled quite naturally to think of metaphors about cultural littering and moral pollution. Perhaps most discouraging of all, one feels one's influence over one's own children slipping, and one's efforts to transmit traditional values to them undermined. The latter lament is expressed poignantly by Walter Berns:

> . . .unfortunately, in the present intellectual climate, education in this area is almost impossible. Consider the case of the parent who wants to convince his children of the impropriety of the use of the four-letter verb meaning to copulate. At the present time the task confronting him is only slightly less formidable than that faced by the parent who would teach his children that the world is flat. Just as the latter will have to overcome a body of scientific evidence to the contrary, the former will have to overcome the power of common usage and the idea of propriety it implies. . . . Now, to a quickly increasing extent, the four letter verb—more "honest" in the opinion of its devotees—is being used openly and therefore without impropriety. The parent will fail in his effort to educate because he will be on his own, trying to teach a lesson his society no longer wants taught—by the law, by the language, or by the schools.[18]

So in the end, the aging conservative feels that he is not only an alien in his own land, but a stranger in his own family.

It will be little comfort to him to show, in the manner of Ronald Dworkin, that his attitudes are not genuine moral convictions. He may be happy to admit that there are, or could be, other communities whose customs, practices, and traditions, whose norms of conduct and standards of manners, while greatly different from those of the community he treasures, are equally rational, or if you will, "moral." This is not the point. Our own traditions, he might reply, have been built up by many generations of our ancestors; it would be a waste and a betrayal to let them wither away, to be eroded like the pillars of ancient temples in the sandstorms. Once the radical new changes have taken place, the old way is gone forever, and this, he might add, is an evil of the same sort as the extinction of a biological species.

Then, the final note of bitterness. "All this happened without anyone consulting me," he might complain. "What vote did I have about whether the old ways were to continue or not? What choice, in fact, did anyone have? An overwhelming majority of us, helpless to use the law in our defense, simply watched the changes take place, with growing resentment or passive resignation." "It is not a sufficient answer," says the conservative philosopher, "that social practices will not change unless the majority willingly participates in the change. Social corruption works through media and forces quite beyond

the control of any conscious design at all."[19] Deep changes in the moral
environment, then, are thought to be not simply evil, but also unfair, the
violation of the "rights of the majority to defend its social environment from
changes it opposes." In this way the conservative thesis borrows support
from a new source, an appeal to a kind of moral majoritarianism. It may well
be that certain social changes are free-floating evils, but be that as it may, *that*
is not why the state has a right to resist them by using the criminal law.
Rather it is because these changes are contrary to the will of the majority, and
therefore illicit in their origins. Raymond Gastil puts the majoritarian case for
"the enforcement of morals" succinctly. Likening the moral environment to a
public park, he writes: "Since everyone's likes and dislikes cannot be accommodated in the same square, the obvious basis of decision as to regulation
becomes the desire of the majority of its users."[20] Many conservatives, I
think, would settle for less. Thinking of attitudes that were once virtually
unanimous but now have dwindled and are threatened, they may claim legal
protection only for those central core moral standards to which not merely a
simple majority, but the overwhelming consensus of citizens, have always
paid allegiance.

3. Impure moral conservatism: arguments for the conservative thesis based on fairness

There are at least three forms of the conservative argument for the legal enforcement of conventional morality, two of which are "impurely conservative" since
they appeal ultimately to some consideration other than the inherent evil of
drastic social change as such, and one of which is "pure" since it appeals
ultimately to the supposed free-floating evil of drastic social change. (It is of
course open to writers to combine these arguments in the same tract.) One
impure support for moral conservatism is an appeal to the rights of an overwhelming majority, as such, to prevent unwanted changes in its traditional
way of life. This form of argument, described sketchily in section 2 above, is
essentially based on fairness, for it concludes that it is unfair (and hence morally illegitimate) to alter the moral environment of a community without the
consent of a majority (or at least a quite substantial minority) of its members. If
the changes are evils, according to this view, they are genuine *grievance evils*,
wrongs to determinate persons who have a right to complain that they have
been treated unjustly. This "impure" appeal to the conservative principle in
support of the legal enforcement of established morality is often supplemented
by an appeal to the other element in harm, namely set-back interest. Many or
most of the unwilling majority, it is said, have genuine *interests*, investments of
their own personal well-being, in the perpetuation of the traditional ways, so

that an abandonment of those ways, through either abrupt or gradual changes, would be a setback to that interest, and in virtue also of its being unfair, it would be a genuine harm to people whose prevention would legitimize the use of the criminal law. The appeal to moral conservatism then is only at an intermediate stage in the argument. The ultimate legitimizing appeal is made to the harm principle. (This form of impure moral conservatism will be discussed below in §4.) The third form of conservative argument gets along without an appeal to fairness or to majority rights, or to direct harm to other-regarding personal interests, invoking instead the broadly moralistic principles that the prevention of certain free-floating evils is itself a good reason for legal coercion. Extreme and unwelcome changes in a group's traditional way of life are then held to be among the sorts of free-floating evils that the state has a presumptive right to prevent by criminal legislation.

How should we respond to these arguments? The argument from fairness, I think, is not only defective in its own terms; it can be used to justify far more coercion than even the conservative presumably would welcome, and in the end it can be turned back against the conservative thesis itself. First of all, Gastil's "public square" analogy will not survive scrutiny long. To be sure, you cannot have a band concert, transcendental meditation sessions, carnivals, six-day bicycle races, automobile traffic, and public promenades all at the same time in the same small public square, and which activities to permit under these crowded circumstances admittedly is a question of public policy, to be settled in a democracy (within certain constitutional limits) by majoritarian procedures. But there is plenty of room, even in a small public park, for an unlimited variety of thoughts, beliefs, and attitudes. Catholics take up no more room than Protestants, Republicans no more than Democrats, blacks no more than whites. And if we find it easy to accommodate religious, political, and ethnic pluralism, indeed pluralism of every *other* kind, why not moral pluralism too? Why is a vote required to decide whether to let in homosexuals as well as heterosexuals, voluptuaries as well as virgins, secret readers of pornography, pot smokers, and numbers players, as well as Bible students, pipe smokers, and chess players? (Remember that offensive displays, solicitations, and the like *can* be prohibited on liberal principles.) Walter Barnett chides proponents of the conservative position for uncritically assuming "that two or more moralities cannot exist in mutual toleration in the same society,"[21] even while they are willing to concede, however grudgingly, that the whole spectrum of religious differences can easily be accommodated, not to mention the political, ideological, ethnic, aesthetic, and linguistic contrasts. Barnett pounces in particular on Devlin's insistence that every society must choose between monogamy and polygamy. Why could they not exist side by side in the same society?, he asks, and finds it impossible to "see any inherent incompatibility between them."[22] There would simply be "two marital regimes in a society to choose from,"[23] instead of one.

If we remind ourselves, as we constantly must in this discussion, that we are not thinking of offensive public displays or obtrusive nuisances forced on the attention of disgusted captive observers, but only practices and preferences freely exercised in private or in reserved public places before willing observers, our initial doubts about the plausibility of moral pluralism quickly vanish. A neighborhood can be harmonious and attractive for anyone to live in even though it contains Liberal and Fundamentalist Protestants, Roman and Greek Catholics, Reform and Orthodox Jews, Moslems, Buddhists, atheists, and indifferents. Any one of these may disapprove of the religious practices of the others and resent it if they were constantly obtruded upon his attention. But what the others do in their own churches, he will admit, is their business and no barrier to friendly neighborliness with them. How is the case any different when we consider homosexuals and "perverts," crapshooters and drinkers? We would be offended if we could escape being captive witnesses of their disapproved activities only at great inconvenience to ourselves, but what goes on in the privacy of their bedrooms and public meeting places need not sever the bonds of community between us. Our metaphorical public park is not as crowded as Gastil assumes.

But even if we were to grant (as we should not) the aptness of the "public square" analogy, it would not follow in any automatic way that majority rule would be the only morally legitimate procedure for deciding who is to have access to the park. The park commission composed of officials elected in free elections would surely have a right to decide on general policy grounds to exclude military bands, motorcycles, or even bicycles, or as the case may be, to reserve a place and time for band concerts and bicycles, but ban horseback riding, ball games, and unleashed dogs. But when antecedently recognized *rights* enter the picturre, there the majoritarian procedures find their limit. The park commissioners could hardly settle their problem by restricting the park to either males or females, old or young, blacks or whites, socialists or economic conservatives. Neither a majority nor its representatives can be permitted to make its decision in that fashion. How then could a majority rightly make its decision on the equally irrelevant ground of sexual preferences or private reading tastes?

Finally, the majoritarian argument backfires against its proponents in another way. If we are going to use the political analogy at all, we should take it seriously. Democratic theory endorses the moral propriety of majority rule only when minorities have been left free to try to become majorities if they can. Gastil himself observes that "The right to try to form new majorities is the basic right given to individuals in both the majority and the minority that makes meaningful the rights of either."[24] Trying to become a majority presumably requires efforts to *persuade* one's fellows to join one's cause, but that opportunity is hardly open to the person whose favored activities are deemed criminal and banned on pain of punishment. When the minute vegetarian party loses an election and is thus shown to be a very tiny minority indeed, this is not followed by the legal prohibition of vegetarianism and the jailing of the party's leaders. How then does the analogy extend to (say) homosexuality? (Actually the analogy is not only inconsistently applied by conservatives, it is flawed from the beginning in any case. "Moral minorities" do not necessarily even wish to persuade a majority to their styles of life, but only to persuade the majority to leave them in peace.)

Whatever principle of fairness the moral conservative uses to justify the legal prohibition of unestablished minority styles of life, he will be hard put to explain why the principle doesn't establish with equal cogency the fairness of sweeping totalitarian restrictions. In particular, if it is fair to enforce moral conformity on conservative grounds, why is it not fair to enforce religious conformity in religiously homogeneous communities on the same grounds? Surely the moral heterodoxies of today's swingers are no more odious to moral conservatives than were the damnable heresies and sacrileges of rival religious sects to true believers in days gone by. And when we subtract from the sum total of our moral code that rather substantial part of it that coincides with the universal moral minimum (that is, its prohibitions against force, violence, and fraud) what is left can hardly be deemed more essential to the identity of our community than religious fidelity was to the homogeneously pious communities of our ancestors. So the argument from the need to preserve a way of life would apply *a fortiori* to religious nonconformity. And indeed a precisely parallel argument for the legal prohibition of religious unorthodoxy was abandoned historically only after a couple of centuries of indecisive warfare between mutually intolerant sects.

It would be impossible, moreover, for the conservative argument to stop short of crossing the line between the prohibition of a disapproved sort of conduct and the prohibition of speech advocating that conduct, or even speech advocating the permissibility or the legalizing, of that kind of conduct. If speech is to be left free while conventional immoralities are to be prohibited, the case for the prohibition must be based on other than conservative grounds. One newspaper article advocating the legalization of marijuana could do more to weaken the barrier to the spread of pot smoking than a hundred youths who smoke in the public park or a thousand youths who smoke unobserved in their private quarters. One article by a respected psychoanalyst or anthropologist defending the reasonableness in some circumstances of adultery could do more to weaken the norm against that practice than a thousand circumspect liaisons.

Once more, how is the conservative argument to stop short of justifying, again on grounds of "fairness," the enforced regulation of hairstyle and the prohibition of long beards and styles of clothing of those who advertise themselves as nonconformists? Do not these *visible* deviations from prevailing standards weaken those norms as much as the existence of deviant attitudes, tastes, sex lives, and reading and entertainment preferences that are only indulged in private?

Considerations of fairness, when they do have a bearing on these issues, seem to oppose rather than reenforce the conservative argument. If we assume, as seems natural, that human nature comes in different sizes and shapes, so to speak, that there are deep and morally significant differences among normal people in respect to basic temperament and emotional needs, then to insist that only some of these types of character, even if they are the most common ones, are entitled to their satisfaction, would seem to be unfair to the others, a form of discrimination as arbitrary as racial prejudice. Suppose most people wore a size nine shoe. If making shoes in any other size were forbidden by law, wouldn't that be unfair to those who happen to have unusually large or small feet? Mill's case for "experiments in living" was only partly based on utilitarian considerations, his own protests notwithstanding. It is not *fair* to a young person not to let him try on a large variety of lifestyles in his search to find one that best fits his inherited propensities and distinctive needs.

The shoe-size analogy is not wholly apt. I must admit that not all is relative in this area. There are certain kinds of human character and modes of life that I would hate to see triumph in the Darwinian struggle that a liberal state would permit. I do not view with equanimity the prospect of a community whose majority is primarily devoted to lotus-eating, or to the exclusive reading of pornography, and the like. But I don't understand why conservatives who share these particular attitudes of mine pessimistically assume that in a fair fight the better values would inevitably be at a disadvantage, so that only the values they believe to be superior need the added help of the state's iron fist. Do they really believe that pornography seriously threatens to make the human race forget Shakespeare, or that many, most, or even all people would prefer a steady diet of mass-produced stories generated by some simple formulas to Saul Bellow's novels or the political memoirs of Henry Kissinger or David Stockman? (When did a publisher ever give a pornographer a two million dollar advance?)

I would hate to see us become a nation of pornography readers for the same reason I deplore the widespread consumption of bad literature of any kind (I mean literature that is bad on certain *literary* grounds). People who enjoy trite and obvious novels written by formula—potboilers, "good guy-bad guy" Westerns, sentimental tear-jerkers, gothic romances—tend to lack discrimination and independent judgment in real life. They will be as easily manipulated by advertisers and politicians as they are by hack writers, for their responses to stock stimuli in art and life are unthinking knee-jerks. They are as likely to be incapable of discriminating nuances of feeling in their dealings with others as the pornography-addict is incapable of meeting the challenge of a genuine love affair. Requiring courses in good literature in our schools receives its primary justification from the power of literature to enlarge our insight, through vicarious identifications with plausible characters, into "the varieties of human ideals, outlooks, . . . and experiences."[25] Stereotyped pseudo-literature has the very opposite effect. So if the bad effects on feeling and judgment of a habitual preference for pornography are the grounds for prohibiting it, then they equally justify the criminal prohibition of all cynically hack-written pseudo-literature. Proper education in the feelings should be compulsory, but for children only. For adults it is never too late for education, but much too late for compulsion.

But to get back to fairness, when *is* the "fight" between contending lifestyles a fair one? No parliamentary body legislates these things; we have no "moral constitution" specifying the permissible means of persuasion; there are no written rules of procedure analogous to those governing judicial proceedings. But if the idea of fairness is to have any application to the processes of cultural change, I should think that it would rule out all influences on the outcome but the perceived merits and demerits of the alternatives. He who would reform our moral environment by fair means should be prepared openly and forthrightly to express his dissent, and attempt to argue, persuade, and offer reasons, while continuing to live in his own preferred way with persuasive quiet and dignity, neither harming others nor offering counterpersuasive offense to tender sensibilities. On the other hand, a citizen uses illegitimate means of social change when he abandons argument and example for indoctrination and propaganda, force and fraud. If the latter are the things that make the contest unfair, then it is surely unfair to use the power of the state to affect moral belief *one way or the other*. (Again, the example of religious doctrines and observances in a religiously pluralistic society makes a good model.) A contest is fair when neither contender has an unfair advantage; it can hardly be fair when the referee forcibly sides with one of the contenders.

4. Impure moral conservatism: arguments for the conservative thesis based on harm to interests

In one of his more memorable passages, Mill wrote that "There are many who consider as an injury to themselves any conduct which they have a

distaste for, and resent it as an outrage to their own feelings. . ."[26] It would
be absurd, of course, to claim that one had been personally "injured" or
wronged by the private conduct of some stranger on the sole ground that one
disapproves of it or "has a distaste for" it. But moral conservatives of the
"impure" variety to be discussed in this section present a much more plausible ground for their fancied personal grievances. Some disapproved-of private conduct wrongs them, they claim, precisely because it *harms* them, and
harms them because it sets back a genuine, at least partly other-regarding
interest they have in living in a certain kind of (homogeneous) community,
namely a community in which persons do not behave in the disapproved-of
way, even in private. Preventing such harm to them, they claim, legitimizes
criminal prohibitions of the disapproved-of conduct of the others, under the
harm principle. What can I, as a liberal, say to a person who regards his
neighbor's religious and/or moral nonconformity to be not simply something
he disapproves of, but something that causes him harm by setting back an
interest he has in living in a community of a certain sort?

My problem in replying to this conservative use of the harm principle can
be traced to its origin in Volume one of this work.[27] In that volume I argued
that to harm a person is to set back his interest and violate his right. The
concept of an interest was only partly analyzed, but I characterized a person's
interests as "distinguishable components of his good." What is *in his interest*,
in short, is what is good for him, and that in turn is what promotes the whole
economy of his more ulterior interests. To *have an interest*, in turn, is to have a
stake in some outcome, just as if one had "invested" some of one's own good
in it, thus taking the risk of personal setback or harm. I argued then[28] that a
person could have genuine interests not merely in future states of himself
(e.g., wealthy, knowledgeable, virtuous, powerful) and the means thereto
(money, health, self-control), but also "other-regarding interests," some in
the well-being or ill-being of specific other persons desired at least in part as
an end it itself ("vicarious interests"), and some in more impersonal outcomes
like victory of a political cause, discovery of the cure for a disease, the
extension of astronomical knowledge, or the construction of a cathedral, also
desired partly as ends in themselves and not solely as means to some ulterior
self-regarding purpose of the desirer. (Some of the latter interests are of the
"collective" type, interests each person in a group has because all the others
do). I argued then that harm to other-regarding interests of both the vicarious
and the relatively impersonal types is not only possible, but, in the case of
vicarious harms at least, common and familiar, especially when love has
created a stake in another person's good. A parent may have an important
personal interest in the well-being of his child so that whatever harms the
child, *ipso facto* harms him.[29]

But now a certain amount of slippage begins to take place. Suppose a parent has what *resembles* a "vicarious interest" in his child's achievements, but it is not an interest in the child's good *simpliciter*, but rather an interest that the child achieve his own good in one particular, obsessively desired way, say by becoming a doctor or a nun. We can imagine that a parent has long dreamed of his son or daughter being (say) a doctor, that he deliberately started a family with no other aim than producing a doctor, that from their early childhood he has tried to instill that ambition in his children, that he regards it as the final aim of his own life, in support of which he has invested not only his savings but his own deepest hopes, resting his chance of personal fulfillment on the outcome. It is clear that he has an enormous stake in his child becoming a doctor, that that goal is one of his *interests*, in the sense of this book. Suppose then that he reads this book and learns, after his son has rejected medical school for the life of a poet and vagabond, that he has been *harmed* by his son. It would of course be absurd for the state to exercise coercion against the son to prevent this harm to the father, but the harm principle might seem to recognize a *prima facie* moral claim in the father to such "protection."

The next example reveals slippage in a more dangerous direction. All his life, Terrence Truview has dreamed of becoming a founding member of a community of like-minded puritan fundamentalists. Together with his comrades he works and saves feverishly and single-mindedly for twenty years, buys a remote plot of land, moves his worldly goods to the new utopia, labors around the clock constructing a church building and modest homes. Twenty more years pass, and the pioneer settlement has grown into a municipality of twenty thousand like-minded souls with a political government of its own, a town council, public schools, and a police force. What is absent are such hateful things as television sets, movie theaters, rock music, hard liquor, and the like. Terrence Truview is proud and content. His dominant life ambition has been fulfilled. He has invested his hopes in an outcome that has materialized. He has achieved his own good.

Then it is discovered that a member of the second generation, one Farley Fairjoy, has been secretly reading romantic novels in the privacy of his quarters, occasionally drinking a can or two of beer, and listening (at low volume of course) to popular music on his tiny radio. He is warned by the town elders that he must desist. But he points out to them, respectfully but firmly, that he is entirely discreet in his enjoyments, neither injuring nor directly offending any of his neighbors. He ends his defense rhetorically by quoting Thomas Jefferson: "It does me no injury for my neighbor to say there are twenty gods or no god. It neither picks my pocket nor breaks my leg."[30] Deeply wounded, Terrence Truview rejoins that *he* for one, and presumably

a majority of the others, has been harmed in a perfectly literal sense, since
their paramount interest in living in a community of a certain sort has definitely been set back. Then quoting Feinberg instead of Jefferson, he departs
for the town council meeting to introduce criminal legislation against the
possession or use of novels, beer, and radios.

When I wrote *Harm to Others*, I assumed that any supporting argument for
legislation like that proposed by Terrence Truview would tacitly invoke
either the offense principle or some form of legal moralism. It didn't occur to
me that supporters of the so-called "enforcement of morality" might prefer to
argue in such subtle and indirect ways from the harm principle itself. If that
had occurred to me in time, I no doubt would have tried to control the
damage to my liberalism by adding another "mediating maxim for the application of the harm principle," one which would place constraints on the way
appeals to harm prevention can be made in those quite common circumstances in which interests are opposed. In those circumstances, a statute
protecting one set of interests would necessarily lead to the setback of the
interests that conflict with the protected ones. My problem at this point is
twofold: how to formulate the mediating maxim so that it does the desired job
cleanly, and how to support that maxim against the charge that it is merely an
ad hoc repair job.

At the conclusion of my unfortunately sketchy account of conflicting interests,[31] I formulated the following mediating maxim to guide legislators in
their use of the otherwise intolerably vague harm principle: "Where opposed
interests of different kinds are related in such a way that if the law is silent
then the one will be set back to a certain degree, whereas if the law protects
that one then the other will be thwarted to the same degree, the legislature
should protect that interest which is the more *important*. Relative importance
is a function [I continued] of three different respects in which opposed interests can be compared: (1) how "vital" they are in the interest networks of their
possessors; (2) the degree to which they are reenforced by others interests,
private and public; and (3) their inherent moral quality." We can imagine,
first of all, that in our present example interests of the Truview type and
interests of the Fairjoy type tend typically to be of equal vitality in their
possessors' interest networks. Secondly, I did not intend the reenforcement
test to warrant simply counting hands in a community to determine how
many persons had interests of one of the conflicting types and how many of
the other. Rather this test is to measure the convergence of radically different
kinds of interest behind each of the conflicting interest-types, and we can
safely imagine that that test too is indecisive in the present case. Finally I
restricted the "inherent moral quality" test to certain extreme and untypical
cases (if there are any) where "all reasonable persons" can recognize some

interests as sadistic or morbid and hence "less worth protecting" than any of the great miscellany of potentially conflicting innocent interests. I am willing to assume what seems obvious, that in the present example both Truview's and Fairjoy's interests are of the morally innocent, nonsadistic sort.

We need therefore a fourth test of the relative "importance" of conflicting interest-types if the harm principle is to be usable at all in cases of this kind. Those of us who would like to be liberals if we can do so coherently would of course prefer that the supplementary test favor Fairjoy's interest, somehow, over Truview's, even though Truview's interest in more widely shared in the political community in question. We might be tempted at the start to characterize Fairjoy's interest as self-regarding and Truview's as other-regarding (see Vol. I, pp. 70–79), and then affirm the greater importance, as a general matter, of self-regarding over other-regarding interests. That hasty move, however, would have the absurd consequence that when A's entirely self-promoting financial interest conflicts with B's equally vital altruistic or public-spirited interest, A's interest should automatically take precedence. We must, therefore, distinguish subkinds of interest in both the self-regarding and other-regarding genera with the purpose of identifying the relevant classes of which Fairjoy's and Truview's conflicting interests are members. At the very least we should discount the importance of those self-regarding interests that are *selfish*—that is, interests in acquiring personal advantages unreasonably at the expense of others (see Vol. I, pp. 73–74). Of course we cannot prejudge the question of whether Fairjoy's or Truview's interests are selfish without begging the question that is before us. Perhaps it is better to assume, *ex hypothesi*, that neither is selfish. That would help preserve the initial impression of their conflict as close or even tragic. But we would want to exclude from the list of important interests those that are thoughtlessly greedy or cruelly indifferent to the sufferings of others.

Fairjoy's interest in drinking beer, reading novels, and listening to popular music, or, more generally, in securing a certain kind of life-style *for himself*, is a predominantly self-regarding interest. To be sure, no man (and that includes Fairjoy) is an island, and his interest in achieving that life-style generates instrumental interests in the noninterference and even active cooperation of others. Other people must continue to manufacture radios, brew beer, write novels, etc. And Fairjoy might very well have a partly derivative, partly independent, social interest in sharing his pleasures with others. But there is a fairly clear sense in which Fairjoy's interest is, and Truview's interest is not, a predominantly *personal interest*, an ulterior interest in how he is to live his own life. For the most part, the other-regarding interests it spawns are instrumental.

In contrast, Truview's interest is predominantly other-regarding, an inter-

est in how other people, including Fairjoy, live *their* lives. But its membership
in the other-regarding category alone is not what makes Truview's interest less
important than Fairjoy's. Rather, it is the particular subclass of other-
regarding acts of which it is a member that has this consequence. Let us focus
then on a distinction between two ways A can have an other-regarding interests in B. On the one hand, A's interest in B might be what in Volume one (pp.
70–79) I called a *vicarious interest*, an interest in B's well-being as an end-in-itself
(as in love) or in B's ill-being as an end in itself (as in "disinterested hate" or
malice). For our present purposes, we can exclude the malevolent interests
from the class of vicarious interests and make vicarious interests benevolent by
definition. (The "importance" of the malevolent interests might well be discounted anyway by the "inherent moral quality" test.) On the other hand, A's
other-regarding interest in B may be an interest in some state or condition of B
other than the advancement of B's own interests. What A wants for B and has
an interest in bringing about in that case is quite independent of what B wants
for himself or what is in B's interest, though A may have an independent
(vicarious) or derivative (instrumental) interest in B's concurrence as well. We
can characterize A's ulterior interest in B's life-style as a predominantly *external
interest*, and one that may well be in conflict with B's own personal interest.[32] I
think that a case can be derived from a more-than-liberal consensus that the
personal interests are more important, more worth protecting in general than
the external ones.[33]

In the case of the father's external interest in his son's becoming a doctor,
there is a conflict between the son's interest in living his own life in one way,
and the father's interest in his son's living his life in another way. Both
interests are equally interests, equally components of their possessor's good;
moreover, it is conceivable that they are equally vital interests representing
equally great stakes; and they are surely equally innocent interests. Still, if
we must choose the more important interest, it seems to me, we must choose
the son's, precisely because it is a personal interest rather than an external
one. The son's interest in how he lives his own life is more important than the
father's interest in how another person lives his life, other things being equal,
because the life in contention is *his* life, not someone else's. I don't think this
judgment is strictly *ad hoc*, having as its sole merit that it eliminates some
harm-principle support for the legal enforcement of conventional morality
and prevailing religion. Rather I strongly suspect that this judgment derives
from a moral consensus of persons on both sides of the controversy over the
legal enforcement of morality, at least insofar as they attach preponderant
value to personal autonomy, as we presumed in Volume three. This proposed new measure of the comparative importance of competing interests is
designed to capture the intuitive force of Mill's final comment on the person

who considers another's disapproved-of private conduct to be a personal injury to himself:

> . . . there is no parity between the feeling of a person for his own opinion [or practice or values] and the feeling of another who is offended [even harmed in his external interest] at his holding [doing] it, no more than between the desire of a thief to take a purse and the desire of the right owner to keep it.[34]

To the believer in *de jure* personal autonomy (and that includes most of us, at least implicitly) he is the "right owner" of his own life, and even the genuine interest of other parties in how he lives it in private, though more respectable than that of "thieves," is of comparatively little importance.

The conflict between the Truviews and the Fairjoys of the world is perhaps trickier to deal with than that between parents and their grown children, but I think it can be resolved in the same way. The conflicting interests are equally interests, equally vulnerable, equally vital, and equally innocent. But Fairjoy's interest is a purely personal one. No direct reference need be made to any other parties in specifying what it is an interest *in*. The only implied behavior of others is their noninterference. Truview's interest is an interest in there not being others in his community who behave privately in certain ways, have private pleasures of certain kinds, or cultivate values of certain sorts. His external interest in how others live their lives and choose their values conflicts with Fairjoy's personal interest in how he lives his *own* life and selects his *own* values. When two persons each have interests in how one of them lives his life, the interests of the one whose life it is are the more important. I should think that the denial of this judgment is virtually tantamount to a denial that personal autonomy, so long celebrated by philosophers of diverse sorts, has very great moral relevance to political controversies. I concede that there are difficult borderline cases for the distinction between personal and external interests, but, vague as it is, the mediating maxim that employs it would close the door at least part way to a much too easy victory for the partisans of illiberal coercion.[35]

In summary, one person can have a genuine interest in the private life of another of an "external" sort, for example an interest that he have "correct values" as an end in itself. "Incorrect behavior" of that other party, even when private and discreet and having no direct adverse effect on any one else's personal interests, can "harm" the first party's interest, in the sense simply of affecting it adversely or setting it back. But since legal coercion would set back an interest of the nonconformist that is more *important* than the external interest of the first party, the nonconformist does not *wrong* the first party in pursuing that interest, and the first party is not harmed in the sense of this book, that which combines set-back interest and violated right.

The harm principle, therefore, will not legitimize criminal "enforcement of morality" in the cases we have been considering.

This sketchy argument has been rejected by Professor Eugene Schlossberger, whose arguments[36] deserve attention here, since they may require us to further modify our position. Schlossberger is quite unconvinced that personal interests are always more "important" than competing external ones. First, he makes a case for the profound *personal* importance some impersonal or external wants (Schlossberger calls them "world-oriented wants") may have. Indeed, our most important self-regarding wants "depend ultimately on ways we want the world to be, upon general values." "My desire to publish a groundbreaking paper, to take just one example, depends essentially on a vision of knowledge and understanding as general goods. For I would not have the kind of interest in philosophy that I in fact do, including my interest in such 'self-regarding' activities as increasing my knowledge of philosophy, did I not desire that the frontiers of knowledge be pushed back." In short, my important personal interests, those of the most ulterior kind (see Vol. I, Chap. 1, §§4–6), tend to presuppose "general values against which the world can be measured independently of my participation in it." But Schlossberger is too cautious to maintain that each and every important self-regarding desire presupposes a particular world-oriented desire, but only that "in order to have self-regarding desires significant enough to be protected . . . one must have at least some world-oriented ones." Without such interests, we can behave in one way rather than another, only "as heliotropes follow the sun."

Having thus shown that world-oriented interests are important, Schlossberger concludes that "I have as *legitimate* an interest (whether or not it is as *strong* an interest) in the world's being a morally acceptable world as I do in my having enough to eat." Here the conclusion employs one example (acceptable moral actions and feelings of others) while the premises employed another (the expansion of the frontiers of knowledge). The former, being more probably an example of an "external" interest, seems more likely to clash with the personal autonomy of other people than would the latter. But then Schlossberger moves on to examples of competing personal interests that he thinks lack great importance and fare poorly when compared to the "world-oriented wants" with which they are likely to clash. One is that of a private individual whose "interest" in masturbation clashes with another person's "interest" in living in a world without masturbation. As Schlossberger envisages this clash, *A*, by using the law to prevent *B* from masturbating, prevents *B* from living his life as he wishes, but alternatively and equally, "by masturbating *B* prevents *A* from living *A*'s life as *A* wishes." This is supposed to be a counterexample to the claim that personal interests are more important, *ceteris paribus*, than external ones. Schlossberger's other example he presents as follows:

> Suppose that it is truly, objectively wrong to eat pork, and that a given Rabbi gives an irrefutable argument for this. Moreover, he argues persuasively that his desire to live in a sanctified society is frustrated by *C*'s consumption of pickled ham [presumably in private]. Now *C* accepts the Rabbi's argument; he agrees that eating pickled ham is immoral, and prevents others from achieving an important good, namely living in a sanctified society. "But", says *C*, "I like the taste of pickled ham. So I'm immoral; too bad."

Here again the examples are selected (or invented) to fit the point. In both, the personal "interest" (or passing fancy) is not vital, and it is presented as not merely "personal," but self-indulgent and unattractive. In the ham-eating example, there is even admitted "immorality." What a contrast these examples make with Mill's example of a "religious bigot," who "when charged with disregarding the religious feelings of others [retorts] that they disregard his feelings by persisting in their abominable worship or creed."[37] In Mill's example there is a clash between a personal interest in religious worship and (perhaps) an equally genuine external ("world-oriented") interest in having a religiously homogeneous society, interests alike in their vitality and innocence, and differing only in that one is personal and the other external. In examples of this type, it is clear to the partisan of personal autonomy that since both interests cannot be protected, the personal interest should prevail.

What are we to say, however, when the clash is between one of Schlossberger's "world-oriented interests" and a merely self-indulgent one that presupposes no higher impersonal principle or moral commitment? What of my interest in being able to drink a bottle of beer whenever I feel like it, when that interest clashes with the puritan's more widely held interest, of equal vitality and innocence, in living in an alcohol-free society? The puritan's interest is a personal one, but it may presuppose an equally vital interest of a world-oriented sort that there *be* an alcohol-free society, whether he lives in it or not. My beer-drinking interest looks paltry and petty compared to that. But fine moral discriminations among competing interests of equal vitality and innocence are out of place. Once an interest qualifies as "innocent," that is, not sadistically or morbidly intending other people's pain or harm as its ultimate goal (see Vol. I, Chap. 5, §6), then it is an unrewarding exercise to try to attach weights to conflicting interests on the legislative scale according to their more subtle moral properties. If the desire to drink beer (or to masturbate, or to eat pickled ham) is to be dismissed as "merely" self-indulgent, though its moral innocence is otherwise duly acknowledged, then we might with equal justification dismiss the puritan's interest that beer not be drunk (or the corresponding interests of Schlossberger's anti-masturbator and rabbi) as officious busybodies' interests or gratuitous meddlers' interests, for it is difficult to understand how a desire for a pure society could become so powerful as to make its object a component of a person's own good, without an element of that morally unsavory sort. But when the name-calling is over, both sides would have to acknowledge that the distinctions between morally attractive and morally repellent motivation, and between personal and external desires, cut across one another, and that there is no feasible way of generalizing for all or most examples a "weight" on the legislative scale for whole classes of innocent external and personal interests, "on the whole" and "by and large."

The added weight of the personal interests comes not from any necessary inherent moral superiority of self-regarding concerns but rather from the protection personal autonomy gives to the area that is one's own proper business. The beer drinker's "interest" (if his taste preference could ever amount to such a status) is reenforced by his general interest in liberty, that is in being himself the one to decide whether to drink or not, and what to drink when he has a choice. That in turn might very well presuppose, as Schloss-berger suggests, one of his impressive "world-oriented interests" in the existence of a community in which everybody's autonomy is equally and fully respected, and also a self-regarding interest, equal in its comprehensiveness to the puritan's interest in living in a sanctified society, in living in a liberal community where everybody honors an established tradition of respecting the personal autonomy of everyone else, and diversity is cultivated and welcomed. With all that in the background, the beer-drinker's interest seems more prepossessing on the scales.[38]

5. Pure moral conservatism: arguments for the conservative thesis based on the need to prevent free-floating social-change evils

When a writer makes a strong case for the preservation of his community's traditional ways, even by legal force if necessary, he may be appealing (as in §4) to an other-regarding *interest* of his own and his neighbors in the preservation of the old ways, or he may be appealing to a widely held *judgment* that change would be an evil even if not exactly a harm. Very likely the distinction will not have occurred to him, and, even if it has, he may find it too vague to apply to the case at hand. In order for the preservation of traditional patterns to be an ulterior interest or focal aim of anyone's, that person must invest a very great amount of hope and desire in it, and, in most cases, even effort and dedication (see Vol. I, Chap 1, §3). Otherwise the dreaded changes, if they should occur, will only disappoint him, but not detract from his well-being. Needless to say, this degree of "investment" is psychologically difficult to achieve, and with the exception of truly dedicated workers whose cause is a passion (as in our example of the fundamentalist pioneer in §4), most moral conservatives rest their case on the importance of preventing largely free-floating social-change evils.

It would seem then that, for the most part, cultural change in a democracy is at most a free-floating evil. So we shall assume, at any rate, in this section. Impersonal evils, however, cannot be personal grievances, or violations of individual rights. In some cases, of course, one person is justified in using force against a second to prevent the second from harming a third. One need not, therefore, have a personal grievance of one's own to have a moral justification for coercion, provided that one acts to protect the rights of another. But *no one at all* needs "protection" from the occurrence of a free-floating evil or can claim the prevention of the evil as *his* due. So invasions of the interest that persons are presumed to have in their own liberty, if done in order to arrest cultural change, cannot be justified on the grounds that individuals must be protected from harm, nuisance, or unjust exploitation, but rather on the quite distinct *kind* of ground that certain alleged free-floating evils must be prevented.

There are three lines of liberal response to this conservative mode of justification. First of all, the cultural changes in question may not be evil at all. Not all changes are changes for the worse. It is often enough clear in retrospect that severe changes in a traditional way of life were all for the better. How many of us now regret the passing of theocratic puritanism, or strict racial segregation? Yet those changes were as deep and revolutionary in their time as any now foreseen by the gloomiest conservative. The characteristic conservative argument, however, as we have noted, is not that any given way of life is uniquely rational, but rather that any severe change in a traditional culture is evil *as such*, even though it might seem on other grounds to be an improvement. Lord Devlin clearly held the view that *any* change in the essential norms of a society is a change for the worse. That too was the view, at least in respect to religious dissenters seeking legal rights, of Lord Thurlow, a nineteenth-century English Lord Chancellor, who said to a group of dissenters: "I'm against you by God, Sir, I'm in favor of the established church; and, if you'll get your damn religion established, I'll be in favor of that."[39] Quite explicitly it was the *establishment* as such that Lord Thurlow was "in favor of," not any particular set of religious doctrines. The same sorts of preferences are expressed about other cultural norms by Ernest van den Haag in a paradigmatic statement of the conservative thesis:

> Every community has a right to protect what it regards as its important shared values. In India, I would vote for the prohibition against the slaughtering of cows. In Israel, I would vote for the prohibition against the raising of pigs for

slaughter. In the United States, where a certain amount of sexual reticence has been a central value of traditional culture, I would vote for the rights of communities to protect their sexual reticence.[40]

With the generosity of one who enjoys the benefits of historical hindsight, I can grant the conservative a small part of his thesis, if only for the sake of the argument that can be employed against him. Let it be allowed then that there is some loss (cost, "evil") involved in *any* drastic cultural change as such. Nevertheless, a given drastic change might yet be a great improvement *on balance* even when one takes account of the cost. Other things being equal, it was perhaps a regrettable thing that the puritan way of life ceased being dominant, or that the ante- and postbellum Southern ways of life had to go with the wind, or that Victorian double standards were finally purged from the cultural body. But "other things" were not equal. Repression, exploitation, and hypocrisy were great component evils, and their reduction was a gain that far outweighed the losses we can grant in charity to the conservative. In the case of looming changes that are now the subject of controversy, neither side has the benefit (yet) of hindsight, and both must concede that only time will tell. But the verdict of history may never be uttered if all change is forcibly blocked by the criminal law.

The second line of liberal criticism is that legal enforcement is hardly required to preserve some parts of the status quo whose change would be on balance evil. The entrenched majority has great advantages in the free competition of life-styles even without the help of the state.[41] Merely social pressures to conform to those traditional norms that are thought to be indispensable by the great majority will be difficult to resist and the norms themselves highly resistant to erosion. The most sacred of the norms, those that are unqualified taboos, for example those forbidding mother-son incest, are not likely to lose their power in an epidemic of contagious violation. Criminal enforcement is utterly redundant in their case.

The third liberal line is perhaps the most important theoretically. Even if a given social change would be an evil on balance, and even if it were necessary to use the criminal law to prevent it, it would be morally illegitimate to do so anyway. Legal enforcement would be illegitimate in almost all conceivable cases, not only on the grounds of unfairness presented in section 3, but on the very general ground that the need to prevent free-floating evils, while always a relevant reason for action, is not the kind of reason that can have enough weight to justify invasions of the interests (the interest in liberty, among others) of specific, particular, flesh and blood human beings. That is not to say that reasons in the free-floating category never have *any* weight. Preventing a free-floating evil is not simply morally irrelevant, neither here nor there, or totally beside the point. On the contrary, it does have some weight as a reason for coercion and must be rebutted or outbalanced by reasons on the other side. But the reasons on the other side, as we have seen, are reasons of another *kind*, reasons of a sort that are generally more weighty. The need to prevent an impersonal evil that no one "suffers" is usually not as weighty a reason as the standing presumption in favor of liberty, and the general case against invading the interests of specific real persons. That is very much like saying that males as a group are heavier than females as a group, though in a given case, a heavy female might weigh more than a light male. I think it is even more like saying that human beings tend to weigh more than mice, even though in an extremely rare case a given bloated mouse may weigh more than a premature human infant. At any rate, even though some free-floating evils are real evils and even great evils, it remains true that insofar as an evil is free-floating, that subtracts from its weight on the scale of reasons.

When a person has been harmed in one of his vital interests, or even when he has been seriously inconvenienced to his great annoyance, a *wrong* has been done to him; he is *entitled to complain;* he has a *grievance* to voice; he is the *victim* of an *injustice;* he can demand *protection* against recurrences; he may deserve *compensation* for *his* losses. But no one is entitled to complain in the same way when a free-floating evil is produced by another's action. Who is wronged when the adult brother and sister discreetly go to bed together? Where is the injustice when a grown man in the privacy of his chambers enjoys lascivious thoughts over his pornographic magazine? Who is the victim when a religious person omits one of his required observances or when a person of rectitude experiences feelings of vindictive glee at the sufferings of another? Who needs protection against widespread false beliefs about some ancient emperor? Who should be compensated if the Colorado cave fish becomes extinct? On the other side, all of us are harmed by criminal prohibitions to whatever extent they invade our "interest in liberty," and certain identifiable individuals are especially harmed by coercive interference in their lives, and even by criminal punishment. To justify such palpable harms on the ground that they are necessary to prevent even greater free-floating evils is to imply that the evils inflicted on persons are less serious evils than states of affairs that harm no one, being only regrettable subtractions from the net value of the universe—a judgment, it seems to me, that could only rarely be true, and in its application to the "enforcement of morals controversies," one that is downright perverse.

There is a special offensiveness in invoking the evils of social change to justify inflicting harms on individuals. Moral arguments of that kind fly in the face of our understanding of personal autonomy. If I am forbidden on pain of criminal punishment and public humiliation from acting as I prefer in ways that harm no one, in places where I offend no one, on the ground that in

so doing I would be subtly changing the moral environment of my fellow
citizens, I am being asked to acquiesce to a demand that would utterly
demean my autonomy. Surely a person's autonomy, whatever else it may
consist in, precludes his thinking of his activities, practices, beliefs, and
preferences as no more than part of others' "environments." How can I have
any personal autonomy if my neighbors can claim a *right* to have me think,
feel, and privately behave only in ways they approve? There is nothing
offensive to autonomy in the practice of limiting some people's liberty for the
sake of other people's interests; using persons as "means to an end" can be
inoffensive when the "end" is the protection of other persons, but morally
odious when the "end" is anything else.

6. Some second-thought conservative grievances

There are still two lines of defense open to the conservative who relies on the
prevention of severe social change as such in his defense of the legal enforcement of morals: he can deny that the social changes that he thinks evil would
be exactly *free-floating* after all, or he can admit that they are free-floating but
insist that they are such great evils that the necessity to prevent them has even
greater weight on the scales that the presumptive case for liberty. To take the
first line would not necessarily be to abandon legal moralism for the harm and
offense principles, for the conservative might wish to claim that one can have
a personal grievance against the conduct of others on grounds other than that
the conduct harms, offends, or unjustly exploits anyone. I confess that I
cannot see how a person whose interests have not been adversely affected,
and who is still able to live a good life, can have any personal grievance
against the people in his "social environment" when they discreetly live their
own lives and form their own views in ways that he finds regrettable. He
might protest that, to our discredit or to the universe's loss, a way of life is
about to become extinct, but that is a mere complaint, not a grievance. If he
presses the analogy to the abrupt extinction of a biological species he is on
shaky ground. The more obvious biological analogy, as we shall see, would
be to a species' evolution of new traits, rather than to its destruction, and who
is wronged in any way by that?

A more plausible way of arguing for a grievance even without a harm is to
argue that persons brought up in a traditional way of life often order their
own lives in all good faith in reliance on the old ways being continued.
Emotionally unprepared, then, for drastic changes, they are left high and dry
in their declining years, not only disappointed but righteously embittered by
changes which are in their eyes betrayals.

The sense of grievance in these cases is understandable, even when the aggrieved party can show no genuine harm to his interests or rude affronts to his sensibility. Understandable, perhaps, but justifiable? I think not. No one ever signed a "social contract" with such people, or made a solemn vow, or even an informal promise, to keep things unchanged. If aggrieved parties believe otherwise on ideological grounds, then they are victims, in a way, of their own conservatism.

Still another ground for fancied grievance without harm or offense has a certain superficial plausibility about it until it is subjected to critical scrutiny. Imagine a conservative who reasons as follows: I concede that immoralities done discreetly in private by individuals or consenting adult groups do not cause me personal harm, and since I am not a direct witness to such goings on, they do not cause me offense in a way that the offense principle could be expected to take into account. What I am worried about is the offense that will be caused me *in the future* if the conduct in question becomes more and more widespread and increasingly tolerated by the general public. I am protected by the offense principle now, but as more and more people are converted to the deviant conduct, or develop tolerance and even respect for it, the conditions for the application of the offense principle to the conduct in question will no longer be satisfied. In particular, the extent of the offense will no longer be great, and susceptibility to shock and outrage will no longer be attributable to a majority or even a large minority, much less "almost any person chosen at random."[42] Then the deviant minority will go public with impunity, and people like me, though still technically in the majority, will be the captive witnesses of scenes that offend and dismay us. Homosexuals will walk arm in arm down public streets and kiss and pet on public park benches; pornography sections will be in every drugstore and supermarket; visible and audible reminders of the offensive changes will keep us constantly irritated and harrassed. At that point, it won't do to talk about "free-floating evils"; our offense will be personal enough, but we will no longer qualify for protection from the offense principle. In those circumstances, when we complain that our "moral environment" has been polluted, we will not mean simply that regrettable things are occurring in secret behind locked doors, but rather that disgusting changes are taking place (no doubt at an accelerated rate) in the world of common perception.

The first response to this lament should be an attempt to offer comfort and reassurance. Not everything that is tolerated and respected when done in private can be witnessed without offense even by those who morally accept it. All of us are sometimes naked in our bathrooms and bedrooms, but we still do not tolerate nakedness in public. Married sexual intercourse is not considered immoral by anyone, but it is still not accepted on the public streets. If liberty prevails, homosexuals may indeed become increasingly bold. Homosexual couples may behave in public as their heterosexual counterparts do. But what reason is there to think that they will be able to go beyond the limits we now impose on heterosexuals without causing near-universal offense? And permission to operate bordellos, pornographic cinemas, adult book-stores, and the like, does not imply license to litter, to solicit by personal confrontation, to advertise in garish or tasteless ways, or to convert pleasant neighborhoods into ugly, noisy, tawdry ones while immune to the possibility of control by zoning restrictions. Still, when all of that is said and done, one must concede to the worried conservative that there is no assurance that the changes he fears will not produce visible effects that will offend him. We can worry, for example, that standards of "tastelessness," "ugliness," "garishness," and "tawdriness" will themselves be eroded.

So the best way to reply to this conservative's "grievance" is to grant that his fears have some substance, but urge him to use methods short of the criminal law to support his own tastes and standards. There is indeed something odd about his lament when one thinks of it as an *argument* for criminalization, even an argument with true empirical premises. For if he begins by accepting the harm and offense principles as mediated by the various supplementary maxims and standards argued for in Volumes one and two, then he cannot very well demand exemption later, as a kind of after-thought, when he realizes how those standards may affect him. What he is arguing for now is the (or a) principle of legal moralism, and he is arguing for it on the grounds that the offense principle as properly mediated does not give his sensibility sufficient protection. He can hardly do this after having granted the cogency of the reasons that support the various restrictions medi-ating the offense principle's application. That is uncomfortably similar to accepting the rules of baseball as useful and fair, and then having a "second thought" about them upon realizing that against teams with a certain kind of strength the rules might lead one's own team to lose. Closer to home, it is like accepting the unsupplemented harm principle, but then having second thoughts when one realizes that a certain kind of behavior now prohibited because it is harmful may one day cease to be harmful, so that it may eventually have to be permitted. That is the exact analogy to the present conservative argument, for its advocate accepts the offense principle until he realizes that one day a certain kind of public activity now prohibited because it is offensive may cease to be sufficiently offensive to warrant prohibition. The reply to that is that if the conduct does cease to be sufficiently offensive, why then prohibit it? The conservative's answer can only be that even though the conduct is not sufficiently offensive to warrant prohibition on principled grounds, it will nevertheless be very offensive to *him*.

7. Cultural change as a free-floating evil: some misleading models

The final argument for the conservative position may be the most difficult to evaluate. It is available to the conservative who has accepted all my conclusions up to this point (unlikely fellow!). He can agree that the majoritarian arguments for the legal enforcement of morals fail, and that other arguments based on fairness do no better. He can agree (*pace* Schlossberger) that where there is a genuine interest in opposing social change, that interest is not as important, *ceteris paribus*, as the conflicting personal interest in living one's own life as one pleases. He can agree that voluntary private immoralities that *wrong* no one (even though they may incidentally set back some interests) are at most free-floating social-change evils, and further that the need to prevent evils in that category is *in general* a reason of a kind inferior to the need to satisfy genuine individual grievances. He can agree, finally, that free-floating evils cannot themselves be the ground of personal grievances. His last stand must be that some (admittedly uncharacteristic) free-floating evils are such great evils that the need to prevent them *as such* is a weightier reason than the case for individual liberty on the other side of the scales. All the conservative can do at this point is present relevant examples in a vivid and convincing way; the relative "weight" of acknowledged reasons is not otherwise amenable to proof. Some of the most impressive of his examples, unfortunately, appeal either to sentimentality or to such misleading models for cultural change as biological extinction and genocide. It is only because conservatives tend to misconstrue the nature of social change that their examples of serious social-change evils have an initial impact.

It is surely an unobjectionable generalization that wherever there is (1) technological change, (2) no geographical isolation from the influence of alien cultures, and (3) an absence of severe totalitarian controls, human culture in all its aspects will be in a process of natural and constant change. A "way of life" (whatever plausible interpretation we give to that phrase) enjoys no immunity from this process. The moral conservative either denies or deplores that fact. He thinks of his group's way of life as it exists at a given moment of time as a kind of collective treasure, a precious inheritance, which, like any other thing of value (an art object, a national park), requires preservation and "protection." When he tries to imagine the world without this treasure, his head spins and his emotions rebel. It is like thinking of Glacier National Park without its forests, or the world without whales and elephants, or the human population without its Chinese or French or English. One can sympathize with these concerns up to a point, but the arguments the conservative uses for

legal enforcement forfeit much of that sympathy by their gross misinterpreta-
tion of the process of social change and their flawed use of analogy.

The most common error in the reasonings of the moral conservative can be
called the Rip Van Winkle fantasy. Like the rest of us, the conservative sleeps
only a third of a day rather than twenty years at a time; yet that period is
sufficient for him to suffer the recurrent nightmare that he will awaken in a
society of barely recognizable aliens, dressed in exotic costumes, speaking a
nearly unintelligible tongue, and engaging openly in unsavory though harmless amusements. His nightmare is that of sudden cultural extinction; his
model is that of the disappearance of the dinosaurs (or of one of our current
threatened species), or of the genocide committed against the Tasmanians
and attempted against the Jews. Ways of life can be destroyed too, he insists,
and our devotion to individual liberties and our preoccupation with the prevention of crimes of fraud and violence should not be allowed to blind us to
the danger.

Cultural change, when it happens naturally, however, typically happens
one step at a time. The favorite conservative analogies are completely inappropriate in that respect. Genocide is a relatively quick and enormously harmful
and wicked way to bring about the disappearance of a cultural group. More
typically, an unforced assimilative process like the Chinese absorption of the
Jews, or a natural evolutionary process, like the change of Saxons into En-
glishmen, is unabrupt and harmful to no one.[43]

Even when social change is gradual in this way, and almost every link in
the process is voluntary, so that individuals do not suffer harm or distress, the
moral conservative is likely to find a generalized social harm or "harm to
institutions." There is an ambiguity in the latter phrase that makes it especially subject to trickery. When we deplore the "harm" suffered by an institution, we may mean that the institution which formerly served human needs is
now crippled in its functioning so that particular flesh and blood individuals
will suffer as a result. But the conservative, when *he* deplores harm to an
institution, may have a further meaning in mind. He may grieve for the loss
of the institution as such, quite apart from whether it leads to further harm to
the interests of individuals. In the primary sense, as we have seen (Vol. I,
Chap. 1, §§1,4), only beings who have *interests* can be "harmed" or "benefitted," and thus become the objects of our pity or concern, our benevolent
satisfaction or envy. When inanimate objects like rocks or bicycles, or abstractions like institutions, are said to be harmed, this is often an indirect way of
referring to the harm suffered by those who have an interest in the mainte-
nance of those objects. When the moral conservative rues the "harm" done to
social practices and institutions though, he will not be placated by the
thought that, after all, few individual interests will be harmed. He grieves for

the loss of the practice as an evil in itself, quite apart from its connection to human interests.

Very often we hear that pornography, aberrant sex, and the like, do great public harm by undermining valuable social institutions, for example by "harming the family." Even if the family as we now know it should in time become extinct, however, and even if that would be an evil, it doesn't follow that any given individual would be wrongfully harmed in the transitional process. The analogy to the extinction of species and cultural groups is helpful here. There is, after all, a morally crucial distinction between "destroying" a species by permitting it to evolve naturally over the centuries into some new and different species, and destroying it by shooting all its members. The family, like all social institutions, is always evolving in new directions. If each link in the chain of change is voluntary, then there is no unconsented-to harm and no personal grievance, even though witnesses may understandably shed a prospectively nostalgic tear over the departure of the old ways and their distinctive values.

Indeed even now a steady process of change is working on the family. Law cases are producing precedents where before the law had no need to venture. New legal rights, duties, liabilities, and immunities for unwed cohabiting men and women are thereby being created, and new statuses for their children. Unwed liaisons, often thought to be alternatives or successors to the family, are thus becoming more like the original families they were thought to replace, even as easier divorce and new assignments of sex roles are changing the surviving traditional families. Tomorrow, everything will be familiar and recognizable, and the day after tomorrow too, but when Rip Van Winkle wakes up a generation from now he may think a revolution has occurred. Those who have stayed awake during the transition, however, will not notice anything exceptional, and many of us will find to our pleasure that new options have been opened in a society whose institutional forms respond to special needs.

There is yet another useful application of this point. Suppose that in an ethnically pluralistic society higher birth rates permit some ethnic and religious subgroups to grow faster than others, so that over a century or so they greatly increase their relative size and their cultural influence in the society. The process in time may lead to drastic changes in the makeup of a whole people and its common culture, and that change may seem to some to be objectively regrettable. But who is harmed? Who can voice a personal grievance? On the other hand any step taken now to interfere forcibly with the process will trample on thousands of toes.[44]

Abrupt and revolutionary change in a people's way of life causes dislocation, trauma, and alienation, but natural social change is not abrupt. A better model

would be that of the evolution of one biological species out of an earlier one—
the horse from *Eophippus*—or closer to home, the steady change and eventual
disappearance of a natural language. The ancient Etruscan language is now
unknown; it evolved into Latin, which is now "dead"; and Latin, in turn,
through the steady accretion of small changes that characterize all living languages, became French, Spanish, Portuguese, Italian, and Rumanian. Is there
anyone who would shed a tear for the loss of Etruscan, or of the ancient Saxon
tongue?[45] Were there ever any peoples in this history who were suddenly
stripped of their mother tongue and rendered mutually incommunicative?

Hear the descriptive linguist—

> Vocabulary comes and goes . . . That portion . . . which changes most freely
> is sometimes referred to as "slang." But even staid and dignified words are
> constantly being created and continually passing out of active use, to be pre-
> served in literature which is dated by their very presence. While certain types of
> words are more transient than others, none are absolutely immortal. Even the
> most familiar and commonly used words, which might be expected to be most
> stable, have a mortality rate of about twenty percent in a thousand years.[46]

Any natural language, according to this formula, will change its entire vocabulary in 5,000 years. A central element in a people's way of life (if the
people itself survive as recognizably "the same," a doubtful possibility), its
traditional language, then will be extinct, replaced by an altogether new
language. If that happened overnight, the change would shatter and disintegrate a community, but over the longer period, only a few pedants—
"linguistic conservatives"—even notice. As for the hundreds and thousands
of minor constitutive changes over the long period, few of them would have
occurred but for a perceived utility to someone. Not all change, of course, is
for the better, but socially harmful or inconvenient changes do not often
stand the test of time.

It took most of the eighteenth century for the majority of linguists and critics
to learn that lesson. Led by the indefatigable Jonathan Swift, one English critic
after another spoke of the need to "fix the language" once and for all and render
it impervious to debasing change and corrupting foreign influences. Many
advocated establishing an academy on the French model. "It is curious," writes
one historian of the period, "that a number of men notable in various intellectual spheres in the late seventeenth and early eighteenth centuries should have
been blind to the testimony of history and believed that by taking thought it
would be possible to suspend the processes of growth and decay that characterize a living language."[47] Indeed, Daniel Defoe, in his work advocating an
English academy (*Essay upon Projects*, 1696–97) seriously advocates criminal
sanctions to "protect" the language: "The reputation of this society [academy]
would be enough to make them the allowed judges of style and language; and
no author would have the impudence to coin without their authority. Custom,

which is now our best authority for words, would always have its original here, and not be allowed without it. There should be no more occasion to search for derivations and constructions, and it would be as criminal then to coin words as money."[48] Fortunately, Defoe did not have his way. Our living language is as untidy and illogical as ever; change has not been arrested; and the English language in only a few more centuries will be so different that Defoe would barely understand it. But then Defoe will not be present to be frustrated and distressed.[49]

Change in a language must be tolerated, the moral conservative might reply, because attempts to thwart it will be self-defeating. Moral change, however, is another matter. Would you be as willing (he asks triumphantly) to have us "evolve" (he would prefer the words "decay" or "degenerate") into a wholly homosexual society? Can you view that prospect with liberal equanimity? In reply we must ask the moral conservative whether we are to imagine these momentous changes occurring *tomorrow*. (I wake up in the morning and gradually learn during the course of the day that I am the last heterosexual left in the world.) But surely that would not happen as an immediate consequence of the withdrawal of criminal prohibitions today. There would be rather striking changes, however, reasonably quickly, if municipalities passed civil rights laws for homosexuals (on the model of similar laws for blacks) and the estimated 10% of the population with that generally despised disposition came out of their closets, demanded "gay studies programs," and gay history courses, and recognition for homosexual clubs, societies, and political lobbies. But that would simply be for the rest of us to acknowledge the truth, and no longer deny what we have always known. What terrible social consequences might we expect from this new candor? The more hysterical conservative response that respectability for homosexuals would in due time threaten male-female bonding and the family, and eventually even our human reproductive capacity, "curiously assumes" (in the words of John Boswell) "that all humans would become exclusively homosexual if given the choice."[50]

The conservative, however, needn't be that naive. He might press us more realistically and inquire whether we can honestly contemplate an increasingly visible homosexual character to society even in a more distant time, long after we have departed the scene, so that *we* will not have personal grievances to voice. Would not this radical change in our way of life be an inherent evil, to be prevented now while there is still a chance, even if no individual human interests need protection from it? It is preposterous to imagine a future homosexual society, intent on its selfish pleasures and negligently failing to reproduce the species. Surely equal rights pose no clear and present danger of *that*. More likely what would result would be a society in which there were three possible types of primary personal attachments, male-female, male-

male, and female-female. No effort would be made to conceal the homosexual relationships, and no stigma would attach to them. Everyone would take these differences in stride as we now take the differences (say) between Catholics, Protestants, and Jews in our religiously pluralistic society. No one would attach any particular significance to them, until finally, in a century or two, our indifference would approach that of the ancient Greeks who, according to John Boswell, did not see homosexuality as something that needed a name, much less a dirty name.[51]

The disappearance of our current prevalent attitudes toward sexual deviance (attitudes compounded of spontaneous pre-rational repugnance, prejudice against what is perceived as alien, and terrified anxiety) would indeed be a change so drastic and in so central an area that "we might without exaggeration say that our way of life had changed its essential character" and become another way of life. Surely that is what we would say if the revolutionary change took place *overnight*. If, on the other hand, the changes were imperceptibly gradual and continuous, taking a full generation's time or more, those of us who lived through them would probably prefer to say that our society's way of life had survived despite undergoing extreme changes. The greater the continuity of change, the more likely we are to think of the subject as unchanged in essential identity. Similarly, the less drastic the change of properties, the more likely we are to think of the subject as having survived the changes it underwent. But of the two criteria of preserved identity, continuity of change is more important even than degree of change. Thus English is the "same language" it was eight hundred years ago though much changed, whereas the changes that led us to classify Portuguese as a separate language from its mother Spanish may have been no greater in degree, but much more abrupt. If *Eohippus* had been capable of preserving records of its continuous evolution into the modern horse, horses might think of themselves as the same species as their forebears though much changed.[52] But what does it matter whether we say that a thing is the same thing as it was only with very different properties, or a new thing altogether? Or whether a "way of life" is simply in a new and different phase, or has replaced its predecessor as an utterly new way of life? The important distinction for moral purposes is not between essential and accidental change, but between continuous growth and abrupt termination. The former is hardly ever, and the latter almost always, an "evil."

8. The concept of a "way of life"

The social costs of criminalization are so sobering that we might well ask the moral conservative what it is about a society's traditional "way of life" that makes it so worthy of protection even at such a price? The phrase "way of life" is a general term of rhetoric rather than an invention of social science like the barely more precise terms "culture" and "folkways," or a term with a more specific referent like "religion," "morality," "technology," and "language." On the one hand, it is used in a sweeping way to include all the major diverse elements in a national culture. On the other hand, it is used to evoke sentiment and loyalty, often singling out elements in the larger scheme that are useful for that purpose. Thus The American Way of Life (a glittering phrase whose function is similar to that of a flag or anthem) was once said to include baseball and apple pie. Russell Baker associates the phrase with a pleasant detached home "on a tree-lined street in a town that was drawn for a *Saturday Evening Post* cover in 1938."[53] The house has a porch and the porch has a swing on which sits a wholesome family sipping tall glasses of home-made lemonade. If the family has a daughter she might be alone on the swing with "the boy next door" doing a little "smooching," but she would much prefer taking him into the kitchen to watch her make fudge than tolerating his "getting fresh." Of course this picture doesn't fit the whole American reality in 1938 or any other year, but those large sections of the population trapped in sordid tenements or dust bowl farms were expected to aspire to such a way of life themselves (as they usually did) and to "the American Dream."

In theory it would be possible to use the law to "protect" even such trivial though deeply sentimental elements of a way of life as baseball and apple pie. One can imagine for example the requirement of special license fees for amateur soccer teams, higher taxes on soccer balls, eventually even criminalization of soccer if it should threaten to become too popular a rival to baseball. Similar steps could be taken to control the production and sale of Greek bacclava or kadaif if they should threaten to usurp the traditional role of fruit and pumpkin pies in American family holiday celebrations. In fact, however, no conservative advocates using coercion to protect currently prevailing tastes in cuisine, sports, amusements, folkways, games, music, and the like. Any one of these elements alone would seem too trivial to warrant coercive protection, and even all of them together can change and grow, incorporating foreign elements and improvements, provided that the change is so gradual and steady that only old-timers can realize that it has happened at all. And that is indeed how "ways of life" tend to change when coercion is kept out of the picture.

The term "way of life," vague as it is, and rhetorically focused as it often is on sentiment-evoking trivia such as food items and amusements, is generally given a much more comprehensive use. It normally refers to a congeries of overlapping categories, some of which are more important than others, and few if any of which are essential. If styles of cuisine and sport are considered too trivial to enforce, there is a sense in which religion (in the United States and some other Western countries) is considered too important. Religious convictions and loyalties have proved to be the beliefs that people have been most willing to die for, and indeed where in the past bloody and inconclusive religious wars, inquisitions, and persecutions have taken their toll of lives without achieving much else, designers of modern states have been determined to sever all connection between religion and compulsion. Hence, loyal worshippers in quite different sects—in churches that have fought and persecuted one another in the past—live side by side in neighborly domesticity, sharing all of the *other* elements, in a common way of life.

In between these extremes of cultural practices that are beneath and those that are above coercion falls a spectrum of other elements in a people's way of life. Which are its characteristics "life-styles"? Does the woman stay home to manage the household or join the man in the work force? Do the children work from an early age or extend their formal schooling to and beyond adolescence? Does the husband spend evenings with his family around the piano or television set, or with "the men" at the local tavern? Do the unmarrieds have sex promiscuously, or in informal, relatively stable liaisons, or not at all? There has always been great variation in people's actual behavior, but "official" national self-images and ideals to be emulated are often simplistically uniform and archaic. Other elements in a way of life include the prevailing norms of manners (Do students address their teachers by their first names?); styles and rules of speech; fashions of clothing and rules of dress (Are men required to wear neckties in fancy restaurants? Are women forbidden to wear slacks in church?); traditions and rituals; legends, flags, and anthems.

Prevailing life-styles, at first, may seem no less trivial than one's choice of sport or taste in pastry, and no less ludicrous as objects of protective legislation. Nevertheless, the various "family protection bills" submitted to the United States Congress in 1982 and had just such goals. They proposed to forbid the use of federal funds for "textbooks and other materials that do not reflect 'traditional family' sex roles, to wit: Daddy goes to work and Mommy stays home and does housework"; they permit school boards to "prohibit the mixing of boys and girls in sports or any school activity, even in regular curriculum classes such as science, mathematics, vocational education and home economics";[54] and they increase parental authority in the home by permitting states to disregard the Federal Child Abuse Prevention and Treatment Act and guidelines regarding spouse abuse, as well as watering down the definition of child abuse in the Federal law. Despite the common references to crime statistics in the speeches of the advocates of these measures, moral conservatism seems to provide the best account of their motives, and even their explicit arguments refer more commonly to the need to protect "family values" and traditional ways from corrupting change than to the need to protect people from harm.

Part of a society's way of life, of course, is its prevailing morality, and that may be what conservative legislators claim to be preserving from change by introducing "family protection bills" and the like. Whatever else a morality is, they insist, it is no trivial thing like baseball or apple pie, and it is a central, indeed essential, element in the complex called a "way of life." We can agree that within any group's morality there is a sector of absolutely first importance without which the society would dissolve into anarchy, and which therefore calls out for support, vindication, and criminal enforcement. But that sector (Hart's "moral minimum") is what permits any group of individuals to be more than just that, but a society or community as well. But the moral minimum is not the section of a community's morality that makes it the distinctive community it is, and distinguishes it from other societies with other life-styles and other traditions. Rather the moral minimum is the morality the society has in common with all other actual and conceivable societies. The moral conservative would "protect" not only the common moral minimum, but other moral rules he thinks essential to the distinctive identity of *his* society. And preserving that identity, he thinks, is reason enough for legal restrictions, even for coercive force through the criminal law.

9. Summary: grievance and non-grievance morality

Much of what we call morality consists of rules designed to protect individual interests from being thwarted or individual rights from being infringed. Individuals can plausibly demand from their fellows respect for their privacy, dignity, and autonomy; help or rescue when they are in danger; abstinence from the arbitrary use of force or coercion, from wantonly inflicting injury or causing distress, and from unfair exploitation even perhaps when it leads to wrongful gain for the exploiter rather than wrongful harm to the exploitee. We can even demand that our neighbors not be nuisances, inflicting inconveniences on us short of actual injuries. Whenever one of these rules is violated there are assignable persons who can voice grievances in protest, and press for some sort of remedy or censure.

On the other hand, much of what we call morality consists of rules designed to prevent evils of a kind whose existence would not be the basis of any assignable person's grievance. No one can complain on his own behalf, or vicariously for another, if someone has evil thoughts (short of the intention to act on them) or false beliefs, or violates his own religious duties. If these things are evils, they are evils that "float free" and are incapable of grounding personal grievances. The free-floating evils do not hurt anybody; they cause no injury, offense, or distress; they are not in any way unfair. At most, they are matters for regret by a sensitive observer. To prevent them with the iron fist of legal coercion would be to impose suffering and injury for the sake of no one else's good at all. For that reason the enforcement of most non-grievance morality strikes many of us as morally perverse.

The social-change evils feared by the moral conservative are for the most part non-grievance evils. The extinction of the early Saxon language (with who knows how much unique poetic power) was such an evil because it occurred in such a fashion that it harmed no one along the way. So was the disappearance of *Australopithecus* in the evolution of *Homo sapiens*. So was the merging of the various German and Celtic tribes into the peoples of modern Europe, and of their pagan religions into the mainstream of Christianity. So were the vanishing of the New England theocratic village life-style, the antebellum Southern plantation way of life, and the double-faced Victorian standards of sexual propriety.

A final distinction must be made between the evil that consists in substituting the worse for the better and the change whose evil consists in the pace and the manner in which the transition is made, irrespective of the comparative values of the starting and finishing points. The conservative position on social change is not that any given way of life is inherently superior but rather that any severe change in a traditional culture is evil *as such*, even though it might be an improvement on other grounds. We have conceded to him (at least for the sake of the argument) that there is some loss in any extreme cultural change. Nevertheless, we have insisted, a given severe change might yet be a great improvement on balance, even when one takes account of the alleged cost. The cost even of drastic change, however, is not very great to begin with, if the change is analogous to the natural growth of a language or the evolution of a biological species rather than to the abrupt and violent obliteration of a race, religion, or over-hunted breed. Where there are no individuals who can voice personal grievances over an unforced change, then tears shed in advance over the "destruction of a way of life" are more sentimental than moral or humane.

29A

Autonomy and Community

1. Apparent conflicts

It is commonly maintained by conservative writers that the personal autonomy so treasured by liberals is incompatible with certain community values most of us would be loath to give up. Since the incompatibility is real, these writers insist, the liberal's uncompromising endorsement of autonomy carries an exorbitant price. Some of these tensions I will be unable to deny, but, for the most part, I think that liberalism can be defended by showing that it does not bear the heavy costs it might at first appear to. I will try to argue, in short, that one can preserve one's allegiance to personal autonomy in the way that liberalism requires while fully acknowledging the central and indispensable importance of community in human lives.

First, a disclaimer. This book defends only liberalism in a narrow sense—a thesis about the proper scope of the criminal law—whereas most of the arguments against liberalism to be considered in this chapter are directed at a wider worldview called "liberalism" to which I am not logically committed. Still, there is more than an accidental linguistic tie, or a merely sentimental association, between the narrow and broader theses of liberalism, and historically liberalism in the narrower sense has rarely been found apart from the more comprehensive liberal ideology. A reader might well be justified then in suspecting some covert affinities with the wider view among supporters of the narrower, even in the absence of logical entailment. But there is no reason why a modern liberal, especially a defender of a liberalism of limited scope, should feel committed to traditional theories that are now clearly inadequate or absurd—classical liberal theories of human nature and motivation and outdated accounts of the nature of society and the relations between social groups.

The classical liberal *ideals*, perhaps partly because of their vagueness and flexibility, remain the most appealing part of traditional liberalism. These include not only *liberté* and *egalité*, but also, not least for being last, *fraternité*. It has been notoriously difficult for the liberal to reconcile liberty (and its underlying value, autonomy) with equality, but here we will address the problem of reconciling autonomy with the cluster of values represented by "fraternity." These values include group memberships and loyalties, cooperativeness, civic spirit, public participation, and piety in a broad sense.[1] (It will not do to identify fraternity with an indiscriminate intimate sort of personal *love*, and then, as James Fitzjames Stephen did, dismiss it as an inappropriate social ideal.)[2]

The felt tensions within the broader liberal ideology have been described not only as conflicts between liberty and fraternity, but also, in alternative language, between autonomy and community, and between "individualism" and "communitarianism." When these clashes are thought of not simply as internal tensions within liberalism but as essential conflicts between rival ideologies with battle lines drawn, the ensuing debate may impress the bewildered observer as a tiresome controversy between partisans of largely compatible or complementary goods, in which the rivals exhibit merely a difference of emphasis, much like the endless debates over "nature" versus "nurture" when the subject is the explanation of human behavior. Often each partisan defines the other's position in the most extreme way, so that his own, presented as the only alternative to an absurdity, wins by default. Communitarianism, for example, is not infrequently presented as the alternative to an "individualism" that is defined in terms of utterly absurd doctrines, such as that each person is an atom, or island, whose essential character is formed independently of the influences of social groups and who is in principle entirely self-sufficient. Actually, which of these views is correct, "individualism" or "communitarianism," depends on the question each is thought to answer, and since there are many such questions, it is possible that one doctrine is the answer to some of them, and the other to others. And some questions may be so misleadingly formulated that communitarianism and individualism are not conflicting answers at all.

It will be the tentative thesis of this chapter that in most cases of apparent conflict between autonomy and community, the opposing values can be satisfactorily reconciled, but that in the few cases of irreconcilable conflict, it is not implausible to urge that autonomy be given priority. Communitarian critics have argued that liberal ideology is in irreconcilable conflicts of at least five kinds with the deliverances of common sense about the importance of community. I shall discuss three of these under separate headings in the sections that follow, and the others incidentally in the course of other discussions. The first objection to liberalism, to be discussed in section 2, is that it presupposes an inadequate individualistic conception of human nature, one that cannot be reconciled with the social nature of man. The second objection, discussed in section 3, is parallel to the first. It charges that liberalism gives insufficient weight to the value of fidelity to *tradition* in human life, that is to the temporal dimension of community. The third objection, discussed in section 4, is that liberalism ignores the basic human need to *belong* to communities, and the severe *alienation* that results when that need is unfulfilled, as it would be, so the argument goes, in a perfectly liberal society. Other objections charge that the immense importance of civic virtue and public spiritedness cannot be reconciled with the liberal emphasis on autonomy and self-fulfillment (discussed *in passim* in this chapter and in Chap. 33) and that liberalism finds no place for what Madison called "the spirit of locality" (also discussed *in passim*).

2. The social nature of man

To allay any possible misunderstanding, the liberal should begin by acknowledging the bedrock importance of community to human nature and well-being. (See Vol. III, Chap. 18, pp. 46–47.) Whatever else a human being is "by nature," he is essentially a social product. He is born into a family, itself part of a tribe or clan and a larger political community, each with its ongoing record or history, his first concepts shaped by a language provided for him by the larger group of which he is a member, his roles and status assigned by social custom and practice, his membership and sense of belonging imprinted from the start. He finds himself, as Alastair MacIntyre puts it,[3] "embedded" in a human culture not of his own original design or "contractual agreement," but one that is simply given. As soon as he has any conception of himself at all, he thinks of his identity as determined by his membership and group-assigned roles. He may form purposes of his own, but even those that are nonconformist or rebellious can only be understood against the background of community practice and tradition. His original purposes, values, and conceptions, all socially assigned, play a decisive role in his deliberations even when, as a budding adult, he chooses to change them. A complex modern community will even provide him with anti-traditionalist traditions to identify with and be comforted by.

Of all the shared cultural artifacts, none is more central in shaping our individual identities than language. We come into existence biologically programmed to receive a language, and our "linguistic community" promptly provides one, bearing the mark of social practices and habits of mind which we learn "with our mothers' milk." In the Cartesian period it was widely assumed that our thoughts came first, and that only then did our acquired language, a transparently neutral vehicle, permit us to convey them to others. But since Charles S. Peirce and (especially) Ludwig Wittgenstein,[4] it has become the more common view that language is "a necessarily public institution within which human selves are formed and by which people constitute the world they live in . . . Shared practices, actions, reactions, and interactions among people provide the foothold upon which all . . . self-descriptions of our mental life must rest. Language is first of all public and firmly rooted in what we do together."[5] We are, in short, as much the products of our linguistic tradition as we are the users and masters of a language, since the use of that language itself presupposes an elaborate background of group practice and tradition.

It is absurd, therefore, to think of an individual as formed prior to and independently of his socialization in a particular social group, capable of living in isolation from any community, speaking his own private language, starting from scratch with no base in a tradition. That, I think, is beyond controversy. What is doubtful, I think, is whether the liberal commits himself to such absurdities by ascribing to individuals a sovereign right of self-government within their own proper domains. (See Vol. III, Chap. 19, for a detailed account of "personal sovereignty.") It does not seem implausible on its face to suppose that the liberal can give up the excesses of individualism, acknowledge the social nature of man, and still hold on to what is essential in his normative theory, the doctrine of the human right of autonomous self-government within the private sphere. It will be my strategy in what follows, in any case, to argue for the compatibility of communitarian conceptions of human nature with personal autonomy.

There are two forms of individualism that communitarian writers reject. The first is an ontological theory about the status of individuals and social groups; the second is a psychological theory about the essential constituents of human nature. The simple-minded individualist ontology that is rightly rejected by communitarians is one that treats all social groups as mere aggregates of individuals, like the random collection of strangers on a subway train, and concludes therefore that the individuals are "logically prior" to the groups since the groups simply *are* nothing but this individual, plus that one, plus that one, etc. The individuals can and do exist apart from their random aggregations, but the aggregative groups obviously cannot exist apart from the individuals who compose them, because that is all there is to the groups; they can be analyzed without remainder into their ultimate parts. This interpretation may do for mere aggregates of people, but it is naive to think of complicated groups, ongoing communities, structured institutions, chartered organizations, churches, clubs, unions, informal neighborhood societies, etc., as mere aggregates. They are, to be sure, composed of people, and without people there could be no communities. But they are people and *more*—people in complex relations to one another, people with common purpose or values, people united by bonds of affection or loyalty, people occupying roles, discharging responsibilities, exercising rights, all assigned by rules or customs known and acknowledged. If individuals are the component "parts" of communities, as the individualist rightly insists, then communities clearly are more than the sum of their parts.

There is a more sophisticated mistake at the other extreme that communitarians sometimes commit. Perhaps they fall into it because they have not fully expunged individualism from their minds but only "kicked it upstairs." That mistake is to infer from the fact that communities are not mere aggregates of ordinary flesh and blood individuals that they must therefore themselves be some sort of super-individuals with minds and bodies of their own, and rights and duties not reducible to those of any constituent officials, representatives, or ordinary sorts of individuals. Sometimes communities are said to be "organisms" in their own right, with some ordinary individuals serving as their heads, others as their limbs, others as their loins. The individual parts come and go like the cells in ordinary human bodies, but the organism survives them all and continues its own independent career.

Sometimes ontological individualism is nothing more than a common-sense rejection of this fanciful organic theory, just as communitarianism is sometimes nothing more than the common-sense rejection of the naive theory that treats all social groups as mere aggregates. These two common-sense positions are not incompatible, and I dare say, are both true.[6] Humans are essentially social, and their communities are structured associations of individuals, not super-individuals themselves. The individual is a social being through and through, and much of what we think of as essential in him is inconceivable without his relations (membership, belonging, allegiance, status, inherited culture, etc.). On the other hand, a social group is indeed nothing but a collection of individuals, not merely aggregated,[7] but in often complex, sometimes hierarchical, relations to one another. Any analysis of individuals and societies, then, that makes too stark a contrast between them, either by considering individuals as self-sufficient and "logically prior," or by treating groups as moral organisms, is radically deficient.

The extreme individualist theory of human nature that communitarians rightly reject ascribes an anemic, "thin," or 'empty" self to individuals by treating them as if they were, or could be, in isolation from the communities that shape and nourish them and provide the purposes and allegiances that contribute to their characters. Commonly, the communitarian criticism employs the concept of personal "identity"—not the metaphysical concept that has traditionally puzzled philosophers—but rather the concept that social scientists use to describe how individuals think of themselves. Usage is vague and shifting, but there are at least two ways of construing "identity" when used in this sense. The first construes it as a comprehensive notion comprising *all* the descriptions of a person that he accepts as true and, at least to some minimal degree, significant parts of his self-conception. Thus a person's full identity may include being a woman, a mother, an Italian-American, a Roman Catholic, a liberal, a redhead, a short person, an intellectual, a devoted daughter, a dancer, and a potter. The other interpretation construes "identity" as a narrower and more clearly normative concept: the roles, allegiances, commitments, statuses, or other descriptions that are most central to one's conception of one's self, those with the most important place in one's "self-image" or "self-definition." (Obviously, the distinction between one's comprehensive and one's normative or essential identity is vague, a matter of degree, and depends on the extent to which self-descriptions can be rank-ordered.)

A monk or priest, asked who or what he is, might reply straight off that he is first and foremost a faithful Roman Catholic. That he stems from an Italian ethnic group might be way down his list, one of those merely accidental truths of no great significance to him. We can contrast him with an Italian restaurant owner who mentions his ethnic affiliation straightaway but who regards his "faith," lax and conventional as it is, as merely incidental to his ethnic membership, a part, but not a central part, of his comprehensive identity. That he lives on the New Jersey side of the New York-New Jersey border, while also true of him, may not be part of his normative identity at all if he is no "Jersey patriot," and in this he may differ from some of his neighbors.

Michael J. Sandel, in a recent influential work, argues forcibly for the central place in our "identities" of community allegiances—"those more or less enduring attachments and commitments which taken together define the person I am".[8] Sandel is an excellent writer and is very persuasive in his particular account of our social natures: "Living by" our community allegiances, he writes, "is inseparable from understanding ourselves as the particular persons we are—as bearers of this history, as members of this family or community or nation or people, as sons and daughters of that revolution, as citizens of this republic . . . To imagine a person incapable of constitutive attachments such as these is not to conceive an ideally free and rational agent, but to imagine a person wholly without character, without moral depth."[9] So far so good. But Sandel then proceeds to argue that "the liberal" is logically committed to the denial of these profound though obvious truths, and in this task, I think, he is less successful.

"The liberal" who is Sandel's primary target is one who derives his liberal principles ultimately from Kantian or Rawlsian premises. Now Kant's conception of a person as an unknowable "thing in itself" is, to be sure, a conception of a self "without character," but that is because Kant *defines* it that way as an abstraction from a person's full identity to be *contrasted* with his "merely empirical self," the character that is formed in the world of cause and effect and is open to our observation. Kant did not mean to deny that we have empirical selves or that group memberships and social roles are essential to their "identities." His metaphysical conjectures are simply not part of an account of human nature. Similarly, Sandel attacks Rawls (his favorite target) for the "thinness of the deontological self" in Rawls's argument, as if the abstract self-interested rational chooser behind a veil of ignorance that Rawls uses as an illustrative device in his derivation of the principles of justice were a seriously intended portrait of human nature in all its appetitive and purposive richness. Rawls's methodological abstraction behind the veil of ignorance is a mere heuristic device, not a "picture of the self." It functions to explain, in vivid imagery, what Rawls means by calling the principles of justice "rational." It may indeed be impossible for a human being to exist at all without the aims and attachments that Sandel regards as so important, but Rawls would have us imagine not that his hypothetical chooser lacks such loyalties and preferences, but only that he doesn't *know*, during his deliberations, what they are. To reply that such ignorance too is psychologically impossible is to miss the point in much the manner of the critic of traditional social contract theory who rests his case on the lack of historical evidence for an original contract, or the literalist reviewer of Swift's *Gulliver's Travels* who complained that he couldn't believe a word of it.

In any case, one need not be either a Kantian or a Rawlsian to be a liberal. Sandel implies that all forms of liberalism, however supported, have certain common failings, and at the root of these failings he always finds the same deficiency. He prefers "a view that gives fuller expression to the claims of citizenship and community than the liberal vision allows."[10] This view, he adds, is provided by communitarian citics, who

> unlike modern liberals, make the case for a politics of the common good. Following Aristotle, they argue that we cannot justify political arrangements without reference to common purposes and ends, and that we cannot conceive of ourselves without reference to our role as citizens, as participants in a common life.[11]

Again, I do not understand why a liberal is logically precluded from valuing the "common good" and even pursuing it as one of his own ends in collaboration with his associates. Moreover, while we are all participants in *some* "common life" or other, there need not be a perfect overlap of common purpose. For some, the primary "common life" is embedded in the neighborhood community, for others in their families. For still others, it is the scientific community, the black community, the gay community, the church, or even perhaps an "atheist community." To be sure, they are all Americans (or Frenchmen, or whatever), and loyal citizens, but their loyalties may well be based on their mutual respect and their devotion to the ideal of a national community in which an unrestricted myriad of social groups prosper and flourish. *That* "common good" is hardly alien to the pluralistic liberal tradition. One of its great enemies is the intolerant predominant subcommunity that chokes off or absorbs weaker subcommunities and soon identifies its own parochial values and traditions with those of the national community.

Liberals and communitarians, Sandel points out, sometimes give different reasons for the same policies, for example "where liberals might support public education in hopes of equipping students to become autonomous individuals, capable of choosing their own ends and pursuing them effectively, . . . communitarians might support public education in the hopes of equipping students to become good citizens, capable of contributing meaningfully to public deliberations and pursuits."[12] Again, this is a false opposition. First of all, liberalism is a theory about the limits of state power, not about the content of education for children. Many virtues should be inculcated in children that could not be rightly enforced upon adults. Secondly, though the liberal does wish to enable all children to develop the rational skills necessary for self-government and to become capable of "choosing their own ends," he can consistently urge that children should be brought up and educated in such a way that the common good *becomes* one of "their own ends." I think Amy Gutman had a similar point in mind when she pointed out that the liberal's "sense of justice," spelled out in part as equal opportunity for all voluntary associations in a harmonious pluralistic society, can be part of a person's own "identity": "My commitment to treating other people as equals, and therefore to respecting their freedom of religion, is just as essential a part of my identity as my being Jewish and therefore celebrating Passover with my family and friends."[13] Gutman's liberal sense of justice manifests itself in a concern for the equal good (or equal opportunity to pursue that good) of all constituent subcommunities. There seems to be no justice then in Sandel's claim that a liberal cannot make a case for the politics of the common good. At the most, he might claim that the liberal has his own distinctive conception of the public good as consisting in the harmonious flourishing of diverse groups united by bonds of mutual respect and loyalty to a tradition of tolerance and brotherhood.

It is not an attraction of Sandel's theory that he thinks of the public good as definable independently of social justice. If the most comprehensive public good is some function of the good of constituent social groups, then it must require some constraints on the pursuit of subgroup goals if only for the sake of other subgroups and overall harmony and stability. Brian Barry puts the point well: "Any theory that does not simply amount to 'my project right or wrong' or 'my country right or wrong' must be prepared to apply an external standard to the pursuit of commitments that form part of people's self-identities . . . Sandel's argument should be turned on its head. It is exactly when 'devotion to city or nation, to party or cause' run deepest that the constraints of justice on the pursuit of those allegiances are most needed."[14] That is why the "public good," so important to political activities, as both the liberal and the communitarian would have them, should not be conceived of as something independent of justice, but rather as something inextricable from that favorite liberal value.

In summary, there is nothing in the liberal devotion to personal autonomy that precludes his appealing to the common good in his political arguments, or from conceiving that public good in terms of the goods of constituent groups, each constrained by the principles of justice and fair play. Injury to the good of a community or subcommunity is ultimately harm to the interests of its individual members, but some of the interests vulnerable to such damage are "collective interests" in Postema's sense (see Chap. 28, §9), that is, common and interdependent interests belonging to each individual only insofar as he regards himself as a member of the group. Moreover, there is nothing in the liberal's ideology that *need* blind him to the social nature of human beings and the importance to all of us of community memberships. He may insist, like Mill (see Vol. III, Chap. 19, §2), that individual self-fulfillment is the good for individual human beings, and that personal autonomy is its essential prerequisite. But he can, indeed he must, concede what is plain fact, that most of what we fulfill when we fulfill ourselves are dispositions implanted by our communities, and most of what we exercise when we exercise our autonomy is what our communities created in us in the first place.[15] Some of the communities responsible for shaping our identities and making us (in part) who we are, for example our families and nations, were not chosen by us or by some unencumbered rational precursors of ourselves. But the selves we inherited in part from these communities might nonetheless be free to select some of their subsequent affiliations and to freely exercise their autonomy in making new communal commitments, with new consequences for their personal identities. Self-creation (see Vol. III, Chap. 18, §3, pp. 33–36) is possible within this community-created setting, even though the self in its capacity as creator is itself a social product. We cannot rebuild ourselves completely, starting from scratch, or lift ourselves by our own bootstraps, but we can use our autonomy to change our course in search of our own deeper currents—which are themselves partly the product of community. This is a capacity well short of omnipotence, but not one to be sneezed at.

3. Tradition

The value of tradition is not something commonly emphasized in liberal tracts, so it is important here to derive and explain that value and also to state clearly what attitudes the liberal might consistently hold toward it. I have already acknowledged the essential place of community membership in human affairs and the natural impulsion toward communal life in all of us. Perhaps the most important of all the many kinds of communities are those that are the most unified and durable—the "communities of memory", as Robert Bellah and his associates[16] call them, those that are in a way constituted by their past, and so structured that they do not forget their past. The main way of assuring that continuity with the past is maintained, according to Bellah, is for the community frequently to "retell its story, its constitutive narrative," the legends and histories that distinguish it from other groups, and define and reenforce its own ideals. The group's story may consist of exemplary tales of heroic conduct that express favored conceptions of character and virtue, or "painful stories of shared suffering that sometimes create deeper identities than success."[17] Ethnic and racial communities are examples of communities of memory, as of course are religious communities "that recall and reenact their stories in the weekly and annual cycles of their ritual year, remembering the scriptural stories that tell them who they are and the saints and martyrs who define their identity."[18] Actual historical descent from the heroes and martyrs of the constitutive narrative, of course, is not necessary. Western Europeans are not the literal descendents of the characters in Bible stories, but their affiliation with a common religious tradition creates the requisite "spiritual bond." Similarly, nation-states have bonds of memory that unite citizens with earlier figures who may not be their literal ancestors.

There is more to a community of memory, however, than its constitutive narrative. Bellah and his associates also speak of "practices of commitment . . . ritual, aesthetic, ethical . . . which define the patterns of loyalty and obligation that keep the community alive."[19] Ceremonies, celebrations, holidays, mourning rituals, recitations, public readings, and symbolic renewals are among the formal practices that contribute to the vitality of the association and its preservation.

Family groups only rarely and transiently achieve the status of "communities of memory." Dynasties may appear to be exceptional cases of historical traditions based on family, but they are usually only strands of full families. For most ordinary families the care of the past is precarious; intergenerational unity is unstable; membership is constantly scattered and diluted. "Families can be communities, remembering their past, telling children the stories of parents' and grandparents' lives, and sustaining hope for the future—though without the context of a larger community that sense of family is hard to maintain. When history and hope are forgotten and community means only the gathering of the similar, community degenerates . . ."[20] An important part of the difficulty of maintaining separate family narratives, of course, is the merging of families through marriage in each generation. Every time this happens a new family's history is compounded, so to speak, of two prior ones, and each history is accordingly diluted. The sense of a single ongoing tradition is quickly lost, especially if the newly merged "stories" do not sit well together. In any event, in subsequent generations, the doubling occurs again and again, and mere families, not having institutional structure, lack officials to maintain and give order to their ever increasing archives. Perhaps that is no reason for denying, however, that families through one, two, or three generations are frequently "communities of [short] memory," whose traditions are genuine enough, though brief.

Once we put aside the relatively clear cases—churches, ethnic groups, nations, families—the vagueness of the concepts of "community of memory" and "tradition" is revealed. We speak, for example, of "scholarly traditions" (Aristotelianism, empiricism) and the "traditions" of particular scholarly disciplines ("The traditional assumption academic psychology is . . ."). Then there are cultural and institutional traditions (e.g., the common law tradition, the American theatrical tradition). There are traditions of institutional types ("The traditional Western university issues degrees at commencement ceremonies at which the faculty wear traditional caps and gowns.") and traditions of particular institutions of those types ("At our college the tradition calls for the students to wear blue gowns and for the ceremony to be held at the old town church.")[21] There are traditions within traditions (Protestants and Catholics are united in a common Christian tradition, but they are separated by divergent traditions of various kinds.) Doe, Roe, and Moe might glory in their common American traditions, but Doe and Roe both also celebrate the traditions of the labor union movement, while Moe, a corporate executive, glories in the traditions of the General Motors Corporation. Doe then is a more natural associate of Roe than of Moe, but he is in another way more like Moe than like Roe, since he and Doe are both Catholics, while Roe is a Protestant. So our traditions unite us and separate us in overlapping and interlocking ways. In a large modern nation, at least, the broadest community is a complex network of subcommunities, many of which have their own "constitutive narrative" and thus their own traditions. We are all in traditions, and whether we are conscious of it or not, they shape the way we interpret the world. As Bellah *et al.* say "There is no other place to stand."[22] But in a modern pluralistic society, we may find ourselves interpreting our lives through diverse traditions, including even those of groups with which we are not formally associated. Even playing a role within all the subtraditions to which we are consciously committed may be a little like riding separate trains along divergent tracks.

A geological metaphor, irresistible to most sociologists, is apt for the bewildering diversity of traditions in a modern society. There are exposed *layers* of tradition, simultaneously visible from many viewing locations. Thus the Reformation (evangelical churches) coexists with the Enlightenment (the A.C.L.U.); thirteenth-century Scholasticism can be seen in the same cliff wall with nineteenth-century Romanticism. Majority traditions don't collapse and die; rather they become minority traditions and go their own way. The rock wall is tilted and all the strata show. "Our tradition" is a tradition of traditions, an impure mixture, whose very impurity gives solid support to the surface layers and nourishment to their soil.

In a pluralistic society, some traditional affiliations are voluntarily chosen by those who wish to associate themselves with them. At one extreme, it resembles choosing one's groceries in a supermarket. The traditions are displayed, and we select those that best fit our predispositions and tastes. There are other traditions, however, that we are born into, and we find ourselves already fully and indelibly shaped by some of them when we come to self-awareness. It is traditions of the latter kind to which Alasdair MacIntyre, in his penetrating study of the impact of social life on individuals, attaches such great importance.[23]

A human self, according to MacIntyre, derives its unity from the coherence of a "narrative" connecting its birth to its life to its death as beginning to middle to end. A human life is a narrative-unfolding that takes place in what he calls a "setting"—an institution, or a practice, or "a milieu of some other human kind."[24] (Note MacIntyre's use of the singular here, implying a rather tight unity of background settings.) "But it is central to the notion of a setting as I am going to understand it that a setting has a history, a history within which the histories of individual agents not only are, but have to be, situated, just because without the setting and its changes through time the history of the individual agent and his changes . . . will be unintelligible."[25] Full intelligibility then requires that we place an episode to be explained in a set of narrative histories, both of the individuals involved and of the settings in which they act. Individual life narratives are embedded in larger institutional processes and literally cannot be understood in part or whole except as part of these larger histories. "What I have called a history is an enacted dramatic narrative in which the characters are also the authors. The characters of course never start literally *ab initio;* they plunge *in media res,* the beginnings of their story already made for them by what and who has gone before."[26]

MacIntyre then expands his theatrical metaphor in much the manner of the ancient Stoic philosopher, Epictetus.[27] "We enter upon a stage which we did not design and we find ourselves part of an action that was not of our making."[28] MacIntyre proceeds to put the metaphor to a use that is reminiscent of, though not identical to, that of the ancient Stoics, who emphasized that our duties are determined by the roles we play. Indeed, they suggested that a role is *defined* by the duties that constitute it. A father is a man whose duties are to . . . A soldier is a person whose duties are to . . . And so on. Ours not to choose the role; what is up to us is to play the assigned part well. But that is Epictetus. Here is MacIntyre:

> I can only answer the question "What am I to do?" if I can answer the prior question "Of what story or stories do I find myself a part?" We enter human society, that is, with one or more imputed characters—roles into which we have been drafted—and we have to learn what they are in order to be able to understand how others respond to us and how our responses to them are apt to be construed . . . I am never able to seek for the good or exercise the virtues only *qua* individual. I am someone's son or daughter, someone else's cousin or uncle; I am a citizen of this or that city, a member of this or that guild or profession; I belong to this or that clan, that tribe, this nation. Hence what is good for me has to be the good for one who inhabits these roles. As such I inherit from the past of my family, my city, my tribe, my nation, a variety of debts, inheritances, rightful expectations, and obligations. These constitute the given of my life, my moral starting point. This is, in part what gives my life its own moral particularity.[29]

The theatrical metaphor, as MacIntyre demonstrates, is apt and remarkably fruitful.[30] In our twentieth-century world, however, it is easy to exaggerate both the moral centrality and the inevitability of role assignments. I have frequently tried, with little success, to persuade American students of the plausibility of the Stoic doctrine of "my station and its duties." They can understand that as sons and daughters they have inherited certain duties toward their parents, and how other duties derive from voluntary agreements with spouses, partners, employers, and the like, or from voluntary undertakings, like committing oneself to a career of one kind or another. But they dismiss as antiquarian relics the notions that one has little choice in the selection of one's "stations" and that conflicts between the duty of the natural self and the duty of a particular role are always to be settled in favor of the role-duty. Surely in a modern nation-state it is no longer plausible to maintain that one's position as a farmer, or soldier, or mother, or teacher, or vagabond, is rigidly assigned and unchangeable in the way one's status as man or woman, or son or daughter, are. We no longer "discover" our stations and their duties by simply observing our parents' place in the world and our heritage from them. The characteristic problem of modern youth is to *decide* what role-commitments to undertake from among many alternatives. Older societies were quite different in that respect: As Alan Ryan writes, "Odysseus could not have decided that he did not like fighting, or argued that his talents were better suited to a career as a stand-up comic."[31] Even more alien to modern students was the Greek tendency to interpret tragic dilemmas as conflicts between equally real duties attached to different roles, never as conflicts between "pure conscientious action" (a modern notion) and a role-duty, in which "conscience" or "decency" or "compassion" urges one course and role-duty the other. The Greeks, according to Ryan, "made almost everything of the objective, role-fulfilling activity and made little of the project of the person who filled the role, save insofar as his project was identical with what the role prescribed."[32]

It is unfair to saddle MacIntyre with a simplistic Stoicism, since his more sophisticated views are avowedly Aristotelian, but these examples show how easy it is to exaggerate his genuine insights while attempting to apply them to modern society. A corrected emphasis (no more than that would be required) would make more of the role in modern life of the various "intermediate"[33] subcommunities that are located in the center of a spectrum running from family at one end to racial or ethnic group and nation at the other. We must locate nearer to the family end such relatively noninstitutionlized groups of smaller scope and function as neighborhood associations, local churches, charitable societies, social clubs, schools and alumni groups, recreational societies, offices, shops, labor union locals, fraternal associations, professional societies, political "causes" and parties, and so on. These groups play an important part in the communal life of modern individuals, and membership in them, or association with them, is more apt to be voluntary than the "roles into which we have been drafted" that MacIntyre emphasizes. And given our social natures, they are often a basis of our "good" if not a source of important duties, or inherited debts. To be sure, in the passage quoted MacIntyre mentions guilds and professions as well as families and nations, but these are no longer roles into which we are drafted, like son- or-daughterhood or national citizenship.

In the modern world, then, it is no longer true that I can decide "what am I to do?" only by considering first who I am, what roles I have been drafted into, what stories I am a part of. In respect to many life dilemmas, we cannot know "who we are" *until* we decide what to do. Should I, a Protestant, marry this Catholic woman and adopt her faith? Should I, an umemployed Minnesota iron miner, move to the Sunbelt and seek a slot in the computer industry? Should I do this even if it means abandoning my local subcommunities? Even if it means leaving my parents behind? These are problems that call for modes of reasoning other than an automatic deduction of duty from station, because it is no longer clear to people what their 'stations" are. Not in our time, for better or worse, will we return to a society in which each person had, in MacIntyre's words, a "given role and status within a well defined and highly determinate system of roles and statuses"[34] from which he could read off his identity. When the problem at hand is to choose a role or seek a status, then one must do something other than merely consider who one is.

What MacIntyre says about our genuinely inherited roles of kinship and citizenship, however, is profoundly and importantly correct. I doubt whether there is as tight a connection between even these roles and one's personal good as he claims in the quoted passage,[35] but I think we must concede to MacIntyre that our fixed *inherited* roles do indeed bring with them a "variety of debts, inheritances, rightful expectations, and obligations." The full impact of this observation is brought home by MacIntyre's interpretation of collective responsibility for past atrocities. He dismisses "those modern Americans who deny any responsibility for the effects of slavery upon black Americans, saying 'I never owned any slaves' . . ." and "the Englishman who says 'I never did any wrong to Ireland; why bring up that old history as though it had something to do with *me*?' " or "the young German who believes that being born after 1945 means that what Nazis did to Jews has no moral relevance to his relationship to his Jewish contemporaries." All these examples, he says, "exhibit the same attitude, that according to which the self is detachable from its social and historical roles and statuses."[36]

What we must say to this, I think, is that there are selves and selves, and some are detachable from certain roles that others are not detachable from. More important, there are historical roles and historical roles, and some are more difficult for anybody to detach himself from than others. A Protestant may become a Catholic, and a fourth-generation family farmer may leave the ancestral plot to become a computer engineer. But there is no gainsaying MacIntyre's point that by the time one has an adult awareness of the world, it is for all practical purposes too late to cease being, in certain fundamental respects, an American, Englishman, or German, as the case may be. If one tried to "detach" oneself from one's group membership in one respect, one would also have to deny features of one's identity that are deep and fundamental. Perhaps such radical "disownings" are possible; if so they must be rare and exceedingly difficult.[37] It is not just a matter of renouncing benefits that come unjustly from one's countrymen's ancestors' exploitation (say) of slaves. That would be hard enough. Rather it is renouncing membership in a group which stands, as a group, in a moral relationship to another group. What was done by that group as a whole, the group as a whole is responsible for, and that responsibility applies distributively to all members of the group across generations, just as the national debt can remain to be paid many decades after the passing of the generation that originally incurred it. Thus MacIntyre concludes: "What I am, therefore, is in key part what I inherit, a specific past that is present to some degree in my present. I find myself part of a history, and that is generally to say, whether I like it or not, whether I recognize it or not, one of the bearers of a tradition."[38]

That may be taking the point too far. The German youth may have renounced most of what he takes to be distinctive of German culture, and he may have chosen thereby to become a very *untraditional* German. A particular ex-German Jew to whom he stands in a special moral relationship may actually be an atheist. Neither then is a "bearer," willing *or* unwilling, of a tradition. Rather each is a member of an ongoing transgenerational community, a quasi-juridical entity, similar in its unity to a team or a company, that distributes its "debts" to all its members whether they like it or not.

It is surely not *my fault* that black Africans were cruelly impressed into slavery by Americans. I am not *to blame* either for the sufferings of the slaves long before I was born or for the residual harms inherited by present blacks from the earlier condition. Certainly I am not *guilty* of these historical atrocities. Fault, blame, and guilt do not transfer in the absence of actual wrongful conduct and intention.[39] But MacIntyre is right: I cannot completely escape responsibility. I wear the same "uniform", after all, as those early American slaveholders. Our "team" persists through history and I remain (quite indelibly in fact) a part of it, so that I inherit its record and become implicated in it. I am not to blame except insofar as *we* are; and as a kind of corporate group, we are indeed to blame. It follows that certain moral attitudes toward blacks would be highly appropriate in me: on occasion some embarrassment, a need to give reassurance, a kind of deep personalized regret—almost a vicarious remorse—and a feeling of shame. Being ashamed of one's national forebears is no more irrational, after all, than being *proud* of one's ancestors or countrymen or any other people with whom one is closely associated—those with whom one naturally identifies, or, failing that, those with whom one is naturally identified by others. We are proud or ashamed of others when somehow, by some mechanism or another, their conduct reflects on us. Speaking in our name, though before we were born, our government behaved atrociously (so the American, Englishman, and German in MacIntyre's examples might reason); and even now it is our name, a name that rightly attaches to us still, that is tarnished by the historical record. Thus shame can be appropriate even when one is not personally at fault, and a sense of personal guilt would be morbid.

That we do unavoidably inherit some of our group roles from the past, that they often carry debts and obligations with them, and that they often become a fixed part of our identities is undeniable. MacIntyre says that these thoughts "are likely to appear alien and even surprising from the standpoint of modern individualism [from which] I am what I myself choose to be."[40] Only a very narrow individualism would recoil at them, however, and, in any case, not the sort of individualism to which liberalism is wed. We must remember that liberalism is essentially a doctrine about the uses of state power and the limits of enforceability. As such, it still has a point even within a modified MacIntyre framework. Liberalism insists that there is an area of individual autonomy, that is of rightful self-rule, but that is not to say that individuals before they have any properties at all can select for themselves any properties they wish, or that we can separate ourselves from our aims or purposes or commitments, or that we can step out of our skins. Our self-identities may well be, more or less, as MacIntyre says they are, but these selves may also be the owners of rights and the rightful determiners of their own lot in life. What liberalism *is* committed to saying about tradition is that the state should leave community traditions alone, neither restrict them nor enforce them. Rather it should let communities work out their own historic courses, write their own stories, find their own pattern of evolution, conduct their own argument (without force) with dissidents and reformers. That is not only the state role that is *just* for all (as the liberal emphasizes); it is also the best way for the traditions themselves to flourish.

Welcome support for the latter point comes from MacIntyre himself. In a passage that could have made John Stuart Mill cheer, he explains how his conception of tradition differs from that of traditional conservatives:

> Characteristically such theorists have followed Burke in contrasting tradition with reason and the stability of tradition with conflict. Both contrasts obfuscate. For all reasoning takes place within the context of some traditional mode of thought, transcending through criticism and invention the limitations of what had hitherto been reasoned in that tradition; this is as true of modern physics as of medieval logic. Moreover, when a tradition is in good order it is always partially constituted by an argument about the goods the pursuit of which gives to that tradition its particular point and purpose.
>
> So when an institution—a university, say, or a farm, or a hospital—is the bearer of a tradition of practice or practices, its common life will be partly, but in a centrally important way, constituted by a continuous argument as to what a

university is and ought to be, or what good farming is or what good medicine is. Traditions, when vital, embody continuities of conflict. Indeed when a tradition becomes Burkean, it is always dying or dead.[41]

The same point was made over and over by Mill.[42] When a tradition is rigorously policed against change it becomes frozen in orthodoxy, its vital role in human lives snuffed out. Lovers of tradition, then, following MacIntyre, might well make common cause with Millian liberals.

4. Alienation

The characteristic social malady of our time (it has been said for over a century now) is the disintegration of traditional communities and the resultant widespread estrangement or "alienation" of individuals. Karl Marx used the term "alienation," which was already commonly used in theological works in reference to man's cosmic condition,[43] to describe the worker's plight under capitalism in which he is "related to the product of his own labor as to an alien object."[44] Social scientists generally use the term in a much wider sense to describe in general the feelings of restless loneliness an individual, almost *any* individual, will feel when he is cut off from membership in communal groups. There does seems to be a natural human need to associate, to belong, to "identify with", to be accepted, to acquire both memberships and status within a group. If, as Sandel and MacIntyre have argued so well, a good part of our own sense of identity is reserved for our affiliations and memberships, our identities will be narrow or "empty" when our social ties are cut, so that the result will be not only estrangement and depression, but a kind of depersonalization as well.

One writer speaks of our social impulses as a "need for domesticity", adding "we need to be at home."[45] Think of a youth from a small midwestern town who leaves behind his family, his neighborhood, his Four H club, his church, to seek his way in New York City. There he finds a tumultuous sea of strangers, with exotic faces and accents, many organized groups but none that appear initially inviting, and no place, at least at first, where he can feel at home, accepted, belonging, secure. Of course New York is not really all that bad, and in time our lonely visitor will find hospitable groups of like-minded individuals to accept him. In the meantime, however, his estrangement may be very oppressive, a kind of intense loneliness, but more than that, for it will not be cured by chance encounters with pleasant and friendly individuals or even random aggregates of individuals, for what he craves is a place in a more or less organized group (or in two or three). If, for one reason or another, he cannot satisfy *that* craving, his estrangement will grow in severity until, at its limit, he is driven to suicide.[46]

Perhaps because this kind of experience, though less extreme, is becoming more common, a nostalgia for the old small-town ways has recently found expression in our literature and popular culture. This is to be contrasted with one of the predominant literary trends of an earlier period (still with us) in which the cruelties and hypocrisies of "Main Street" were exposed and condemned. In contrast to the alienated youth who can find no place to feel at home, the older literature featured sensitive youths who felt suffocated by hometown pressures toward conformity, their individuality stifled by overwhelming togetherness, their creativity smothered by "herd reactions," their privacy invaded by busybodies.

There seem at first sight, then, to be two opposed ways of looking at the small-scale communities of family, neighborhood, town, and so on. One can think of the idealized, small, self-contained world as cozy or as stifling, and the wider world of the big city as alienating or as liberating. We can condemn the smaller groups for their crushing cohesiveness, and their loyal members as mindless conformists who cannot think for themselves, or praise them as sanctuaries from loneliness, a sense of exclusion, and perpetual outsidership. We can rally behind the banners of autonomy, freedom, and individuality, or those of community, brotherhood, and civic virtue. We can cite as "the characteristic evil of our time" either alienation *or* social oppression. But these are, like so many of the issues that bedevil our subject, false oppositions. There are clearly two ways of missing the ideal. Individuals can be *assimilated*, herd-like, into groups at great cost to their individuality (the danger Mill emphasized), or they can remain *isolated*, mere atoms or islands, at great cost to the human need to belong and to "be at home" (the danger given equal emphasis by Tocqueville).[47] But there is no reason to think that one or another of these evils is inevitable, and that we must line up then behind the one we think is the lesser evil. The alternative to assimilation and isolation is *integration* of the individual into congenial groups that do not smother or trap him, but leave his integrity and his freedom, except for his voluntary commitments, intact.

Individuals differ, of course, in need and temperament, and a community that is smothering to one person may be exactly what another needs. Moreover, there are, even more obviously, differences among the groups themselves, so that one would stifle most people, while another would stifle very few; one family would be oppressive to most, while another would seem cold and unconcerned to most. The solution to the problem of maladaptation is the same in both cases. Society should provide an abundance of subcommunities of all kinds, catering to all needs and tastes, and our political and economic superstructures should be encouraging to such a proliferation, deliberately adopting subcommunity-building policies. It is less important that we have a strong, comprehensive, ideologically uniform community playing a prominent role in the daily life of its citizens than that we have an abundance of subcommunities which together provide at least *some* place for everyone. The psychological need for a unifying ideology amidst all this healthy diversity would be satisfied by a liberal state built on a creed of mutual tolerance and respect for rights. Such a creed, as our national experience has shown, is amply capable of generating its own nourishing traditions, its folk heroes and exemplary stories.

The true opposition is not between partisans of individuals and partisans of communities, but between supporters of diverse intermediate subcommunities, on the one hand, and supporters of a uniform and united, comprehensive, public community on the other. This is an opposition between individuals organized in small groups, as is natural to the species, and Society with a capital S, organized to take unto itself all the functions that separate groups would ordinarily discharge, one superfamily, superchurch, and superassociation, in which all the majority traditions become the *only* traditions, and in which mindless conformers can all find a comfortable place.

Many social commentators have noted that totalitarianism, the characteristically twentieth-century form of political tyranny, typically comes about by moving into a void caused by the collapse of intermediate associations and widespread alienation. This can happen in two ways. First of all, if the loss of an array of associations leaves most of us depersonalized and hungry to "belong" somewhere, we all become parts of a "faceless mass," ready for manipulation into a totalitarian supercommunity. If a great diversity of receptive subcommunities is not present in a society, the powerful craving for membership will naturally cause people to move into the corrals of an omnicompetent government if that is the only way they can find the social solidarity and sense of belonging that they need. The totalitarians respond to the alienated persons' needs not by restoring the diverse and balanced array of intermediate associations, as a sophisticated liberal would or should recommend, but by replacing them altogether with a single unified state apparatus. Robert Nisbet describes the result:

> This new order is the absolute, the total, political community. As a community it is made absolute by the removal of all forms of membership and identification which might, by their existence, compete with the new order. It is, further, made absolute by the insistence that all thought, belief, worship, and membership be within the structure of the state . . . What gives historical identity to the totalitarian state is not the absolutism of one man or of a clique or a class; rather it is the absolute extension of the structure of the administrative state into the social and psychological realm previously occupied by a plurality of associations . . .[48]

The other recipe for totalitarian success also involves the destruction of diversity and balance among private institutions. Social relationships start at the level of the family and "the small informal social groups which spring up around common interests and cultural needs."[49] Given the social nature of man, these intermediate associations are, as we have seen, vital to individual well-being. But the number of associations extends, Nisbet tells us, to the larger associations of society, to the churches, business associations, labor unions, universities, and professions. These too are vital to individual well-being, though each is "potentially omnicompetent in relation to its members."[50] In an unstable system one of them might grow in power to the point where it absorbs it rivals, leaving no way to generate alternative institutions to satisfy the unmet needs of minorities. Soon, an all-powerful private institution absorbs the state itself and forcefully imposes its structure on the ordinary life of citizens. Perhaps this was the pattern in Iran.

By whichever route totalitarianism threatens, the way to prevent it is to foster the independence and development of "this array of intermediate powers in society, this plurality of 'private sovereignties' . . ."[51] If the threat is primarily from widespread alienation, the remedy lies in providing ample opportunities to citizens to "belong" where they feel most "at home". If the danger stems primarily from the overblown power of a "private sovereignty," the remedy is more checks and balances from rival associations. Sandel and others are misleading, then, when they argue that state enforcement of established traditions is the most effective bar to creeping totalitarianism. He may be right when he claims that "intolerance flourishes most where forms of life are dislocated, roots unsettled, traditions undone."[52] But to establish one among many is also dislocating, for to enforce one tradition is to weaken the others, diminishing for many the opportunity to belong and be at home, thus spreading more alienation. On the other hand, if everyone is absorbed into the majority tradition, then it becomes dangerously powerful on the Iranian model, ready to capture or demolish all of the intermediate associations not already in its power. The most stabilizing arrangement would also be the most just, a form of social union in which diversity flourishes, differences are respected, and rights honored.

5. What communities are

The word "community" has been having a vogue. It is now used so indiscriminately that it would be wise to specify a relatively narrow and precise sense for the sake of clarity. We hear talk for example of "the speech community" (of English speakers), "the university community," "the European community" (of nations), "the law enforcement community" (but not "the criminal community") "the gay community," "the black community," "the mathematical community," "the scientific community," "the business community,"

"the Catholic community," "neighborhood communities" (as opposed to neighborhoods), "retirement communities" and many more. It would be helpful to have an explanation of what, if anything, these various uses have in common, or what some important subset of them have in common, and why other possible applications of the term "community" seem to be excluded.

I think it is useful to think of "community" as a concept subject to degrees. Different social groups differ in the extent to which they are communities, or, if you will, in the degree of their "communitiness." We could begin then with a relatively strict definition, and then stipulate that to the extent that any social group resembles this model of a "perfect community" it partakes of communitiness. In that way we might avoid tedious disagreements about whether or not a group with certain agreed-upon characteristics *really* is a community. This tack might also explain why we are reluctant, though not adamantly unwilling, to apply the label of community to certain other cases.

We can begin with the relatively formal definition of a community proposed by Robert Bellah and his associates: "A community is a group of people who are socially interdependent, who participate together in discussion and decision making, and who share certain practices [thought to be good in themselves] that both define the community and are nurtured by it. Such a community is not quickly formed. It almost always has a history and so is also . . . defined in part by its past and its memory of its past."[53] Note that to the degree that a group lacks a long memory (like most families for example), it falls short of perfect communityhood. Similarly, social interdependence tends to make a group more like a community, and some groups are moreso than others. Common decision-making is less frequent in large communities, but a group that does poorly by this criterion might do redeemingly well by the others. A business association, insofar as it values its activities as means to profits only, lacks what Bellah calls "practices" (or "practices of commitment"). But some business associates might think of their work *also* as a "calling," or intrinsically valuable activity, and to that extent their association may resemble a community even though they earn their livings from it.

Bellah *et al.* contrast their strict conception of a community with what they call a "lifestyle enclave," defining it as follows: "Members of a lifestyle enclave express their identity through shared patterns of appearance, consumption, and leisure activities, which often serve to differentiate them sharply from those with other lifestyles. They are not interdependent, do not act together politically, and do not share a history. If these things begin to appear, the enclave is on the way to becoming a community. Many of what are called communities in America are mixtures of communities in our strong sense and lifestyle enclaves."[54] Clear examples of life-style enclaves are "retirement communities" (so-called) and a "youth culture." The members of a retirement settlement may have little in common except mutual convenience and similar tastes in consumption and recreation. Their bridge and golf games are not a "calling," an intrinsically valuable form of work. Rather they are just part of a "style"—a pleasant way of living with no further significance. Bellah attributes to many retirees an interpretation of the directive to "love thy neighbor" (American style). They "consider that responsibility fulfilled when they love those compatible neighbors they have surrounded themselves with, fellow members of their own lifestyle enclave, while letting the rest of the world go its chaotic, mysterious way."[55] There is little give and take, little common enterprise or joint deliberation in the mere enclave. The "members" (if they can be called such) express together a shared selfishness rather than cooperative efforts in a larger cause. They are closer to being a mere aggregation of individuals thrown comfortably together than a perfect community.

One possible dimension of "communitiness" is not mentioned explicitly by Bellah. To whatever extent a social group is *organized* it tends to be a community. It would no doubt be going too far to insist that organization (itself subject to degrees) is either a necessary or a sufficient condition for a community, but organization does help bring about the other community-making characteristics. One of the functions of the American Philosophical Association, an organization with headquarters, offices, a budget, and a constitution, is to mould the loose collection of American professors of philosophy into something like a community. Organizations are community builders and reenforces. One of the features of an organization is that it has a "spokesperson"—some official or officials delegated to speak in its name. An organization, in turn, often claims to speak in the name of the community it represents. Individual persons may be members of either the community or the organization, or (quite commonly) of both. Sometimes the level of organization in a community is low; the rules are more like customs or loose conventions, and there is no official constitution, or budget, or officers. Yet it can qualify as a community anyway because even in its (relatively) unorganized way, it satisfies the other criteria, and various members, even all of them, can be understood to be speaking for the group.

There is, as I have said, a law enforcement community but not a criminal community. Why should that be? The answer apparently is that criminals are a mere aggregate of individuals or small groups of individuals acting independently. They are not organized like police departments and can have no official spokesperson. They are more like music lovers, dog owners, or stamp collectors, people who *separately* do the same kind of thing, than like a congregation of worshipers, a faculty of scholars, or a department of police. The Mafia, on the other hand, may very well have many of the defining traits of a community, though Bellah would no doubt withhold the term "practice" in his sense from the money-grubbing raison d'être of the Mafia.

A school basketball team falls well short of being a perfect community for other reasons, even though it does have some of the elements in high degree. It offers its members a sense of belonging, and though it is united only by a single common interest, it creates strong ties and, in certain limited contexts, the purest of communal loyalties—one for all and all for one. But a school basketball team is not a community in the strict sense because it is too limited and partial an overlapping of lives. In contrast, a long and well-married couple may come very close to a complete sharing of lives. Its "members" may be united by the strongest bonds—love and affection, common property, common values, common responsibilities, common experiences, and common friends. And yet they may be *too* well married to be a genuine community of two, for a certain degree of separateness of the parts is necessary if the whole is to be considered a community.

A more general point emerges that was well appreciated by Aristotle. In his discussion of the *polis*, the city-state community that embraces all the other constitutive social groups, Aristotle emphasizes that a community is a unity in diversity, requiring that its members remain distinct and separate persons in their own right even though unified in an intimate way by their common values, beliefs, and interests. The members must share some things in common but not other things (Aristotle criticizes Plato for making his Guardians share too much in common),[56] since they are "a harmony of distinct but complementary persons,"[57] not a merger of separate persons into one. So we can attribute to Aristotle too our conception of an integration of persons that is a mean between the extremes of assimilation and isolation.

We can now summarize some of the ways in which social groups can fall short of perfect community in Bellah's strict sense:

1. The association can be too transient (as in *ad hoc* committees).
2. The bond between members can be too narrow, involving too small a part of their whole lives (as in school teams).
3. The unifying interest can be too general and comprehensive, a mere lowest common denominator. (That is why there is no such thing as "the feminine community" or "the masculine community"—though there may well be "the feminist community.")
4. The common interest, goal, or value can have too slight a hold on members' loyalty (imagine a junior high school alumni society).
5. It can fail to provide a tradition, something to take hold of, or to believe in.
6. It may not be based on any common convictions, ideals, or values (like a life-style enclave).

7. It can lack organization and have no suitable "spokesperson" (like "the criminal community").

8. It can have too tight a unity (as in the very well married couple).

A social group can fail in some of these ways but not in others, and therefore be "more or less of a community."

The strict conception of community is important for many theoretical purposes, and especially in understanding alienation. But less strict conceptions of community can be important too, and especially for making a point about a society's political stability. In the strict sense of community, most of us are members of only a few communities—perhaps a church and a university (if one is a teacher-scholar), perhaps a favorite charitable-fraternal society, a political lobby, and an amateur chamber ensemble. Perhaps. But in a less exact sense of community, many of us can be members of dozens of communities at the same time—church subgroups, neighborhood protective associations, single-issue political or moral action groups (the American Civil Liberties Union, Planned Parenthood, Right-to-Life societies, the American Society for the Prevention of Cruelty to Animals, the Women's Christian Temperance Union, the National Rifle Association), college alumni associations, recreational societies (hunting and fishing associations, garden clubs, chamber music societies), professional groups and subgroups (the American Medical Association, the American Orthopedic Association, the American Bar Association, the Society for Law and Psychology), regional and local units of labor unions, philanthropic societies, small face to face groups and large national associations, ethnic or racial societies. In a pluralistic national society the list goes on and on. We can think of many of these groups as "imperfect" or only "approximate" communities in Bellah's strict sense, or as communities proper in a less strict but equally useful sense. That doesn't matter. What is important is how central it is to the liberal vision of a just society that there be as many of these groups as possible, and that they be permitted to thrive or decay, as their members' enthusiasm or apathy determines, without outside intervention in any form.

6. Overlapping memberships

Society does not consist, as the discredited old individualism had it, of isolated atoms, or solitary individual islands. But neither does it consist, as our uncompleted picture might suggest, of islands of *clusters* of individuals, or free-floating "molecules." Large overarching communities are needed to protect and further unify the smaller ones which are to a large extent their subcommunities, for it will not do for each of us to be at home in one of Bellah's small perfect communities if we are hostile strangers with only tenuous bonds to the millions of people in other subgroups who are, after all, our fellow citizens. Large comprehensive communities, whether political, like municipalities and nations, or larger "private sovereignties" like nationwide professional or religious associations, are not communities in the strict sense, but they are often communities of communities, as the Roman Catholic Church, for example, is an organization of many local church communities and church-sponsored organizations, and the A.F.L.-C.I.O. is composed of hundreds of "locals." We have already seen how important it is as a barrier to totalitarianism that there be an abundance of diverse organizations. In this section we shall see how the large associations, and other groups that are not themselves "perfect communities," contribute to the communal unity of disparate subgroups and help build a comprehensive community united by a network of interlocking bonds.

Why is it important that there be overarching communities, and in particular a supreme national community? We have very little choice in the matter, to begin with. We are all thrown together willy-nilly, all 230,000,000 of us, and efficient transportation and communication in a common language make us *de facto* associates. Also we *need* one another, on a quite massive scale, for we must be able to count on people in addition to those in our small restricted communities for economic cooperation and emergency help. Most of our dealings in the world are with strangers, and when strangers cannot be presumed to be trustworthy, there is a Hobbesian state of nature with all its celebrated incommodities. Moreover, "in unity there is strength" and in strength, security. In addition to these obvious needs, however, there are more subtle ones. What writers call "alienation" can be cured by acceptance in small genuine communities, but when one's trust, fellow-feeling, and common purposes and values are restricted to the members of a local group, and one is estranged from the other groups and masses of people one sees every day, there can be an almost equally destructive state of mind, whether we call it "alienation" or something else. Uncorrupted partiotism, free of chauvinism and bellicosity, answers to a genuine human need.

One technique for building and strengthening a comprehensive national community (indeed a probably indispensable technique) is to provide an ideology that all can accept, assigning ideals to which all can pledge allegiance, and a tradition of heroes and ancestral sufferings that all can learn. I shall discuss that form of community building in the next section. In this section we shall consider how a healthy network of private associations, including many that are only "more or less communities" in the strict sense, can unify as well as divide us—all of us. Another way in which unity is increased is by the phenomenon of institutional splitting or traditional containment. Protestants separate from Catholics, liberal Protestants from conservative ones, high church from low church. Professional associations splinter into more specialized societies. The American Philosophical Association, for example, has now spawned dozens of societies devoted to more specialized forms of philosophizing, some of which stay under the umbrella of the parent organization, some of which become in a sense "rivals" to it. But there is a unity preserved in this form of increasing diversification. New communities become communities within communities, sharing generic allegiances with both parent and other split-off sibling groups. Catholics and Protestants, after all, both are Christian, and their common faith can unite them even as less fundamental differences separate them. Jews and Christians have in common "the Judeo-Christian tradition," which provides a basis at least to build further community.

A more interesting way, perhaps, in which larger unities are built out of local diversities is the phenomenon, in a liberal society, of overlapping memberships. It is highly likely that any two people will be similar in some important respects and different in others, some of their needs complementary, some convergent, some conflicting, some of their interests identical, some reenforcing, some opposed, as is true of their talents, their ideals, and convictions. Thus a fellow member in one organization may profoundly disapprove of one of your other favorite groups; he may be an ally in one cause, an enemy in another. But he is just one person, after all, not two or more persons, so there must be some uniformity in your manner of dealing with him. You must have *some* sense of common purpose, some residue, at least, of respect for him, for you are fellow members of at least one among many organizations.

In an open pluralistic society with an abundance of subcommunities, near-communities, and community-like intermediate associations, the people become great joiners.[58] When each person is a member of many groups, the phenomenon of overlapping membership is greatly magnified. The naturally diverse needs and attitudes of the people will unite some in one context and separate them in another. We accept their support willingly in one group on one issue while feeling them strangers in another, and rivals in a third. But again, each is a single person, for all his diverse relations to you, and it is that single person who is a fellow citizen in the overarching community.

Let us take for illustrative purposes an artificial model of how overlapping membership might work. Suppose there are exactly ten associations open to persons: the American Civil Liberties Union (A.C.L.U.), a Right to Life Society, the Music Appreciation Society, the American Society for the Prevention of Cruelty to Animals (A.S.P.C.A.), the Women's Christian Temperance Union, the Voluntary Charity Society, the Chamber of Commerce, the Wilderness Society, the Historical Preservation Society, and Citizens for Growth (a builders' lobby). While attitudes of members may be nearly uniform toward the purposes for which the organization was formed, they can remain highly diverse, nearly random, on issues of other kinds. Thus there may be as many animal haters as animal lovers in the Temperance Union and as many drinkers as teetotalers in the A.S.P.C.A. Let us trace the membership patterns of only ten citizens, each of whom is a member of five of the available associations, as indicated in diagram 29A-1.

Most of the ten share memberships and causes with all of the others, and most of the common memberships are repeated two or three times. These overlapping memberships knit the collection of groups itself into a closer community than would otherwise be the case, much as overlapping strands of string contribute strength to a stretch of rope. The intergroup bonds are more like strands of gossamer, "a filigree of threads and crossthreads," than like hoops of steel, but they are better than nothing and can keep the overarching community-in-the-making from flying apart under the slightest pressure. To the members of one group, the other groups cease seeming entirely alien, and the members of divergent organizations with overlapping memberships develop the habit of civility and greater skill at handling conflicts and compromising. Group members learn to respect the outsider; for all they know he may be an insider in another of their groups.

7. The idea of a liberal community

A great interlocking network of private associations is a more accurate model for a national community than millions of separate "atoms" or "free-floating molecules." The tightly organized groups of individuals that are the "molecules" in one of these pictures are tied into a more or less stable (though perhaps "less" than "more") social entity of which the "molecules" are in some sense the parts. While all that is helpful, however, it is not sufficient to mould the individuals into the comprehensive community each of them needs. What is needed is some common ideology, providing a common set of national goals and ideals, and some collective "vision of the good." At this point, the communitarian will argue that liberalism cannot provide the requisite ideology since, by its own choice, so to speak, it is neutral between competing conceptions of the human good. The role of the state according to liberalism is to protect the rights of individuals, alone or in association, to pursue their *own* visions of the good, free of unjust interference from others. It is an abuse of power and a usurpation of function for it to establish one set of dogmas, or prescribe one form of worship, to regulate private tastes by

A.C.L.U.	Right to Life	Music Appreciation Society	A.S.P.C.A.	Women's Christian Temperance Union	Voluntary Charity Society	Chamber of Commerce	Wilderness Society	Historical Preservation Society	Citizens for Growth
Abel	Baker	Abel	Abel	Charles	Abel	Dock	Baker	Baker	Abel
Baker	Fox	Charles	Baker	Dock	Early	Gimbel	Charles	Charles	Early
Charles	Gimbel	Dock	Early	Gimbel	Fox	Hemp	Dock	Hemp	Gimbel
Dock	Hemp	Early	Fox	Hemp	Gimbel	Fox	Fox	Iron	Hemp
Early	Iron	Jones	Jones	Jones	Iron	Iron	Iron	Jones	Jones
and	and	and	and	and	and	and	and	and	and
others	others	others	others	others	others	others	others	others	others

Diagram 29A-1. Overlapping memberships.

coercive law, or to proscribe the expression of unorthodox or unpopular opinions. But if liberalism will not take sides with one of the competing conceptions, the argument continues, then it cannot provide the necessary unifying vision, and society will remain a tenuously balanced congeries of constitutive "molecules" rather than the tighter, more stable union we all require.

The liberal will reply that his doctrines *do* contain a unifying "vision of the good," but that ideal is a *social* good, a conception of how individuals should live together. Its conception of the *individual* good is necessarily abstract and variable. The good for individuals consists in the fulfillment of their individual natures, and given the natural diversity of human beings, the nature of the fulfilling life will vary from person to person and is best left to individuals and the groups in which they are "embedded" to work out on their own. The protection of diversity is itself a community interest, the liberal will add, for reasons similar to the reasons why a balanced portfolio is a prudent investment, or why a diverse gene pool protects a species from disease epidemics.

The communitarian will have at least three kinds of reply at this point. He might claim, first of all, that the liberal's neutral vision of the (social) good is one that keeps people separate rather than draws them together, so that it can hardly be as effective a community-builder as more partisan ideologies would be. The liberal will rejoin that his social creed actually builds more communities, but smaller ones, living in mutual tolerance and respect. The bonds of understanding and forbearance among these diverse subcommunities are what tie them together into a national community. Thus the faith that makes Mennonite villages and hippie communes parts of the same overall community is their devotion to the rights of the other group, as of all groups, to go their own way in peace. But perhaps there would a much tighter, more unified national community if we were *all* Mennonites, or all hippies, or all Marxist-Leninists, or all puritans, or all mystics, if that were possible. In a sense that is true. But Aristotle's point becomes relevant at this juncture: a group can have too much unity to be a community. A corporate merger of companies, after all, is not a community of companies. A community, at least in the sense of the word in which it stands for a form of grouping that answers to a basic human need, is "a harmony of distinct but complementary persons." In the liberal vision, a community is a harmony of mutually respectful often radically different individuals.[59]

Secondly, the communitarian might reply that the liberal's social ideal is vacuous. Respect for the rights of others is fine, he may concede, but it is hardly a full picture of the social good. If all that any of us did was to forbear from interfering with the rights of others, then none of us would ever *do* anything. And if our sole moral conviction were that to interfere with liberty

without proper cause is wrong, then no one would have a very practical guide
to how he ought to live his life. But the liberal rejoins that his theory does not
purport to be a full guide to the good life. It is an answer to a more limited
question about the scope of rightful state power. It doesn't offer a full moral
code, but only a stricture on state enforcement of codes. Not that it necessarily limits state functions to enforcement. The liberal state can consistently
use public *education* to foster respect for rights; to inculcate patriotic pride in
being part of a nation that scrupulously preserves individual liberties, a
tradition for which heroes have died; and to urge public service, charity, and
cooperation—virtues that a liberal can praise as consistently as anyone else.
The objection of vacuousness is a charge not simply that liberalism doesn't
give warrant to these governmental functions, but that it *cannot* (consistently).
But limitations of government coercion do not have these further restrictive
implications. We can use our *de jure* autonomy, with benign governmental
encouragement, to make moral commitments and autonomously choose to
help one another. To be secure in one's human rights is not necessarily to be
selfish or antisocial. The liberal ideology, in short, is not so much vacuous as
formal, and the formal framework *can* be filled in by the ideals of sociality so
treasured by the communitarian.

The communitarian might now concede that the liberal ideology is neither
divisive nor vacuous, but at worst only incomplete. He might still complain,
however, that it is insufficiently inspiring to mould a powerful sense of
national community. He might point to times and places in history when
patriots have given their lives for their God, or their king, or their "country
right or wrong," and then question whether similar devotion could ever be
shown toward an abstract system of rights. On this point there can be no
other proof of the pudding but its eating. Liberal rhetoric is hardly in short
supply, and, while little of it is poetic, much of it is passionate. Pericles'
funeral oration and Lincoln's Gettysburg Address may not compare in elo-
quence to the speech Shakespeare gives Henry the Fifth at Agincourt (where
the appeals are to comradeship in arms, to honor, fame, and glory) but they
have dampened many an eye in the rereading. There is genuine ardor in the
liberal slogan attributed to Voltaire—"I disapprove of what you say, but I
will defend to the death your right to say it," and inspiration in John Stuart
Mill's celebration of human diversity in *On Liberty*. I think there is little doubt
that people can be and are in fact moved by the more eloquent liberal appeals,
and moved toward brotherhood and community. American patriotism, for
example, might be compounded of a number of elements, including love of
place and love of ancestors, but among those elements are gratitude for
liberties unknown by one's ancestors in foreign lands, and pride in the American system of constitutional rights itself. How many have meant when they

say "I am proud to be an American" (or an Englishman, etc.) that they are proud to participate in a system where each is free to pursue his own good, and a hundred flowers may bloom?

A system of liberal rights, where citizens are truly devoted to it, can strengthen the sense of national community in two complementary ways. Each person respects the rights which he recognizes in every other citizen, so people are respected derivatively as *right-holders* and potential moral claimants. But above and beyond this, each may respect (in a less narrowly legalistic sense) the other as a brother, a comrade, a fellow citizen, because each presumes that the other is a person who respects *his* rights in turn, and like him respects the rights of all the others. Each senses that the other is an equally voluntary participant in something valuable and reciprocal. "I would respect your rights *in any case*," one might say to the other (any other), but "I respect *you* not only as a right-holder but as someone with whom to share a common good, someone with admirable social virtues (indeed, mainly *liberal* virtues like open-mindedness and tolerance of differences) that I welcome and 'feel at home with,' a person who is 'one of us' and one of our (right-respecting) kind." In such a way the social good is crowned with honest brotherhood.

I have tried in this section to defend liberalism from the charge that it *cannot* provide a unifying, community-building ideology. But of course no proof can be given that *only* the liberal ideology can create and bolster community. In smaller, more homogeneous societies, in particular, there have been united communities and powerful nations that were highly illiberal. Instead of showing that liberalism is uniquely correct (no small undertaking), I have tried only to rebut arguments that it is *necessarily* inadequate. Liberalism is compatible with community, but is that all that can be said for it? As a matter of internal logic, I think it is possible that that *is* all that can be said for it. Very likely it is not possible to demonstrate its inherent moral superiority to the various nonliberal alternatives. But as a practical matter, in our particular historical context, I think a great deal more can be said for it. For historical societies like our own, the products in large part of inconclusive religious wars and tempestuous political struggles, with large and diverse populations unable to reconcile their differences except by grudging tolerance, no other ideology will work as well. No other ideology would be neutral toward the substance of the differences, and a partisan state would be more divisive than unifying in its effect.[60]

Still, the communitarian might point to the fuller sense of cosmic orientation that the nonliberal ideologies can provide the alienated soul. Octavio Paz is typical of Latin American and European intellectuals who look to a political ideology for some larger comfort of this sort, some statement of exactly what one's place is in the larger order of things. He comments in his recent *Reflec-tions*[61] on the historical novelty of the United States' allocating "ultimate ends"—"questions as to life and its meaning" to "the private domain." The liberal and very American Naomi Bliven responds: "I cannot imagine any other arrangement, certainly not a government functionary probing the state of my soul."[62] This remark is an expression of the deep hostility and suspicion toward the very idea of a partisan governmental ideology, perfectly natural in a country founded in part to provide refuge from enforced orthodoxies and unanswerable government functionaries. Bliven grows more pensive, however, as she considers Paz's further comments on this matter, but her reply again gives natural expression to the liberal temperament:

> [Paz] remarks . . . that the absence of a single dominant belief and of a sense of national historical purpose makes it difficult to say what all our activity is for— what we are about collectively. *I am not sure there is any advantage in a culture that is easy to sum up.* I think we have another way of being American. My school memories suggest that being an American was a matter not of belonging to a collectivity with a shared faith or mission but of becoming a certain kind of person—for example, one who was not snobbish.[63]

One way in which a political ideology can help build a national community is to say what all the national activity is for, what collective faith or assigned mission gives it its single ultimate point. Another way, which Bliven reminds us can be equally effective (or more effective in an already pluralistic society), is to celebrate the liberal virtues (respect for human rights, open-mindedness, lack of snobbery) which provide us not with a single joint mission, but with an essential style of pursuing our several missions.

8. Remaining tensions between community and autonomy

Often what is hastily described as a conflict between individual autonomy and community is actually a conflict between an individual's practice and general majority attitudes, as for example, the conflict between Jones's right to read racy novels in the privacy of his chambers and the "traditional sexual reticence" of "the American people in general." The latter collective is a somewhat comprehensive grouping, ill-defined, and despite its majority inclinations, quite heterogeneous, with numerous dissenting subcommunities, whose members rub shoulders peacefully enough with majority people in other subcommunities. Reference to "community" in this context is a misleading way of invoking majority disapproval, even without harm or direct offense, as a reason for restricting or invading autonomy. The liberal, needless to say, will be unimpressed with this "reason" and unable to see any difficult conflict. He will be even less impressed with the pure legal moralist's argument that the fact that an individual does such things at all is itself an evil of a free-floating kind that the universe would be intrinsically better without. That can hardly be a decisive reason, even if true, for legal coercion, so long as personal autonomy is respected at all.

It is different when the "community" in question is smaller and better defined, and when genuine "collective harm" (see Chap. 28, §9) is caused to its members by the nonconformist. Even in the latter case, the liberal, though sensing the genuine conflict of interests, will side with the nonconforming individual on the ground that interfering with his autonomous rights is a more serious harm, *ceteris paribus*, than the collective harm his discreet nonconformity causes the others (see Chap. 29, §4). But there are some oppositions of this kind in which the conflict is genuine and close, and, in still others, the communitarian is quick to point out, decisions in favor of the community do not outrage liberals.

Liberals cannot always be counted on to complain, for example, about restrictive covenants enforcing decorative uniformity or standards of upkeep on the members of a residential community, even when it means that some property owners are denied the liberty of decorating or building as they see fit, and others are legally compelled to mow their lawns or paint their houses. The most natural way of interpreting these conflicts is as oppositions between an individual's separate interests and the collective interests he may or may not share with the other community members. These interests have to be carefully balanced by legislators and courts, and factors in addition to "seriousness of harm" and "avoidability of offense" considered. For example, it is highly relevant whether the recalcitrant homeowner entered the agreement with full understanding and free will, and whether he has any reasonable alternative to staying in the community should he choose to leave.[64] Very rarely will the prevention of an alleged aesthetic free-floating evil (like the disappearance of a traditional style in its traditional place) be invoked in the argument, and even when it is (as in our Nantucket example, Chap. 29, §1) it will be only one of the factors cited.

Still, some extreme communitarians will take the case of aesthetic enforcement in neighborhoods as a kind of model for the enforcement of traditional practices and beliefs of all kinds. This is the point, I think, in the following somewhat Hegelian passage from Roger Scruton:

> . . . for a long time it has been recognized that a man may not deal freely with his house, and not merely because some ways of dealing with it directly 'harm' his neighbors. [I assume Scruton has in mind such harms as depreciation of property values.] He may not demolish it, alter it, even (on occasion) redecorate it, without the consent of legally authorized bodies. And the reasons for this might be entirely aesthetic, matters of local character, "traditional appearances"—in short a public

expectation as to how a man's property should *look* . . . The ascendance of the aesthetic in matters of planning is of immense significance. For it shows the law enacting a will for visual continuity that can have no other legitimate origin than in the vested power of the state, conceived not as a means to individual freedom, but as the expression of social consciousness . . .[65]

A less obscure account of the source of the authority to enforce neighborhood codes, and one that is more congenial to the liberal, cites the power of the state to enforce the right of individuals in association to protect a good common to them all. Each of them agrees to maintain his property in the traditional way and receives a promise in return from the others to do the same. This not only keeps each person's property values high (an interest each has quite independently of the others) but protects an interest that all have interdependently, that is an interest that derives from community membership. There is no policy reason not to enforce such agreements except in cases where they unreasonably exclude outsiders (as racial restrictions do) or are imposed in hindsight on previous owners who are unwilling to go along, or when the harm inflicted on nonconformists, given the alternatives open to them, is disproportionate to the gains to the others (e.g., if the required paint contains an ingredient that makes the homeowner ill, and he cannot relocate without great cost to his other interests).

It surely doesn't follow from the fact that neighbors, in protection of their own interests, have a right "as to how a man's property should *look*," that they have a right "as to how a person's life should *be*, how he should behave in private, or what he shall believe. It is possible to imagine neighbors having a collective interest in these matters too, but as we have seen, (Chap. 29, §4), the harm to that interest, however great the number of those who share it, will be less important, *ceteris paribus*, than the harm to the coerced party. In general, collective harms must be treated (under the harm principle) in the same manner as other harms, and weighed carefully on the balancing scales. For Scruton, the state's expression of social consciousness is preemptive, and individual rights are not strong enough even to create a problem. Even acknowledging the natural importance to most people of group traditions, there is no need to take sides in these conflicts in so absolute a manner. Collective interests *are* among the important interests of individuals, and a good thing too. But their promotion can come at too great a cost, in some circumstances, to other individual interests.

When these conflicts seem about to occur, it would be a great mistake to assume automatically that there are irreconcilable differences among the contending parties. This facile assumption is one of the false "dualisms" exposed by Amy Gutman in her important criticism of communitarianism. The basic "appeal of liberal politics," she reminds us, is "for reconciling rather than repressing most competing conceptions of the good life."[66] She reminds us of the success, for example, of liberal licensing schemes for allowing porno-graphic bookstores (a nod to the liberals and to pornography readers) while regulating the location and manner of sales (to protect traditional neighbor-hoods). (See Vol. II, Chap. 8, §2.) Thus individuals in local communities are protected against unwanted changes in their neighborhoods, and dissenting individuals in those neighborhoods are permitted access to the disapproved materials, *both*. That is quite another thing from automatically enforcing the majority wishes, as such, of the most comprehensive community—the city or the nation.

There are of course much harder conflicts to reconcile than the bookstore example. The interests of individuals alone can conflict with the interests of individuals in association in myriad ways. Sometimes, the "association inter-ests" are not "collective interests" in the sense we have given that phrase, but only convergent independent interests, like the interests senior citizens have in the peace and quiet of their condominium complex, which may lead them to attempt to ban pet dogs and cats. Merely convergent interests would probably not impress a communitarian as much as genuinely collective interests would, for example, preserving the traditional form of services in their church, but a liberal would have no basis for such a comparative evaluation. Still, the liber-al's own balancing scale might disclose (and the communitarian might agree in the case at hand) that dogs and cats may legitimately be banned, and yet he may come to a different judgment about the legitimacy of barring families with small children from a particular neighborhood, a case in which the interests of family members would weigh more heavily than those of pet owners in the other case. And then there are harder cases of individuals versus neighbor-hoods than the restrictive covenant examples mentioned earlier. Sometimes neighborhood associations will request courts to issue preventive injunctions, even when there was no restrictive covenant, not on the grounds that a volun-tary contractual agreement would otherwise be breached by an untraditional building, but rather that the building would be an intolerable affront, spoiling the community's heritage, and should be banned on those grounds alone. Alternatively, an ordinance might be proposed in a local legislative body to prohibit buildings of a certain sort or to empower a board to grant or withhold licenses in accordance with community-protecting directives.

Whatever the legal mechanism employed, the problem of protecting the traditions of neighborhood communities is complicated by the fact that these communities overlap and intersect almost inextricably when their members reside in crowded urban areas. When the traditions in question are tied to a place, it is often impossible for the law—and especially for the criminal law—to act on the wishes of a neighborhood community to preserve itself without stomping, inadvertently as it were, on the interests of outsiders. Something must give, individual rights or "community values." The law in a liberal society will almost always back the "outside" individuals, but this need not be a tragedy for the (already somewhat scattered and interpenetrated) community members. Often as not they can preserve their traditions unforcibly with ingenuity and the willingness to tolerate minor inconvenience.

An example is in order, and *New York Times* correspondent J. Anthony Lukas provides a timely one. He made a detailed study of Charlestown, Massachusetts, a predominantly Irish-American suburb of Boston. This over-grown neighborhood community, he finds, is a case study of a deep moral rift in American society between the values of "equality" (his term for what I have called personal autonomy, a rightful individual liberty universally and equally possessed by all) and "community"—"the warmth, intimacy and comfort of family, church, tavern, and neighborhood that lies at the heart of what many Americans call home."[67] There have been many times and places in American history when individual liberty was stressed more, and other times and places when community had no near rival. Lukas gives examples of the latter:

> The communal intensity of Winthrop's Massachusetts was rooted in the "cove-nant," the sacred compact that each cluster of settlers made with God and with each other. By the very act of joining the congregation, the Puritan accepted not only one God and one religion, but one polity, one law, one allegiance. The towns they formed could not tolerate diversity: Sudbury enacted resolutions to bar "such whose dispositions do not suit us." Dedham banned "the contrarye minded."

To our modern minds this seems an ugly picture, one of narrow provincial-ity, even bigotry. But Lukas reminds us that "the notion that communities ought to control their own destinies—even at the expense of outsiders—was a deeply held American value with an ancient and honorable pedigree."

So long as the conditions of colonial America persisted, and settlement was clustered in small, relatively self-sufficient farming communities, the Puritan way, illiberal though it was, seemed morally defensible. Outsiders with different values would have no reason for joining, and even dissenters in the towns could leave on their own for more congenial towns or frontier farming land. For those who willingly stayed at home, the distinction between auton-omy and community must have seemed vanishingly small, since the free exercise of their autonomy corresponded with their promotion of the commu-nity values they shared with the others. The very "identity" of the selves that were self-governing was provided by their community allegiance. But of course the conditions could not, and did not, last long. Economic life became more complex and specialized, and waves of immigrants spilled over and around them, weakening both their isolation and their independence. From the beginning, however, the chief destructive pressures on the rigid, self-contained Puritan communities came from the national government. Ironically, the enforcement of individual rights conferred by the national constitution and its earliest amendments functioned actually to promote community, but broad rather than narrow community. It helped knit together diverse sectarian communities into a stronger, more cohesive national community. It weakened residential exclusiveness in such a way that differences between subcommunities remained, but the diverse groups were themselves bound more securely together by a common respect for established rights. That common bond, as well as increasingly common experience and growing economic interdependence, created a more unified "American people," even as millions of immigrants with different cultural backgrounds poured in to add variety to the mix. Through this whole long development, the ideals of the earlier communalism continued to exist and flourish. "Local control" and "individual rights nationally enforced" were the basis, as Tocqueville put it, of "two separate political systems in America," and in the Civil War they came into irreconcilable conflict.

The liberal has every motive to encourage the growth of private associations, large and small, including neighborhood communities. For given the social nature of man, autonomous individuals will exercise their autonomy by seeking common cause with like-minded associates, and in the promotion of group projects, find their self-fulfillment. But there is no necessity that community protection and development *must* come into conflict with the human rights of individuals. Sensible planning and flexibility often reconcile these values, and when the conflict seems starkly irreconcilable (as in the Civil War conflict between local control and freedom from slavery), the moral case for individual rights is likely to be decisive.

At the present time, and for the foreseeable future, local communities will not be geographically isolated (with some exceptions like Amish farm areas and the larger black ghettos). Rather they will be found scattered or diluted throughout cities, or pocketed and defensive amid shifting and unstable urban populations. What can the individual Irish-American do to preserve his traditional community ways as blacks, Hispanics, and other ethnic groups gradually move into his territory? He can join Irish cultural associations and clubs, even if it entails a longer drive, and some inconvenience, to get to meetings. He can find an Irish tavern, with a predominantly Irish-American clientele, including many of his friends and relatives, even though the surrounding territory is no longer ethnically homogeneous. As for the newcomers, he can form new overlapping communities with them based on their common territorial interests, just as he has always been willing to do with non-Irish Catholics in his church. Not all community values require common territory and neighborhood homogeneity.

There will remain tensions, as recent American history shows. Neighborhood schools will change their character as the neighborhood changes its population. One's children's playmates will have different accents and vocabularies, different manners, different concerns, and their different style will rub off on one's children. In a liberal state whose law stays clear of such problems except to enforce the basic rights of autonomy, the tensions will have to be controlled by voluntary actions within communities. Where there is good will and ingenuity, individual rights and community values can both be preserved, though the latter will no longer be tied so directly to territories. The pace of change will be slowed so that disparate groups will absorb traits from one another, and private associations devoted to ethnic traditions will flourish even in alien neighborhoods. The famous "melting pot" metaphor is an unfortunate one. Where community *integration* occurs, each individual (or subgroup) preserves his own individual integrity, but develops bonds of attachment and respect to others. The result is a strengthening of community in the Aristotelian sense of "a harmony of distinct but complementary persons." And a new neighborhood community can emerge that overlaps the two older communities which remain distinct. Thus the integration of the larger regional or national community is also strengthened.

It is naive to expect neighborhood integration always to work out so smoothly. More often than not there is no control over the pace of the influx of outsiders; change is drastic and abrupt; there is menace and danger in the air. Good will in the established group is overcome by the instinct to fight or flee. Those are the circumstances, apparently, that Lukas has in mind when he writes that conflicts between racial justice and neighborhood self-determination "rise to the level of genuine tragedy . . . precisely [because] . . . these are not choices between right and wrong, or between judicial dictatorship and sound social policy, but between competing values, between right and right." In the precise conflicts that Lukas has in mind, or at least in the most difficult of them (for example *de facto* racial segregation versus enforced busing), he is undoubtedly correct when he finds "right" on both sides. Surely there are claims on both sides that are morally worthy of respect. But it is doubtful to me either that the claims represent distinct and incommensurate sorts of values, or that they very frequently are absolutely equal in moral cogency. The claims of community are the claims of like-minded individuals to preserve a form of association that is interdependently valuable to all of them. These can be made to seem expressions of individual autonomy, since each individual can invoke his right to "choose his own lot in life" as he pleases, in this case to share a certain form of life with others. The individual's claim to racial justice, which sometimes seems to conflict with others' right to their community ways, can also be seen in a certain light as a communal (or subcommunal) right, since individuals (as Sandel and MacIntyre keep reminding us) come in communal groups and are hardly imaginable apart from them.

Moreover, while instances in which the conflicting moral cases balanced out equally on the scales are conceivable, that is unlikely in the actual cases we are considering. Thus talk of "genuine tragedy" is hyperbolic. When legitimate interests of one group appear to conflict with the basic rights of another, the basic rights must always triumph. This is clearly seen in the case of the Civil War, in which a well-established traditional way of life, founded upon black slavery, could no longer possibly be upheld morally. Perhaps it was a shame that a tradition ended and a community had to be restructured from scratch, but there is no doubt that the destruction of an essential community practice was less an invasion of personal autonomy than slavery had been. And Southerners are no less of a community, and the country as a whole much more of a community, now than before.

De facto racial segregation in public schools is an unjust barrier to equal opportunity, and, as such, it can be argued, a violation of basic rights, but it is by no means as severe a violation as slavery. On the other hand, it is not as essential to the communal interests that support it as slavery was to the Southern plantation. Some of the most treasured aspects of ethnic community, as we have seen, can be preserved, even without common territory, and most of the rest can survive if there is genuine hospitality and cooperation shown to newcomers. To invoke the honored name of community for a policy of "fight or flee" is as Orwellian an obfuscation as calling antagonism "brotherhood," or standoffishness and exclusivity "fraternity" or "civic spirit." The best way to "defend neighborhoods," in the end, is by a policy of neighborliness.

9. Summary

If liberalism implied that community values were not part of human beings' central sense of identity, that communities were mere aggregations of isolated atoms, that community life was not embedded in traditions, that alienation was not a necessary consequence of isolation from communities, or that it was of no serious consequence in any case, then liberalism would be untenable. There is no denying, furthermore, that liberals in the past (most of them well back in the past) have held these and similar doctrines. But there is no reason why liberalism, defined in terms of its normative commitments, need continue to carry such useless baggage. The liberal no less than the communitarian can insist that the individual whose autonomous right of self-government is so important to him is a social being through and through, and that many of his more important interests he shares with others in communities large and small. His community memberships, his assigned roles, his group allegiances form an important part of his conception of who or what he is. In a familiar sense, therefore, they form part of his *identity*, the "true self" that rightfully determines his lot in life. Some of these affiliations he inherits and never loses. He comes into existence with his character already fixed or nearly fixed in these respects. In other ways, however, the "fixing" remains for him to accomplish over his lifetime. In modern societies, at any rate, his vocation or trade, his political orientation, even his religious conviction, can be largely up to him to determine. His human nature determines that he has a basic need for community membership, and his specific inheritance provides him with a distinguishing profile of aptitudes and temperamental proclivities, but he will have to seek, on his own, the means to fulfill them. However he manages to do so, it will be within communities, and in cooperation with others.

The liberal who is determined to protect the liberty of individuals to experiment, to make their own life-decisions and moral commitments, must therefore also insist on the right of small subcommunties to grow in rich and diverse profusion. When the political state usurps the natural functions of these "intermediate associations," absorbing them into itself or forbidding individuals to combine and associate within them, it tramples on the most important of individual liberties, with all the dire consequences of which liberals have long warned us. The corollary of the doctrine that individuals must be left free within the zone of their autonomy (see Vol. III, Chap. 19, §1) to think and act as they wish, is that the communities of individuals must also be left free in their coordinated activities. For there to be nonconforming miniorities there must be communities of nonconformers, united by the very characteristics that separate them from the majority.

Liberals are also likely to emphasize the existence of wide differences among otherwise similar individuals in need and temperament. Some of us are more endangered by coercive pressure within overly cohesive groups, others by alienation because of isolation or exclusion from groups. The moral of this story too is that the more abundant, diverse, and receptive the social groups open to individuals, the better off the individuals are.

It is a mistake, however, as Gerald Postema emphatically points out,[68] to think of all human associations—and particularly those associations we call communities—as answering primarily to antecedently formed interests and needs of separate individuals, which then converge and reenforce themselves in association. Very often the community comes first, so to speak, and its collective interests emerge as a consequence, not a prerequisite, of member-

ship. This account applies especially to families, ethnic communities, nations, and the other communities that individuals are born into, and can
leave, if at all, only with the greatest difficulty. Since affiliation with communities of this kind too can form an important part of individual self-identity, a
political state intent on protecting individual interests will protect the collective interests of individuals in communal association.

Many practical problems in liberal states result from the apparent clash of
interest between the intermediate associations so valued by an enlightened
liberalism, and their members or other individuals. When genuine interests
are opposed, all of the usual dilemmas of interest-balancing can arise. One
way of obviating these moral conflicts is (again) to have available an immense
variety of alternative associations, or the opportunity of forming such groups.
Often, however, it is not easy for an individual to extricate himself from a
whole network of crisscrossing subcommunities, so that if he is forbidden by
law to deviate from the requirements of one of his communities, he has the
impossible option of relinquishing his right to be different, or else moving
and thus straining or snapping other valued associational ties. When the
continuation of his deviant ways is banned by the state, enforcing the community requirement, and the harm and offense principles are not directly or
obviously involved, then either the restrictive community must argue that it
has been harmed by the deviant's discreet practices as such, or else that his
nonconforming ways are a free-floating evil which the state has a right to
forbid, as such. Liberalism, as developed in this work, cannot accept the
latter reason because of the strong presumption that free-floating evils (assuming this *is* one) are not as serious evils as harms, and it cannot accept the
former, on the ground that harms to a personal interest are more serious than
harms to merely external interests, even when there are many more of the
latter than the former. (Again, see Chap. 29, §4.) In many cases, however,
spokesmen for the community cannot ingenuously claim that community members are in any way *harmed* by the nonconforming conduct. They wish only
to point out that the conduct, even though discreet, is strongly disapproved
of by a majority either of the complaining community or of the larger, most
comprehensive community. But it is no reason whatever to restrict A's behavior simply because B disapproves of it, in the absence of harm or offense. In
effect, that sort of argument would simply make unpopular nonconformity,
as such, criminal, with no further justification required.

When community interests clash with the individual interests of outsiders,
the situation does not differ in principle from ordinary interest-conflicts
between individuals. Community interests tend to be a very important kind
of interest, so they can weigh heavily on the balancing scales. But very often,
especially when territorial possession and residential homogeneity are not

essential to the preservation of a community, outsiders' interests can be accommodated at small cost, and the community interest does not exert its full weight on the scales. And when the outsider's interest is a fundamental one, like equal educational opportunity or freedom of movement, it has the status of a basic right and must prevail over whatever interest of lesser status cannot be reconciled with it.

Important as it is to human beings in modern societies to live in the midst of a thriving network of private associations, their peace and stability cannot be secured if there are not other social ties, not only forming bonds *within* the separate groups but also *between* them, making them into a unified national community and not a mere assemblage of "free-floating molecules." In part this unity is created by subgroups preserving their "sibling" ties to other subgroups of the same parent group, and partly by the phenomenon of random overlapping memberships. But adequate overall unification probably requires more than these threads of webbing. General loyalty to a common ideology is probably also necessary, with the traditional exemplary tales and legends that usually cluster about such an ideology. Liberalism is as capable as any other ideology—and in the complex modern world, with its immense and diverse national populations, probably a good deal more capable than its rivals—of providing such unification.

30

Strict Moralism: Enforcing True Morality

1. Critical versus conventional morality

Unlike the moral conservative, the strict legal moralist honors morality for its own sake, not simply because of its central place in a group's traditional way of life. The morality he wishes to enforce by law then must be *true morality*, a collection of governing principles thought to be "part of the nature of things," critical, rational, and correct. True morality, so understood, provides the standards and principles by which to judge the actual institutions of any given society, including its *conventional morality*—the rules and principles actually established in that society, for better or worse. That a given rule, standard, or customary practice is part of the established morality of a group is not a good reason for enforcing it by means of the criminal law, on this view, unless it is also a correct rule of morality, capable of satisfying a transcultural critical standard. On the other hand, if the established rule does satisfy such a test, then that is a very good reason, on this view, for enforcing it.

Even the liberal can be a "strict legal moralist," as the latter view has been so far defined, provided he holds that there is and can be *no harmless wrongdoing*. For if all wrongdoing necessarily harms or endangers the interests and violates the rights of others, then there is a perfect coincidence between what is "truly immoral" and what is "harmful" in the liberal's sense. Anthony Woozley, to mention only one distinguished writer, expresses the perfect coincidence view when he boldly maintains that "a question of [true] morality is a question about there being a harm, or risk of harm, or intended harm to somebody which is produced or manifested in conduct of such and such a kind."[1] Since Woozley denies that there can be any (true) immoralities that do not cause or threaten harm, it is no surprise that he further holds that there can be no immoral conduct "from which the law should *a priori* be excluded,"[2] a conclusion that sounds, paradoxically, like that of the strict legal moralist. Clarity would be served, then, if we added to our definition of strict legal moralism the tenet that there *are* harmless immoralities as determined by a "natural" or correct standard. That condition would not be satisfied by Woozley's view, which we can therefore exclude from the scope of the present discussion. On the other hand, I have grudgingly acknowledged that some behavior can involve or produce evils—"free-floating evils"—that are subject to adverse criticism by "correct" standards, even though they harm (wrong) no one in particular (though as a group these evils are much less significant than genuine grievance evils). We can concede this point to the strict moralist, however, while denying his central claim that free-floating moral evils can rightly be prevented by the criminal law.

The strict legal moralist takes free-floating moral evils much more seriously. (Oddly, some of the samples that he characteristically takes *most* seriously, like sexual deviance, do not strike many liberals as intuitively evil at all, much less as "true immoralities.") Typically, the true immoralities, as the strict moralist conceives them, even when private and harmless, are such evident and odious evils that they should be forbidden on the ground of their evil alone. As we have seen, the argument has a perfect simplicity; a single premise yields a single conclusion. Such and such activities are inherently immoral; therefore they should be prohibited even when private and harmless to individuals.

More often than not, strict moralism also deploys a version of the retributive theory of punishment. Not only should the criminal law prevent true immoralities, including the more odious of the free-floating ones, but it is an end in itself that the wrongdoer, even when his wrongdoing is victimless, should suffer the pains of punishment. The full theory of strict moralism, then, has three tenets: (1) true moral evils may rightly be prohibited by the criminal law even when they are free-floating; (2) some of the more serious true moral evils *are* free-floating; (3) it is an end in itself that moral wrongdoers, even when their misdeeds wrong no one, should be punished.

Strict legal moralism as we have defined it comes very close to the description Bertrand Russell gives of what he calls "puritanism"—

> We may define a Puritan as a man who holds that certain kinds of acts, even if they have no visible bad effects upon others than the agent, are inherently sinful, and being sinful, ought to be prevented by whatever means is most effectual— the criminal law if possible . . . This view is of respectable antiquity; indeed it was probably responsible for the origin of criminal law. But originally it was

reconciled with a utilitarian basis of legislation by the belief that certain crimes roused the anger of the gods against communities which tolerated them, and were therefore socially harmful . . . But nowadays even Puritans seldom adopt this point of view . . . The laws in question can, therefore, only be justified by the theory of vindictive punishment, which holds that certain sins, though they may not injure anyone except the sinner, are so heinous as to make it our duty to inflict pain upon the delinquent.[3]

The puritanical position on legally enforcing the ban on certain nonharmful immoralities, as Russell describes it, has become a steadily more *pure* kind of strict moralism. In the beginning, harmless immoralities had to be prevented and punished not only because they were true immoralities but also, given the precedent of Sodom and Gomorrah, because they endangered the community. But in more recent times the argument frequently stands unbolstered by further appeals to social harm and danger, and the appeal is to strict moralism through and through.

2. Pure moralism in the strict sense

The most characteristic argument for the strict moralistic position in its pure form involves the imaginative use of examples. The strict moralist must find actual or hypothetical examples of actions or states of affairs that are not only "evil in the generic sense" (see Chap. 28, §6) but *morally* evil as judged by "natural" objective standards, and perfectly free-floating, that is not evil simply because harmful (in the liberal's sense), offensive, or exploitatively unfair, but *evil in any case*. Then, if the example is such that the liberal, reacting spontaneously, would be embarrassed to have to oppose criminal prohibition, the example has telling probative impact. Indeed such arguments, while technically *ad hominem* in form, have as much force as can normally be expected in ethical discourse (see Vol. 1, Introduction, §6). This strategy requires that the strict moralist cite some plausible (though admittedly uncharacteristic) free-floating moral evils that are such great evils that the need to prevent them *as such* is likely to be accepted by the reader as a weightier reason than the case for individual liberty on the other side of the scales. All the legal moralist can do at this point is present relevant examples in a vivid and convincing way, pointedly reminding the reader of certain principles of critical morality that he holds in common with the legal moralist and takes equally seriously. The relative "weight" of acknowledged reasons is not otherwise amenable to proof. More exactly, the legal moralist offers *counterexamples* to the liberal thesis that personally harmless transactions between consenting adults in private cannot be evils of sufficient magnitude to justify preventive coercion.

Let us begin with the standard liberal example of the pornographic film or the nude stage show. Imagine that the advertising for these entertainments is perfectly honest and straightforward. On the one hand, it is not lurid or titillating in a way that would offend passersby; on the other hand, it does not conceal the nature of the shows in a way that would mislead customers into expecting something that is not pornographic. Imagine further that children are not permitted entrance. Since neither compulsion nor deception is used to dragnet audiences, everyone who witnesses the show does so voluntarily, knowing full well what he is in for. No one then can complain that he has been harmed or offended by what he sees. The shows therefore can be banned only on the ground that the erotic experiences in the minds of the spectators are inherent evils of a free-floating kind.

The playfully skeptical legal moralist can now begin to alter these hypothetical paradigms until his liberal adversary begins to squirm. He asks us to suppose, for example, that the voluntary audience is thrilled to watch the explicit portrayal on the stage of sexual intercourse, or even "sodomy and other sexual aberrations." Imagine live actors and actresses performing live sex for the delectation of live voyeurs. Well, surely this would be degrading and dehumanizing for the actors, protests the liberal. In that case, the state has a right to make sure that the actors too, and not only the audience, are voluntary participants. But why shouldn't some contracts between producers and actors be capable of passing the test of voluntariness? No doubt the actors' work would be unpleasant, but let us suppose that it is well paid. People have been known to put up, quite voluntarily, with great discomfort for the sake of earning money. Could sexual exhibitionism be that much worse than coal mining? Maybe it could. But should it not be up to the free choice of the actor to decide whether a certain amount of public degradation is worth ten thousand dollars a week? It would be paternalistic to prevent him from doing what he wants to do on the ground that we know better than he what is good for him. Liberal principles, then, offer no grounds to justify the legal prohibition of such diversions. That may not embarrass the liberal (very much), but other counterexamples lie in wait for him.

Imagine a really kinky live sex show primarily for voluntary spectators who prefer their sex with sadomasochistic seasoning. William Buckley eagerly takes up the argument from here:

> Does an individual have the right to submit to sadistic treatment? To judge from the flotsam that sifts up in the magazine racks, there is a considerable appetite for this sort of thing. Let us hypothesize an off-Broadway show featuring an SM production in which the heroine is flailed—real whips, real woman, real blood—for the depraved. One assumes that the ACLU would defend the right of the

producers to get on with it, trotting out the argument that no one has the right to interfere with the means by which others take their pleasure.

The opposing argument is that the community has the right first to define, then to suppress, depravity. Moreover, the community legitimately concerns itself over the coarsening effect of depravity.[4]

That the community has the right to define and suppress depravity as an inherent evil is, of course, the moralist thesis here at issue. That the community can be concerned with "coarsening effects," on the other hand, is the sort of consideration a proponent of the harm principle might invoke if he thought on empirical grounds that people with coarsened characters tend to cause harm to unwitting victims, so it is a consideration that can be put aside here.

Vicarious sexual pleasures of a "depraved" sort are not the only examples of private enjoyments found repugnant by some legal moralists. Professional boxing matches are another case in point. Here some of the liberals themselves are among the most denunciatory. *The New York Times* published an editorial demanding the abolition of professional boxing altogether shortly after the bloody first Frazier-Ali fight.[5] One of the many indignant letters to the editor that followed denounced *The New York Times*, in turn, on familiar liberal principles:

> Ali and Frazier fought of their own free choice. Neither of them has complained that he was forced to submit to brutal and dehumanizing treatment. Those who paid money to see the fight did so willingly and most of them thought they got their money's worth. . . . [W]hat was immoral about this fight? No rights were transgressed. Those who disapprove of professional boxing were not forced to watch.
> . . . The parallel to declining civilizations of the past referred to in your editorial is without any basis in fact. The contestants in the cruel sports that were practiced in the dying days of the Roman Empire, for example, were not free men with free choice . . .[6]

The liberal author of that letter is set up for the last of the ingenious moralistic counterexamples to be considered here. Irving Kristol has us consider the possibility of gladiatorial contests in Yankee Stadium before consenting adult audiences, of course, and between well-paid gladiators who are willing to risk life or limb for huge stakes. The example is not far-fetched. We can imagine that, with closed circuit television, the promoter could offer twenty million dollars to the winners and ten million to the estates of the losers. How could we advocate legal prohibition without abandoning the liberal position that only the harm and offense principles can provide reasons of sufficient strength to override the case for liberty? Kristol has no doubts that the liberal is stuck with his huge free-floating evil and can urge prohibition only at the cost of hypocrisy:

I might also have [used the word] . . . "hypocritical." For the plain fact is that none of us is a complete civil libertarian. We all believe that there is some point at which the public authorities ought to step in to limit the "self-expression" of an individual or a group even where this might be seriously intended as a form of artistic expression, and even where the artistic transaction is between consenting adults. A playwright or theatrical director might, in this crazy world of ours, find someone willing to commit suicide on the stage, as called for by the script. We would not allow that—any more than we would permit scenes of real physical torture on the stage, even if the victim were a willing masochist. And I know of no one, no matter how free in spirit, who argues that we ought to permit gladiatorial contests in Yankee Stadium, similar to those once performed in the Colosseum of Rome—even if only consenting adults were involved.[7]

The example of the gladiatorial show, at first sight, satisfies the requirements for argumentative cogency. Almost anyone would concede that the bloody contest would be an evil, and most would be willing to concede (at least at first) that the evil would be in the non-grievance category, since in virtue of the careful observance of the *Volenti* maxim, there would be no aggrieved victim. Moreover, the evil involved, in all of its multiple faces, would be a moral one. It is morally wrong for thousands of observers to experience pleasure at the sight of maiming and killing. It is an obscenely immoral spectacle they voluntarily observe, made even worse by their blood-thirsty screams and vicarious participation. If we reserve the term "immoral," as some have suggested, for *actions*, then the immoralities are compounded and multiplied, for the promoter acts immorally in arranging the contest, advertising it, and selling tickets; each gladiator acts immorally by voluntarily participating; and millions of voluntary spectators share the guilt.[8] If all these individual moral failings can be coherently combined, they add up to a social evil of great magnitude indeed. And yet it seems at first sight that the evil is a non-grievance one, since no one can complain in a personal grievance that he has been wronged.

From liberals who are determined to avoid hypocrisy, Kristol's examples will elicit at least three types of reply. First, Kristol is entirely too complacent about the problem of determining genuine "willingness" and "voluntary consent." The higher the risk of harm involved, the stricter must be the standards, one would think, for voluntariness. (See Vol. 3, Chap. 20, §5.) When it is a person's very life that is at issue, the standards would have to be at their strictest, especially when the life involved is clearly of great value to its possessor, unlike the life of the would-be suicide suffering from a painful terminal illness. Perhaps, as we have seen, the state would have the right, on liberal principles, to require such things as psychiatric interviews, multiple witnessing, cooling-off periods, and the like, before accepting a proffered consent as fully voluntary. Kristol talks glibly of finding "willing" public suicides in "this crazy world of ours," not noticing that an agreement is hardly consensual if one of the parties is "crazy." To exploit a crazy person in the way he describes is not distinguishable from murder and equally condemned by the harm principle. On the other hand, we must admit that a self-confident and powerful gladiator need not be "crazy" to agree to risk his life before the howling mobs for twenty million dollars. There could be a presumption that such a person doesn't fully understand what he is doing, or is not fully free of neurotic influences on his choice, but these hypotheses are rebuttable in principle, and in some cases that we can easily imagine, with only minor difficulty and expense rebuttable in fact. The liberal's second and third responses (below), then, are the more pertinent ones.

In conceding to the legal moralist that the wholly voluntary contest *is* an "evil" we are not making that judgment primarily because of the injury or death, the utterly "defeated interest," of the losing contestant. That result is an "evil," one might say, because it is regrettable that anyone had to be injured in that way, but so long as we adhere to the doctrine of the absolute priority of personal autonomy (see Vol. 3, Chap. 19), that sort of evil is always more than counterbalanced (indeed it is as if cancelled out) by prior consent to the risk. The primary evil relied upon by the legal moralist is not that anyone was harmed (i.e., injured *and* wronged), for no one was, and not that anyone was injured even without being wronged, since that "otherwise evil" is nullified by consent, and there would be an even greater evil, indeed a wrong, if consent were overruled. The fatal maiming of the loser was an "evil" (regrettable state) that he had an absolute right to risk. In reaffirming that right we are making it clear that we are not backtracking on our opposition to paternalism. The acknowledged evil that makes this case a hard one for the liberal is apparently a free-floating one, an evil not directly linked to human interests and sensibilities. That evil consists in the objective regrettability of millions deriving pleasure from brutal bloodshed and others getting rich exploiting their moral weakness (see Chap. 32). The universe would be an intrinsically better place, the strict legal moralist insists, if that did not occur, even though no one actually was wronged by it, and there is no one to voice a personal grievance at it.

The liberal who is sensitive to the charge of hypocrisy may, in the end, have to reply as follows. Gladiatorial contests and "voluntary" submission to torture are among the most extreme hypothetical examples of non-grievance evils that the legal moralist's imagination can conjure. There seems little likelihood that they will ever occur, at least in the foreseeable future. Yet they seem to be convincing hypothetical examples of very great evils. A liberal might treat them as the limiting case of the "bloated mouse" that has more weight than the undernourished human being (see Chap. 28, §8). The need to prevent them would be, in his view, one of the very weightiest reasons for coercion that one could plausibly imagine from the category of (merely) free-floating evils. He could then concede that the question of whether they could legitimately be prevented by state coercion is a difficult and close one, and admit this without hypocrisy or inconsistency. He would still hesitate to resort to legal coercion even to prevent the greatest of free-floating evils, simply because he cannot say who is *wronged* by the evils. At any rate, he can concede that the case is close. But the actual examples that people quarrel over: pornographic films, bawdy houses, obscene books, homosexuality, pros-titution, private gambling, soft drugs, and the like, are at most very minor free-floating evils, and at the least, not intuitively evils at all. The liberal can continue to oppose legal prohibitions of them, while acknowledging that the wildly improbable evils in the hypothetical examples of Buckley and Kristol are other kettles of fish. The liberal position least vulnerable to charges of inconsistency and hypocrisy would be the view that the prevention of free-floating evils, while always a relevant reason for coercion, is nevertheless a reason in a generally inferior category, capable of being weighed on the same scale as the presumptive case for liberty only in its most extreme—and thus far only hypothetical—forms.

The preceding paragraph describes a rather uncomfortable fallback posi-tion for the liberal who wishes to preserve without hypocrisy what he can of his liberal principles in the face of Kristol's vivid counterexample. Before he settles in to that position, however, he would be well advised to look more carefully at the complex of images and associations we experience when we ponder the example that is supposed to appeal to our "intuitions." What exactly is it about that example that we are responding to when it inclines us toward Kristol's conclusion? Inevitably, I think, we import into the example a nightmare of unconsented-to indirect harms. We naturally set the example in a brutal society full of thugs and bullies who delight in human suffering, whose gladiatorial rituals concentrate and reenforce their callous insensitivity and render it respectable. We cannot hold an image of these wretches in our minds without recoiling, for each of them alone will seem threatening or dangerous, and thousands or millions of them together will be downright terrifying. It is highly difficult, if not plain impossible, to think of wide-spread indifference to suffering as a mere private moral failing unproductive of further individual and social harm. And so we move quickly (too quickly) in the direction of Kristol's conclusion, ready to endorse with enthusiasm his judgment that the gladiatorial contest would be a huge evil, and to accept uncritically at the same time that the evil would be free-floating.

The immorality of the participants in Kristol's story, then, is not like that of the solitary taboo-breakers or other harmless wrongdoers who can righteously rebuff our interference with the claim that what they do is none of our business. Rather it is an inseparable component of our spontaneous reaction to the story that the wrongdoing and "wrongfeeling" in it powerfully threaten basic human interests and are therefore quite assuredly everybody's business. I have insisted (Vol. I, pp. 65–70, *infra*, Chap. 33) that moral corruption as such is not a relevant ground for preventive criminalization, but when the moral dispositions that are corrupted include concern about the sufferings of others, then the interests of others become vulnerable, and the corrupting activity can no longer be thought to be exclusively self-regarding. Nor are we considering here the mere "speculative tendency" of actions to endanger others, short of a clear and present danger that they will. When the bloody maiming and slaughtering of a human being is considered so thrilling and enjoyable that thousands will pay dearly to witness it, it would seem to follow that thousands are already so brutalized that there is a clear and present danger that some innocent parties (identities now unknown) will suffer at *their* hands. Indeed, it may be too late, in Kristol's gladiator example, to prevent such harms by prohibiting the show. If seventy thousand people will fill Yankee Stadium and enough others will attend closed television showings in theaters to permit the producer to pay thirty million dollars (my example) to the gladiators and still make a profit, then we are as a people already brutalized, and legal coercion, at best, can only treat the symptoms and slow their spread.

Kristol might reply to the above argument as follows. "*I* am writing the story," he might say, "in order to make *my* point. And in *my* version of the story, the spectators, for all their love of gory thrills, are not dangerous to other people. None of them would ever be likely to commit battery, mayhem, or homicide. Perhaps providing them with an orderly outlet for their savage passions makes them even less dangerous than they would otherwise be." In any case, he might say, they resemble in their motives and actions the dutiful wife of the dying invalid who secretly welcomes his sufferings but would never do anything to cause them herself (Chap. 28, p. 23), or the honorable bigot who values whites more than blacks but would never intentionally violate the rights of a black (Chap. 28, p. 32). The participating spectators then are, *ex hypothesi*, harmless to others. They all witness the spectacle voluntarily, and the gladiators themselves participate voluntarily, and no third parties are endangered or directly offended, so no one has a grievance. Yet it remains a monstrous moral evil that people should get pleasure in this way from the suffering of others, an evil whose prevention justifies prohibition, even though it is free-floating.

So might Kristol rejoin. But then the liberal reader might reply: "I never thought to interpret your example in *that* way. Indeed, it is highly unlikely that one could cultivate genuine joy at others' suffering without himself becoming more of a danger to others, and it is wildly improbable that hundreds and thousands of spectators could come to be bloodthirsty without constituting a threat to at least *some* of the rest of us. Perhaps what you ask us to assume is psychologically impossible. But never mind; I agree that it is at least *logically* possible that people should be capable of such decompartmentalization in their responses. So have it your way. But now my problem is that the original intuition to which you appealed, that the gladiator show is a sufficiently great evil to counterbalance autonomous liberty on the scales, is now substantially weakened. I can still acknowledge that it *is* a free-floating evil that a person derives pleasure from the suffering of others, while now denying that it is the business of the law to interfere." The example of a free-floating evil is now a purer one, but what it has gained in purity it has lost in intuitive forcefulness. Kristol's new mouse would no longer be as bloated as it was. (See also pp. 328–31.)

3. Impure strict moralism: Devlin's social disintegration thesis

Pure strict legal moralism is relatively rare. It seems to be presupposed here and there in specific arguments of writers like Buckley and Kristol, and it is found in pithy passages throughout the work of James Fitzjames Stephen, but I am not aware of a leading writer who has systematically developed it. That is especially surprising when one considers that this relatively rare form of legal moralism is probably the hardest for the liberal to deal with. Better-known writers in the camp of legal moralism seem to prefer "impure" arguments, appeals to the indirect consequences of permitting apparently harmless immoral behavior—its indirect effects on the public welfare and on more remotely connected human interests and sensibilities. The legal moralism of these writers is "strict" in our sense, because the free-floating evil they focus on is immorality as such. Immorality is free-floating for them in the sense that it would be an evil, even apart from its indirectly harmful consequences, which are themselves incidental and contingent and often not produced at all in individual cases.

Very often, however, the moralism of these writers fails to be consistently strict, when the morality they wish to enforce (to judge from their arguments) is the conventional morality of their society, whether or not it conforms to the true critical morality that is "part of the nature of things." Patrick Devlin, the most famous and influential of twentieth century legal moralists, is a case in point. Devlin is not consistent about the morality he aims to enforce, but insofar as it is conventional morality as such, then either immoralities are not

free-floating, and the ultimate appeal in Devlin's arguments is to the *harm* of
social disintegration, or else the genuinely free-floating evil to be prevented is
not true immorality as such, but the drastic change in a community's traditional way of life that would result from the change in its established morality. In the former case, Devlin's commitment is to the public harm principle
and is consistent with liberalism. In the latter case, Devlin is a legal moralist
of the moral conservative stripe. In neither of these interpretations, then, is
his view to be called "moralism" in the strict sense. If on the other hand it is
"true morality" that Devlin wishes to enforce, he can be a consistent strict
legal moralist, though perhaps, as we shall see, not a "pure" one.

Devlin's famous Maccabean Lecture in Jurisprudence read at the British
Academy in 1958[10] was a response to the report produced by the Committee
on Homosexual Offenses and Prostitution under the chairmanship of Sir
John Wolfenden. The committee had been appointed by Parliament in 1954
to appraise British law at that time regarding homosexuality and prostitution
and to recommend any changes it thought desirable. The Wolfenden Report
squarely endorses Millian liberalism: "It is not the duty [function] of the law
to concern itself with immorality as such . . . It should confine itself to those
activities which offend against public order and decency or expose the ordinary citizen to what is offensive or injurious . . ."[11] At first Lord Devlin was
as pleased as any liberal. "The only part of the Report relevant [to jurispru-
dence] was the statement which, as I have said, I completely approved, that
there was a realm of private morality which was not the law's business, and
the distinction between crime and sin."[12] Soon, however, Lord Devlin had
second thoughts and reservations, and out of them emerged his celebrated
lecture.

Devlin's first doubt concerns the Wolfenden Report's repeated use of the
phrase "private morality." The report concludes, for example, that "Unless a
deliberate attempt is to be made by society, acting through the agency of the
law, to equate the sphere of crime with that of sin, there must remain a realm
of private morality and immorality which is, in brief and crude terms, not the
law's business. To say this is not to condone or encourage private immorality."[13] Presumably what the report means by a "realm of private morality and
immorality" is a sphere of predominantly self-regarding behavior, not directly affecting the interests or sensibilities of others, in which the autonomous actor is free to follow his own moral judgments and principles even if
they should diverge from the prevalent standards in his community ("public
morality"). And what Devlin and the report both apparently mean by "sin" is
an action that violates the prevailing morality even if it causes no distress or
harm to others. Devlin admits early in his lecture that he has come to have "a
feeling that a complete separation of crime from sin . . . would not be good

for the moral law and might be disastrous for the criminal."[14] The idea of various protected zones of "private morality" had begun to appear anarchic and socially dangerous in its threat to undermine the prevalent public morality. Morality is the foundation of society, he insists, and to replace a building's foundation with another cannot be done without bringing the whole structure down:

> In England we believe in the Christian idea of marriage and therefore adopt monogamy as a moral principle. Consequently the Christian institution of marriage has become the basis of family life and so part of the structure of our society . . . It has got there because it is Christian, but remains there because it is built into the house in which we live and could not be removed without bringing it down.[15]

Devlin translates his doubts about the Wolfenden Report into three questions. The first is: "Has society the right to pass judgment at all on matters of morals? Ought there, in other words, to be a public morality, or are morals always a matter for private judgment?"[16] This first question is very badly misworded. Obviously society has the right to "pass judgment" on *some* matters of morals. No liberal would deny that there should be judgment, indoctrination, even public enforcement of the other-regarding sector of morality, and that the condemnation of violence and fraud must not be weakened. The question is not whether society can pass judgment at all in matters of morals, but rather which matters of morals are its proper business; not whether morals are always a matter of private judgment only, but whether they are ever a matter for private judgment only.

Having misformulated his opening question, Devlin proceeds to give his famous answer:

> . . . society means a community of ideas; without shared ideas on politics, morals, and ethics, no society can exist. Each one of us has ideas about what is good and what is evil; they cannot be kept private from the society in which we live. If men and women try to create a society in which there is no fundamental agreement about good and evil they will fail; if having based it on common agreement, the agreement goes, the society will disintegrate. For society is not something that is held together physically; it is held by the invisible bonds of common thoughts. If the bonds were too far relaxed the members would drift apart. A common morality is part of the bondage. The bondage is part of the price of society; and mankind, which needs society, must pay its price.[17]

If the question to which this argument is directed were not so misleadingly formulated, with its basic confusion of "ever" and "never," "sometimes" and "always," this argument could be readily seen for the *ignoratio elenchi* that it is. Society is a community of ideas; without any shared moral beliefs a group of people would be a mere assemblage or collection, not a society or community. But from that truism it does not follow that to be a society, a group of people must share *all* moral beliefs. A common morality is required, but Devlin has not shown that our common convictions about other-regarding morality (what Hart calls the moral minimum) will not do. We cannot live together without any agreement, but it is not the sole alternative to no agreement that there be total agreement. The liberal view that a consensus is required on the moral minimum but not on predominately self-regarding morality, has not been dented by Devlin's argument.

Devlin's second question is the more interesting one. "If society has the right to pass judgment," he asks, "has it also the right to use the weapon of the law to enforce it?"[18] It is his answer to this second question that has won Devlin fame as a leading exponent of legal moralism; it contains his much debated (and by this date, I think it fair to say, discredited) social disintegration thesis, his analogy between "private immorality" and political treason, and his criterion for determining how the moral judgments ("public morality") of society are to be ascertained. Without its *present* "public morality" (not just *any* public morality), Devlin argues, society would disintegrate, and therefore society has a right to preserve every single part of the presently prevalent morality (not just its noncontroversial "moral minimum") by the use of coercive law, "just as it uses it [law] to safeguard anything else that is essential to its existence."[19] At this point, the political analogy occurs to Devlin for the first time, and he declares that "a recognized morality is as necessary to society as, say, a recognized government."[20] Actually, if there is any analogy here at all, it is between the established morality (beyond the moral minimum) and a given political administration, not between that morality and the state itself. We cannot live together as a society without some administration of government or other; but it does not follow that we cannot live together without this particular one.

Nevertheless, having discovered his fancied analogy, Devlin is off and running. Next comes the analogy between "private immorality" (e.g., homosexual relations between consenting adults in private) and political *treason*. If our basic political institutions are subverted, we shall have no government at all and thus fall into chaos and anarchy, becoming easy prey to foreign conquest. If our morality is similarly undone, the consequences will be equally disastrous for our society. Legal coercion is justified long before the danger of social disintegration is clear and present, for "history shows that the loosening of moral bonds is often the first stage of disintegration . . ."[21] Hence, "The suppression of vice is as much the law's business as the suppression of subversive activities; it is no more possible to define a sphere of private morality than it is to define one of private subversive activity."[22] By "vice"

Devlin means acts contrary to the prevalent "public morality," even when the acts are consensual, harmless, unobserved, and thus inoffensive.

How then is the "public morality" to be determined? We cannot expect it to consist of the unanimous opinion of all citizens; that is too strong a requirement. On the other hand, it must be more than the convictions of a bare majority. Devlin seeks a middle course by applying the legal standard of the "reasonable person," the ordinary man in the street ("the man in the Clapham omnibus"), or the typical "right-minded person." Whatever moral judgments a substantial number of such ordinary upstanding persons can be presumed to agree to unanimously can be ascribed to society as its "morality." Indeed, Devlin (how seriously?) makes the standard for determining the moral judgments of society exactly the same as that for determining the guilt of a defendant in a criminal trial: ". . . the moral judgment of society must be something about which any twelve men or women drawn at random might after discussion be expected to be unanimous."[23]

It is not enough, however, that typical reasonable persons agree in disliking a practice. There must also "be a real feeling of reprobation." "Intolerance, indignation, and disgust . . . are the forces behind the moral law, and indeed . . . if they or something like them are not present, the feelings of society cannot be weighty enough to deprive the individual of freedom of choice."[24] It is not clear whether Devlin's "ordinary" or "right-minded" individual is simply any person (presumably excluding criminals, homosexuals, and libertines) chosen at random, or a person independently qualified as right-minded; but, in any case, when that person is filled with loathing at the very thought of certain practices, he speaks for the morality of the community:

> There is, for example, a general abhorrence of homosexuality. We should ask ourselves in the first instance whether, looking at it calmly and dispassionately, we regard it as a vice so abominable that its mere [unwitnessed] presence is an offense. If that is the genuine feeling of the society in which we live, I do not see how society can be denied the right to eradicate it.[25]

It is unclear how "strict" Devlin's legal moralism is. Indeed, it is impossible to tell from his arguments whether strict moralism, or moral conservatism, or fear of public harm is his basic position. In particular, it seems impossible to tell whether the "morality" to which he appeals is established morality as such, or something with greater authority, a true morality whose principles are part of the nature of things. The correct interpretation, I should think, depends on whether his chief emphasis is on the *ordinariness* of the typical person whose revulsion serves as a standard, or to the *reasonableness* ("right-mindedness") of that upright and respectable omnibus passenger. If it is the ordinariness that is emphasized, and we are to consider how any man or woman in our society, chosen at random, could be expected to judge or feel about a given type of conduct, then at most we have a test for determining whether there is a moral consensus in the community, and that would guide us (as inquiring anthropologists) to a description of the prevailing or established (conventional, popular, positive) morality of the group. But since established moralities in this sense vary from community to community and nation to nation, the fact of *this* consensus is hardly conclusive evidence that the agreed-upon judgments are part of true (objective, transcultural, rational, critical) morality. It may be, then, that it is only the established morality as such, whether it is the true morality or not, that Devlin wishes to enforce. On the other hand, he frequently refers to this morality as "the moral law," and he sometimes shows considerable exclusivity when identifying the ordinary or reasonable person.

Insofar as Devlin's emphasis is on the "reasonableness" of the "man in the jury box," he seems to be inclining toward strict moralism and appealing to true morality after all, for what could be a better test of the content of true morality than the considered judgments and outraged feelings of persons known independently to be right-minded and reasonable? Moreover, if we are to take the jury selection process seriously as an analogy, not just anybody selected at random will be qualified to be on the jury. Persons whose fair-mindedness is suspect—criminals, biased persons, uncomprehending persons—can be excluded. The juror in an ordinary legal case must be a reasonable person, but her reasonableness need be no greater than that of the ordinary minimally qualified bloke. One would think that a higher standard than that would be needed if we are to infer the true morality from unanimous jury verdicts.

A more difficult problem for Devlin (which he never addresses) is whether we are to exclude from the pool of qualified jurors those who engage in the very practices being judged. Can we decide, without fatally begging the question, that homosexuals are neither "ordinary," "reasonable," nor "right-minded"? And if not, how can we expect to get unanimous expressions of "intolerance, indignation, and disgust" at homosexuality? Devlin's Clapham omnibus may itself contain several practicing homosexuals according to the Kinsey Report's estimate that 10% of the male population fall into that category. If the 10% figure is accurate, any representative jury of twelve would be more likely than not to contain a homosexual.

The classification of Devlin's view may also depend on whether his chief emphasis is on the deliberate judgment and incidentally attendant emotion of the ordinary reasonable person or, as seems more likely, on that person's disgust and indignation. If the latter, Devlin seems to be invoking the "bare thought" version of the offense principle (see Vol. 2, Chap. 9, §3), making all reference to "morality" quite dispensable. It would be odd, however, for Devlin to attribute to almost everyone (and even odder, to all reasonable persons) an emotional antipathy to a practice that is so powerful that they all need "protection" from the bare thought that the practice is or might be secretly taking place somewhere in the community with legal impunity. Surely, our own earlier conclusion (Vol. 2, pp. 33–34) that such a reaction would require a pathological susceptibility to offense must be closer to the truth.

The view that Devlin defends in his famous essay, then, is not precise enough to be classified with confidence as either strict or broad moralism. It is possible, however, to interpret him as a strict moralist, but in the light of Devlin's clearly "impure" moralistic argumentation, such an interpretation, would require us to explain in just what sense some actions could be "inherently immoral" according to him. After all, if his view is properly classified as "impure moralism in the strict sense," then the conduct whose criminalization it advocates is held to be *inherently immoral*, but the reason given for prohibiting it is not *that*, but rather one acceptable in principle to the liberal, namely its indirect harmfulness, in particular its threat to social solidarity. Devlin's use of the harm principle does not appeal to any direct harm that the immoral acts might inflict on its victims, but to the social harm that he thinks comes from weakening the moral consensus against it (that is, the consensus that acts of its kind are wrong even though "harmless"!). Some actions are "inherently immoral" for Devlin in the sense that they are condemned by (true?) morality even though they don't directly harm or offend anyone. So it is not any directly harmful or offensive consequences of these actions that make them immoral. Neither in all probability is it their status as the object of a collective indignation and disgust of the sort Devlin describes, for consensus is probably the *test* of immorality—our way of ascertaining which acts are immoral—not the *ground* of immorality, the characteristics that actually confer immorality upon them. *Nothing* external to these acts confers wrongness on them; they are morally wrong through and through, in their own character. Nevertheless, because they are also the object of a certain kind of consensus, they must be forbidden by law, not to prevent any wrongful harms they might cause directly, but simply to enforce the consensus, contingent and local though it may be, for that consensus is part of the social bond that unites us as a community, and we will all suffer irreparable harm if the bond breaks. That is the interpretation that would render Devlin's theory coherent as a kind of legal moralism that is at once both strict and impure. Immoralities that directly harm no one may be prohibited by law but only because failure to do so would be indirectly socially harmful. These acts are "immoral" for reasons other than their harmfulness, but it is the harmfulness of weakening the social consensus about them that justifies their prohibition. The *pure* strict moralist would take their inherent immorality to be sufficient reason for prohibiting and punishing them. Devlin requires more reason than that.

Devlin's discussion of the third and final question in his lecture shows his more liberal side. Ought society to use the criminal law, he asks, to prohibit all cases of immorality or only some; "and if only some, on which principles should it distinguish?"[26] Devlin makes it plain here that he claims only that the inherent immorality of an act is always a good and relevant reason for prohibiting it, but that there are usually powerful reasons on the other side that must be counterbalanced if criminal prohibitions are to be justified. Even the person who acts in ways that "every right-minded person is presumed to consider to be immoral" has rights that cannot be trampled by criminal legislation. If a criminal proscription would overrule his *conscientious* behavior, that counts heavily against it. Insofar as enforcement of the law would lead to widespread invasions of *privacy*, that too counts heavily against it. And, in general, liberty has a powerful claim that requires the full weight of the moralistic reason, in given cases, to counterbalance it. Thus, in his particular legislative judgments, Devlin has a consistent way of rejecting severe depredations of liberty. All of this mitigates without canceling his distinctive liberty-limiting principle: It is always a good and relevant reason in support of criminal prohibitions that they will prevent actions the very consideration of which can be presumed to arouse the disgust and indignation of every ordinary reasonable person, and which will be judged immoral by such persons even though they involve only consenting adults and occur in private.

4. What are we to mean by "morality"?

Lord Devlin was a distinguished judge and a respected and influential public figure, so liberals, predictably outraged at his arguments, felt obliged to rejoin with vigor. One of their primary targets was Devlin's apparent conception of the nature of the "morality" which the state, on his view, has a *prima facie* right to enforce. H.L.A. Hart lampooned it without mercy. "For him [Devlin] a practice is immoral if the thought of it makes the man on the Clapham omnibus sick."[27] If that is all morality comes to, Hart asks, what reason can there be to invade private liberty just to vindicate feelings that themselves may be supported by no cogent reasons, or even by no reasons at all? Devlin is committed, moreover, to the view that if only eccentric old women (those formerly called "witches"), interracial association, and adultery were viewed by the ordinary "reasonable" (respectable?) person with intense intolerance, indignation, and disgust—as they are or have been at other times or places—we would be justified in making laws against them.

Devlin could reply, of course, arguing "impurely," that even if his conception is "all morality comes to," that morality is nevertheless the glue which binds us together into society, the weakening of which is as threatening to our community's survival as subversion and treason. Even a racist community like South Africa, he might say, despite its wicked established "morality," has a right to protect itself from social disintergration just as it has a right, even though racist, to protect its national boundaries from invasion. But Hart rightly will have none of this. "It is grotesque," he claims, "even where moral feeling against homosexuality is up to concert pitch, to think of the homosexual behavior of two adults in private as in any way like treason or sedition either in intention or effect."[28] Private "immorality" (if that is what it is) has no element of deliberate betrayal or breach of faith. The homosexual made no prior vow to govern all his conduct in accordance with the spontaneous nonrational feelings and general opinions of his neighbors, so the analogy with treasonable intention is wholly absent. As for treasonable effect, the only trace of analogy is that the indirect effect of private immoralities may be to shift the limits of tolerance and thus lead to moral change. But that change could itself bring the whole moral structure down only if that structure were an assemblage of interdependent parts, impossible to alter in one area, say attitudes toward homosexuality, without also changing entirely, say, attitudes toward murder, battery, rape, and theft—a conception that is empirically absurd.[29]

Devlin can do his cause no good, then, by appealing to conventional (popular, established) morality as such as the rightful object of criminal enforcement, if all that morality consists in is widespread or prevalent *feelings* without rational support. If the simple one-step argument from "*x* is immoral" to "*x* should be criminal" is to have any plausibility, *x* must be immoral by reference to a critical or objectively correct moral principle. Otherwise it might be "immoral" only in the sense that it contravenes a particular group's thoroughly mistaken and even wicked established popular morality. There is no contradiction in describing the conventional morality of a group as itself in some respects truly immoral.

Very likely then Devlin's view is not legal moralism in the strict sense, not unless he tacitly holds a moral epistemology that bases our knowledge of the true morality on the spontaneous feelings of all reasonable people. On such a view, the ground of moral principles might be one thing, and our way of knowing them quite another. The only way we can determine what the content of true morality is, this account might say, is to ascertain the spontaneous feelings of reasonable persons. It is not the feelings that *make* the principles true; rather the feelings are a reliable index (or litmus test) to the truth of the principles. If that is Devlin's implicit view, then he is faced with the absurd consequence that interracial association was truly immoral in the American South and in present-day South Africa, and that burning witches accorded with the requirements of true morality in colonial Massachusetts. He can avoid such absurdities only by limiting his "jury" of reasonable persons to those who have the appropriate moral qualifications, eliminating from the pool, for example, all those who are racists or would-be witch-burners on the ground that they could not be sufficiently "reasonable" to qualify. That, of course, would be a flagrantly circular procedure. And if Devlin is to avoid circularity he must provide non-question-begging criteria of reasonableness specifying characteristics of the reasonable person that go well beyond his spontaneous feelings of revulsion and disgust.

Another liberal critic, Ronald Dworkin, also aimed his attack at Devlin's curious conception of what morality is. Dworkin has no objection to legal enforcement of a consensus of genuine moral convictions, as opposed to mere spontaneous feelings, but he notes that what Devlin calls "morality" is not a collection of moral convictions, or a genuine "moral position," at all. Dworkin's criticism applies a basic distinction which Devlin has overlooked:

> It is true that we sometimes speak of a group's "morals," or "morality," or "moral beliefs," or "moral positions" or "moral convictions" in what might be called an *anthropological sense*, meaning to refer to whatever attitudes the group displays about the propriety of human conduct, qualities, or goals. We say in this sense that the morality of Nazi Germany was based on prejudice or was irrational. But we also use some of these terms, particularly "moral position" and "moral conviction," in a *discriminatory sense* to contrast the positions they describe with prejudices, rationalizations, matters of personal aversion or taste, arbitrary stands, and the like.[30]

A person's opinions qualify as a moral position when he has *reasons* for them that are more than mere prejudices, allergic aversions, rationalizations (based on wholly unsupported matters of fact), or faithful parrotings of authority (or of the neighbor who in turn parrots *him*). These reasons presuppose a reasonably coherent and comprehensive set of general principles to which he can sincerely and consistently give allegiance. It is quite obvious that the aversion to homosexuality of the man on the Clapham omnibus is not a genuine moral position in thise sense. The aversion he shares with other respectable persons to the "abominable" practice may be part of the group's morality in the anthropological sense, but it forms no part of the "moral consensus of the community" in the discriminatory sense. It would surely be more worthy of respect if it did, but I fail to share Dworkin's assumption that it would automatically be properly enforcible if it did, even in those of its parts that condemned harmless wrongdoing.

How is Dworkin's useful distinction related to our earlier one between conventional and true morality? When one purports to be making an objectively correct moral judgment, or invoking a correct moral rule or principle, one is making an essentially controversial claim, taking a stand on what is really the case, popular opinion notwithstanding. Some have described such claims as "prescriptive" as opposed to "descriptive." I would prefer the less pallid term "advocative." When, on the other hand, one purports to be voicing a judgment of a particular group's conventional morality (without personal endorsement) then one truly is describing the group's established code, actual practice, or shared opinions, in the manner of a visiting anthropologist simply reporting a certain kind of cultural fact, without advocacy. But the anthropologist might find a great diversity of "moral" phenomena to describe. On the one hand, he might describe what Dworkin called the group's "morality in the anthropological sense," the actual consensus of attitudes, feelings, and off-the-cuff judgments about the propriety of various practices, including feelings that are only prejudices, parrotings, allergies, rationalizations, and the like. He might also investigate—and here his inquiry would be no less *descriptive*—the group's "morality in the discriminative sense," the consensus (usefully vague word!) of qualified judgments of propriety, those that are held in a critical, reasoned, and consistent way, as well as various norms (standards, principles, rules) that are not only established but supported by a consensus of reasoned opinion. These distinctions are rendered diagramatically below.

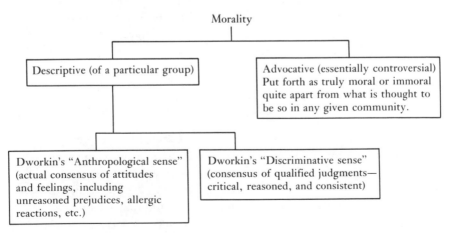

Diagram 30-1. Some senses of "morality."

Moral judgments in the "anthropological sense" may yet be true, as moral rules and practices in that sense may yet be sound, if they should just happen to correspond to true morality. Similarly, moral judgments and norms in the discriminative sense might yet be incorrect if, despite their reasoned basis, they should happen not to conform to the judgments and norms of true morality. Still, one would expect that the discriminating judgments would have a greater chance of being true simply for being discriminating as well as widely held—no guarantee of truth, simply a better chance. If Devlin had taken an advocative stand against homosexuality (for example) and had given convincing reasons for judging it to be truly immoral even when harmless and private, then he would have made the strongest possible moralistic case for prohibition, and his argument would deploy a liberty-limiting principle that is moralistic in the strict sense. Nevertheless, the argument would fail to convince the liberal, even if he were convinced of its premise, for he could find no person who wanted, or needed, or could claim a right to "protection" from the alleged immoralities, even assuming them to be genuine immoralities. Still, the argument might carry some probative force. If Devlin had argued instead from an accurate *description* of a consensus of discriminating judgments in our society that even private homosexual relations among consenting adults are immoral, that would not be as strong an argument for prohibition, because one could always admit that the consensus was genuine and discriminative, yet deny that homosexuality truly is immoral. Still, the argument might be acknowledged as a reason, though a weak and inferior one, for prohibition. The argument would be diluted strict moralism, urging in effect that the fact of a discriminative consensus is *evidence* that the practices in question are *truly* immoral, even though that fact is not part of the explanation why they are so. But Devlin has not done that much (at least if Dworkin's criticism is just). He has argued directly to legal prohibition from the fact that there is a consensus of prejudice and emotional aversion, a fact which, by itself, has no probative force whatever.

5. Devlin's counterattack: the argument from the moral gradation of punishments

In 1963, H.L.A. Hart published the Harry Camp Lectures he had earlier delivered at Stanford University,[31] in which he amplified his criticism of Devlin and further developed his own liberal view. Then, in 1965, Devlin replied to his critics (mainly to Hart) by republishing his original lecture with a new title, "Morals and the Criminal Law," additional footnotes which addressed the criticism, and six new essays which developed his views in more detail. To this book, which has remained the definitive statement of

Devlin's views, he gave the title of his original lecture, *The Enforcement of Morals.*

To a reader two decades later, Devlin's book seems strangely uneven. On the one hand, his responses to Hart's critical arguments are often feeble and perfunctory. On the other hand, when he turns his attack against Hart's own views he argues with fresh vigor. Most present-day readers will probably conclude that there is no salvaging Devlin's social disintegration thesis, his analogies to political subversion and treason, his conception of the nature of popular morality and how its judgments are to be ascertained, or the skimpy place he allows to natural moral change. But he does argue forcefully against liberals on the grounds that their nonmoralistic theories cannot account for certain features of our present criminal law that they would presumably be unwilling to have changed. Those arguments deserve our respectful attention.

Devlin argues that Hart cannot account for the exclusion of consent as a defense to all crimes-with-victims except rape and theft—an exclusion that the liberal is presumed to wish to maintain—and also for the continuance of certain crimes (bigamy is the one to which he devotes most attention) that do not obviously have liberal rationales. Since we have discussed these matters earlier (consent as a defense, Vol. 3, Chaps. 23–27, and bigamy, *supra*, Chap. 28, §4, and Vol. 3, Chap. 24, §7), we can be content in this chapter with a summary treatment of them (§8 below). In this section we can concentrate on the subtlest of Devlin's arguments of this type, one that Hart himself had discovered in James Fitzjames Stephen's 1873 attack on Mill.[32] The argument can be put as follows: The liberal allows no legitimate role to "the enforcement of morality as such" in the making of criminal law. The only legitimate function of criminal law for him is to prevent private and public harms and nuisances. In all consistency then, he should not permit any considerations other than the prevention of harm (and offense) to enter into decisions about the degree of punishment to be assigned to different categories of crime, and to commissions of the same crime by different offenders under different circumstances. And yet it is our traditional practice, which not even the liberal would wish to alter, to treat greater moral blameworthiness (Stephen's term was "wickedness") as an aggravating factor and lesser moral blameworthiness as a mitigating factor in assigning punishment, a practice impossible to justify on the assumption that the aim of punishment, as of criminal law generally, is simply to prevent harmful behavior. If the makers of criminal law can have no legitimate concern with moral wrongdoing as such, then neither should judges deciding punishment have any concern with morality independent of harmfulness. The only admissible kind of reason for punishing one thief more than another is that he stole more money and thus caused more harm.

Hart does not allow himself much space to reply to this argument, revealing perhaps his failure to be much impressed by it. He admits that "the moral differences between offenses should be reflected in the gradation of legal punishments,"[33] but denies that this shows that the whole object of penal statutues cannot be to prevent acts dangerous to society, and that it must instead be "a persecution of the grosser forms of vice" (Stephen's phrase[34] for a condemnation of immoral behavior). The non sequitur in Stephen's argument, Hart maintains, comes from his "failure to see that the questions: 'What sorts of conduct may justifiably be punished?' and 'How severely should we punish different offenses?' are distinct and independent."[35] Given the logical independence of these questions, liberals, he says, "can in perfect consistency insist on the one hand that the only justification for having a *system* of punishment is to prevent harm, and only harmful conduct should be punished, and yet on the other hand agree that when the question of the *quantum* of punishment for such conduct is raised, we should defer to principles which make the relative moral wickedness of different offenders a partial determinant of the severity of punishment."[36]

Hart's claim that the questions of justification for a system of criminal prohibitions and for specific quanta of punishments are distinct and independent simply denies, without further explanation, the assumption behind Stephen's argument, and Devlin is unimpressed. The questions do not seem obviously independent to him. Rather, "They are a division, made for the sake of convenience, of the single question which is: 'What justifies the sentence of punishment?' The justification, he continues, must be found in the law, and there cannot be a law which is not concerned with a man's morals and yet which permits him to be punished [in part] for his immorality."[37] "It is an emasculation of Mill's doctrine," Devlin concludes, "to say that it is to apply only to the making of law and not to the administration of it."[38] The liberal then is placed in a dilemma: either he must approve legislation prohibiting "harmless wrongdoing," or he must disapprove of even partial adjustments of sentences in accordance with degrees of moral blameworthiness.

I think the liberal can escape this trap, and I should like to suggest here how that might be done. Two lines of argument could be used. The first, which is suggested by Hart's sketchy remarks, I shall consider in this section. The second response, which is the more fundamental one, maintains that the first is quite sufficient, but hardly necessary.

For any rule-structured social practice or institution, we can ask "What is it for?", meaning not just how it in fact functions, but how it ought to function, what purposes it must achieve to be justified. Following Hart's earlier work,[39] we can label this proper purpose "the justifying aim" of the practice. Sometimes we cannot specify an institution's justifying aim without referring to moral functions such as the cultivation of good character, moral counseling or instruction, resolution of moral conflict, provision of the means of penitence, and the like. Very likely some such moral function must be mentioned in a full statement of the justifying aims of family law courts, churches, and schools, among other social institutions. For other structured practices, for example team sports, theater, medicine, academic philosophy, and manufacturing corporations, moral functions are not part of the justifying aim. To cultivate character, exhort to virtue, condemn moral failings, inculcate moral teachings, resolve moral dilemmas, etc., is not what structured practices in these categories are for. Nevertheless, even a practice lacking a distinctively moral *raison d'être* cannot do without moral rules for the regulation of its own activities. An amoral justifying aim does not imply an immoral mode of operation.

Consider the organized sport of football. What is its justifying aim? Presumably, a full answer to that question might be to provide exercise, demanding physical challenges, cooperative enterprise, and camaraderie for players, and absorbing, tense entertainment for spectators. To be sure, some might also mention character-building and cite that as a moral function, but the character traits developed, like courage, competitive ardor, cooperation, and patience, are perhaps not the most distinctively moral sorts of virtues. (The miscellany of virtues called "moral" includes everything from saintly self-denial and scrupulous honesty to having a good sense of humor, cheerfulness,[40] and charm. The list shows how treacherously ambiguous and flexible the word "moral" is.) In any case, the cynical judgments of most college and professional players belie the claim that football either does, can, or should be expected to make players better people. It is plausible then to characterize the justifying aim of football in nonmoral terms. But football must be governed by procedural rules, if it is not to become chaotic violence rather than a game. Kicking, gouging, punching, and the like are forbidden by these rules, and the teams that benefit in the game from transgressions are deprived of their unfair gains and penalized accordingly. It is still possible, however, for officials to distinguish between unintentional and deliberate infractions, and between serious and trivial ones. For the more egregious violations, individual offenders are ejected from the game and, depending on the gravity of their offense, suspended for a time from further participation. For minor offenses often a mere warning suffices. It would be unfair to the players as well as disruptive of the game if these distinctions were not made by the rules and enforced by the officials.

No matter what the institutional practice is, and no matter what it is for, there are moral and immoral ways of participating in its activities. Professional philosophy has as its justifying aim the pursuit of truth about certain

abstract questions, the achievement of greater clarity, insight, and understanding. It is not its purpose to exhort people to virtue, punish sin, or
excoriate wickedness. But a philosopher may yet practice his calling unfairly
and immorally if he resorts to plagiarism, doctors texts, or uses abusive *ad
hominem* arguments or deliberate sophistries. Such professional misconduct
violates rules of procedural fairness that govern the pursuit even of nonmoral
aims. The justifying aim of a business corporation is to provide wanted goods
or services and thereby make work for employees and profits for owners. No
mention need be made at this level of distinctively moral objectives. Yet one
can pursue even purely economic goals morally or immorally and violate
governing moral rules by unfair competition, false advertising, collusive
price-fixing, union busting, or tax cheating.

   We can therefore distinguish between the general justifying aim of a structured practice and the rules of fair procedure that govern its activities. Even
when the former has no moral component, the latter may serve important
moral purposes, and may assign penalties, awards, and compensations all in
the interest of fair play. Applying this distinction to the criminal law, we
must seek the justifying aim of a whole *system* of rules and practices, including
legislative authority to prohibit some kinds of acts, police powers, prosecutorial discretion, rule-governed trials, verdicts, sentences, appeals, imprisonment, parole, etc. A liberal would say that the justifying aim of the whole
system is to prevent private and public harms, while insisting that the rules
governing the system's operations at every level must be *fair*. Fairness to the
accused requires gradation of punishments in accordance with two distinct
sets of considerations: the wrongdoer's degree of *responsibility* for his deed and
degree of *blameworthiness* as determined by his motive and circumstances.

   Consider responsibility first. No matter what actions the criminal law may
properly prohibit, it would be flagrantly unfair to convict a person of a crime
when he did not in fact do the prohibited act (perhaps someone else did it, or
perhaps no one at all). On the other hand, when a person calmly and deliberately does what he knows is forbidden, the act can be imputed to him simply
and without qualification, so that there is no injustice (at least of a procedural
sort) in punishing him for the crime. It would be unfair to others if he were
let go when they have been punished for doing just what he did. However, if
the accused has done the prohibited act, but did it inadvertently, accidentally, or reflexively, then it is not true, baldly and without qualification, that
he did it at all. It is grammatically awkward but conceptually correct to say
that the action was his but that the degree of "actness" in the doing of it was
less than full, or that the act can only partially, not fully, be ascribed to him
as his doing.[41] In that case, while some punishment may be justified (perhaps
it would be unfair to others if he were let off scot-free), it would be unfair to

punish him to the same extent as others who did the proscribed thing to a fuller degree. In fact they didn't *do* (in the full sense) the same thing.

The gradation of punishments then can correspond to the wrongdoer's degree of responsibility for his deed. The offender may have been fully responsible, however, for what he did, in the sense that he did not do it accidentally, unknowingly, inadvertently, etc., and yet, because of his motives and circumstances, he may be subject to less blame than the usual offender. Descriptions of his motives may have been excluded at his trial because the jury's sole task was to determine whether he intentionally did what was forbidden, but rules usually give discretion to the judge to consider such matters in sentencing. Two acts of killing might both be clear instances of first-degree murder, equally intentional and equally premeditated, yet one was done out of mercy, at the request of a suffering, aged invalid, and the other out of malice or greed. Both equally violate the law, and the violators are equally guilty. It would be unfair, however, to punish the less blameworthy killer as severely as his more wicked counterpart, since it is unfair (according to the formal principle of justice stated by Aristotle) to treat alike cases that are *relevantly* unlike.

What is it about the degree of moral blameworthiness that renders it a "relevant" characteristic in the application of the formal (Aristotelian) fairness principle? Its relevance derives from its correspondence to an essential function of legal punishment which, as a symbolic device for expressing public reprobation, automatically stigmatizes the condemned offender.[42] If an essential part of the *point* of a sentence of punishment is to express society's moral condemnation of the criminal, then the degree of that condemnation (expressed symbolically by the degree of imposed hard treatment), should match, as far as is practicable, the actual degree of blameworthiness incurred by the criminal for his criminal act. A judge can hardly be permitted to make the moral blameworthiness of a particular criminal the *sole* determinant of his degree of punishment, for there are other social functions of punishment, notably deterrence, that have a bearing on the decision; in any event, concentrating on the moral status of a particular wrongdoer's motives also might obscure the general reprobation a specified punishment expresses toward the general class of actions of which this offender's act was an instance. The punishment expresses condemnation of classes of crimes too, not only of particular criminals for committing those crimes; the act as well as the actor is condemned. Even if the actor's motives were entirely good so that he is not blameworthy at all, the condemnation is to impress on him the community's moral judgment that the *act* he intentionally performed from such innocent motives was nevertheless wrong. Still, other things being equal, it is unfair that a less blameworthy violation of a statute should be condemned more severely than a more blameworthy one. Fairness requires that relevantly dissimilar cases should be treated in appropriately dissimilar ways, and what could be more "relevant" to the degree of moral condemnation expressed by a punishment than the degree of moral blameworthiness of the one to be punished?

The liberal, I maintain, can endorse this line of reasoning, even if in doing so he is interpreted as excluding distinctively moral purposes from his account of the justifying aim of a *system* of criminal law. The criminal law *process*, he can and should admit, is in its very nature a kind of complex "moral machine." Apprehended suspects are fed into one end of the process and either emerge, status unchanged, through various escape hatches along the way, or are processed right through to the other end of the machine, where the moral stigma is stamped on them both by a judge's solemn pronouncements and the reprobatory symbolism of their confinement. Those who are the "raw material" of the process are separated by the machinery into two classes, those who are returned unpunished to their previous lives, and those who are convicted, punished, and thereby morally condemned. The ultimate aim of the *system* which employs this punitive *process* is to reduce the number of wrongful harms inflicted by individuals on one another, but the mode of operation of the moral machinery must be fair, or else it will work to defeat its own built-in goals. That is to say that it would be self-defeating to use stigma-stamping machinery in such a way that admittedly less blameworthy acts are stigmatized more severely than more blameworthy acts, for this confusion of judgments would impede the function of the machinery itself, namely to match stigma to actual blameworthiness.

Even those institutional practices that do not use moral machinery must abide by morally fair procedural rules on pain of incoherence or counterproductivity. For example, the aim of a professional licensing examination (the bar exam, medical boards, certified public accountancy exams, etc.) is to separate the participating individuals into two groups: those who will be deemed qualified to enter the profession, and those who will not. In some cases (e.g., the certified public accountancy exams) all examinees, those passing as well as those failing, are given a score and thus rank-ordered. No moral judgments, explicit or symbolic, are passed on anyone. In that sense the test "machinery" is not moral. Still, it would be unfair to use a testing procedure that qualified incompetent persons and excluded competent ones, or ranked persons of lesser skill higher than skilled ones. Given the nature and goal of the examination, knowledge and skill are the "relevant" characteristics in the application of the fairness principle, so that it would be unfair to treat parties dissimilarly who are similar in these respects, or to treat similarly parties who are relevantly dissimilar.[43] The point applies to these rule-governed practices even though their ultimate justifying aims are not distinctively moral, but rather narrowly professional. The most striking way in which criminal law differs from the professional licensing process is not that it contains a distinctively moral component in its justifying aim, but rather that it employs a constitutive *process* which is in its very nature morally judgmental. "Here is the complex moral machine," the legal philosopher says; "now, for what purposes only should we use it?" If he is a liberal, he can answer, without obvious absurdity, "Let us use it only to prevent individuals, by the threat of its operation, from inflicting certain kinds of harms and offenses upon one another."

In summary: a rule-governed practice or institution will have its own distinctive justifying aim and its own characteristic process ("machinery"). Either or both of these may be distinctively moral or entirely nonmoral. In either case, the operations of the practice must be governed by fair rules, else it will mistreat those people who participate in it, as well as defeat some of its own internal aims. The fairness of its procedural rules is determined in part by their accordance with the general Aristotelian principle that relevantly similar cases are to be treated similarly and relevantly dissimilar cases dissimilarly in direct proportion to the degree of dissimilarity between them. The "relevance" of a characteristic for the purposes of the fairness principle is determined, at least in part, by the functions of the process it superintends—the job assigned (or built into) the "machinery." When those functions are moral (e.g. stigmatizing blameworthy acts) then such moral traits as blameworthiness will be relevant; otherwise not. But the relevance of these moral considerations will be a consequence of the rules of fair procedure that *any* kind of institution, distinctively moral or otherwise, must employ, not necessarily a consequence of an ultimately moral justifying aim. A system of criminal law, whether or not it is assigned a moral justifying aim, employs an inherently moral (judgmental) constitutive process, and that process, in conjunction with the formal principle of fairness, is what underlies the concern with blameworthiness in sentencing.

I believe that the line of argument sketched above is sound and available to the liberal, but it is not really necessary for him to resort to it in reply to the Stephen-Devlin argument, for a much simpler and direct reply is equally handy. As we have seen, even if the justifying aim of the criminal law is entirely nonmoral, it is consistent to require that its operations be subject to fair procedural rules. In point of fact, however, it is a misrepresentation of the liberal position, at least as I have tried to formulate it, to say that it ascribes an entirely nonmoral justifying aim to the criminal law.[44] There is a clear respect in which the liberal's liberty-limiting principle *is* a moral one. The justifying aim of the system of criminal law, on his view, is not merely to

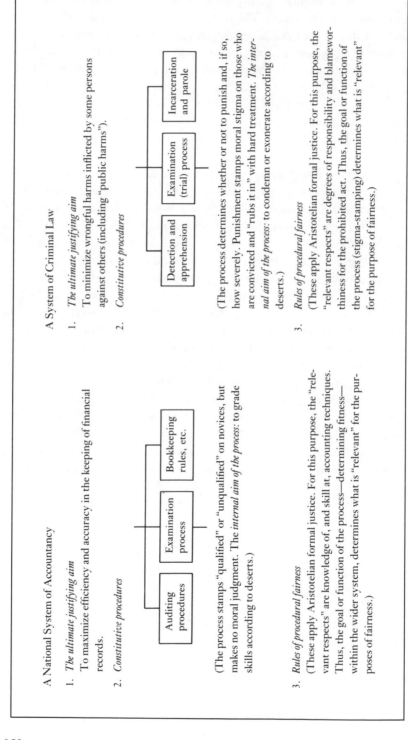

A National System of Accountancy

1. *The ultimate justifying aim*
   To maximize efficiency and accuracy in the keeping of financial records.

2. *Constitutive procedures*

| Auditing procedures | Examination process | Bookkeeping rules, etc. |

(The process stamps "qualified" or "unqualified" on novices, but makes no moral judgment. The *internal aim of the process*: to grade skills according to deserts.)

3. *Rules of procedural fairness*
   (These apply Aristotelian formal justice. For this purpose, the "relevant respects" are knowledge of, and skill at, accounting techniques. Thus, the goal or function of the process—determining fitness—within the wider system, determines what is "relevant" for the purposes of fairness.)

A System of Criminal Law

1. *The ultimate justifying aim*
   To minimize wrongful harms inflicted by some persons against others (including "public harms").

2. *Constitutive procedures*

| Detection and apprehension | Examination (trial) process | Incarceration and parole |

(The process determines whether or not to punish and, if so, how severely. Punishment stamps moral stigma on those who are convicted and "rubs it in" with hard treatment. *The internal aim of the process*: to condemn or exonerate according to deserts.)

3. *Rules of procedural fairness*
   (These apply Aristotelian formal justice. For this purpose, the "relevant respects" are degrees of responsibility and blameworthiness for the prohibited act. Thus, the goal or function of the process (stigma-stamping) determines what is "relevant" for the purpose of fairness.)

Diagram 30-2. Fairness in institutional practices.

minimize harms, in the sense of setback interests, all round. If that is what he advocated he would have no quarrel with the legal paternalist. In fact, his principle permits prohibitory statutes ony when necessary to prevent those harms (and offenses) that are also *wrongs:* those that are unconsented to, involuntarily suffered, and neither justified nor excused. The criminal law, he insists, must serve a profoundly moral purpose, namely the protection of individuals' moral *rights.*

It does not follow, however, from the fact that the only legitimate purposes of the criminal law are moral ones that any and all moral purposes are equally legitimate, or legitimate at all, as reasons for criminalization. "Only moral considerations" does not imply "all moral considerations." The liberal, if I have interpreted him correctly, holds that

1. All of the justifying aim of the criminal law consists of moral considerations.

But this does not commit him to

2. All moral considerations are part of the justifying aim of the criminal law.

One might charge with equal cogency that the liberal is committed to the belief that all animals are dogs by his belief that all dogs are animals. Even though the liberal justifying aim might be entirely a moral one, then, he might yet reject "immorality as such" as a proper target of legislation.

Let me spell out this point a little further. The liberal does not advocate the criminalization of actions simply on the ground that they are likely to have adverse effects on the interests of other parties, for that would lead to the prohibition of dangerous acts that are fully consented to by the parties who are endangered. A criminalizable action must be more than harmful in this minimal sense; it must also be wrongful. But there may well be actions that are morally wrong yet do not *wrong* anyone, that is, do not violate anyone's rights. Even if there are such actions, since they don't wrong anyone in particular, they have no "victims." Nor are there any people who can express personal grievances against the wrongdoer for his wrongful conduct. It follows that the liberal, unlike his moralistic critics, cannot endorse the criminalization of such actions,[45] even though it is open to him to agree with the legal moralists that the actions in question *are* morally wrongful. Immorality as such, therefore, is not a sufficient ground for legitimate criminalization, according to the liberal. The only legitimate ground, to be sure, is a thoroughly moral one, namely the protection of moral rights; but not every conceivable moral ground would be a legitimate one for criminalization. That is what is meant by saying that, for the liberal, the criminal law is not concerned with enforcing "morality as such," but only with protecting the rights of others, that sector of morality I have called "grievance morality."

We can now reply directly to Devlin's contention that "there cannot be a law which is unconcerned with a man's morals and yet which permits him to be punished for his immorality." The liberal does *not* urge that the legislators of criminal law be unconcerned with "a man's morals." Indeed, everything about a person that the criminal law should be concerned with is included in his morals. But not everything in a person's morals should be the concern of the law, only his disposition to violate the rights of other parties. He may be morally blameworthy for his beliefs and desires, his infractions of taboo, his tastes, his harmless exploitations, and other free-floating evils, but *these* moral judgments are not the business of the criminal law.

The consistent liberal then must make important concessions in replying to Devlin. When he approves gradations in punishment based on different degrees of *blameworthiness* (as opposed to responsibility) he must not permit the types of blameworthiness which he excludes at the legislative level to sneak in the back door at the sentencing level. In both cases the moral blameworthiness that *is* relevant is the harm-threatening, right-violating kind, dispositions to feel or act in ways condemned by grievance morality. And in both cases also, moral blameworthiness based on the principles of nongrievance morality must equally be excluded.

Suppose, for example, that there is a municipal ordinance against jay-walking for which the penalty for violation is "up to $100 and up to 30 days in jail." John Doe is convicted of jay-walking for rushing across the street to get to a dental appointment on time—a relatively innocent motive. He is fined $10 and let go. Richard Roe jay-walked with a "lustful heart" to keep within discreet ogling distance of a beautiful woman he was following. The judge sentences him to a $100 fine and 30 days in jail. Thus jay-walking with lascivious motives is punished more than jay-walking with "innocent" motives even when the disapproved motives have no tendency to harm others.[46] Of course, the liberal condemns this way of grading punishments on the same grounds that he would condemn a statue that made "discreet ogling" itself into a crime. The behavior in question cannot be punished separately as an independent crime for the same reason it cannot be the basis for increasing the severity of a penalty for another crime, namely that the law has no business at any level enforcing non-grievance morality. Devlin is at least right in insisting that the legislative and administrative questions must be treated alike in this respect. The liberal would be inconsistent if he defended a rule that made lascivious motivation an aggravating condition in the commission of crimes, while staunchly opposing legislation creating independent crimes of lasciviousness. But the liberal is not inconsistent when he permits malice, spite, or cruelty to aggravate (these being morally blameworthy precisely because they cause harm to others), or when he recognizes mitigating excuses based on diminished responsibility.

The liberal also can and must concede that the criminal *process* in its very conception is inherently moral (as opposed to nonmoral)—a great moral machine, stamping stigmata on its products, painfully "rubbing in" moral judgments on the people who entered at one end as "suspects" and emerged from the other end as condemned prisoners. The question the liberal raises about this moral machine is: "which actions should cause their doers to be fed into it?", and his answer is: "only those actions that violate the rights of others." There is no doubt in his mind that the law may "enforce morality." The question is *which* morality (or which sector of morality) may it properly enforce?", and he restricts the criminal law to the enforcement of "grievance morality." His answer would not be plausible if he did not restrict criminal liability to the doing of actions that deserve condemnation, since legal punishment itself expresses such condemnation, though not everything for which a person might be condemned morally can legitimately be made a basis for criminal liability. But it would be no departure from the moral aims the liberal assigns to the whole system of criminal law (protecting rights) for him to approve of judicial consideration of degrees of responsibility and blameworthiness in sentencing. As we have seen, even undertakings without ultimate moral purposes, like philosophy discussions, business enterprises, and football games, use moral procedural rules to govern the pursuit of their nonmoral objectives, and permit moral gradations in assigning penalites for violations of those rules. All the more so, then, given the moral purpose that the liberal attributes to the criminal law, should the law permit such gradations too. Given that moral purpose (the protection of rights), even Lord Devlin would have to agree that there is no clash between it and the moral gradation of penalties. That is to say, more precisely, that there is no inconsistency in asserting that

1. The law should forbid only actions that violate the rights of others,

and

2. The legal process should always respect the rights of the accused.

6. Stephen's original argument

I return now to James Fitzjames Stephen's original argument, for it raises a number of interesting issues, at least one of which was not fully resolved in the Hart-Devlin debate. The object of criminal legislation, he tells us, is to support the full moral system that is in place in the community—in a nutshell, to promote virtue and prevent vice, as they are generally understood in the community. In principle, at least, the legislature may use the criminal law to promote not only those virtues that consist in the disposition to respect and promote the rights of other people, but also those that consist in the disposition to avoid and prevent free-floating evils that wrong no one. Stephen hastens to reassure us, however, that the criminal law should not be used to enforce the virtue of chastity or to "indict a man for ingratitude or perfidy",[47] not because these are illegitimate uses of law, but because they are expensive, inefficient, and counterproductive means to a legitimate goal. "Such charges are too vague for . . . distinct proof . . . and disproof. Moreover, the expense of the investigations necessary for the legal punishment of such conduct would be enormous."[48] Such practical considerations, Stephen maintains, are "conclusive reasons against treating vice in general as a crime."[49]

It is otherwise, however, when such a vice as unchastity "takes forms which every one regards as monstrous and horrible."[50] Stephen refers here to actions that produce a widespread revulsion not because they are believed to be harmful violations of the rights of others, but because they are inherently revolting, apart from their direct effects on others. If these free-floating evils are great enough, Stephen affirms, it doesn't matter that it is extremely difficult and expensive to apprehend and punish *them*. Why should that be? Part of the answer, Stephen says, is that harm prevention is not the only proper ground for criminalization. The law as it exists now and has always existed makes no sense unless we also ascribe to it as part of its rationale the gratification of "the feeling of hatred—call it revenge, resentment, or what you will—which the contemplation of such conduct excites in healthily constituted minds."[51] Stephen then supports this interpretation by citing examples of criminal conduct in which factors mitigating the blameworthiness (perhaps a better word would be hatefulness) of an act decrease the punishment for that act, even though those factors would actually be aggravating if our sole purpose in selecting the degree of punishment were to deter harmful acts. That the criminal succumbed to an overpowering though common temptation, for example, should be an extenuating circumstance (or at least not an aggravating one) if we wish to modulate the fierceness of our punitive response to match the degree of our natural resentment, but if our aim is to deter others, then the greater their temptation, the greater the amount of punishment we need to threaten them with.[52]

Now I have no doubt that we do often assign lesser punishments in individual cases than we would assign were our sole purpose to deter others, and that we do this out of consideration of the criminal's degree of blameworthiness. The way I would express this, however, is somewhat different from Ste-

phen's. I would say that this is one example among many of a procedural rule
of fairness actually constraining the direct pursuit of a justifying aim. I
cannot deny, therefore, that there is a tension in any system of criminal law
between its ultimate justifying aim and the rules of fairness that constrain its
procedures. (Perhaps it is different in some of the other examples like football, where the fairness-rules more directly contribute to the fulfillment of
the justifying aim.) This tension creates a problem both for the liberal view of
the scope of the law and for the alternative view advocated by Stephen and
Devlin. If either side were to argue that there is no ultimate justifying aim
beyond the inherent goals of the punitive machinery then the problem would
not arise, for there would then be no goal beyond condemning or exonerating
the accused according to his deserts, and the severity of the punishment
would be determined entirely by the degree of the offender's blameworthiness and the corresponding degree of symbolic condemnation given to "similar cases." If Doe's crime, for example, is different in no morally relevant
respect from that of Roe, who is serving a sentence of one year's imprisonment, then the proper sentence for Doe is also one year's imprisonment
whether or not the crime they both committed is becoming more widespread
and more and more people have become tempted to commit it.

Both Stephen and the liberal, however, do allow for a justifying aim
beyond that which is implicit in the nature of punishment itself. The liberal
ascribes to criminal law the ultimate aim of reducing the extent to which
wrongful harms are inflicted on individuals and the public generally. Stephen
and Devlin add to this the aim of reducing the amount of inherently hateful
or immoral conduct whether or not that conduct wrongs or harms others.
The ultimate purpose of the criminal law system in both theories is to reduce,
by direct incapacitation and deterrent threat, the occurrence of actions of the
appropriate kinds. Their only disagreement at this level is over which kinds
of actions *are* appropriately discouraged by legal means.

Now suppose that John Doe commits an act of a kind that is properly (and
actually) prohibited during a mounting epidemic of such acts. Neither the
legal moralist nor the liberal need have any objection to a rule that permits a
judge to increase the degree of punishment in such circumstances so as to
strengthen the deterrent threat in the face of rising temptation to perform the
prohibited acts. Presumably both would urge that there be some reasonable
ceiling to the judge's discretion to increase the sentence in this way. Neither
would be committed, for example, to approve of hanging and disembowel-
ment as a sentence for illegal parking. But neither is prevented by what is
essential in Devlin's theory from approving an increase, decreed by emergency legislation or resulting from discretion judges already possessed, (say)
from $25 to $100 to help solve a mounting traffic crisis. (The penalty might

be announced as "up to $100.") According to the rules of procedural fairness applied to the operations of the stigma-stamping machinery, it would not be fair to punish Doe more severely than Roe for doing exactly what Roe had done in a way that was different in no morally relevant respect. Perhaps ideal candor would have the judge tell Doe: "I am sentencing you to pay a fine of $100 even though yesterday I fined Roe only $25 for doing exactly the same thing. $25 of this fine is to be considered your punishment, and that is the degree of punishment you deserve. The other $75 is an added tariff, not punitive in intention, but necessary to discourage others, in these increasingly difficult times, from doing what you did." I have some doubts that such a breakdown of costs would make the unlucky offender feel a great deal better, but it would perhaps make that part of his penalty that seemed undeserved seem less arbitrary.

My purpose here is not to try to resolve the tensions between deterrence and desert that trouble any theory which recognizes as a justifying aim the deterrence of some undesired sorts of conduct by the use of punishment, a process that has its own internal morality. I emphasize here only that the problem exists to the same degree for Stephen and Devlin as for Mill and Hart. The liberal assigns the law the aim of deterring wrongfully harmful behavior. The legal moralist would use law also to deter inherently immoral acts performed voluntarily or consensually in private. The one wishes to prevent grievance evils; the other would also prevent certain free-floating evils. But deterrence is central to both theories, and deterrence can conflict with procedural fairness in determining sentences equally in both theories.

What interests me most in Stephen's position, however, is an intriguing paradox. For him, the ultimate justifying aim of criminal law is twofold: to minimize hateful evils whether harmful or not, and also to provide orderly outlets for feelings of vengeance, hatred, and resentment against the wrong-doer. He has no objection to creating crimes without victims mainly because (if I interpret him correctly) the legislation creating such crimes is justified by the need to gratify the desire for vengeance that arises so naturally in right-minded people. But if a crime has no victim who is there to want revenge? I wish to pursue this question in the next section of this chapter, but I will generalize it so that it not only covers vengeance but also more respectable forms of retribution. The question I shall investigate is whether the concept of retribution in any of its many forms can have coherent application to the punishment of a victimless crime. If "retribution" makes no sense applied to such punishment, then there is a plain conflict between legal moralism, the view that we may properly punish acts of harmless wrongdoing, and the retributive theory of punishment, the theory that punishment is only justified when it is retributive.[53]

The committed legal moralist, of course, may respond to this conflict by saying "So much the worse for the retributive theory," just as the retributivist can respond "So much the worse for legal moralism." I cannot resolve that impasse. But if the incompatibility could be established, it would be a devastating argument against Stephen, and, since some other legal moralists also purport to be retributivists, the alleged incompatibility should have more than a little interest for them.

7. "Retribution" for wrongs without victims

The word "retribution" has come to have various senses in the writings of moral philosophers, but it seems to have originally meant "paying for" injuries one has wrongfully caused or "paying off" one's victims or their kin in exchange for their vengeance, and thereby perhaps starting a blood feud. Punishment and compensation were fused in the earliest moral conceptions and legal systems, and that original confusion still survives in our talk of wrongdoers "paying for" their crimes, or of (what is a different but related idea) the retaliating victims "paying the wrongdoer back" by returning his harm back upon him. Restoring the moral equilibrium is a concept hardly distinguishable in its earliest uses from "balancing one's books," and it still survives as a root metaphor in ordinary conceptions of punishment.

In the light of this history one can understand the dictionary entries that define "retribution" as "something given or extracted in recompense," and "recompense" as "an equivalent or a return for something done, suffered, or given."[54] The word "retribution," in virtue of its embodiment of the repayment metaphor, is one of a family of closely related and often interdefinable terms including "requital" (to make suitable return), "retaliation" (to pay back for a wrong), "reprisal" (retaliation for damage or loss suffered), "reciprocation" (return in kind), and "revenge" (rataliating in order to "get even"). One wonders who would have the standing to demand that retribution be returned upon a sinner whose wrongdoing was wholly self-regarding? If *no one* has a grievance in consequence of another's evil thoughts or private vices, who then can demand his own "satisfaction" through the other's suffering? How could punishment be a "return in kind"? How much suffering would constitute "payment" for one's sins? Who could "get even" with the self-regarding sinner, even symbolically or vicariously? In those early senses of "retribution" that employ the commercial repayment metaphor, retribution for wrongs without victims does not seem to make sense. Retribution in its original senses is a logically suitable response only to "grievance evils." The person who has the grievance "gets even" (by subtraction from the wrongdoer, usually, rather than by addition to the victim).

The philosophical theory of punishment called "retributivism," however, has given a variety of new and technical senses to the term "retribution," all of which bear some semblance to the original, but which depart from it in significant respects. To the ordinary nonphilosopher, perhaps, "retribution" suggests "revenge." In legal punishment, it is often thought, the state exacts vengeance vicariously on behalf of the wronged victim of the crime, thereby obviating the need for private vengeance and the danger of perpetual feuds. Revenge in turn is often thought of primarily in psychological terms and identified with "satisfaction" or vindictive pleasure in the mind of the wronged party when he contemplates the suffering that has been inflicted on the responsible criminal. This sort of gloating *schadenfreude* is offensive to those moralists who are disposed by their principles to deny that it can ever be right to take pleasure in the sufferings of another, and many who have been called "retributivists" (e.g. Kant and Hegel) have been careful to dissociate their own views from it. These nonvindictive retributivists justify punishment as retribution (in some sense) but insist that it must be inflicted calmly and rationally (not in anger) as the expression of a moral judgment, and that its primary justification "be found in the fact that an offense has been committed which deserves the punishment, not in any future advantage to be gained by its infliction."[55] The moral concept of *desert* (or "fittingness") then replaces the disreputable idea of vengeful retaliation. Retribution as "deserved suffering" in turn has been given various interpretations by philosophical retributivists, and some of these interpretations, when applied to ordinary crimes (with victims) have at first sight an intuitive plausibility. But most of these are no more plausible than revenge is when applied to "harmless sins" and other free-floating evils.

Perhaps that form of nonvindictive retributivism (if I may use that phrase) that has the greatest initial plausibility is that which purports to apply principles of distributive justice to crime and punishment.[56] It is intolerable to a victim of a crime, or the next of kin of a victim, or to any disinterested observer to see the perpetrator enjoying the fruits of his ill-gotten gains, or even just continuing to live freely in pursuit of his own happiness, while the victim from whom the gains were wrongly extracted is dead, disabled, or impoverished. That state of affairs will be intolerable even to the enlightened person who has forsworn the more primitive sorts of vengeance, and it will be intolerable because it is *unfair* that a "wrongdoer prosper . . . when his victims suffer, or have perished."[57]

It is offensive enough to distributive justice that good persons, for whatever reasons, should have fewer of the means to happiness than bad persons, but the outrage is multiplied many times when the disparity is explained as a consequence of the bad person's mistreatment of the good. Punishment of the wrongdoer then helps to rectify the disparity. It cannot in the worst cases restore the moral equilibrium entirely. The victim, if he is dead, cannot be brought back to life, and if he has suffered keenly during his mistreatment, that suffering cannot be nullified or cancelled out as if it had never occurred. Very often the wound produced in the wronged one cannot be repaired or even compensated for, either because the means of compensation are not available or because the harm in its very nature is not morally compensable. Nevertheless, from the standpoint of distributive justice, the repellent dispro-portion between the circumstances of the wrongdoer and those of his victim can at least be reduced to some degree by the punishment (and official moral condemnation) of the wrongdoer. But again, as Hart has pointed out,[58] where the wrongdoer had no victim, the concept of distributive justice in terms of which the present notion of retribution is understood has no intelligible application.

A more plausible way of applying the retributive theory to harmless wrong-doing is to punish the latter for its *disobedient* character. The person who disobeys even wholly self-regarding moral rules thereby flouts the authority of the rule-maker or commander, and for *that* characteristic of his act he must "pay." Someone must exact retribution. Since by hypothesis no one else is harmed, perhaps it is the rule-maker who can demand punishment as *his* due. But is the authority who lays down the rule necessarily "wronged" or "harmed" by acts of disobedience? The answer seems to be no when we think of political and legal authorities. Criminals usually cause harm to aggrieved victims, but the legislators whose laws they break do not thereby acquire personal grievances at the wrongdoers. *Their* rights have not been directly infringed. Sentencing judges may be righteously indignant at the convicted criminal standing before them, but they do not put *themselves* among the wronged parties on whose behalf the indignation is expressed. Why then would they claim personal grievances when the crime is victimless? If legisla-tors and judges could plausibly hold themselves to be personally wronged by disobedience as such, then merely private or victimless wrongdoing would not be free-floating after all, since wronged parties who were genuinely aggrieved by it would exist. Indeed, there could be no such thing in principle as a "victimless crime."

Let us remind ourselves what sorts of examples we are talking about when we speak of victimless immoralities—private vices, secret thoughts, moral corruption of another without danger to his other interests, defamation of the long dead, secret mistreatment of a corpse or descecration of a sacred symbol, incest between adults, capricious squashing of a single beetle in the wild, voluntary participation in degrading sexual exhibitions or gladiatorial con-tests, etc. Before these acts are criminalized, what are the commands or rules they "disobey"? If the acts are true evils, then, presumably, it is *moral* rules that they break, that is, the rules of true morality. Not all moral philosophers would take the next step and argue that all valid rules must stem from an authoritative personal rule-maker. Moral rules may carry their own authority, as rules of logic and mathematics do, quite apart from what anyone has said about them. Those who deny the autonomy (in this sense) of morals are nearly unanimous in identifying the authoritative moral rule-maker with God. Moral rules are valid, on this view, because they have been decreed by God, not the other way round. Do "victimless immoralities" of the sort we have been considering then make a "victim" in the appropriate sense out of God? If they do, then perhaps some sense can be made of legal punishment construed as retribution—a restoration of the moral equilibrium between the wrongdoer and his commander or rule-maker.

There are at least two reasons, even given the usual theological assumptions, for doubting this account. Why, we might ask, does disobedience to rightful authority, as such, harm or wrong the person in authority? We saw above that human judges and legislators claim no personal grievances when their authoritative orders are disobeyed. Why should it be any different with the supreme moral commander? One good answer to this question is that the relation between God and those He commands is a much more intimate one than the distant and impersonal relation between political authorities and citizens, more like that between parental authorities, perhaps, and their children. Still, when Johnny disobeys his parents' rule and steals candy from his playmate Billy, only Billy is directly wronged. Johnny's parents will be angry and disappointed, but can they claim that a wrong comparable to the wrong done to Billy was done to themselves? The answer, though not perfectly clear, probably depends on whether they think of Johnny's act as deliberate wrongdoing, motivated by envy, greed, or malice towards Billy, and only incidentally an infraction of their rules, or whether they think of it as a deliberate *rejection* of their authority, a defiant rebellion, and therefore a conscious personal estrangement. Not every episode of moral wrongdoing, either with or without victims, can be thought of as a rejection of divine authority in a parallel way, though at least one paradigmatic bout of disobedience has been so interpreted, namely the fall of Lucifer.[59] Any punishment of Lucifer by God could be thought of, I suppose, as a retributive "paying-back" for a wrong done to God even if the interests of others were not involved. Yet it is not because Lucifer's behavior was disobedient *merely*, but rather that it utterly flouted God's authority as an end in itself and even challenged and usurped it.[60]

Even if it is conceptually coherent to think of each and every private episode of (otherwise) victimless immorality as a direct wrong to God, and hence of punishment as "retribution" on God's behalf, there still seems little point, and no justification, for using the resources of the all-too-human political state for such purposes. Just as God's authority over human beings must be thought of in highly personal terms, so must His "retribution." No merely political leader has ever made a persuasive claim to speak, *qua* political leader, for God, and the claim to be the instrument of God's highly personal purposes is a piece of swaggering presumption, not to say insolent usurpation. If God decrees "retribution" for all private acts that are incidentally noncompliant with His own Will, He has his own resources. The human criminal law is hardly necessary.

Leaving the theological theory aside, there are still other conceptions of retribution whose application to purely victimless wrongdoing is not conceptually distorted, but the lack of incoherence is virtually all that can be said for them when so applied. I have in mind various subtle theories of how punishment can restore a moral equilibrium—theories that do not essentially require that a moral relation between persons has been disrupted by the crime, and do not rely on the commercial "repayment" model: Hegel's theory of punishment as the "annulment" of the wrongdoing, or erasing or blotting out of the moral record-sheet;[61] G.E. Moore's theory of "organic unities," according to which the intrinsic value of a whole sequence of events (including a wrong act and a later punishment) may be different from the sum of the values of its parts;[62] and theories, based often on aesthetic analogies, of an intrinsic "fittingness" between doing moral evil and undergoing suffering for it.

Defenders of these varieties of retributivism are likely to concede that inflicting suffering on an offender is not "good in itself," but they will also point out that single acts cannot be judged simply "in themselves" with no concern for the context in which they fit and the events preceding them which are their occasion. Personal sadness is not a "good in itself" either, and yet when it is a response to the perceived sufferings of another it has a unique appropriateness. Glee, considered "in itself," looks much more like an intrinsically good mental state, but glee does not morally fit the perception of another's pain any more than an orange shirt aesthetically fits "shocking pink" trousers. Similarly, it may be true (the analogy is admittedly imperfect) that "while the moral evil in the offender and the pain of the punishment are each considered separately evils, it is intrinsically good that a certain relation exist or be established between them."[63] In this way, the nonvindictive, noncommerically modeled retributivist can deny that deliberately inflicting suffering on a human being is either good in itself or good as a means and yet find it justified nonetheless as an essential component of an intrinsically good complex. Perhaps that is to put the point too strongly. All the retributivist needs to establish is that the complex situation preceding the infliction of punishment can be made better than it otherwise would be by adding the offender's suffering to it.[64]

These theories of retribution rely heavily on analogies to moral and aesthetic intuitions—orange and shocking pink do not go together, the last note of Beethoven's Fifth is absolutely required (a strong sense of "fits") by the notes that immediately precede it, glee does not morally match pain, compassion is morally called for by the awareness of another's suffering, etc. If we are asked how we know these things, we can only reply that anybody can, and everybody does, just *see* that they are so. Some of us, but by no means all of us, will express skepticism about the similar claim that one can "just see" that inflicting suffering on the sadistic murderer is uniquely called for by the wickedness of his crime. Despite its moral trappings, the judgment may seem to have a suspicious connection to the primitive lust for vengeance. Others might locate its element of plausibility in its implicit appeal to the notion of retribution as the rectification of distributive unfairness, which we discussed earlier. But when we come to apply this aesthetic-modeled retributivism to the harmless wrongdoers we have been considering in this section, it loses whatever trace of self-evidence it had in its other applications. Hardly anyone will claim that he can "just see" that the harmless wrongdoer's suffering added to his sin will make a complex moral whole whose value is greater than that of either component considered separately. It is bad enough, many will say, that the voluntary spectator at the pornographic show should wallow in erotic delight at the degrading performances of voluntary participants, but to add pain and suffering to his subsequent experience, or to theirs, though it will have no beneficial effects, is only to make matters *worse*. Without an aggrieved victim, I have argued, it is doubtful that the moral evil of a "harmless" action can ever be serious enough to counterbalance the loss of freedom to do it. Whatever the reader may think of the intuitive case for that comparative judgment, he will probably agree that the intuitive case for the intrinsic fittingness of *punishment* for such acts is a good deal weaker still.

In the end, I suspect, it is best to interpret Stephen as no kind of retributivist at all, despite his injudicious use of words like "vengeance." Stephen does not think of punishment as paying the harmless wrongdoer back, getting even with him, or in any of the more traditional senses, restoring the moral equilibrium. Such retributive conceptions seem to require that the wrongdoer had a victim. Stephen thinks of sodomists' behavior as hateful and advocates punishment as an expression of the hostility they deserve. That hatred need not be a retributive emotion. It is not hate together with a sense of grievance, not hate on behalf of a victim, self or other. Rather it is hate as the automatic response of right-thinking people to *inherently* odious conduct, harmful or not. It is a familiar fact that the thought of what a person takes to be "unnatural sex" may fill him with disgust or repugnance, as the thought of eating "evil-tasting" food does. But *hatred* is another thing. Stephen teaches the liberal to identify one of the moral presuppositions of his own political position, that *it is not appropriate to hate people except (at most) for their disposition to harm and wrong others.* But then that is a lesson, I think, that most "right-thinking people," liberal or not, do not have to learn.

I conclude that the liberal restriction of criminal law to the prevention of harmful wrongs and the enforcement of "grievance morality" can survive the argument from the moral gradation of punishments as formulated by Stephen and Devlin, and that Stephen's case for the legitimacy of victimless crimes, insofar as it rests on the notion of "retribution" for free-floating evils, will not survive scrutiny.

8. Consent as a defense in criminal law

As was mentioned above (§5, p. 45), Devlin has another argument directed at what he claims is liberal inconsistency. The liberal should permit the genuine consent of the party who would otherwise be a "victim" to count as an exculpatory defense to any charge of criminal wrongdoing based on harming others. That, of course, is because liberalism employs the *Volenti* maxim in mediation of its application of the harm principle. Our present criminal law does allow consent to be a complete defense to the charge of rape, false imprisonment, and the various forms of theft (burglary, robbery, larceny, embezzlement, etc.), but no other crime that consists of one person imposing harm on another is similarly excused. Thus assault,[65] battery, mayhem, and all forms of homicide remain unexcused and unjustified even when there was a perfectly willing "victim." That shows at most, of course, only that our present law is not based on exclusively liberal principles, not that it *ought not* to be based solely on such principles. The liberal can with consistency maintain that fully valid consent ought to be a defense to all the crimes that are defined in terms of individuals acting on other individuals, including battery, mayhem, and murder, just as he maintains (usually with more confidence) that collaborative behavior ought never to be criminal when the collaboration is fully voluntary on both sides and no interests other than those of the collaborative parties are directly or substantially affected. (The latter position excludes as proper crimes sodomy, bigamy, adult incest, prostitution, and mutual fighting, among other things.) Devlin shrewdly aims his argument, however, at the liberal who wishes to maintain his liberalism and the current law's restriction of the consent defense *both*. Against such persons his attack has the form, *prima facie*, of a cogent practical argument.

Hart replied to this argument, as we have seen (Chap. 28, §5), by arguing that the traditional exclusion of consent as a defense to battery, mayhem, and homicide expresses a commitment not to legal moralism but to "physical paternalism." That contention is at least a relevant rejoinder to Devlin's argument construed as an argument for legal moralism, but it will not do, of course, as a rejoinder to the argument construed as an attack against liberalism, for liberalism, at least as I have defined it, rejects both moralism and paternalism. Hart's reply to Devlin is ineffective in any event, since it is by no means clear whether the law excludes consent as a defense to battery, mayhem, and homicide because (a) the harms associated with these crimes are always and necessarily bad for a person whatever he may think about the matter (paternalism), or (b) killing, beating, and maiming a person are inherently immoral things to do whether or not they seem beneficial on balance for the person in the present case (moralism). Contrary to Hart, I think that the moralistic reconstruction (b) is probably the more accurate account of legislative motives, though no doubt it can be reenforced in large measure by paternalistic considerations. The moralistic account, at least, seems more applicable to those frequent cases of requested euthanasia where what is requested quite clearly *is* in the interest of "the victim," and his consent clearly is voluntary. Those who concede the beneficial and voluntary character of the killing, yet rest their case against permitting it rigidly on the moral commandment "Thou shalt not kill," are committed to the moralistic, not the paternalistic, rationale. Moreover, in cases of consensual collaboration, the moralistic argument seems the more likely reconstruction. Adult brother-sister incest, for example, need not be harmful to either collaborator; given contraceptive protection it need threaten no third parties; and given privacy, it need cause no offense. The argument for making it a crime must rest simply on the claim that it is "just wrong *per se.*"

The liberal must reply to Devlin that *in principle* he is solidly in favor of the universal use of the consent exculpation in crimes involving relations between individuals, but that in some cases, for reasons entirely consistent with liberalism, he is reluctantly opposed to a judicial policy that would make the defense freely available. Thus we have already argued that bigamy and usury (Vol. 3, Chap. 24, §7) when freely consensual ought not to be crimes, but that dueling (Vol. 1, Chap. 6, §1) and slavery (Vol. 3, Chap 19, §§5 and 6) should be forbidden categorically because of insolvable problems of verifying voluntariness, and that other *prima facie* consensual crimes be kept on the books to protect third parties from harm or offense. Consistency requires the liberal in each category of crime either to uphold the consent defense or to reject it for acceptable liberal reasons (protection of third parties or skepticism about voluntariness).

The Devlin argument from the exclusion of the consent defense cannot then be replied to in a wholesale way but requires a systematic survey of all two-party interactive crimes and a piecemeal effort to apply liberal principles to each. That large task cannot be undertaken in this place (though it has been done in large degree in scattered sections of this book wherever specific traditional crimes are discussed in detail). A cursory survey of the role of consent in some representative crimes might be in order here, however, just to show that the liberal program sketched above is by no means hopeless. First, the crimes for which consent *is* a defense.

Rape. (See Vol. 3, Chap. 25, §7.) The harm in rape consists in undergoing a sexual act under compulsion or coercion quite against one's will. Take away the compulsion and coercion and add willing collaboration, and you have eliminated the harm altogether. Genuinely voluntary consent does just that, and for that reason, it always does (and should) exculpate.

Theft. (See Vol. 3, Chap. 25, §6.) The source of harm in all crimes involving theft is a transfer of property against the will of the original owner. If the transfer is done with the consent of the owner then it is either part of a legitimate business transaction or else a gratuitous gift. Since free exchange and gift-receiving are not in the appropriate way harmful, they are not (and should not be) crimes. Hence, voluntary consent entirely exculpates.

False imprisonment. (For complications, see Vol. 3, Chap. 19, §7.) Confinement is not unlawful, for the most part, if it was done with the voluntary consent of the person confined and if the consent is treated as reasonably revocable. "Thus, a farmer who chained his wife to a bed while he went to town was held not guilt of false imprisonment where there was unmistakable evidence that she had requested him to do so, whatever the reason for this request may have been."[66] (Very likely, however, the agreement to treat the basic request as absolutely irrevocable, or as irrevocable within an extended period of time, would not be a defense for the farmer if he kept his wife chained for a month or a year.)

In the common law, kidnapping was a crime even without ransom demands. Simple (nonextortionate) kidnapping was defined as "The forcible abduction of a man, woman, or child from his own country, and sending him into another."[67] (In some early American statutes transportation out of the state was sufficient.) The most common form of simple kidnapping at one time was the "shanghaiing" of sailors to serve against their will on the crews of sailing ships. If a sea-captain were later charged and tried for kidnapping, he would surely have had the consent defense available, for the harm of simple kidnapping consists entirely in being made to live and work against one's will in a different job in a different locale. If the sailor freely consented to the terms of his new employment (which include irrevocable confinement for long periods on a seagoing ship), then there is no harm for which to punish his employer.

So much is straightfoward. But now we come to some more controversial crimes.

Murder. The harm in homicide is the complete destruction of the person. There are some circumstances, however, in which death is more of a deliverance than a harm. While it is always possible, even likely, that a person who believes he is in such circumstances is mistaken, nevertheless the circumstances are common enough, so that we can assume that death requests *can* be entirely voluntary and rational, and that the killer in these instances does not "wrong" a "victim." We can treat these cases as parallel to rape, theft, and false imprisonment. The harm consists in being wrongfully deprived *against one's will*, of one's life. If there was genuine (uncoerced, fully informed, competent) consent, then *that* harm did not exist. So, in principle, the liberal is in favor of permitting the consent defense even to homicide. The defender of the traditional limits on the consent defense would argue that the dissimilarity between the ways it applies to rape (say) and to murder reflects a basic disanalogy between the harms in those crimes. Take away the victim's unwillingness in rape, and you have no victim and no harm, but only a sexual act which cannot be thought of as an evil or a harm in itself. But take away the willingness (indeed, eagerness) to die from a case of murder and what is left is something quite different, namely death, which is an evil in itself. The liberal's reply to this is that death is not to be judged "in itself" but rather in relation to the living person's circumstances that precede it, and in some of these circumstances death is plausibly judged to be a blessed sole alternative to intolerable suffering and despair.

Suppose, however, that we do reintroduce the consent defense to homicide charges (as James Rachels, in effect, has urged—see Vol. 3, Chap. 27, §2). Suppose further that it becomes apparent in time that murderers of all varieties have been encouraged to use a new defense when other defenses don't apply (as they have been encouraged to try the insanity plea when nothing else can work). Perhaps, in time, enough murderers will get away with this abuse of the new defense so that their numbers, combined with the number of proper acquittals, encourage ill-motivated murderers to pose as mercy killers, and manipulate or counterfeit the consent of their victims in advance. This in turn significantly weakens the deterrent effect of the homicide law, thus harming (destroying) indeterminate third parties who might otherwise not have been killed. On some such grounds as these (and there are numerous other "practical difficulties" with the scheme to recognize consent as a defense to homicide),[68] the liberal could with consistency uphold the *status quo*. The argument, it is important to note, is a harm principle rationale, not a moralistic or paternalistic one, since its bottom-line appeal is to the interests of third parties.

To be sure, one could argue on the other side that eliminating the consent defense to rape would increase the number of convictions in rape prosecutions, discourage men from having sexual relations, even consensual ones, outside of marriage, and thus greatly increase the deterrent effect of rape laws. By such means, the total number of rapes would be reduced, and thousands of third parties who would otherwise be victims of rapes could be saved from that fate. This would be a definite gain in terms of the harm prevention but at substantial costs to individual freedom of choice, the trustful spontaneity of affectionate relationships, and other values. Similar costs are being paid now, the liberal might point out, and usually much more severely suffered, because consent is excluded as a defense to homicide. The point is that *wherever* there is a defense allowed to a crime, criminal defendants will be tempted to fake its conditions in their own cases, thus weakening deterrence somewhat, but that this is one cost to be reckoned among others, as we balance and reconcile conflicting human interests. Our legislative deliberations at this level need not implicate any liberty-limiting principles beyond the harm principle.

The liberal could also raise practical objections of the sort we have discussed in connection with Rachels' "modest proposal" (Vol. 3, Chap. 27, §2). It might be unfair to the conscientious and humane mercy-killer himself to make him assume the risks of proving the "victim's" consent if he is to escape conviction. A better scheme might be to provide licensing procedures whereby the authenticity of consent is determined in advance so that the mercy-killer would kill (or petition specialists to kill for him) only with prior state permission, thus minimizing his personal risks, and removing the problem almost entirely from the province of criminal law. (In an analogous way, marriage, in the past, has been thought of as official license to have sexual intercourse regularly with a given partner, so that sexual acts are legitimized in advance by official permission, and the issues of "consent" and "rape" need never arise.) The only point that need be emphasized here is that the liberal with consistency can advocate similar schemes in respect to euthanasia to take the strain off criminal proceedings and prevent the weakening of the deterrence to morally unjustified killings. Mafia assassins, muggers, barroom brawlers, angry vengeance seekers, and other "ordinary murderers" would not be likely to apply in advance, with their prospective victims, for state permission to kill!

Mayhem. Most American states have statutes against "mayhem," now construed as the deliberate and malicious maiming or disfiguring of another. To
maim is to inflict permanent damage on the victim by amputating in whole or
in part a limb or organ (e.g. removing an arm, leg, eye, or testicle) or by
injuring (e.g. blinding) him. When political enemies set upon Sir John Coventry in 1670 and slit his nose in retaliation for obnoxious remarks he had
uttered in Parliamentary debate, their offense could not be labeled "mayhem"
since they did not permanently disable him. The so-called "Coventry Act"
was quickly passed by Parliament extending the offense to disfigurement,
such as the removal of ears or noses.

One would think that the ground for excluding consent as a defense to
mayhem would be at least in part paternalistic, since maliciously disabling
and disfiguring could hardly be good for a person whatever his wishes might
be, or so it would seem. The English common law conception of mayhem,
however, built its motivating rationale into its very definition, and made it
plain that the rationale had no element of benevolence in it, paternalistic or
other: mayhem, according to the English common law, is "maliciously depriving another of the use of such of his members as may render him less able, in
fighting, either to defend himself or to annoy his adversary."[69] Mayhem, in
truth, was a crime against the state consisting in rendering "the person less
efficient as a fighting man (for "the King's army").[70] The prohibition of
mayhem was intended to protect citizens from a public harm which was
simply the setting back of the public interest in national defense by weakening the king's forces.

It is an odd person indeed who would request his own maiming, but
persons have had various motives for doing so, and some persons have been
odd enough to act, apparently voluntarily, on such motives. Perhaps in the
earlier days of the common law, a frequent motive would have been to escape
conscription—a not altogether irrational trade-off when one considers the
carnage of war. If *A* pays *B*, a surgeon, to remove his arm so that he might
escape conscription, then *B* becomes a party to a fraud perpetrated against the
state, and it is no wonder that *A*'s consent is no defense for him. Fraud was
also involved in the famous *Wright's Case*[71] of 1604 in which "a lusty rogue"
had his left hand amputated by a companion "in order to get out of work and
be more effective as a beggar," and consent naturally failed to exculpate the
maimer. No different in principle are those modern cases in which the motive
for requesting the maiming is to defraud an insurance company. The private
harm principle is quite sufficient to cover all of these cases where the consent
to mayhem is both intelligible and thoroughly dishonorable.

In a smaller number of cases, the harm principle rationale is not clearly
applicable, yet the exclusion of the consent defense continues, probably for

paternalistic reasons. It will be very difficult to comprehend the motive for consent in these cases, and the suspicion of nonvoluntariness will be strong. Nevertheless, the liberal would permit the consent defense out of respect for personal autonomy, subject to appropriately stringent standards of voluntariness.

Recent examples involving comprehensible motives, apart from the insurance fraud examples are usually cases concerning the transfer of bodily organs. Jesse Dukeminier gives some examples:

> In some foreign countries live persons are not permitted either to give or to sell their spare organs when delivery is to take place during life. In Italy, such a statutory provision exists as a result of an incident which occurred in the 1930's when a rich man bought a testis from a young Neopolitan and had it transplanted by a surgeon. The public outrage resulted in the passage of a law prohibiting the sale or gift by a live person of an organ if removal of the organ could produce a permanent deficiency. The Italian law was modified in 1967 to permit the removal of kidneys from live persons for transplantation . . . [In America] criminal law sets limits on the ability of a patient to give his informed consent to a surgical operation that is not for his [medical] benefit . . . Under some circumstances . . . the removal of an organ, even with the donor's consent, may constitute the crime of assault and battery or the crime of mayhem.[72]

Devlin might seize on some of these examples as embarrassing to the liberal, because the prohibitions seem plausible (to him), and yet third party interests are not involved. But I, for one, find no discomfort in the position defended at length in Volumes 3 and 4 that in the absence of third party interests, an autonomous person should be free to choose the uses of his own body, subject to the usual strictures about voluntariness. Where the motive for self-mutilation or consent to mayhem seems mysterious and incomprehensible, the presumption of nonvoluntariness because of psychological impairment is very strong. Where the motive is intelligible, however, it is usually benevolent (the willingness to sacrifice oneself or to take great risks to save another) or else mercenary. To make it a crime to assist a person in his self-sacrificial service to another seems utter folly. As for the mercenary cases, even the Neopolitan youth who sold his testicle for cash had a moral right to do so (and his surgical friend a right to help him implement his will), provided that the agreement with the millionaire was not coercive or "unconscionable" in part because of the disparity in bargaining positions. (See Vol. 3, Chap. 24, §5.)

Battery. When one professional boxer lands a punch on another's face during an officially sanctioned match, he has not committed battery since the other boxer voluntarily consented to the risk of such blows in advance. There is, therefore, at least this one kind of example of consent exculpating a party charged with battery. (Consented-to surgical operation is another.) Blows landed in an entirely informal scuffle are also privileged when the exchange is part of a friendly contest of strength or skill, and there is no intent to hurt or injure the other party. In the unlikely event of criminal prosecution for assault and battery, one of the contestants could successfully cite, in his own defense, both the voluntary and the harmless character of the contest. The law is less lenient, however, when blows are struck in anger with intention to hurt or injure, or in conscious indifference to the risk of injuring the other person. If the angry brawl occurs in a public place, then both combatants have committed the common law offense, of *affray*, the essence of which is disturbing or frightening the public ("a mutual fight in a public place to the terror or alarm of the people").[73] The consent of the other party is clearly no defense to *affray*, but equally clearly, its exclusion is explainable on liberal principles, since, in effect, the crime consists in one's collaboration with another party to cause either genuine public harm (putting third parties in real jeopardy) or at least the alarming or disturbing apprehension of such harm. The harm principle (in the former case) and the offense principle (in the latter) are quite sufficient to explain the crime.

Where both parties agreed to fight (perhaps one as the challenger and the other the accepter), the exclusion of the consent defense is sometimes explained by the maxim, "It takes two to fight." That is, each party's consent was necessary to produce the social harm that resulted, and neither party, therefore, can exculpate himself by citing the other's equally voluntary participation. In other cases the initiative is entirely on one side, and the other party participates only for his own protection. He can therefore plead self-defense (a quite different defense from consent), provided he did not provoke the other party's attack by abusive or insulting action. If the one party merely defends himself, then the combat is not truly mutual and there is no affray, but the attacking party, who cannot plausibly claim his target's "consent," will be liable for assault and battery.

So far, the traditional crimes of battery are explainable on entirely liberal grounds. A more difficult case is that in which the combat is genuinely mutual, both parties assume risks of harming and being harmed, both parties angrily land blows, and the whole episode occurs in a private place unknown to the wider public. The traditional law finds both combatants guilty of assault and battery and disallows the consent defense for each. The rationale for the law *could* be paternalistic or moralistic, or both. But there are also considerations available to the liberal that tend to support—given certain factual assumptions—the exclusion of the consent defense (see the fuller discussion in Vol. 1, Chap. 6, §§1 and 2). They parallel the reasons for outlawing traditional dueling, which is the same sort of combat, though more formal, deliberate, and lethal. In the first place, in subcommunities where the cult of machismo (the working-class counterpart of the Code of Honor) is strong, the loss of face from refusing to fight makes the voluntariness of all acceptances of challenges suspect. More important perhaps, there is a social interest in preserving civility and restraint in interpersonal relations, in maintaining personal security and freedom from anxiety generally, and in keeping physical injuries to a minimum. If the law offered no strong discouragement to violence—even mutually voluntary violence—these social interests would be set back and socially harmful consequences would result. The liberal cannot be charged with inconsistency if he supports rules that keep these public harms in check.

9. Summary

Strict legal moralism, or legal moralism in a strict and narrow sense, is the view that the criminal law may legitimately prohibit certain actions on the sole ground that they are immoral. Not just any kind of free-floating evil is sufficient; it must be a specifically *moral* evil, an infraction of the rules or principles of morality. When we speak of "morality," however, we may be referring to "true morality"—a system of rational norms that apply equally to all nations and communities, including standards for criticizing the conventional norms that may be established at a given time and place—or we may be referring to the conventional norms of our own community in our own time. If it is conventional morality to which the strict moralist refers, his argument may be dismissed quickly, for there is nothing in the idea of conventional morality as such that commands the respect he wishes. Established rules can be, and often have been, absurd, cruel, or unjust. We have therefore stipulated that the morality the strict moralist wishes to have enforced is true morality. Since some liberals might agree with strict moralism if that is all it advocates (since some liberals think of harm prevention as the generating principle of all true morality) we have in the interest of taxonomic clarity attributed to strict moralism the additional tenet that some truly moral evils are not grievance evils at all, but evils through and through, whether or not they are harmful or offensive to anyone. And finally, the strict moralist typically holds that some harmless infractions of true morality are so heinous as to justify the punishment of the offender as an end in itself.

The advocate of a purely moralistic theory in the strict sense does not argue for these propositions by deriving other bad consequences from the moral evils he condemns, but instead rests his case entirely on the intuitive plausibility of the direct inference from "X is a moral non-grievance evil" to "X may legitimately be prohibited by the criminal law." These "pure" (one-step) arguments, when supported by vivid hypothetical examples like the gladiatorial contest in Yankee Stadium, are the most difficult ones for the liberal to cope with, since he must admit that the evils are both genuine, odious, and of the non-grievance kind. The liberal then should be willing to concede that the desirability of preventing such evils is a consideration of some weight on the scales, while insisting nevertheless that its weight is insufficient to counterbalance the case for liberty, since it is impossible to name anyone who can demand "protection" from the evils in question.

Impure forms of strict moralism produce additional reasons for prohibiting even free-floating immoralities, including the alleged social harm of not prohibiting them (e.g. the weakening of communal ties). When *only* these supplementary arguments are produced, it is sometimes not clear whether the view defended is strict moralism at all (as in the work of Lord Devlin). Despite his repeated use of such terms as "sin" and "the moral law," it often appears that the morality Devlin finds it legitimate to enforce is that which happens to be established in the community, and the basic principles which serve him as premises are the public harm principle and the principle of moral conservatism.

Devlin is at his most impressive when he abandons the defense of his own position and attacks what he claims to be inconsistency in his liberal critics. The argument from the moral gradation of legal punishment is his most formidable one, but it fails because it does not acknowledge (a) that an institutional practice may have a nonmoral justifying aim and yet be bound to rules of fair procedure in its operations; (b) that the criminal law may employ an inherently moral "mechanism" in the sense that its essential mode of operation is to issue symbolic judgments of (moral) condemnation and to "rub them in" with punishment, and yet not be justified in doing its work on every kind of conduct a legislature may deplore; and (c) that the justifying aims of a system of criminal law may include the moral one of protecting citizens' rights from harmful invasions and yet with consistency exclude the enforcement of the non-grievance sector of morality. James Fitzjames Stephen's original version of the argument runs into still another difficulty. He explicitly adopts a rather primitive form of the retributive theory of punishment but cannot explain how retribution, in *any* sense, can apply to crimes without victims. Since the retributive theory of punishment is the third tenet of our stipulated definition of "strict legal moralism" it would seem that the full doctrine of strict moralism is internally inconsistent. If the retributivist tenet is detached from the other two, then it becomes impossible to adopt both moralism *and* retributivism, as Stephen and others have attempted to do. Finally, Devlin's claim that *liberals* are inconsistent, based on the law's exclusion of the consent defense from some crimes, is an effective argument against some liberals, but not against those who would permit the defense for all crimes except where doing so would be harmful to third parties, or where because of difficulties in confirming voluntariness, it would not be workable. The latter *is* a consistent liberal position.

We turn next to another class of free-floating evils and a possible liberty-limiting principle of a moralistic kind that would justify prohibiting just these evils even when harmless. Such a liberty-limiting principle has not been defended by any well-known writer, but it seems at least as persuasive (for whatever that is worth) as the other forms of legal moralism we have considered. I refer to the possible position that the free-floating evils that the criminal law may rightly be employed to prevent are those which commonly are called "exploitation" and are thought to be evil not simply because they sometimes cause wrongful harm, but because they produce wrongful gain.

31

Exploitation With
and Without Harm

1. The concept of exploitation

Exploitation is an evil that is not typically free-floating. More often than not, perhaps, it is harmful to the interests of the exploitee. Very commonly it coerces or deceives him, or takes advantage of his personal incompetence, in which cases it is not voluntarily consented to, and therefore, when harmful, is a wrong to the person it exploits. But a little-noticed feature of exploitation is that it *can* occur in morally unsavory forms without harming the exploitee's interests and, in some cases, despite the exploitee's fully voluntary consent to the exploitative behavior. In these cases there is no wrongful loss for the exploitee, who can himself have no grievance. If the exploitation in these cases is, as it seems to be, a moral evil, then it is a free-floating one, and the principle that would legitimize its prohibition is a quite specific form of strict moralism. We can label that liberty-limiting principle (on the model of "the harm principle" and "the offense principle") *the exploitation principle*. It makes stronger claims to our acceptance, in my opinion, than most other forms of legal moralism and must therefore be taken very seriously. We shall consider it carefully in Chapter 32, after a more thorough examination in this chapter of the concept of exploitation itself.

The word "exploitation" when used pejoratively puts a stamp of disapproval on whatever it is applied to; it is in this understood sense of its use that exploitation is not only an evil but a moral evil, a kind of injustice. Pejorative exploitation is always a relation between two or more persons or groups, and in its more complicated forms (to be considered below, §3), it can involve morally altered relationships among three or even four parties. In its non-pejorative sense, on the other hand, the word "exploitation" usually refers to opportunities and resources rather than people, as when one is told to exploit one's own talents or make the most of a situation. To exploit something, in this most general sense, is simply to put it to use, not waste it, take advantage of it. Even in this general nonpejorative sense the exploiter is always a person; diseases, landslides, and tropical storms have never exploited anything. The kind of exploitation with which we shall be concerned here, however, is interpersonal exploitation, in which both exploiter and exploitee are persons. When "exploitation" refers to a relationship, it tends most frequently to be pejorative. Thus, exploitation of a person is normally a way of using someone for one's own ends, which is somehow wrongful or blameworthy, whether it wrongs the other person or not.

Another important distinction is the difference between A exploiting a person, B, on the one hand, and A exploiting F, some characteristic or circumstance of B, on the other.[1] The exploitation of F may be exploitation in the wholly nonpejorative sense of using for a purpose, as when a film director "exploits" the peculiar intensity of an actor to bring out the proper passion of the character he is portraying, without of course exploiting the actor himself. One exploits a person by exploiting his traits or circumstances, but one can "exploit" his traits or circumstances without exploiting *him*. Thus Bruce Landesman contends that so-called exploitation films "exploit the vulgar tastes and prejudices of the audience, but . . . it may sound too strong to say that audience members are exploited."[2] I think Landesman is right about this because the audience's fully voluntary participation is not typically contrary to their interests, their judgments, or their consciences, in the way that pandering to certain moral weaknesses tends to be. Nevertheless, we may be inclined to condemn it as pejoratively exploitative of vulgarity, even though it exploits no persons, since it strikes us as a peculiarly offensive kind of wrongful gain analogous to profiting from the suffering or misfortunes of others. Even the use of mere traits or characteristics, then, can be pejoratively exploitative when it is somehow an unjust use, and morally repugnant exploitation, though typically of persons, may in some cases be exploitation only of their traits or circumstances.

Many of the leading examples of exploitation, of course, are also examples of coercion. The concepts are quite distinct in sense but have a large overlap in application. Some proposals by A are coercive in their effect on B in that they close or narrow B's options, and they are also instances of A exploiting B's vulnerability for A's own advantage. To determine whether A has coerced B we look to the effects of his conduct on B's options. The expected effect on A's own interests (his profit or gain) is only relevant to the further and partially independent question of exploitation. If we define exploitation in terms of A's profit through his relations to B, then not all exploitation involves coercive mechanisms. In fact there are four possibilities:

1. A's act can be exploitative and coercive, as when his proposal effectively forces B to act in a way that benefits A.
2. A's act can be exploitative and noncoercive, as when he takes advantage of B's traits or circumstances to make a profit for himself either with B's consent or without the mediation of B's choice at all.[3]
3. (More dubious) A's act might be nonexploitative but coercive. Perhaps an example would be when A, a policeman, calls out to the murderer in hiding, B, to come out with his hands up or face lethal fire. This is a proper and justified use of coercion, but only minimally exploitative, that is a "taking advantage," in this case, of B's vulnerability. It shares in common with all exploitation a kind of opportunism, but it is not an exploitation of a person or in any way blamable.
4. A's act can be both nonexploitative and noncoercive, as in an ordinary commercial exchange from which both vendor and purchaser expect to gain (but not at one another's expense).

We shall be concerned primarily with noncoercive exploitation in this chapter and will consider the other combinations only where useful for purposes of comparison and contrast.

Put very vaguely, all interpersonal exploitation involves one party (A) profiting from his relation to another party (B), by somehow "taking advantage" of some characteristic of B's, or some feature of B's circumstances. When the exploitation is coercive, the characteristic of B that is taken advantage of is his lack of power relative to A, as when A, for example, is in a superior bargaining position. The word "exploitation" is a technical term in Marxist economic theory,[4] in which it refers to the coercive process by which capitalists hire workers for bare minimal wages because the workers have no alternative except to starve. Then all the wealth created by the workers' labor ("surplus value") goes to the employer. This of course is a case of superior power exerting its force extortionately to produce harsh employment contracts to which the employee's agreement is considerably less than fully voluntary.[5] There are other examples of exploitation, however, which, as John Kleinig has noticed, do not violate the exploited party's autonomy—

> A sponger may exploit another's generosity; children may exploit the love of their parents; a man may exploit the insecurity of a woman; advertising firms may exploit the gullibility of the public; politicians may exploit the fears of the citizenry. It would be difficult to argue that these cases of exploitation involve coercion. Rather they involve one party's playing on some character trait of the other for the purpose of securing some advantage.[6]

The key phrase "play on" is very apt. The skilled exploiter plays on the other's character in the way a pianist "plays on" a piano. *A* may say afterwards to *B:* "You are what you are [generous, loving, insecure, gullible, or fearful, as the case may be]. I don't change that, or infringe on it, or exert pressure on it. Rather, I *use* it to my profit. *You* have no complaint. At most you might be envious of my gain. But I didn't force anything on you; I simply used you as you are."

Common to all exploitation of one person (*B*) by another (*A*), whether the exploitation be coercive or not, is that *A* makes a profit or gain by turning some characteristic of *B* to his own advantage. That characteristic could be simply a vulnerability to force or deception; it could be some other kind of weakness; or it could be a strength. It could be a trait, or it could be a circumstance. It could be a state or an underlying disposition, a virtue of character or a flaw, a skill or a failing. In any case, what is necessary is that *A* use it for his own gain. Characteristically *B* loses, but not always. The essential point is that because of something about *B*, which *A* uses in a certain way, *A* profits. Thus there are three elements in all incidents of exploitation about which we can raise further questions:

1. How *A* uses *B*,
2. What it is about *B* that *A* uses,
3. How the process redistributes gains and losses.

In addition, exploitation (in the pejorative sense with which we are here concerned) is assumed to be *unfair* ("taking unfair advantage") or otherwise subject to adverse criticism.

2. The elements of exploitation (A): ways of using the other person

The first element, what Kleinig called "playing on" another, is also called "using" the other, or, in some cases, "manipulating" the other. It would hardly mark an advance in our philosophical understanding, however, if we were to define this element of exploitation as "manipulation," since many dictionaries define "manipulation," in turn, in words that could serve as well to define noncoercive exploitation, and thus we would have too small a circle of interdefinable notions. (To manipulate, says Webster's dictionary, is "to control or play upon by artful, unfair, or insidious means, especially to one's own advantage.") Moreover, manipulation may suggest too active a form of intervention for some sorts of noncoercive exploitation. The exploiter (*A*) uses more passive techniques when he simply agrees to do what *B* wants and thereby exploits *B*'s greed, recklessness, or foolishness without any "manipulation" at all. Indeed he may simply respond to what is entirely *B*'s initiative from the outset. Nonmanipulative exploitation can be illustrated by examples from both competitive and noncompetitive contexts. Thus, in response to *B*'s proposal, *A* says: "Do you really want to bet $1,000 that you can beat me at billiards (gin rummy, one-on-one basketball, etc.)? All right, I'll be happy to take your money, that is 'exploit your foolishness'." Imagine that *A*'s remark is more than the usual bravado of conventional badinage. His self-confidence is entirely well founded. We can imagine also that *A* has not tricked or misled *B* into underestimating *A*'s talent, and *B* has no illusions or misconceptions under that heading. *B* has never lost a match of this kind before, though he has never played anyone of *A*'s caliber. He is young, brash, and cocky— precisely the traits that *A* will exploit—but he is free of all coercion, and he knows exactly the risks he is taking.

For an example that is morally parallel from a noncompetitive context, consider the following. *B* is a professional beggar who is led to believe on good evidence that he could improve his business if he had only a stump instead of an arm. So he offers *A* $1,000 to amputate his quite healthy arm. *A* replies: "I think that your values are cockeyed. How could you prefer a higher income to a healthy left arm? Still, it is *your* arm, and if you want me to exploit your foolishness, I will be happy to do so." And he does.[7]

One could argue, of course, that in each example *B* consents out of ignorance, so that his action is not fully voluntary after all. In the first example *B* believes that he can win, a belief that is proved false by the event, showing that he labored under a voluntariness-diminishing misconception after all. And in the second example, one might argue that *B* falsely believed that his increased profits would adequately compensate him for the loss of his arm when in fact, let us suppose, he keenly regrets his action in later years. The reply to this argument from ignorance (or mistake) in the first example is that it gives so strong an interpretation of the ignorance condition for nonvoluntariness that no wagers or contests of skill could ever qualify as fully voluntary on both sides. To be sure, *B*'s prediction or anticipation of the outcome turned out to be false, but his belief that he *could* win (given nearly equal skill, fierce competitiveness, and a little bit of luck)—that is, the belief that he had a *chance* to win—might well have been correct even though he lost. And while his taking the risk of losing might have seemed unreasonable to more cautious friends and observers (it was not a risk any of them would have taken), it was not patently irrational, as would be required to vitiate its voluntariness. Much the same may have been true of the second example. *B*'s belief that he would not come to regret his choice may have been false and even unreasonable in the eyes of others. But again it was a matter of choosing to risk a future development that no one could foresee with certainty; if the risk were not manifestly irrational (as we may suppose) there is no reason to deny that it was fully voluntary.

The fact of B's voluntary consent to the risk in these examples, however, does not automatically relieve A of all responsibility for subsequent harms to B. It is at least a somewhat disingenuous reply for A to say "B brought it all upon himself. I was a mere passive instrument of his will,"—for, as Kleinig points out, A actively chose or agreed to be the instrument of B's purposes and cannot escape responsibility for his own free choice. Kleinig's view, which we shall discuss further in Chapter 32, is that exploitation of another's rashness or foolishness is *wrong*, even when because of prior voluntary consent it does not violate the other's right, it does not wrong him, and it does not treat him unfairly. It is wrong because the actor (A) believes on good evidence that it will probably set back B's interest, and deliberately choosing to be an instrument of another's "harm" (setback to interest) for one's own gain is often something we ought not to do, even though the other can have no grievance against us when we do.

More active forms of noncoercive "using" or "playing upon" another person involve a great miscellany of manipulative techniques that fall short of out-right coercion or misrepresentation. A can offer inducements, employ flattery, beg or beseech; he can try alluring portrayals or seductive suggestions; he can appeal to duty, sympathy, friendship, or greed, probing constantly for the character trait whose cultivation will yield the desired response. If he finds it and thereby persuades the other to consent, the other cannot complain of being forced or tricked into it. After all it was his own true, flawed but autonomous self whose utilization produced the consent, not some overpowering external force, or deceit.

3. The elements of exploitation (B): exploitable traits and circumstances

The next factor to be considered turns our attention away from A to B and the traits and circumstances in virtue of which he is exploited by A. Virtually any traits or circumstances are in principle exploitable provided only that they are causally relevant to the exploiter's purposes. Exploitable traits include virtues (excellences) and flaws, both self-regarding and other-regarding, and also occurrent mental states of relatively brief duration whether or not they instantiate underlying dispositions of character, such as particular states of joy or grief, anger or love. A can exploit such self-regarding character flaws in B as recklessness, cockiness, or intemperance, as well as other-regarding flaws like greed, vindictiveness, or enviousness. A can even exploit B's self-regarding virtues, for example taking advantage of his cautious prudence by a bluff, challenging B to a match A knows he (A) cannot win in order to impress some third party with his own bravery or self-confidence. When B wisely but predictably declines the challenge, A gains his objective. B's other-regarding virtues especially—his unwillingness to cheat, free-load, or break his word, his generosity and tendency to trust others—make him vulnerable. Indeed, any trait or circumstance of B's that A can subsume under a reliable generalization makes B reasonably predictable, and it is precisely in his predictability to one who has studied him closely that he becomes vulnerable. By capitalizing on his knowledge of B's character and his present circumstances, A gets B to respond in the desired manner without using any force or deception whatever. He knows for example that B, a conscientious type, can be trusted to do his share of the work, so that A can get away with doing less than his own, or he predicts that B, a cocky sort, will wager in an unequal contest, so he arranges such a contest and pockets his profit.

Other-regarding moral flaws. Exploitation of another party's defect of character is likely to seem the least blamable form of noncoercive, nonfraudulent exploitation. Even fraudulent exploitation of another's moral defects, while of course blamable on balance, seems to have a mitigating character. Consider, for example, so-called "confidence games." These swindles exploit a weakness in their victims and trick them by deliberate deception and misrepresentation. Sometimes the victim is badly harmed and the fraudulent exploiter is rightly seen as a heartless villain who deserves severe punishment. But often there is a pleasing element even in the fraud when the victim's exploited trait was itself a moral flaw, particularly when it was an other-regarding moral flaw, like cruelty or greed, so that the victim was hoist with his own petard and is seen to have got what he had coming, even though it was wrong for the con-artist to have given it to him. One of the reasons practical jokes at their harmless best are so amusing is that they exploit some flaw in their victims, as in the story of the prissy London office worker who was excessively protective of his precious derby hat. Every day he found that his head had grown as (unknown to him) his waggish colleagues substituted identical hats of gradually diminishing size, each with his name and the correct size on the hat band. Despite the deceptive methods and the victim's involuntary role in the joke, the actual harm done (as opposed to perplexed anxiety induced) was minimal, and the trait exploited was unattractive. Now if we add to these elements some profit to the jokesters and subtract the element of fraud, we have a case of noncoercive exploitation that can also please the observer and lead him, at the very least, to modify his adverse judgment of the exploiter.

A noncoercive, nondeceptive, and nonmanipulative case of a similar sort is suggested by a little noticed newspaper report. The exploiter in that story may seem entirely blameless because the traits of his "victim" that he turned to his own advantage are themselves other-regarding flaws. According to the published report, an Italian engineering company seemed to be "exploiting" the Libyan dictator, Colonel Muammar Qaddafi, by turning to its own advantage a somewhat malevolent Libyan scheme and making its profit at Qaddafi's expense.

> One of . . . Qaddafi's latest plots calls for the building of a wall 187 miles long to seal off his country from Egypt. He plans to hire thousands of Kenyans to build this "El Fateh Line" in North Africa to prevent border attacks by the Egyptians. Engineers say privately that Qaddafi is nuts, that building a wall on shifting sands in territory physically altered by periodic sand storms is silly—"but they're willing to take his money."[8]

If the engineering firm had made its appraisal known to Qaddafi (and not merely "privately") and Qaddafi's acceptance of the unreasonable risks were entirely due to his own headstrongness rather than to any information or expert opinion being withheld from him, then his "consent" to the operation would be largely voluntary, and the Italian firm could not be charged with defrauding him. The firm might yet be morally censured for wrongfully exploiting him but for the fact that his wall scheme was part and parcel of a general foreign policy that was alleged to involve, among other unsavory elements, large-scale assassination plots around the world. The exploitation of another's evil propensities pleases us in much the same way that the morally apt practical joke does, and even more for being profitable.[9]

Moral virtues, conscientiousness, and trust. It is very much otherwise when the exploited trait is a virtue, when for example, a freeloader takes advantage of the dutiful laborer or the law-abiding fare-payer and profits, not necessarily at their expense, but *only* because they were honorable enough to forgo themselves the easy gains of the cheater. When A cheats on his phone bill, he may not cause much harm to anyone, since the phone company will pass on its losses in dilute form to all its customers. Evading payment exploits the company's trust and also the cooperative forbearance of the other customers who do pay their bills. As we shall see in §5, this kind of cheating is generally thought to be the clearest example of *unfair* advantage-taking.

When A and B are close friends, A may sometimes be tempted to exploit B's friendship for his own advantage. When he passes off a burdensome chore to B in full confidence that B will do it, if only out of friendship, he may well be subject to the charge of taking unfair advantage of his friend. Perhaps he has asked for a favor that he himself would resent having to grant were their roles reversed. This exploitation of B's virtues—friendly good will, loyalty, and trust among them—for his own convenience strikes us as morally akin to cheating or freeloading. On the other hand, A "exploits B's friendship" in a blameless (and hence a not genuinely "exploitative") way when he simply uses his relationship with B in a way that costs B no unreasonably burdensome inconvenience. B (or his influence) has become a compliant instrument of A's, but B does not feel wrongly used. Loaning his influence costs him little, and he is likely to reassure A that "that's what friends are for."

Misfortunes and unhappy circumstances. When A, a publisher, exploits a widow's grief (through the pitiless glare of publicity), or when A, as a circus owner, exploits a grotesquely deformed person's appearance by exhibiting him, for a salary, in a sideshow, the results are repugnant. In these cases, it is unfortunate circumstances or characteristics rather than character traits that are utilized, and even if there is voluntary consent the result is morally ugly, for one person's profit is made possible only because of another's suffering, without diminishing that suffering. The moral repugnance is likely to be greater still if the exploitation is coercive, when, for example, the circus owner has arranged things so that the grotesque person can find no other work and then offers him a job at low pay as the only alternative to permanent unemployment. Exploiters are typically opportunists; they extract advantage from situations that are not of their own making. Coercers, on the other hand, are typically makers rather than mere discoverers and users of opportunities. (The model coercer is the gunman who *creates* an exploitable situation by using his weapon to back up a threat). One technique for profiting from the misfortunes of others combines the opportunism of the typical exploiter with the manipulative intervention of the typical coercer, by means of the "coercive offer." (See Vol. 3, Chap. 24.) Quite clearly the coercive proposer *exploits* his superior power and his victim's desperate need in order to get what he wants from him, but the transaction in which this happens is not an example of *noncoercive* exploitation, which is our main interest here.

The noncoercive exploitation of another's unhappy circumstances is often called *cashing in* on them. When a crime wave strikes a neighborhood, businessmen will soon appear on the scene to capitalize on property owners' anxiety by selling them various protective devices and services, thereby making a good thing (profit) for themselves out of an objective evil. Cashing in is exploitative in the blameworthy sense only when it is also unproductive. If it indeed provides a useful service at a reasonable price to those in need, then it is not exploitative, even though it makes opportunistic profit; but if it capitalizes on hysteria to sell unneeded, expensive devices, then it takes advantage of that flawed state of mind in an exploitative fashion, though it does so without clearly violating anyone's rights.

Consider the uproar when Hollywood's MGM film studio announced plans to base a movie on "the Yorkshire Ripper," who had slain thirteen women in five years of terror. The film company was denounced by the Labour MP for Leeds for "cashing in on other people's tragedies . . . ," while the *London New Standard* editorialized: "Leeches suck the blood of others and get fat by it. MGM executives are proposing to exploit the vile deed of a man who has brought fear and misery to countless women in the North in order to make a 'contemporary mystery thriller' to titillate audiences inured to horror on the screen and ready for new depravities."[10] Again, if the Hollywood studio cashed in on the tragedies productively, there could be no complaint, despite its opportunism. If the movie was of high dramatic quality, appealed to the higher sensibilities of its audience, and conveyed a morally edifying message, then it would produce valuable and redeeming results. But if it simply pandered, in the easiest and most obviously profitable way, to a widespread taste for cinematic blood and gore, that would not be "productive" in the redeeming manner. The pattern in this example is typical of much objectionable "cashing in." Advantage is extracted by a first party from the personal tragedy of second parties by means of a book or film or other communication that panders ("unproductively") to the bad taste or other flawed responses of third parties.

Pandering is all the more repugnant when it is accompanied (as it often is) by self-serving and cynical posing. One can share Jack Kroll's indignation in his review of the film *Class of 1984:* "One of the nastiest movies of our time, it pretends to be horrified by endemic violence in our schools while actually exploiting violence with a cold-blooded cynicism that's worse than the violence itself."[11] In contrast there was no "pandering" involved in the opportunistic publication throughout the world of a photograph of the assassination attempt on the Pope in Rome in 1980. The quick-witted professional news photographer just happened to be on the scene at the time and captured the event in an accurate and dramatic picture. He quickly "cashed in" on the event by selling the photograph to news services for a high price. If charged with cashing in on a great misfortune, he could reply that he was paid for providing the world with a helpful supplement to the journalistic accounts of an important historical event.

More unfortunate circumstances: credulity born of desperate need. Another example of exploiting a person's unhappy situation in a direct two-party case may be closer to the mark. About 70,000 Americans a year learn that they have cancer, and a sizable proportion of them do not survive the disease. Many are told by their physicians at a certain point that while symptoms can be treated and the progress of the disease slowed down, cure is impossible. It is no wonder then that thousands of terminal cancer patients are willing to take a chance on any advertised cure no matter how low the probability of its success. After all, they have nothing more to lose and everything to gain. And it is no surprise that there are promoters of unproven "wonder drugs" who are willing to exploit their desperation for profit. The most famous of the scientifically disreputable but popular cancer cures is laetrile (also called vitamin B-17), an extract of apricot pits. The Federal Drug Administration and many private laboratories have tested laetrile on animals and found no evidence of its alleged effectiveness. Most cancer specialists have long considered its promotion to be outright quackery. Because its therapeutic value was unproven, the F.D.A. refused to license its use. That decision caused a roar of protest from what had already become a powerful laetrile lobby, and within five years legislatures in twenty-three states had passed legislation legalizing the sale and use of laetrile.

A liberal case for such legislation can be made even on the assumption (now well confirmed) that laetrile is worthless as a cancer cure. In moderate doses laetrile is harmless. If its use legally required a medical prescription, it would not be likely to cause any harm (or indeed to have any significant effect on health one way or the other). Legislatures could require that a warning label (e.g., "The Surgeon-General has determined that there is no evidence that laetrile is an effective medication for cancer") appear on every bottle, to obviate fraudulent misrepresentation and assure that patient consent is "voluntary." Prescriptions of laetrile could be legally restricted to patients who have been certified as terminal. Thus, if a dying patient chose to cling to what he believes is his last desperate chance of survival, no paternalistic intervener would deprive him of his hope. Only the disease itself will do that. "Under the Government's nodding supervision, the purity of the product might then be assured, the flourishing black market in laetrile—which has netted some of its pushers millions of dollars—would finally be broken, and the nostrum could be given despairing patients beyond all hope of conventional medicine."[12] In 1977 the editor of the *New England Journal of Medicine*, arguing on liberal grounds for the legalization of this worthless drug, told the press: "If a patient suffering from incurable cancer comes to me and says to me he wants to go on a pilgrimage to a shrine [one offering the hope of a miraculous cure] I wouldn't deny him that right."[13]

The primary consideration against legalization is the argument from exploitation. Pharmaceutical companies, druggists, even some physicians, would make large and legitimate commercial profit from the sale of the product. These profits would not exactly be at the expense of the customers, since the drug is harmless, and they freely pay their money to keep alive their hope—an exchange that seems reasonable to them if not to us. Yet some parties will be turning to their own advantage the misery and desperation of others, achieving a gain for themselves only because of others' misfortunes. That is a form of parasitism that tends to offend the objective observer, whether ultimately justifiable or not. It is not pleasant to behold the strong and healthy making their living off the desperate hopes of the powerless.

"Human weaknesses." Another class of conditions whose exploitation is morally suspect are moral weaknesses, largely self-regarding character flaws that incline a person to act against his own interest, his own judgment, or his own conscience, whenever there is temptation to do so. *A* exploits the moral weakness of *B* when he deliberately provides that temptation and takes his own profit from the consequences. Lord Devlin has claimed that "All sexual immorality involves the exploitation of human weaknesses,"[14] and finds considerable support for this opinion in the *Wolfenden Report* which he is criticizing. The latter, in its chapter on the English crime of "Living off the earnings of prostitution," states:

> It is in our view an oversimplification to think that those who live on the earnings of prostitution are exploiting the prostitute as such. What they are really exploiting is the whole complex of the relationship between prostitute and customer; they are, in effect, exploiting the human weaknesses which cause the customer to seek the prostitute and the prostitute to meet the demand. The more direct methods . . . are not the only means by which the trade is exploited; that it continues to thrive is due in no small measure to efforts deliberately made to excite the demand on which its prosperity depends . . . At the present time, entertainments of a suggestive character, dubious advertisements, the sale of pornographic literature, contraceptives, and 'aphrodisiac' drugs (sometimes all in one shop), and the sale of alcoholic liquor in premises frequented by prostitutes, all sustain the trade, and in turn themselves profit from it . . .[15]

I assume that both Lord Devlin and the authors of the *Wolfenden Report* considered sexual congress with prostitutes to express a "human weakness" because they thought of it as something typically opposed to the customer's interest, his prudential judgment, and his conscience; the customer typically only succumbed because of the enticements and allure of the commercial exploiters. In other passages, however, Lord Devlin seems to make a stronger claim, that the impulse to illicit sexual conduct is a human weakness even when it is not in any way dangerous to the actor (apart from rendering him or her liable to criminal prosecution) nor contrary to his or her conscience. This stronger and more puzzling claim won the sympathy of the American authors of the *Model Penal Code* and, for a time, at least, of a majority of the United States Supreme Court (which had clearly been influenced by the *Model Penal Code*). Professor Louis B. Schwartz, co-author of the *Code*, wrote that its antiobscenity provisions were not aimed at any "sin of obscenity" as such, but

obliquely at a "disapproved form of economic activity—commercial exploitation of the widespread weakness for titillation by pornography."[16] As
Schwartz proceeds to point out, the criminal prohibition of obscenity, so
regarded, takes on the "aspect of regulation of unfair business or competitive
practices."

> Just as merchants may be prohibited from selling their wares by appeal to the
> public weakness for gambling, so they may be restrained from purveying books,
> movies, or other commercial exhibition by exploiting the well-nigh universal
> weakness for a look behind the curtain of modesty.[17]

Justice Brennan quoted that passage with approval in his opinion in *United
States v. Ginzburg*,[18] upholding Ginzburg's conviction (and five year sentence)
for violating a federal obscenity statute. What aroused Justice Brennan's ire
and that of some of his colleagues was not that obscene materials were produced, disseminated, used, and enjoyed (the justices in this case do not
appear to be excessively prudish), but rather that persons should derive a
profit from "the sordid business of pandering . . . to the erotic interest of
their customers."[19] In the absence of any argument that the erotic interest as
such is a human weakness, this use of the word "pander" begs the question.
We *cater* to people's wishes, we *minister* to their needs; but we can *pander* only
to their weaknesses, flaws, and follies. In fact, pandering can be well defined
as noncoercively exploiting the moral deficiencies of another by providing
him the services he voluntarily seeks, even if it should be contrary to his
interest or conscience. The legal writers quoted above speak of "human
weakness," because that term is less censorious than "moral weakness," and
their concern is not to censure the weak party so much as to condemn the
exploiter who profits by serving him.

While there may be genuine doubt that the erotic interest is a human
weakness, there can be no doubt at all that any *addiction* is a moral weakness
that renders some human beings especially vulnerable to exploitation by
others. But the sort of exploitation I have in mind cannot plausibly be said to
be voluntarily consented to; the addict's exploitation is by means of still
another kind of "coercive offer."[20] "I'll pour you a drink if you give me a
dollar," said to an alcoholic with his last dollar in his pocket, may in effect
leave him no choice but to hand over his dollar, the compulsion stemming
from his own addiction rather than from an external threat. A better example
of an undoubted human weakness that is frequently exploited *noncoercively* by
others is the desire knowingly to bet against the odds in certain forms of
structured gambling for the sake of the thrills involved and the (not too much)
less than even chance of winning large sums of money. Surely the slot-
machines that one sees everywhere in Nevada exploit a human weakness in

this way. Hardly anyone is addicted to them even in an appropriately figurative sense, and some even profit occasionally from playing them. But it is a statistical truth that most plays are losing ones and that the machines will win in the long run. Profit is assured for those who "play upon" the very human propensities of the passersby, who indulge them in many cases against their better judgment "in a weak moment."

Notoriety: more three-party cases. Another sort of human condition that lends itself to exploitation by others is sheer notoriety, or the state of being interesting to others. Exploitation of this condition, as we have seen, is often a relation among three parties, or groups of parties. In these cases the primary party whose traits or circumstances are exploited is not the same as the party (or parties) from whom the profit is derived, although the latter party is also "used" for the exploiter's gain. Norman Mailer's book, *The Executioner's Song,*[21] a "true life novel" based on the career of Gary Gilmore, the Utah murderer who insisted upon his own execution, illustrates the genre well. The first half of Mailer's book is mainly a narrative of Gilmore's life, loves, and crimes, derived in large part from his own words in tapes and letters. Book Two of the "novel" introduces the cast of "literary ambulance-chasers" bent on using the Gilmore story to make as much money as they can. Diane Johnson's review claims that Mailer's book succeeds in both describing and exemplifying the moral ugliness of this brand of exploitation—

> . . . now enter hordes of people sensing a buck to be made out of Gilmore's refusal to appeal his death sentence, and big money if he gets executed. Into the lives of the sad, consternated people of Provo come reporters, TV people, film people, media lawyers, contracts, names they've heard of (David Suskind, Louis Nizer), names they haven't (Lawrence Schiller) [Mailer's partner]. . . . Once you are in the mind of Schiller who becomes the protagonist of Book Two, it becomes obvious why Mailer has kept himself out of the narrative. This account of the exploitation of the poor convict and his relatives is so appalling that the author of the end product—the book you are reading—must seem to be innocent of it, must seem not to be writing it at all, let alone making a reported half a million for starters out of it. It is the "carrion bird" Schiller who must seem the bad guy . . .[22]

Why should the efforts of journalists to make a profit by selling to their customers the inside story of interesting events and a truthful account of notorious persons strike us as "appalling?" After all, the writers did not stage the events; they simply report, in an organized and interesting fashion, what has already happened and offer their accounts to third parties who voluntarily, indeed eagerly, pay the price. Nobody was tricked; no one was coerced; there was not even much active noncoercive manipulation of motives. But in the end the writers are enriched; those whose careers they used to their advantage are dead, demoralized, or devastated; and only because personal tragedies have occurred has a profit been made at all. The writers have exploited, that is, turned to their own advantage, the misery of others, just as the carrion bird converts to his own substance the victims of misfortunes in which he had no role.

The carrion bird of course performs useful services. Why then is he such an appalling symbol for human beings? Perhaps it is because none of us can be comfortable in the presence of others who have a stake in our misfortunes, especially in those *unnecessary* misfortunes, which unlike inevitable death and taxes, come only to those whose deeds or luck are terrible. Physicians also make their livings off the sufferings of others, but their function is to cure, repair, and prevent, and not *simply* to make a profit for themselves.[23] Mailer and Schiller did nothing *for* Gilmore and his family,[24] and for that matter they did nothing *to* them either; rather they took them and left them much as they found them, having used them exactly as they were to make a killing for themselves. If they are to escape Diane Johnson's charge of blamable exploitation it must be on the ground that the book and television series they produced were useful public services of disproportionate and overriding value, that they were more like the photograph of the attempted assassination of the Pope than the film based on the story of the Yorkshire Ripper. The case may be close, but the book itself reveals that *intentions* may be predominantly exploitative even when results are not.

Four-party cases: Playboy centerfolds. There remain certain common uses of the term "exploitation" that are more difficult to analyze. Other examples of alleged three-party exploitation are especially puzzling. Consider for example the common complaint of feminists that centerfold photographs of nude female models in such magazines as *Playboy* "exploit women" (as opposed to merely exploiting their traits). The exploiter in this case must be the publisher. He presumably makes a gain by means of the photographs well beyond what it costs him to pay the model. Those from whom the profit is made is the readers (or voyeurs), mostly males who willingly pay the purchase price at least partly in order to look at the photographs. If we can agree with Lord Devlin, Professor Schwartz, and Justice Brennan that the taste for that sort of thing in the male audience is a "human weakness," then it will follow that the publisher makes his profit by pandering to a human weakness. He exploits his male readers by turning their lust to his advantage.

But how does that process exploit women? The only woman directly involved is the model, and like any other contractor or employee her relatively weak bargaining position could be exploited if the publisher offered her an inadequate fee for her labors. That would be to "take advantage of her" in the manner of Marxist (coercive) exploitation. But in fact that cannot be what feminists mean, for the models often receive pay in four figures for only a few hours work, even though they can usually be replaced by any of dozens of understudies eager for their chance to be "exploited" in turn. The only obvious sense that I can discern in which the nude models are exploited is the relatively innocuous one in which all persons whose characteristics or skills are used by others for profit are "exploited." The attractiveness of the model is turned to the advantage of the publisher, but if her role in the process is voluntary and she is paid a fair wage, then the exploitation is not at her expense, and *ceteris paribus* it is not unfair to *her*.

It is clear then that if any women are exploited by the nude photographs they must be persons other than those who do the posing. Some women not directly involved in the transaction feel that *they* have been exploited (perhaps vicariously) insofar as they share the characteristics of the model that are being turned to another's gain, that their own sexual attractiveness is cheapened, and that this is demeaning to them. That state of affairs may well be a bad thing, particularly if we accept the premise that the interest of the ogling male betrays a "human weakness," but it rather stretches the meaning of the word "exploitation" even beyond the limits of its extensive elasticity to use it in this way. At the worst, *Playboy* centerfolds may be degrading to women, but they are not on that ground exploitative of them.

A better explanation of the prevailing usage is that proposed by Alan Buchanan.[25] The element of exploitation in the nude photographs, on his view, is not so much vicarious as causally indirect. The centerfolds contribute to an environment in which more direct and familiar types of exploitation of women by men is encouraged, and it does this by spreading the image of women as sexual playthings. The pictures then have a direct causal influence on the way the woman's role is conceptualized in society and that in turn makes certain kinds of exploitation possible. The exploitation involves four sets of parties: the publisher, the model, other women (the victims), and other men (the direct exploiters). Both the publisher and the model, on this account, are *indirect* exploiters.

Other four-party cases: Newsweek's Reaganomics cover story. Exploitative journalism quite frequently alters the moral relations among four parties or groups of parties, so the *Playboy* example is not unusual in that respect. In some of these examples, no person is directly exploited, though personal traits or circumstances are wrongfully utilized, and the party who is wronged is quite other than those whose traits or circumstances were manipulated to the exploiter's advantage. Consider the complaint, for example, expressed in a 1982 letter to the editor of *Newsweek*[26] from Republican Representative Robert Michel about a *Newsweek* cover for an issue on Reaganomics that showed a poor, haggard, small, female child. The cover, said Michel, was exploitative, and ". . . while it may be acceptable practice in Hollywood to exploit little children to get the usual reflex emotional response from viewers, reputable journalists do not indulge themselves in pandering to the emotions."

Let us assume for the sake of the argument that Michel's charge is justified. What does it imply for our scheme of conceptualization? The incident was a "four-party case" involving (1) the exploiter (*Newsweek*), (2) those whose "usual reflex response" was pandered to or "exploited" (many readers), (3) the child whose sad-eyed visage was exploited too, and (4) the Reaganites whose policies were put in a bad light. Were the readers and the child "exploited" in different senses of the word? Maybe we should say that the persons of the readers were not exploited but only their vulgarity or knee-jerk sentimentality. (That can be bad enough.) Similarly, we could say that the person of the child was not exploited (since she was neither coerced, deceived, nor harmed, and perhaps, like the *Playboy* model, she was amply rewarded for her trouble), but then only her "situation" was exploited. Even on these assumptions the behavior of *Newsweek* could be criticized as wrong, and wrong in a special way, not necessarily implying the violation of anyone's rights, but involving only the unjust extraction of gain from another party's circumstances. (The cover presumably did help *Newsweek* sell magazines.) That is how we might leave the example if the fourth parties were not to be considered. The only parties who could claim to be treated unfairly in this example were the Reaganites. In that case, *they* were the victims of the exploitation that took place, although they were not the parties exploited! Only in the very trivial sense tha their *vulnerability* was exploited were they, or any feature of their circumstances, "exploited." But in that sense it is *necessarily* true (but trivially) that every victim of exploitation is an object of that exploitation.

4. The elements of exploitation (C): redistribution of gains and losses

The third element in exploitation is some redistribution of benefits and harms among the related parties. The one essential feature under this head is that the exploiter himself be a gainer. Exploitation in the usual pejorative sense is the wrongful turning to some advantage by one party (*A*) of some trait or circumstance of another party (*B*). There is a variety of ways in which *B*'s interests might be affected by the process, but without gain for *A*, there is no exploitation. This requirement may seem subject to exceptions and will have to be weakened somewhat to be altogether secure. *A* may exploit *B* for great "gain" all of which he then gives to charity. Clearly, to accommodate this example we must dilute the sense of "gain" so that it includes gain either for oneself or for some person or cause that one chooses to benefit. In order to preserve the gain requirement, in short, we must employ an admittedly extended sense of "gain" including both gain in the strict sense and fulfillment of one's aims, purposes, or desires, including altruistic and conscientious ones. The "gain" in question, moreover, need not be a *net* gain if there should happen also to be attendant losses. The Hollywood film producer who requires an aspiring starlet to sleep with him as a condition of a screen test *has* exploited her even though he contracts syphilis from her as a result. One does not always profit in the long run from one's immediate advantage-taking.

We would not normally speak of exploitation either (at least in any blamable sense) when *B* himself gains from the use to which *A* puts him. *B*'s not gaining, however, may also be too strong a requirement. *B* could gain from his own exploitation, I suppose, but be badly used because *A* gained disproportionately. (American universities are often said to exploit the student-athletes they recruit from the ghettos even though they offer them the opportunity to play football for four years and to attend various classes from which they often can derive little benefit. That is because the universities profit immensely from the arrangement, while the gains of most of the players are soon dissipated.) Herbert Morris provides a different kind of example of an exploitee's gain.[27] He has us suppose that *A* "exploits" *B* for great profit, all of which he uses to set up a trust fund for *B* himself. In the face of these examples then, we must weaken our initial point. We do not normally speak of blamable exploitation of a person when that person gains from the process, *except* when that gain is disproportionately small compared to the exploiter's, or when it comes from a paternalistically motivated return of the gain from the exploiter. *B* might complain in the latter case that *A* took unfair advantage of him but then paid him back with the ill-gotten gain. The repayment does not make it false that the exploitation did occur, but it does partially remove or mitigate its blameworthy character. In Morris's example, however, there is not exactly a "repayment," since it was *A* not *B* who chose what to do with the funds gained by exploiting *B*, so that *B* does not get to use the money in the way he prefers. In that case clearly it remains true that *B* was taken advantage of, despite *A*'s paternalistic generosity.

In the most general nonpejorative sense, physicians "exploit" sick persons by turning to their own profit the unhappy circumstances of their patients. But they achieve this gain by helping the other party, and unless the fee charged is extortionate, the patient cannot complain that he was exploited since he too profited from the process. Typically, of course, the physician does not rub his hands in gleeful anticipation of his fee when he encounters a person with a serious ailment; his mind is entirely on the cure and his motives may be commendably humanitarian and sympathetic. But even in the rare case of the ambulance-chasing physician motivated entirely by greed, his patient cannot complain of exploitation if the fees were standard and the treatment beneficial. At the most, we can say that the physician's motives or intentions in that case were "exploitative"—all he cared for was what was in it for him. But even then it cannot be true that his *conduct* exploited his patient in any blamable sense that provides the patient with a moral basis for complaint.

When, on the other hand, *B*'s interest is adversely affected (and he is in that sense "harmed") by the profitable use to which *A* puts him, then that may be exploitative. In that case we can say that the exploitation not only benefits *A* but is also *at the expense of B*. Now we can even speak of *B* as a "victim" of *A*'s exploitation. But if the exploitation was noncoercive yet harmful (a setback to *B*'s interest)—if *A* received *B*'s voluntary consent to the conduct that proved "harmful" to *B*—then the subsequent setback is not unfair to *B*. It is not an injustice *to him;* it gives him no grievance; it does him no wrong. Yet it may demean or degrade him; it may present him to the world in an unfavorable (though not inaccurate) light; it may cost him dearly. The exploiter may not be answerable to *him* in that case, but, as Kleinig reminds us, he may nevertheless be answerable to third parties or to his own conscience, or subject to adverse criticism generally.

Perhaps the most philosophically interesting pattern by which exploitation may distribute losses and benefits is that of actions in which *A* uses some trait or circumstance of *B* to make a gain for himself, but *B* is *neither harmed nor benefited* in the process. *A*'s conduct neither helps *B* nor is at his expense, and yet it clearly exploits *B*, even in the strongly pejorative sense. The two most familiar species of this puzzling genus are *parasitism* and certain unrepresentative instances of *unjust enrichment*.

Parasitism. Noncoercive exploiters are often parasites; they make their livings by attaching themselves to others, and, without necessarily injuring their hosts, take their own gains as byproducts of the host's activity. (Recall Zeno Vendler's driving-in-the-fog example, Chap. 28, p. 14.) The dictionary recognizes a sense of "parasite" in which the parasite may even be an invited guest ("one frequenting the tables of the rich and earning welcome by flattery"), in which case the host's consent is voluntary; he doesn't mind at all being used. Indeed, he has a use in turn for the flatterer, and the exploitation in this case is not only consensual; it is also mutual. If the relationship is also mutually productive, if it is genuinely advantageous for both parties, then it resembles not so much parasitism as the biological process of symbiosis, the living together of two dissimilar organisms in a mutually beneficial relationship. We are not inclined to use the word "exploitation" at all for such cases unless it is to indicate that the trait taken advantage of by at least one of the parties is some sort of defect, or weakness, or symptom, as when one party is paid to whip the other, a sexual masochist. The need for flattery is itself both a character flaw and a human weakness; hence we can speak even of the well-paid parasitic sycophant as an exploiter. The paid flatterer, moreover, is not a productive parasite. He lives off his host's vanity and contributes nothing of genuine substance in return, like the drug provider who lives off his host's addiction and provides only more addiction-strengthening drugs in return.

It is not easy to conceive of mutual exploitation, but there are many personal relationships that approximate this description. Even the most familiar near-examples are complex in structure: *A* treats *B* in such a way that it would be properly characterized as "exploitation" were it not for the fact that *B* is treating *A* in such a way that it too would be characterized as "exploitation" but for the way *A* is treating him. Two types of "personal symbiosis" may be distinguished.

(1) Single-stranded cases. *A* exploits *B*'s characteristic *F* and thereby exploits *B*. In virtue of this activity and as a part of the very same process, *A*'s characteristic *G* is exploited by *B* who thereby exploits *A*. Here personal exploitation (as opposed to wrongful utilization of traits or circumstances) is cancelled out, and we might better say that there is no exploitation at all. A possible example would be a university department hiring an unqualified instructor from a minority group to placate the affirmative action officer, thus "taking advantage" of that person to the detriment of his or her self-esteem. The hired instructor, fully aware of his or her own lack of the requisite skills, accepts the job anyway, thus taking advantage of the department, for the sake of his or her short-term gain. One and the same transaction—the hiring proposed by one party and accepted by the other—is "exploitative" of both parties.

(2) Double-stranded cases. *A* exploits *B* by doing *x*, while during the same time period of *A*'s activity, *B* exploits *A* by doing the distinct and unrelated act Y. Even in this case, if each party's "gain" is in the form of monetary profit, the gains may be uneven, so that on balance one party exploits the other more than he is exploited, or the profits may be equal, canceling out the "exploitation." Thus if *A* panders to *B*'s lust by selling him pornography for a $100 profit, while *B* exploits *A*'s credulity and cashes in on *A*'s misfortune by selling him laetrile for $100 profit, then they might as well combine the transactions into one simple trade, and the pecuniary gains cancel out. But if the gains are incommensurable as opposed to monetary, and the actions

unrelated, there may be more sense in describing their relationship as mutually exploitative. Mr. *A* exploits Mrs. *A*'s trust by having an affair during the
same period when Mrs. *A* exploits *his* impatience with bookkeeping by squan-
dering their savings in lavish and self-indulgent expenditures. Here each is
quite independently exploiting the other.

The parasitic profiteer who is most clearly a noncoercive exploiter is the
person who operates either with the consent of his "host" or, more likely, not
against the will of the host, the latter being either ignorant of, or indifferent
to, his own exploitation, which in turn is neither harmful to him nor in any
way beneficial to him. The Mailer-Schiller exploitation of the Gilmore family
fits this model approximately. So do all cases, generally speaking, in which *A*
attaches his profit-sucking tubes to some vulnerable place in the social nexus
and extracts some advantages from events that occur in *B*'s life, without
depriving *B* of any gain or inflicting any loss upon him. If this way of taking
profit is to be condemned as exploitation, as opposed to ordinary commercial
initiative, it must be partly because of the particular traits or circumstances of
B's that are utilized by *A*. If they are moral virtues like cooperativeness or
trustworthiness, or innocent personal weaknesses, or tragic personal losses,
then the utilizer is said to have "exploited" them for his own personal gain,
but if they are other-regarding moral flaws, or routine or happy events, then
the word "exploitation" may be considered too harsh and judgmental. Even if
the utilized traits or circumstances are of the inappropriate kind, their employment may not be blamable exploitation if they are used not only to make a
profit for *A* but also to produce some valuable public service like information,
education, or increased employment. But if the only "gain" other than the
exploiter's personal profit consists (say) in the gratification of the unsavory
tastes of third parties, then the parasitic profiter's gains will seem ill-gotten,
even though the party from whose traits or circumstances the gains were
derived was not wronged (not *personally* exploited).

Unjust enrichment. Sometimes the gain in exploitation comes from deliberate
advantage-taking. In pure parasitism, for example, the exploiter deliberately
takes advantage of the other party's situation. In other cases, however, the
exploiter's gain comes through the inadvertent receiving of benefits and conse-
quent refusal to make restitution. The latter category includes some of the
cases known to the law as "unjust enrichment." *A* has been "enriched" if he
has received a benefit (in almost every case from *B*, the plaintiff), and the
enrichment is "unjust" provided that retaining the benefit would be unfair.
When *B* has "officiously" conferred the benefit upon *A*, then he is not later
entitled to restitution. Thus companies are not entitled deliberately to send
unordered goods to persons and then sue for payment of the bill or return of

the product. Nor is a benevolent gift-giver entitled to sue for the return of his gift when his feelings toward the recipient have changed. These legal rules accurately reflect moral intuitions and are grounded in socially useful policies. If a zealous and crafty book dealer deliberately sends me a twenty dollar book that I did not order, along with a bill requesting full payment, there is no unfairness if I retain the book and ignore the bill. I could hardly be accused of "exploiting" the book dealer to my own advantage when the traits of the dealer from which I took my advantage were his cupidity, officiousness, or deceit. If I keep the book, "the joke is on him." The very scheme by which he meant to exploit me—to take advantage of my carelessness, gullibility, or some other "human weakness"—was turned back upon himself. Moreover, the rule barring restitution for officious benefits prevents me from being inundated with unordered products and charged with the immense inconvenience of returning them all to their senders. Of course tbere is no further point in prohibiting officious conferrals by the *criminal* law. Simply barring restitutional remedies is sufficient to deter unsavory commercial practices and to "protect persons who have had benefits thrust upon them."[28]

When conferrals of benefits are deemed "nonofficious," on the other hand, the courts will order restitution of the benefit to the unwitting benefactor on the theory that were *A* to insist on retaining the benefit, that would be for him to *exploit* some weakness, innocent mistake, or unavoidable misfortune of *B*. If *B* overpays his debt to *A* by mistake, for example, and *A* knowingly retains the overpaid amount, then he can be said to have "exploited" *B* by taking (or maintaining) advantage of *B*'s error.

In most cases *B* not only loses from *A*'s unjust enrichment, but his loss is exactly the same as *A*'s gain. An example of *A*'s gain coinciding exactly with *B*'s loss would be overpayment of a debt to *A* because of a "mistake of fact" by the debtor *B*, where "the payee would be unjustly enriched by the amount of the overpayment if he were permitted to keep it and the payer would be unjustly deprived of that amount if he were not permitted to recover it."[29] But there is no necessary relation in unjust enrichment between *A*'s gain and *B*'s loss, and there are numerous interesting cases where *A* is enriched unjustly, that is in a manner that is unfair to *B*, even though *B* suffers a smaller loss or even no loss at all. In these cases *B* sues to "recover" *A*'s gain rather than to be compensated for any loss of his own. Dan Dobbs explains very clearly the difference between restitution of unfairly retained benefits and compensation for damages:

> The damages recovery is to compensate the plaintiff, and it pays him, theoretically, for his losses. The restitution claim, on the other hand, is not aimed at compensating the plaintiff, but at *forcing the defendant to disgorge benefits* that it would be unjust for him to keep.[30] (italics added)

Dobbs then considers the defendant who, as "a conscious wrongdoer," comes upon the plaintiff's missing boat, worth $5,000 at the time, "and sells it to someone else at a very good price above the market, say for $10,000."[31] In this case,

> the plaintiff has lost a boat worth $5,000. He could have sold it on the market for such a price and he could replace it on the market for such a price. If he has no special damages, his recovery of damages would be $5,000, because such a sum represents his loss and would fully compensate him. But the bad faith defendant has sold the boat for twice its market price, whether by luck or clever bargaining or the location of a special customer. The defendant thus has gains resulting from his tort [the tort of wrongful conversion]. If it is unjust for the defendant to profit from his tort, he should be made to disgorge these gains. That is exactly what the law of restitution will force him to do. *The plaintiff in such a case obtains a windfall, but this is thought to be acceptable because it is the major means of avoiding any unjust enrichment on the defendant's part.*[32] (italics added)

The defendant in the Dobbs example has walked into his own trap, and the order that he disgorge his ill-gotten gains for the advantage of the plaintiff has a pleasing moral symmetry to it. In a way the plaintiff has "exploited" *him* to make a "windfall profit," but the traits and circumstances thus turned to the plaintiff's advantage were moral flaws and wrongdoing, turned back on the wrongdoer himself. The very same scheme that was meant to profit the defendant at the plaintiff's expense has boomeranged and profited the plaintiff at the defendant's expense.

Whether we are talking about "unjust enrichment" in the strict sense of the lawyers or in an analogous moral sense, we must notice that unjust enrichment is often a matter of passive recipience rather than active doing or taking. The enrichment is often more like a windfall than it is like reaping the fruits of one's larceny, burglary, or fraud. Consider the author who dumps a messy manuscript on his grossly underpaid and inexperienced typist and demands that it be typed with great care and precision and finished as soon as possible. She takes the manuscript and agrees to the proferred terms. Two days later the author to his amazement hears from the typist that she has finished her job one full week in advance of the deadline, and to his further amazement finds that she has done a perfect job, worthy of the highest paid professionals. The author now feels that unless he pays her a bonus, he has exploited (taken unfair advantage of) her supererogatory zeal. If he does not pay her more, she has not been wronged (or harmed) and she has no complaint coming, for he will have discharged his side of the bargain anyway. If her labors were disproportionate to her reward, that was her doing, after all, not his. And yet this seems to be one of those strange cases in which a "gratuity" is morally mandatory. But for her consent to the promised fee, his failure to pay an additional amount would be unfair-on-balance to her, and even though she freely consented to his terms, his gain is "unjust." How could the law possibly rectify this injustice? Unlike overpayment of a debt, the gain in this case cannot be returned, so restitution is impossible. And legal pressure to make the author pay more than he originally agreed would interfere with contractual commitments as well as encouraging "gratuitous conferrals" in illicit commercial strategies. Consensual exploitation, it seems, is often not subject to legal correction.

5. Fairness and unfairness

What is the difference between one person merely "utilizing" another for his own gain, and one person exploiting the other? The correct short answer to this question, of course, is that there is an element of wrongfulness in exploitation that distinguishes it from nonexploitative utilizaion. It is more difficult to characterize the nature of that wrongfulness however, and the problem in its full complexity cannot be settled here. In some cases the wrongfulness appears to be identical with *unfair* treatment of the exploited party, or treatment that would be unfair but for the exploited party's consent. In other cases unfairness may be incidentally involved as one of the consequences of the exploitation, although the wrongdoing that renders the treatment exploitative is, as Landesman shrewdly suggests,[33] a distinctive and irreducibly independent kind of wrongdoing, quite separate from the unfairness of the subsequent gains or losses. In still other cases of exploitation there may be no unfairness to the exploited party at all, neither inherently nor consequentially, neither actually nor hypothetically ("unfair but for his consent"). Landesman gives two convincing examples of the latter. Exploitation films exploit the tastelessness or vulgarity of their audiences in a shameful way, yet they give their audiences exactly what they want for a reasonable agreed-upon price, so they could hardly be unfair to those audiences. Neither will it do to say that but for the audience's voluntary consent the films would have been unfair, as if there were an element of *prima facie* unfairness in their showing which consent overrides, as there is for example in the case of the rash challenge, the foolish request for an amputation, or the overzealous typist. Similarly, when a parasitic exploiter extracts profit from the misery of another without coercion or deception, there may be something morally repugnant about his gain, but it seems implausible to interpret the wrongfulness as unfairness to the party whose misfortune was "utilized."

Perhaps there is a wider genus of "injustice" of which unfairness to a mistreated party is only one species. In that case we might say that it is *unjust* that one party cash in on another party's misfortune, or by appealing to another party's vulgarity or prejudice, even though the wrongful gain is neither unfair to the exploited party nor such that it would be unfair but for his consent. On the other hand, gains earned by taking advantage of the other party's desperate credulity, his self-regarding foolishness, rashness, or stubbornness, or his moral weakness, are not only unjust in this generic sense but also specifically unfair as well (or would be so but for consent). Having made this disclaimer, I shall now proceed to discuss the relation of exploitation to injustice, with special attention to the cases where the form of injustice *is* specific unfairness to the exploited party.[34]

How then do we distinguish merely turning another person's situation to our own advantage from unfairly "taking advantage" of him? In treating this question, we must remember that even the fair use of another, in a given instance, might not be morally justified on balance, all things considered. In judging the use to be fair we imply only that the used party himself has no personal grievance. It may have been wrong for other reasons for the second party to use him as he did, but it was not wrong because his *rights* were violated. Moreover, A's use of B might be unfair to B and yet justified on balance, all things considered, as the least of the evils A had to choose from in the situation. There is always a presumption in favor of fairness and against unfairness, but there is no necessary correspondence between on-balance justification and fairness. They are quite distinct notions, and, in this imperfect world, only imperfectly linked.

Fairness and unfairness, while not as comprehensive concepts as justifiability on balance and unjustifiability on balance, are nevertheless internally complicated themselves. One and the same act may be fair in some respects and unfair in others, or fair to some affected parties and unfair to others. What we must mean by (unfair) exploitation is "profitable utilization of another person that is either unfair on balance to him, or which in virtue of its other unfairness-producing characteristics *would be unfair on balance to him but for his voluntary consent to it.*"

To determine then whether a given suspect case is an instance of unfair exploitation, and to evaluate it morally from the various relevant standpoints, we must determine:

1. Whether A used the situation of B for his own gain, and
2. in case B did not consent, whether A's use of B was unfair to B, and
3. in case B did consent, whether but for that consent A's use of B would have been unfair to B.

If the answers to (1) and either (2) or (3) are affirmative then the case can properly be described as an instance of exploitation. But then we can raise still another question about it,

4. Given that A has exploited B, was he justified on balance, in the circumstances, in doing so?

In case the answer to (3) is affirmative, and our case therefore is one of consented-to exploitation, we can ask still another question,

5. Is A subject to adverse moral criticism for his exploitation of B even though B had voluntarily consented to his actions? That is, was A's use of B morally wrong (or "unjust" in itself) even though it was not unfair-on-balance to B?

A fuller account of the characteristics that distinguish exploitation from mere profitable utilization would follow the outline of exploitation's main structural elements, listed above, and their main combinations and variations. Which ways of using or "playing upon" another's traits or circumstances (discussed in §2 above) tend to be unfair to him? Which traits and circumstances of B (discussed in §3 above) are such that their utilization by A tends to be unfair to B? Which ways of changing the balance of gains and losses between the parties (discussed in §4 above) tend to be exploitative and which not? It may be impossible to give precise answers to these questions in the absence of a complete normative moral theory, but we can hope to say of certain elements that, insofar as they are present in a relationship between A and B, that relationship tends to be unfairly exploitative, and, insofar as they are absent, that relationship tends not to be unfairly exploitative. That would not give us a litmus test in the manner of a set of necessary and sufficient conditions, but it would provide a useful start toward a full analysis of the concept of exploitation.

Consider the first element, the nature of A's use of B's situation. It would surely seem that the coercive uses have the greatest tendency to be unfair. When they are disadvantageous to the "victim" (as they normally are), and vitiative of consent (as they always are), they are outright inflictions of harm by A on B for the sake of A's own gain. Subtler forms of manipulation by A, however, may be consistent with B's voluntary consent, and thus not unfair on balance. But insofar as A's profitable utilization of B is the consequence of manipulation, it also tends to be unfair to B. I have in mind consent won by seductive luring, beguiling, tempting, bribing, coaxing, imploring, whimpering, flattering, and the like, short of deceptive innuendo, threats, or coercive offers (which diminish or nullify voluntariness). These techniques do not overpower, nor necessarily deceive by misrepresentation. But they appeal to a weakness in their victim. They bring out his worse rather than his better self, but a real self nevertheless. And they engage that lesser self in persuasion, so that in a sense the victim acts—not against his will—but against his "better judgment" and his initial disposition. If the manipulative process is excessively long, intense, or emotional, the victim can complain after the fact that his consent was not fully voluntary because of fatigue, clouded judgment, or otherwise diminished rational capacity. But these defenses will be in vain if the process simply brings out the lesser self by a kind of direct appeal or lure that does not impair the victim's capacities so much as engage his vanity or greeds.

Less likely to be unfair are fishing expeditions in which A merely hangs his lure within range of vulnerable B, attracting his voluntary agreement to a scheme that is in fact likely to promote A's gain at B's expense. A may initiate the process by making a proposal to B which B after due contemplation, but no manipulative persuasion, readily accepts. Least likely of all to be unfair to B are those agreements which B himself initially proposes and to which A reluctantly responds, as in our earlier example of challenges to contests of skill; yet, as we have seen, these voluntary agreements may nevertheless exploit B in a manner that we would characterize as unfair were it not for the fact of B's voluntary consent. Still, because of that consent the agreement is not unfair on balance, and whether or not the exploiter is subject to censure for his role on other grounds depends upon a myriad of background factors and expected consequences—the full range of considerations that are implicated in all questions of on-balance moral justification.

The second element to be examined in trying to determine whether A's profitable use of B is also (unfair) exploitation is the nature of B's traits or circumstances which A turns to his own advantage. Insofar as they are social virtues (especially obedience, honesty, industry, cooperativeness, friendly good will, or conscientiousness), misfortunes, or human weaknesses, the advantage taken tends to be unfair. Indeed, the clearest of all examples of unfairness are those in which A takes advantage of B's trust by cheating or freeloading, and thus achieves a dishonest gain for himself.

The wrongful exploitation of misfortunes and unhappy circumstances may or may not involve specific unfairness, but in either case it produces a form of unjust gain that offends the moral sense of the observer in a way similar to that of genuinely unfair freeloading. Part of what seems outrageous in the cheating and freeloading cases is that A, who is morally defective, should gain relative to B and others precisely because B and the others are morally superior to him. This puts the moral universe out of joint: untrustworthiness is rewarded and honesty is penalized (or at least unrewarded). There is a similar asymmetry to A profiting because of, and only because of, B's misfortune. A does not necessarily *harm* the grotesquely deformed victim (B) by contracting to exhibit him in his circus sideshow,[35] but he does make a good thing out of another's misfortune. This is a different kind of moral parasitism than cheating is, and surely less egregious, but when it is not clearly productive of social gain, it too offends the moral sensibility.

The same asymmetry is present but less pronounced when the exploited trait is a "human weakness." Pandering gives the customer what he wants, or what he comes to want after succumbing to temptation, so the customer himself can have very little grievance. Surely his complaint, if he has any at all, is substantially less than that of the law-abiding person whose honesty was put unfairly to another's advantage, or even the unlucky person whose personal catastrophe is milked for another's gain. Still, the moral sensibility is offended by A's profits, even when they are not substantially unfair, if it appears that they are possible only as the result of B's lust, gluttony, morbid curiosity, sentimentality, envy, or prejudice. Insofar as the weaknesses in question are "dirty," the money made by exploiting them seems dirty too, and insofar as the existence of these flaws is regrettable, making money out of them seems doubly regrettable. Appealing cynically to others' tastelessness is a way of getting down on all fours with them, and thus demeaning oneself in the process, and a cynically degraded person offends moral judgment even more than the moral weaklings he lives off of. This sort of blamable exploitation is unjust in some generic sense even though it is not unfair to any "victims."

In all the types of exploitation we have considered, the distinctively offensive element is not that B has suffered a loss but that A has made a profit. We are not indignant that B must pay an additional penny on his telephone bill, but that A has made a good thing for himself out of his nonpayment. We are not angry because bereaved B has suffered her loss (which occurred quite independently of anything A did) so much as that A has made a windfall profit. We are not offended at the flaws of character and taste pandered to by the cynical merchant nearly so much as that he lives parasitically off of them. In each case there is a perceived asymmetry between something regrettable and a personal gain that is extracted, quite nonproductively, from it.

It is otherwise when another's moral flaw or undeserved good fortune is utilized. Then there is the rather pleasing moral symmetry of a would-be exploiter being done in by his own untrustworthiness, cruelty, or greed. There is nothing flagrantly offensive, in this case, when the exploitee (B) turns the would-be exploiter's (A's) wrongdoing to his own advantage. And in the other case, when B receives a windfall blessing, we are not offended when A, without harming B, cleverly turns B's good luck to his own advantage. In these cases, not only is there no unfairness, there is also no injustice, or very little injustice, of any kind.

The final set of considerations bearing on the fairness or unfairness of one person's use of another is the effect on the balance of gains and losses of the

From the point of view of fairness:

1. *Depending on how the other party was used:* coercion and deception are worse than manipulation; manipulation is worse than straightworward offers; those offers in turn are usually worse than "fishing expeditions," which in turn are worse than acceptances of unexpected offers originating with the other party.
2. *Depending on which traits or circumstances were utilized:* exploiting trust and other virtues is most unfair; exploiting misfortunes and human weaknesses also tends to be unfair, even when not unfair on balance because of consent; exploiting moral flaws like cruelty and greed, or lucky good fortune, is less so, and in extreme cases, not unfair at all, nor in any way unjust.
3. *Depending on how gains and losses were distributed:*
   a. Where both A and B gain, then the greater the disproportion between A's gain and B's, the more exploitative;
   b. Where B loses, the greater B's loss, *ceteris paribus*, the greater the exploitation;
   c. Where B neither gains nor loses, then the greater A's gain, the greater the exploitation.

Diagram 31-1. Summary of unfairness-tending characteristics.

parties. Insofar as A's use of B is beneficial to B it tends of course not to be unfair to B, and insofar as it is detrimental—"at B's expense" in a strict sense—it tends to be unfair. The interesting cases are the intermediate ones where A's use of B's situation is neither harmful nor beneficial to B but is nevertheless, in a somewhat weaker sense, "at his expense" too. These tend to be less flagrantly unfair than the harmful cases. Still, when A's "parasitic profits" are unshared or shared unfairly with B, or when A has been unjustly enriched, then other things being equal, there is unfair exploitation even without harm.

The "unfairness-tending characteristics" discussed in this section are summarized in the diagram above.

6. Summary: the main categories of exploitation

It is time to draw the leading strands of our analysis together by summarizing the central points about the language of exploitation, and listing the leading categories of blameworthy exploitation whether they are (wrongfully) harmful or not. Then in the next chapter we can consider what role, if any, the law should take in preventing or punishing exploitation when, because it is either harmless or consented to, or both, it is a non-grievance or even a free-floating, evil. First, a summary of our analysis of the concept of exploitation.

1. *A* may simply utilize some traits or circumstances of *B*'s for his own purposes without wrong or harm to *B* or anyone else. Sometimes this is called "exploiting" the other's traits or circumstances, but in this sense "exploits" is nonpejorative, and is just another way of saying "puts to use." Not all use is ill-use. In these cases, *A* blamelessly "exploits" *B*'s characteristics or situation without exploiting *B* himself.

2. In some examples, on the other hand, *A*, by wrongfully extracting advantage from *B*'s traits or circumstances, can be said to have exploited those traits or circumstances in the full-blown pejorative sense of "exploit." In this category we can make an important distinction between two kinds of cases:

   a. By wrongfully exploiting *B*'s traits or circumstances, *A* exploits *B* himself. This is not merely to use *B*'s characteristics; it is to ill-use them in a way that mistreats *B*, giving him ground for a personal grievance.

   b. By wrongfully exploiting *B*'s traits or circumstances, *A* does evil and is blamable for it, but he does not exploit *B* as a person, *only* his characteristics. *B* himself is not wronged and can voice no grievance in his own behalf. Again two subcategories can be distinguished. Either (i) *A*'s exploitation is a free-floating evil directly wronging no one, but producing an injustice that consists entirely in his achieving a wrongful gain for himself, even though that gain is not unfair to the exploited party or to any third party. Certain examples of unproductive "cashing in" on misfortunes, pandering, and harmless parasitism are cases in point, or (ii) *A*'s exploitation of *B*'s traits and circumstances, though not unfair to *B*, is nevertheless unfair to some third (or fourth) party, though that party was not himself exploited by it (except in the trivial sense in which all right-violations, insofar as they are successful, "exploit" the victim's vulnerability.) This untypical case was illustrated by our example of the *Newsweek* cover story.

3. In cases where *B* has consented to *A*'s conduct, then what *A* did can not be unfair on balance to him (even though it may have been a larger injustice simply because of *A*'s wrongful gain). Nevertheless, if *A*'s act (accepting a rash challenge, performing surgical mutilation) is such that but for *B*'s consent it would have been unfair on balance to *B*, then it can still be called a case of personal exploitation (exploitation of *B* as a person), and *A* may be subject to blame for it (he "took advantage of *B*") even though *B* himself can voice no personal grievance, since his rights were not violated. In these cases of consented-to personal exploitation, no wrong is done *B* (in virtue of the *Volenti* maxim); hence no wrongful harm, in the sense required by the harm principle, is inflicted on him.

The evils that are produced, both *A*'s unjust gain and *B*'s set-back interest, are non-grievance evils.

Now we can conclude this summary by listing some of the leading categories of wrongful exploitation. Exploitative acts can be classified in a large
variety of crisscrossing ways: in terms of the mode of treatment employed,
the kind of trait or circumstances utilized, the way the balance of gains and
losses is affected, and no doubt many others. Some of the categories listed
below may come from different classification schemes; I make no claim of
perfect conceptual tidiness for them, but suggest only that the classes distinguished are useful tests for our understanding of the internal dynamics of
exploitative relationships, and important test cases for the discussion in Chapter 32 of the role of the criminal law.

1. *Coercive forcing, deceiving, or manipulating-the-incompetent.* These are familiar repugnant ways of extracting advantage for oneself from another without
his voluntary consent. They invade the other party's interest in liberty and
almost always other important interests as well. Since they advance the
exploiter's own interest wrongfully at the expense of the exploitee's, they are
exploitative (in the full pejorative sense) of their victim as a person, and not
merely exploitative of his situation and properties. The characteristics and
circumstances exploited are the victim's trust and relative lack of power.
There is nothing free-floating about these evils; they have a victim, and the
victim has a grievance.

2. *Unequal contest.* When *A* lures *B* into an unequal contest or an unpromising wager, or willingly accepts *B*'s rash challenge to such a contest while fully
aware of his own advantage, he utilizes (turns to his own advantage) *B*'s
naiveté, imprudence, or rashness. If *A* is subject to blame for his conduct
(and the answer to that question is not clear without a more detailed example)
then that utilization is also exploitation (in the pejorative sense) of those
characteristics of *B*, but since *B* voluntarily consented to the contest he is not
wronged but "*only* harmed" by his defeat. (That is, his interest has been set
back but his rights have not been violated.[36]) He may have been exploited in
that case, but not treated unfairly on balance. The result may be a kind of
injustice without a correlative grievance, in short a non-grievance evil consisting entirely in *A*'s wrongful gain. But if *A* was not at fault (maybe *B* deserved
to be taught a lesson), then there was no wrongful exploitation in any sense.

3. *Freeloading and similar cheating.* By driving in the forbidden lane, or not
paying his train fare, or cheating on his phone bill, *A* secures an advantage for
himself made possible only because of the trusting forbearance of others.
Though their interests may not have been set back in any measurable degree
by *A*'s cheating, the others can complain of being wrongfully used (exploited)

by *A*. The traits that *A* exploited were conscientiousness and trust—normal other-regarding moral virtues—and by exploiting them, *A* also exploited the persons of their possessors. His ill-gotten gains are an evil, but by no means a non-grievance evil, for he has violated the rights of those who forbear from such conduct themselves on the assumption that the others will too.

4. *Manipulated benevolence*. The benevolent virtues—altruism, generosity, kindness, charitableness, friendship, love—are just as much other-regarding excellences of character as dutifulness and trust. But they can stand in a somewhat different relation to exploitation. For example, a loving and devoted spouse may find no higher satisfaction than unquestioning service to his partner. Helping the other unquestioningly is what he *likes* doing. If that trait is cynically exploited by the partner, who makes ever more unreasonable demands on him, the devoted husband may not feel ill-used in the slightest. He has not been wronged or harmed, but his wife exploited his disposition to the fullest for her own selfish advantage. Similarly, the sponger who knows a dependably generous source of gifts, and the friend who squeezes every drop of friendly beneficence from his quite willing and loyal associate, do not wrong anybody, but their own advantage-taking is an injustice anyway. Again, the injustice consists in a wrongful gain in the absence of any wrongful loss. That regrettable state of affairs is yet another specimen of free-floating evil produced by exploitation.

5. *Petard-hoisting*. When *A* exploits the greed, dishonesty, cruelty, or similar other-regarding flaw of *B* to *B*'s loss and *A*'s gain, and does it (as in the Qaddafi example) without force or fraud but with the victim's own cooperative participation, there is no wrong done to the consenting "victim" and no wrongful exploitation of him as a person. Moreover, even the exploitation of his traits may be mere blameless utilization so that no free-floating injustice results. In that case, good comes from evil in a way that pleases rather than offends the moral sense. Even when the means used to help the villain hoist himself involve duplicity, as in the example from the movie *The Sting*, the wrong done him may be mitigated to the point that it it unclear that he was *exploited* at all, though perhaps we should be cautious and allow that there was exploitation, but maintain that the exploitation of a wicked person's wickedness is not exploitation of the more seriously objectionable kind.

6. *Unproductive cashing in*. The moral repugnance of cashing in stems from the perception that a person is making a good thing for himself out of an objective evil, as if he had a stake in something evil and welcomed its occurrence. The evil states of affairs that can be capitalized on are various, but the chief object of our attention has been the misfortunes or unhappy circumstances of others. When *A* exploits *B*'s desperate anxiety over his terminal cancer by selling him laetrile, or exploits *B*'s personal tragedy by making a

"titillating" film about it, he wrongfully utilizes (and therefore exploits) *B*'s unhappy circumstances. On the other hand, if he makes his huge profit by selling an effective drug for the control of symptoms in terminal cancer cases, or by making a sensitive film of high tragedy, or an excellent book of instructive history, out of another person's actual misfortune, the utilization of circumstances is not exploitative—at least not in the sense that would give *B* a moral grievance. *A*'s gain might yet be disproportionately great, in which case it might be said that he exploited *B*'s misfortune wrongfully to some degree. But if he did not overcharge *B* to do so (in the cancer case) or unnecessarily exacerbate *B*'s psychic wounds (in the film-book case), he probably cannot be said to have violated *B*'s rights or even to have exploited *him*, but only to have gained to an unjust degree. A contribution to charity of the exploitative surplus would set the moral balance straight, but that is hardly something *B* can demand. When cashing in is in this way exploitative, it is usually a free-floating evil, an injustice but not one that is unfair (necessarily) to *B*.

7. *Pandering.* To pander is to provide gratification for others' desires or tastes or propensities. The first panderer was Pandarus, the intermediary between Troilus and Cressida in Chaucer's *Troilus and Criseyde*, in whose honor the noun "panderer" came into use for go-betweens in love intrigues; "to pander" came to mean to provide a sexual partner for someone and to cater to someone's lust or other "moral weakness." Today it means not only to cater to others' moral weaknesses but to play upon others' defects of many kinds, with the usual suggestion of exploitation. The exploiter can pander to others' greed, vulgarity, lust, prejudice, or bigotry, all for the sake of his own personal advantage. Pandering too is a form of cashing in on an evil state of affairs. Normally the panderer gives the other parties what they want. He certainly does not treat them unfairly. He pleases them in ways that cause them no shame or regret, so he surely does not exploit *them*. But he does exploit (in the blamable sense) their flawed traits, and his profit from that is an injustice—a free-floating evil for the most part, except insofar as it has indirectly harmful effects on third parties. If political candidate *A* wins the election by pandering to the prejudices of the voters, he does not wrong the voters, but by wrongfully exploiting their prejudices he wrongs *C*, his opponent in the election, and does incidental harm to the democractic process.

Pandering to "human weakness" is a special case that deserves to be treated separately. The weak person doesn't *really* want to do what the panderer tempts him to do, but he succumbs to the temptation, against his better judgment. The panderer has not appealed to his "better judgment" but to his imprudent desires or corrupted tastes; that is precisely why we call the appeal "pandering." Still, the second party (*B*) cannot claim that the panderer (*A*) violated his rights simply by displaying or advertising A's wares. If B has later regrets, he can only blame himself, since the panderer did not force or trick him. Insofar as A has extracted his own personal advantage from B's acknowledged weakness, however, he has exploited that weakness without exploiting B, and his gain is unjust without being unfair to B. Once more, exploitation is a free-floating evil, and that evil consists in wrongful gain.

8. *Harmless parasitism.* Normally when A behaves parasitically in respect to B, A gains something that would otherwise go to B, so that his gain is B's loss. In cases of symbiotic parasitism, the gain A makes out of his relationship to B also benefits B, so that there is no exploitation in either direction unless one party's gain is disproportionately greater than the other's. Cases of an intermediate kind in which A's gain neither harms nor benefits B are relatively rare. The closest example we have found to a pure case was that of driver A guiding his way through the fog by following driver B's red taillights. (See Chap. 28, §3.) The first driver is not harmed by B, for if B had never appeared on the scene, A would have been no better off. Yet despite the lack of harm to his interests, A might understandably feel ill-used. The example is uncomfortably close to the "harmless" freeloading example discussed earlier, except that the element of cheating is not so clearly present. There is a kind of tacit promise made by train passengers to pay their fares and by motorists to stay out of forbidden emergency lanes. Perhaps a similar commitment is involved in the fog-driving case, but that is by no means clear. Driver B is less likely to think A is cheating on him, or taking advantage of his conscientious forbearance, than that A is simply using B's careful driving for his own gain. There may be a fine line between cheating and opportunistic labor-saving, but if there is such a line, it separates cases of A exploiting B from cases of A exploiting B's routine activities. The latter, if somehow evil, is a free-floating evil, not directly unfair to B, whose interests are unaffected by it.

More common instances of harmless parasitism are those in which the parasite's gain from using the byproducts of his host's normal activities is disproportionately great. In these examples, to be discussed below in Chapter 32, A does not violate any of B's rights and does not set back any of B's interests but makes so handsome a gain for himself that an impartial observer's sense of justice is offended. The intuition of free-floating injustice is likely to be stronger if A's technique of profit-making is unproductive of any genuine social value, or produces a disproportionately small social value. The gossip writer, A, who panders to the vulgar curiosity of third parties by simply reporting the routine activities of some celebrity is an unproductive parasite in this sense, but he does not (necessarily) violate celebrity B's rights or treat him unfairly.

9. *Passive unjust enrichment.* Examples range from A's deliberately omitting

to return *B*'s inadvertent overpayment of a debt, to *A*'s exploitation of the supererogatory diligence of his typist be declining to pay her more than the agreed-upon fee. From the moral point of view, the failure to return the overpayment hardly differs from deliberate fraud—cheating *B* out of what is rightfully his. The only difference is an insignificant one: *A* did not premeditate the cheating, nor take any active steps toward his gain at all. Still his "enrichment," despite its passive and unplanned character, was more than simply unjust; it violated *B*'s rights and treated him unfairly. There was nothing free-floating about that evil. On the other hand, the typist has a less direct and personal grievance (if any at all) against her exploiter. She made the agreement with *A* voluntarily, and he kept his side of the bargain. *She* was not wronged, therefore, by the injustice of *A*'s gain, but our sense of justice is rankled by the free-floating evil in this example that consists entirely in *A*'s wrongful gain.

In short, unjust gain appears to be a generic category of free-floating evil that can be produced by voluntary but unequal contests, manipulated (but voluntary) benevolence, unproductive cashing in on another's misfortune, pandering to others' vulgarity or "human weakness," harmless parasitism, and (some) unjust enrichment. And because this evil consists in a kind of injustice (wrongful gain), it can be interpreted as a moral evil, as well as a free-floating one. In that case, the aim of preventing wrongful gain as such is a good and relevant reason, according to legal moralism in a strict sense, for penal legislation prohibiting the appropriate sorts of exploitation—whether or not they unfairly cause harm. Since the other, more usual forms of strict moralism are implausible, and have been rejected in Chapter 30, we are well advised to give the present variant of that principle a distinct name—*the exploitation principle*—and interpret it to claim that those particular free-floating evils that are substantial enough to warrant criminalization of the behavior that produces them are certain types of *unjust exploitation*. That principle is legal moralism's last best hope.

32

The Exploitation Principle: Preventing Wrongful Gain

1. Legal enforcement

What if anything should the law do about exploitation? A large part of the question is easy enough. When *A*'s exploitative conduct is of a sort that could be expected to adversely affect *B*'s interest and is done without *B*'s voluntary consent, then it can be prohibited and punished by law in virtue of the harm principle. If it is the harm principle that legitimizes the prohibition, then the act is forbidden not because it is exploitative but because it is harmful. The harm principle alone could handle most cases of coercive and fraudulent exploitation, since these are objectionable because they harm a victim, or subject him to the risk of harm, without his voluntary consent.

The harm principle also can be stretched without strain to handle the cases of cheating and freeloading discussed in Chapter 31. When a cheater takes unfair advantage of the law-abiding forbearance of others to achieve a gain for himself, he may not directly cause harm to anyone, but if his conduct were to become common, then it would have immensely harmful consequences for social practices and institutions in which all have a stake. The ultimate rationale of rules proscribing such conduct is to protect us from social harms by preventing the frequent occurrence of cheating.

That leaves two troublesome categories: (1) when *A*'s conduct both exploits *B* and adversely affects his interest, but it is done with *B*'s fully voluntary consent, and (2) when *A*'s conduct exploits *B* without adversely affecting his interest (whether or not it was done with *B*'s fully voluntary consent). The former category is not covered by the harm principle as we have interpreted it, for that principle is mediated in its application by the maxim *Volenti non fit injuria*, so that "consented-to harm" is not to count as genuine harm for the purposes of the principle. If such conduct is to be prohibited at all, it would have to be on either hard paternalistic grounds—to protect B from the consequences of his own fully voluntary choices—or else on the grounds that *exploitation per se* is an evil of sufficient magnitude to warrant prohibition even when, because of consent, it does not wrong its victim. As we have seen, such consented-to exploitation might have tended to be unfair in the sense that, but for the victim's consent, it would otherwise have been actually unfair to him. But even though it was not unfair-on-balance to B (because of B's consent), it might yet be called *unjust* from the point of view of A.[1] Thus, one might argue that prohibition is justified to prevent *unjust gain* even when it is not necessary to prevent *unfair loss* (or "harm" in the sense of the harm principle). In that case, the coercion-legitimizing principle would be neither the harm-to-others principle nor legal paternalism, but rather a version of legal moralism that justifies the prevention of immoral gains even when there is no wronged victim.

Invoking the exploitation principle in this manner to justify legal coercion for cases in category (1) could hardly appeal to the liberal who has already rejected hard paternalism, for it amounts, in effect, to a kind of "back door paternalism," equally demeaning to personal autonomy. If B voluntarily challenges A to what in fact is an unequal contest (see Chap. 31, pp. 150 and 202), and A then exploits him by winning the contest and "taking his money," B has consented to the exploitation and suffered adverse effects, but he cannot be protected by the harm principle because A's unjust gain did not violate his right. When A is prohibited in cases like this from doing x to B on the grounds that even though x doesn't wrong B, it does adversely affect his interest, and that therefore A's gains (from B's voluntarily risked loss) would be exploitative, B *is still prevented from doing what he wants and freely chooses to do.* The liberal might well ask why this isn't as much a violation of B's autonomy (even though the prohibition and threat of punishment is addressed to A) as the same prohibition defended on outright (hard) paternalistic grounds? And if personal autonomy is the ultimate trump card when third party interests are not involved, we have just as much reason, in fact exactly the same reason, to judge the prohibition illegitimate in the one case as in the other.

The second troublesome category would even more clearly require a moralistic principle to justify its prohibition, for it includes cases in which there is wrongful gain by A without harm *in any sense* to B. Not only has the exploited party suffered no wrong, but he has not suffered any *de facto* loss, and his interests are in no worse condition than they would be had A not exploited him at all. If, nevertheless, the law were to prohibit (or otherwise render impossible) *A*'s conduct, it must be purely on the ground that exploitation *per se* is a prohibitable evil, that the prevention of ill-gotten gain is as legitimate an aim of the criminal law as the prevention of unconsented-to harm.

The principle that warrants the criminal prohibition of unjust gain (exploitation *per se*) even when it causes no unfair loss (harm) can be called "the exploitation principle" and defined as the doctrine that it is always a good reason in support of a proposed criminal prohibition that it will prevent unjust gain, even when that wrongful gain is not accompanied by any unfair loss. That principle is clearly a form of pure legal moralism since its aim is to prevent a kind of non-grievance evil, and it makes no ultimate appeal to the prevention of derivative harms. It is also a kind of strict moralism since the evils it would prevent are instances of immorality (injustice). It is not the most sweeping form of strict moralism, however, since it would not criminalize any and all immorality, but only unjust exploitation. It is important, as preliminary steps in our discussion, to distinguish the exploitation principle clearly from other, less reputable, versions of legal moralism, and to point out that frequently *it* is the legitimizing principle that is tacitly invoked in support of what at first sight appears to be paternalistic legislation. In the end, the liberal is committed to rejecting criminal legislation that is intended only to prevent "harmless exploitation," because such injustice is a non-grievance, even a free-floating, evil. But he may have to admit that in some instances it can put more weight on the scales than most other types of free-floating evil.

John Kleinig points out that in a number of jurisdictions a sharp distinction is made between self-regarding one-party crimes and two-party consensual crimes. Often the law seems to take a stand against paternalism in the one-party case, once satisfied that the individual has acted voluntarily, and yet refuses to accept his voluntary consent as a defense for his partner in the two-party case. "Thus in some places suicide and attempted suicide have been decriminalized, but aiding and abetting suicide have not. Similarly, possession and use of small quantities of marijuana have been legalized, but not its sales."[2] Sometimes, Kleinig points out, the official explanation of this asymmetry invokes "pragmatic considerations" about the difficulty of acquiring evidence, for example, or "the difficulty of being sure [in the two-party case] that the consent was full, free, and informed."[3] Pragmatic considerations may, of course, be involved in the full explanation, but it is hard to understand how they could include reference to any problem about the difficulty of verifying consent. Why should the voluntariness of an act of consenting be any harder to determine than the voluntariness of any other kind of act, for example the act of shooting oneself or the act of smoking a cigarette? Kleinig is right in suspecting that the true explanation goes deeper and that it is not so much concerned with preventing harm to the voluntary actor or consenter as with preventing exploitation or other wrongdoing by the provider or abettor. But when the abettors or providers do not themselves profit from their role, when, for example, the service is provided gratis out of sympathy or benevolence (as in mercy-killing), the object of criminal prohibition cannot be simply the prevention of exploitation.

In my view, there is at least a certain plausibility in making exploitation an independent target of criminal proscriptions, although, as I shall argue sketchily below, that plausibility is slight, and will rarely, if ever, outbalance the standing case for liberty. But when both wrongful harm *and* wrongful gain (exploitation) are missing, I can see no case at all for criminalization. If *A* plausibly believes he is doing *B* a favor by *giving* him some marijuana, then certainly he is not exploiting *B* for his (*A*'s) own good. And if the transaction followed *B*'s uncoerced and undeceived request, or *A*'s own freely made offer to which *B* happily consented, then, in virtue of the *Volenti* maxim, *B* can have no personal grievance against *A*. If the marijuana turns out to be physically harmful to him, that was a risk he freely assumed. *A*'s kindness to him may then have proved harmful to his health, but it certainly did not *wrong* him. Since no third-party interests are directly involved in this example, it would be an invasion of *B*'s autonomy to prevent the voluntary transaction, and even worse treatment of *A* if he were punished despite *B*'s consent. To punish *A* more than *B* seems downright perverse.

I am not sure that Kleinig would agree with this judgment. He denies that *B*'s consent to (request for) *A*'s action makes *A* a mere instrument of *B*'s will. Since *A* did not have to do as *B* requested, *B*'s consent does not relieve him of all responsibility for the consequences. From this, however, Kleinig concludes that "*B*'s consent to *A*'s act does not change the quality of *A*'s act in any significant way."[4] This seems to me to be an overstatement. To be sure, there is a sense in which all individuals are responsible for all their voluntary behavior. All individuals must answer, at the very least, to their own consciences for what they have done. For agreeing to do what he did for *B*, *A* is subject to moral judgment, at least on some ideal record, and it will be forever to his credit or blame, as a matter of record, that he acted wrongly or rightly, badly or well. What does *not* follow, however, is that *A* is answerable to *B* for the harmful consequences of his agreement to do, without thought of personal advantage, what *B*, with his eyes wide open, and his judgment unimpaired, freely requested of him. That, it seems to me, *is* a significant change in the quality of *A*'s act produced by *B*'s consent. If the law punishes *A* in this example, it can only be on paternalistic grounds: to "protect" *B* from the consequences of his own voluntary choice. The harm principle as mediated by *Volenti* would not justify criminalization, and the harm principle unmediated by *Volenti* collapses into paternalism. Whatever plausibility moralism has as a ground for preventing exploitation is absent in cases like this in which personal gain is not involved. If A were to be punished in this example, it would be for permitting another autonomous person to determine the acceptability of his own risks, and to do so in a manner that is not flagrantly irrational.

The moralistic element in the rationale for criminalization becomes more plausible, however, as A's own role becomes more exploitative. Kleinig's main concern is with cases in which A's own judgment of the probability of harm to B (or the reasonableness on balance of the risk of harm to B) differs from B's. B is willing to take his chance of losing from the transaction he proposes to A, and A thinks that B's willingness to assume that risk is foolish or rash. And yet there is likely profit for A in the proposed agreement, so he is willing (as the saying goes) to "take B's money." His expectation is then confirmed by the event; he acts as required by the agreement and exploits B's rashness for his own gain. B's interests are harmed, but B cannot complain that A wronged him since B consented in advance to A's conduct, without coercion or deception. Kleinig, however, won't let A walk away with his ill-gotten gain. A has blame and censure coming; he had no right to harm B's interests, even with B's consent, if he could have avoided doing so. So, even though B is in no position to complain of A's conduct, we disinterested third parties can condemn A for exploiting B's foolishness, and the moral record will contain the true judgment that he acted wrongfully in doing so. As Kleinig puts it: "The other's foolishness is something *he* will have to bear, but to exploit it is not to leave responsibility for the consequences on the other's shoulders alone."[5]

We can agree with Kleinig's moral judgment against A, however, without agreeing that the law has any business interfering with A and B in cases like this. Our moral disapproval of A is quite consistent with the judgment that it would have been wrong, and disrespectful to B's autonomy, for any third parties to prevent A from doing B's bidding in the first place.

The transactions we have been considering between A and B have three relevant variables that yield eight possible combinations, only four of which are interesting and controversial. The variables are (1) whether or not harm results to B's interests, and (2) whether or not B consents voluntarily to A's action, and (3) whether or not A's conduct promotes his own gain. The eight possibilities, then, are as follows:

1. B's interests harmed; B consented; A profits.
2. B's interests harmed; B consented; A does not profit.
3. B's interests harmed; B did not consent; A profits.

4. *B*'s interests harmed; *B* did not consent; *A* does not profit.
5. *B*'s interests not harmed; *B* consented; *A* profits.
6. *B*'s interests not harmed; *B* consented; *A* does not profit.
7. *B*'s interests not harmed; *B* did not consent; *A* profits.
8. *B*'s interests not harmed; *B* did not consent; *A* does not profit.

Combinations (3) and (4) can be dismissed from the present discussion since both are instances of *A* wrongfully harming *B*, and it is uncontroversial that the harm principle can validate prohibitions of wrongful harm-doing, whether or not the actor profits personally. Likewise, we can rule out numbers (6) and (8). In both these cases, *A* acts in a manner helpful or indifferent to *B*'s interests and without gain to his own. He may make a gift to *B* out of disinterested benevolence, having first asked *B*'s permission ("Will you accept this?"), or he might place money anonymously in *B*'s bank account without *B*'s consent. Both cases are examples of innocent behavior that should raise no problems for the law. Surely no one would argue that officious conferrals should be criminalized.

We have already discussed examples in the four remaining categories in which controversy is possible. In Chapter 31 we considered these combinations in a discussion of the unfairness that is often an element in exploitation. Here we must briefly consider whether there is a point in prohibiting actions in any of these four categories by means of the criminal law. Our discussion can hardly be conclusive, as it must draw on a very limited number of examples in each category, but it will be a start.

We have already looked at an example in the first category (1), that of the rash challenge (or acceptance of a challenge) to a contest or wager. *A* exploits *B*'s rashness and cockiness for his own profit and *B*'s loss. Depending on how we fill in the details, we can make *A* seem blameworthy for the way he uses *B*, or not. Surely Kleinig's tendency to censure exploiters of this kind is *sometimes* justified. Censure is especially appropriate if we think of *A* as exploiting an understandable and not altogether unsympathetic human weakness of *B*'s. But the phrase "human weakness" is subject to various interpretations. In the Devlin-Schwartz usage it refers to a universal tendency to indulge one's lower tastes in defiance of one's own governing standards. But *B*'s cockiness in the present example is neither universal nor inevitable; it is peculiar to *B*, part of his distinctive personality. In fact, it is a character flaw, albeit of a largely self-regarding kind—in short, imprudence. If we forbid others to exploit it at *B*'s expense, we remove one of the most reliable methods of correcting it to *B*'s own long-range benefit. *A* does not merely "take *B*'s money," he teaches *B* a useful lesson. As a consequence, *B*'s cockiness may be just a bit more subdued in the future.

The second category (2) includes cases in which *B* eventually suffers harm from what *A* did with his (*B*'s) consent, even though *B*'s initial consent did not seem to *A* to be a patently unreasonable acceptance of risk at the time. *A* acts either at *B*'s request (e.g., abetting suicide) or on his own initiative (offering marijuana), but with no thought to his own gain and no subsequent profit. No wrongful harm is inflicted upon a "victim" in this example, so the harm principle cannot warrant criminalization, and no moralistic principle aimed at exploitation has plausible application either, since no element of exploitation is involved, neither wrongful loss nor wrongful gain.

In the fifth (5) and seventh (7) categories are the motley cases in which *A*'s gain seems excessive, even though it does not cause a loss to *B*. The gain may come from a transaction to which *B* consented (category 5), such as pandering and passive unjust enrichment, or it may derive from activity for which *B*'s consent was not requested, or even from actions in defiance of *B*'s refusal to give his consent (both in category 7). Let us consider pandering again. Using prostitutes and reading or watching pornography are thought to be shameful by the bulk of the population, including no doubt many of the users themselves. Yet these practices, when voluntary, harm no one's interests and lead to considerable profits for the panderers. The sellers in these transactions are said to pander to a human weakness, but we must note that the exploited trait in question is nothing like the prudential character flaw of the cocky billiards player. Perhaps it is not so much a weakness or a character defect as it is simply a form of crudity or vulgarity, a kind of bad taste. Exploiting it for profit does not harm at all in a strict sense. At most, "Such conduct offends against an ideal of human excellence held by many people; that is why they condemn it."[6] And it offends people of high sensibility to see others getting rich by catering to it.

I can sympathize with that feeling of repugnance, but I cannot think of any principled way of translating the feeling into an argument for repression. Any such argument would be likely to warrant massive interference in human life. It is, after all, offensive to see people making a killing from exploitation films that not only pander to poor taste, but reenforce and further degrade it, or to see people reap profits from the mass production of expensive cosmetics, gossip magazines, or astrological horoscopes, thus exploiting such human weaknesses as vanity, morbid curiosity, and superstition. Other panderers serve our sentimentality, misplaced anger, or wishful thinking. In fact, the service of "human weaknesses" is perhaps our foremost growth industry. An affirmative program to elevate tastes and promote rational ideas of excellence would be a much more economical way of eliminating these evils than wholesale criminalization.

Passive unjust enrichments, like the author's gain from the supererogatory diligence of the underpaid typist in our earlier example (Chap. 31, §4), fits category 5 perfectly. The typist's interests are not harmed by the author's failure to pay a gratuitous bonus, and *a fortiori* the typist is not wronged by the author's keeping exactly to their bargain; and yet his gain from her zealousness is unjust and permits us to say that he took advantage of her. For all of that, the law cannot require the author to return the unjustly received benefit, or its equivalent, without encouraging an avalanche of officious conferrals and devious tactics for extracting profits from unwilling "beneficiaries." And if the law of restitution has no proper role in these cases, then all the more so is the criminal law out of place. No one could bring serious criminal charges against individuals on the ground that they stubbornly keep to the original terms of their bargains. That would make a mockery of the rules of contract.

Examples of cases in category 7 are harder to come by. Here we must think of *A* leaving *B* exactly as he found him, neither better nor worse off, after *A* has made his own gain by turning some aspect of *B*'s situation to his own advantage quite without any consensual agreement. The cases that come most readily to mind are not pure instances of unproductive parasitism, because third parties are involved—book readers or moviegoers—who benefit. I have already characterized the Mailer-Schiller use of the Gilmore tragedy in category 7 terms, but it has other distracting elements that may make it less than pure—the fact that among the traits exploited were grievous moral failings, for example, and that the exploited circumstances included extreme misfortune and suffering. A hypothetical example, therefore, may do better.

Suppose that an author with Mailer's talent writes a book about some lonely hero's inspiring life spent struggling against fearsome obstacles for the sake of some worthy goal. The author makes a huge killing in the bookstores but she never things of sharing a penny it of with the lonely hero. No wrong has been done the man, no promises broken, no harm inflicted. He has been left exactly as he was, no better, no worse, while the author used the hero's life for her own enrichment. Any sensitive observer can feel the injustice in this, but the problem of designing a purely legal remedy defies solution. We could allow suits for restitution, but if they are to put the moral universe back in equilibrium instead of making it further out of balance than ever, they will have to be governed by a novel complex of rules. Saints and heroes would have the right to restitution, apportioned to the degree of their moral excellence, whereas newsworthy villains would get not a penny of further profits from their moral crimes. Those who are newsworthy for reasons other than their moral excellence or moral failings would be rewarded with some intermediate fraction of the author's royalties. Those who are newsworthy because of some great good fortune that came their way would not be allowed to profit (much) more at the expense of the writer who brings their interesting

experience to the public. Those whose sufferings are used to whet the public's curiosity would be given a more generous share. In the end, the public
interest will be no better served by such rules and their inevitable misapplica-
tions than it would be by a system of distributive justice that allotted each
citizen's share of the economic pie directly, according to the principle that
"the good guys get the most, the bad guys the least."

One final point. Our survey strongly suggests that efforts to protect
persons from noncoercive and even, in some cases, harmless exploitation
characteristically invoke in their defense not legal paternalism but rather
legal moralism, a family of proposed justifying reasons that, in turn, is more
of a miscellany than many writers have noticed. As we have seen, legal
moralism is a class of legitimizing considerations that includes the need to
"enforce morality," the need to protect traditional ways of life, to prevent
inherently immoral states of affairs, and to prevent other inherent evils that
happen not to be harms or violations of individual rights. One form of
moralism that is frequently applied tacitly to the problem of consensual
exploitation justifies state interference on what might be called "perfectionist" grounds. (See *infra*, Chap. 33.) Its appeal is to the need to promote and
protect certain ideals of human excellence, even when those ideals are disso-
ciated from human interests and unlikely to produce gain or prevent loss to
any assignable persons. R.M. Hare describes this mode of argument in his
discussion of "whether it is wrong for a pretty girl to earn good money by
undressing herself in a 'strip club' for the pleasure of an audience of middle-
aged businessmen."[7] Questions of gain and loss, benefit and harm, advantage and disadvantage, he reminds us, are likely to seem quite irrelevant to
such moral questions:

> . . . those who call such exhibitions immoral do not do so because of their effect
> on other people's interests; for since everybody gets what he or she wants,
> nobody's interests are harmed. They are likely, rather, to use such words as
> "degrading." This gives us a clue to the sort of moral question with which we are
> dealing. It is a question not of interests but of *ideals*. Such conduct offends
> against an ideal of human excellence held by many people; that is why they
> condemn it.[8]

It is a form of legal moralism, then, to argue that the protection of some
ideal of human excellence can justify the legal prohibition of normally
harmless (because freely consented-to) conduct. One might be employing
this form of legal moralism if one argued that it should be illegal for *A* to
give *B* marijuana gratuitously and benevolently, or for *A* to help *B* commit
suicide entirely out of pity, or for *A* to pander even without personal profit
to *B*'s "weakness" for pornography. The principle that lies behind such
judgments is that it is a legitimate function of the state, through its legal

apparatus, to promote human excellence, cultivate virtues of character, and elevate tastes. This principle seemed self-evident to the ancients, but it is repugnant to modern liberals.

A second kind of moralism builds on the first but applies strictly to instances of consensual exploitation, that is, cases in which A turns some aspects of B's situation unjustly to his own advantage but does so without wronging B, since he either doesn't set back B's interest (as in parasitism) or he has B's consent (as in passive unjust enrichmen) or even B's full cooperation (as in pandering). The nonharmful evil that the law is entitled to prevent, according to this brand of moralism, is unjust gain, even when it is not, strictly speaking, gain at another party's expense, that is, gain correlated with the other party's wrongful loss. *It is bad enough that a person voluntarily undergoes degradation, according to this view, but it is much worse still that someone else should profit from it.* It is the element of deriving gain from an objective evil, even when that evil is not a harm in any relevant sense, that is said to justify, in extreme cases, criminalization. If the evil opposed by the first form of moralism is degradation of an ideal, the evil opposed by the second form is a type of injustice, namely, that which consists in a person becoming better off as a direct consequence of some evil.

I think we can agree that some voluntary transactions are degrading, and that degradation is an evil even when "harmless," and that exploitation of an evil for personal gain is a greater evil still. But none of these evils are necessarily harms, wrongs, invasions of rights, or personal grievances that people can voice on their own behalf. Exploiters can be made, in egregious cases, to disgorge their ill-gotten gains, thus cancelling the distributive injustice, but when restitution is not feasible, the evils that remain "float free," so to speak, without being wrongs to anyone in particular. They are, in a sense, "unjust" without being unfair on balance *to* anyone. Their free-floating character makes it doubtful indeed that they could ever be sufficiently evil to warrant legal coercion by means of the criminal law. That blunt and undiscriminating instrument, unless aimed at serious harms and wrongs, is quite likely to cause more evil than it can possibly prevent.

2. Harm principle rationales for exploitational crimes: insider trading and next-of-kin organ sales

Nevertheless, there are a number of common crimes now in our statute books that are difficult to explain except as efforts to prevent unjust gain, even when it has no proper "victim." For these actual crimes, the exploitation principle may constitute a part or the whole of the most plausible rationale we can reconstruct. In that case, the liberal must either discover or invent a more plausible liberal rationale, or argue that the criminal prohibitions in question are morally illegitimate.

The more typical prohibitions that raise the suspicion of an exploitation principle rationale are various offbeat commercial transactions, like the selling by next of kin of a dead person's bodily organs (cashing in), or the "insider trading" of securities in the stock market (taking unfair advantage)—unjustly profitable activities (it might be argued) that do not always have readily identifiable harmed victims. And, as we have seen (Vol. II, pp. 183–84, and *supra*, Chap. 31, pp. 187–188), Lord Devlin and Professor Schwartz were tempted to urge the criminalization of forms of sexual pandering to "human weaknesses," like the sale of pornography, as forms of unfair business practice (wrongful gain), even when the proscribed transactions are fully voluntary on both sides and arguably harmless. Indeed, there seems to be an undeniable tendency among legislators to assume that "the commercialization of an activity take[s] it outside the sphere of the principle of liberty and subject[s] it to public regulations."9

Part of the problem in identifying anti-exploitational prohibitions stems from the fact that most statutes have multiple rationales (see Vol. 3, Chap. 17, §4), and since the prevention of social harms is usually at least indirectly part of the legislature's motivation, it is rarely clear that the anti-exploitational rationale is essentially involved at all. One can suspect in many cases that the legislators found it offensive to contemplate certain morally unsavory gains and were happy enough to be able to "slap penalties" on them, and yet that they would not have passed the restrictive legislation (that pleasure notwithstanding) but for attendant social harms preventable by the legislation. A couple of examples will suffice to illustrate this possibility.

Insider trading is defined as "trading in securities while in possession of material non-public information . . . using for private gain certain key corporate information that could affect a company's stock, before that information has been disclosed to the public."10 When a company executive (or secretary, for that matter) is privy to a pending merger agreement with another company, he can expect the stock of at least one of the companies to rise sharply once the merger announcement is made. He can then buy at a low price and sell (after the public announcement) when the price is substantially higher, thus capitalizing on his secret information to make a windfall profit at little or no risk. Insider trading is both a civil and a criminal offense, and according to some writers that is because it is "a kind of robbery."11 But while it is unfair that other traders, lacking such information, do not similarly gain, and more unfair still that other insiders voluntarily forgo similar gains rather than violate trust, it is not clear in any given single case who is harmed, as opposed to deprived of a gain, and the robbery analogy is therefore a bit strained. To be sure, insider trading is very much like "playing with marked cards,"[12] except that in a card game cheating is usually correlated in a clear and direct way with another party's loss (not mere failure to gain). Insider trading has more pronounced similarities to other "harmless exploitations of trust," for example driving in an illegal lane to avoid a traffic jam[13] and other cases in which a personal gain is possible only because others can be relied upon to be too honorable to seek that gain themselves (See Vol. I, Chap. 6, §3, and Vol. IV, Chap. 28, §6). Nonetheless, such unfair advantage taking, if widely done by those who have the opportunity and temptation, would have disastrous results for everybody. "[I]nsider trading . . . threatens the foundations of the industry here and abroad. The S.E.C. is worried that if enough people play with marked cards, honest investors won't join the game."[14] The exploitation principle is not really necessary then to the rationale of criminal prohibition of insider trading. The harm principle is quite sufficient by itself.

Another *prima facie* example of the legal prohibition of "harmless exploitation" is the tendency of state laws to forbid sales (especially by next of kin) of cadaver parts, vital human organs that can be transplanted, if little time is lost, from the body of the newly deceased to the body of a needy patient. There are two possible ways in which such sales (as opposed to donations) might be arranged. The agreement can be made in advance by the patient before he dies, or it can be made after death by next of kin, if other laws have assigned them a property right to the bodily part in question. Most American states permit sales of either kind, but some prohibit sales of one kind but not the other, and only Massachusetts prohibits both kinds. Jesse Dukeminier summed up the situation in 1970:

> In almost all states there are statutes authorizing bequests of bodies, or parts of bodies, to medical science. Few of these statutes prohibit sale. Statutes in Delaware, Hawaii, Nevada, New York, and Oklahoma provide that no remuneration should be given the deceased but they do not prohibit the sale of organs by the next of kin . . . sale of cadaver organs by the next of kin appears to be more objectionable than is sale by the decedent himself, but such sales are prohibited by statute only in Massachusetts and Georgia.[15]

Why is Dukeminier so confident that sales by next of kin appear (at least initially) more "objectionable" than sales by the decedent himself, either while he is a stricken patient, or earlier, while he is still of sound body and emotionally undisturbed? Dukeminier could have doubts about the propriety of assigning property rights over bodily organs to mere relations of the person whose organs they were, as opposed (say) to the state, the community, or the hospital. But he does not here voice *those* doubts. He proceeds instead to give sound policy arguments (appeals to harm prevention) to support prohibition of next of kin sales. He introduces these policy considerations, however, by adding them on, so to speak, to a *prima facie* case against such sales derived from "the unsavoriness of the idea." So we must repeat our question in different wording: why is the very idea of next of kin sales of cadaver parts "unsavory"? If the decedent has left no testamentary instructions, or if he has consented in advance, and if the next of kin truly has a property right to the body after its original "owner" has died, then it would seem that the unsavoriness of his sale cannot stem from any violation of another party's rights. Thomas Grey suggests another source of the unsavoriness. He asks whether what makes the idea unsavory is "the same thing that would make it unsavory for surviving relatives to sell rights to a gossip magazine to cover an otherwise private family service for a deceased celebrity."[17] That "thing," it seems to me, is one and the same practice that we have labeled "unproductive cashing in" (Chap. 31, §§3, 6), one of the basic categories of unjust exploitation, and hence subject to adverse moral judgment, though it is not a very convincing ground, all by itself, for overriding private liberties through criminal prohibitions.

Dukeminier, however, does not claim that unsavory cashing in, all by itself, is a sufficient reason for prohibiting the sale of organs by next of kin. He claims, instead, that permitting such sales would have a variety of harmful consequences for medical practice:

> Apart from the unsavoriness of the idea, permitting sales by the next of kin may well result in great anxiety and fear on the part of the patient that his doctors and next of kin would not do everything possible to save him. It does not seem likely that such sales would lead to murder . . . organs will be useful only if they are removed immediately after death, and thus as a practical matter, organs for transplantation can be removed only from persons who die in hospitals. Nonetheless, permitting sales by the next of kin would increase the possibility that the dead man's wishes would not be carried out . . . Moreover, if sales were permitted, donations by the next of kin would probably decline. If payment is made to the next of kin in one case, the next of kin may well demand it in the next, and that demand will usually have to be met so that consent can be obtained. If donations of organs decline as a result, economic resources that could have been used elsewhere in medicine would have to be allocated to payment for organs so that transplantation can continue.[18]

Dukeminier's rationale for prohibiting next of kin sales then consists of arguments of two kinds. The permissive alternative gives an economic incentive to a relative not to carry out the decedent's wishes (as for example when the decedent does not wish "his" body to be cut open), and the general practice of next of kin sales would increase the cost and thus decrease the capacity for medical life-saving. Such sales then will increase wrongs done to unwilling decedents and increase the loss of salvageable lives, both of which are harmful consequences in the sense of the harm principle (though to some extent they seem to offset one another). Both kinds of reason are meant to influence liberal legislators who may have been prepared to overlook the unsavoriness of next of kin sales for the sake of individual freedom, but can be moved by more direct appeals to the harm principle. All legislatures except Massachusetts and Georgia continued (as of 1970) to permit such sales anyway, being unmoved both by the unsavoriness of the practice (as a ground for prohibition) and the claims of harmful consequences. Whatever the actual reasons of the Massachusetts and Georgia legislators (and they were no doubt diverse), there was a harm principle rationale for their prohibitory statutes, even though, in many instances, it may not have been *their* rationale.

More promising examples of exploitation-principle rationales for current criminal offenses might include prostitution (panderinig), and the sale, as opposed to the mere possession or use, of soft drugs. We shall conclude this chapter, however, by examining three more interesting, and utterly diverse crimes: commercial fortunetelling, ticket scalping, and blackmail.

3. Commercial fortunetelling

Telling fortunes for a fee is prohibited by numerous municipal ordinances throughout the country. There might be a case for reconstructing the rationale for this common criminal offense entirely on nonliberal (that is, either paternalistic or exploitation-principle) grounds. If a fortuneteller, A, takes advantage of B's superstitious credulity to make a profit at his expense, it might be argued, that is because B, like the ever hopeful gambler in an analogous case, has freely taken the risk of loss, and must be allowed his folly (provided he *understands* the risk and he is not mentally handicapped or otherwise impaired). If the state interferes with the gullible believer or reckless risk-taker, the argument continues, it can only be to save him from his own recklessness or gullibility (paternalism), or to prevent the party who exploits him from making a sordid or "unsavory" profit from his quite voluntary folly (the exploitation principle). B will suffer losses to A in both the gambling and the fortunetelling examples, but they will not be wrongful losses (since in both cases B freely consented to the transaction); hence the harm principle will not legitimize prohibition of the activities that led to them. Since we have already rejected legal paternalism (Vol. III), that seems to leave only the exploitation principle to provide a valid ground for criminalization.

If B (in the fortunetelling case) acts on A's phony advice or prophesy, he is even more likely to lose than if he plays roulette at the casino. In the latter case he may have a 40% chance or better of winning, but the chances of tea leaves or crystal balls truly predicting future events must, obviously, be less than that. Indeed, if B acts on the advice or prophesy then the profit of A may well be doubly at his expense. Not only will B be out of the fee he paid to A, but he may, let us suppose, apply the prophesy by betting on a losing horse or buying a failing stock. But consider that if precisely the same phony advice is given *gratis*, with precisely the same result, there is no exploitation since *A* does not gain. The transaction in that case could be a severe case of malicious mischief, but since there was no "unjust gain," it would probably not be a crime in most places. Thus the criminalization of *commercial* fortunetelling, it might be argued, seems aimed more at unjust gain than at unfair loss—at preventing a person from profiting from an act that would otherwise (without his profit) be legally innocent however detrimental. For that reason again, it might be supposed, its most plausible rationale is the exploitation principle.

A legislative defender of statutes forbidding commercial fortunetelling might reason in a different way. He might insist that harm (wrongful loss) is frequently caused or threatened in both types of case, both where a profit is made and where no fee is charged, but in the former case it is the further evil of unjust gain that tips the balance toward criminalization, though harmfulness is also necessary. But it is not just the unsavoriness of *A*'s gain as such that tips the balance, he might insist, but rather the unsavoriness of *A's gain at B's expense*. If we hold to the harm principle, he might remind us, even the criminalization of *noncommercial* fortunetelling could in certain circumstances be justified, or if that is too strong, the prevention of the malicious mischief it produces in those circumstances might well be a good and relevant reason for criminalization even though various practical considerations on the other side of the scale outbalanced it. The relevance of wrongful gain in the commercial cases, he might continue, is itself a matter for "practical considerations." If we hold, with our hypothetical liberal legislator, to the unsupplemented harm principle, it is not the moral unsavoriness of unjust gain as such that tips the balance toward criminalization. Rather, it is because only in the commercial cases are we likely to have confidence in our judgments of the wrongdoer's dishonest motivation and the victim's good-faith reliance on him; only in these cases will evidence be strong that the victim's agreement was less than fully voluntary (informed) because of fraudulent misrepresentation; only in these cases can we hope that the deterrent effect of the prohibition will make significant reductions in the type of harm typically caused by fortunetelling. Harmful fortunetelling is rarely done for reasons other than the fortuneteller's personal gain and is rarely harmful but for the fee that constitutes that gain, so (the argument continues) the law needn't bother with the rare cases of mischievous harm produced noncommercially.

In the still rarer noncommercial cases in which probative evidence *is* available of genuinely malicious intent and genuinely detrimental consequences to the victim, perhaps tort suits would be an efficient remedy. But the operational costs of the criminal apparatus in these cases would probably be too

great to justify the meager net reductions of harm. Deterrence will be sufficient, our liberal legislator might argue, if the threat of punishment is aimed
at the most likely right-violating harm-causers—those who are seeking personal gain. That would explain on exclusively harm-principle grounds why
activities that are innocent when done *gratis* become criminal when done for a
fee.

It may be, however, that even the harm principle, when unsupplemented
by legal paternalism or legal moralism, cannot legitimize the prohibition of
commercial fortunetelling. In order for there to be a harm in the sense
required by the harm principle, the perpetrator must both adversely affect
the victim's interest and wrong him, that is violate his rights. But if the
"victim" voluntarily consents to the perpetrator's activity, voluntarily pays
the fee, and voluntarily takes his chances, all in the absence of coercion and
fraudulent deception, then he has not been *wronged*, however adverse the
consequences for his interests. Most reasonable persons who consult fortunetellers presumably do so out of simple curiosity or hope of amusement. They
know that they may be disappointed by the experience, just as they may be
disappointed by any other form of commercial entertainment, but the price
seems to them low enough to justify the risk; if the disappointment is great
enough, they will not repeat the mistake, and, in any case, their *curiosity* will
be satisfied. These people are surely not *wronged* by the transaction, and even
the other element of harm—adverse effects on interest—will be minimal,
consisting entirely in the loss of the money constituted by the fee. If more
losses occur, say through betting on the wrong horse, or proposing to the
wrong woman, the ordinary "reasonable" person will blame himself for his
gullibility and be too embarrassed to charge the fortune-teller with fraud. He
might with equal folly charge the daily newspaper's publication of horoscope
interpretations, or a Chinese restaurant's serving of fortune cookies, or a
racing form's "best bet" recommendation, with criminal mischief.

Many California communities have nonetheless banned such activities as
those listed sweepingly in the City of Azusa's ordinance: "astrology, augury,
card or tea reading, cartomancy, clairvoyance, crystalgazing, divination, hypnotism, magic, mediumship, necromancy, palmistry, phrenology, phrophesy
or spiritual reading"[19] when done for a fee, on the grounds that these forms of
commercial fortunetelling are "inherently deceptive" and therefore not subject
to the protection of the California constitution's free speech guarantee (Art. 1,
2). Clearly, the Azusa city council did not have in mind our examples of
innocent entertainment and curiosity when it passed its ordinance against
fortunetelling. It would make no more sense to condemn the inexpensive and
entertaining type of fortunetelling as "inherently deceptive" than it would be
to condemn outright and in the same terms works of fiction, magic shows, or

fortune cookies. The legislators no doubt had in mind a different sort of customer, a person seriously concerned to learn what the future holds in some respect, and ready to pay a steep fee to find out. It is not easy to distinguish with precision the identifying marks of the two types of motivation for paying fortunetellers, but a convenient clue would be the size of the fee charged and willingly paid. People who can afford it might pay two dollars, or five dollars, or ten dollars to spend a few minutes with a gyspy crystal ball reader, but no one would pay five hundred, ten thousand, or one's life savings for so trivial a thing as amusement or "curiosity." The more serious customer thinks that he is purchasing a valuable commodity, namely, *vital information*, and, in his case, it becomes a matter of serious legislative concern to protect him from phony goods deceptively merchandized.

If the sorts of activities listed in Azusa's anti-fortune-telling ordinance *are* "inherently deceptive," then unsuspecting customers are deprived of thier money (the fee they agreed in their ignorance to pay) on the false expectation that the fortuneteller had genuine knowledge to sell to them, when the fortuneteller knew all along that he had no such knowledge. That would be like selling any other product through false claims knowingly made. It wrongs the customer and takes his money both, and, if he is credulous, it even makes him vulnerable to further adverse consequences like bad bets. So it would seem that *if* such activity is "inherently deceptive," then the harm principle legitimizes its prohibition. If fortunetelling is not necessarily deceptive in every case, then in those cases in which it is not, its prohibition can be legitimized only by legal paternalism or the exploitation principle.

Is fortunetelling inherently deceptive? Justice Stanley Mosk of the California Supreme Court thought not in his majority opinion in *Spiritual Psychic Science Church of Truth v. City of Azusa.*[20] In that case the court overturned a municipal ordinance banning fortunetelling for money ("consideration"), and enumerating, as in the quotation above, sixteen forms of fortunetelling as that term is to be understood in that statute, from astrology to spiritual reading, "or any similar business or art." This enumeration obviously makes the statute too broad and provides Justice Mosk with one of his more persuasive grounds for declaring it unconstitutional, for "spiritual reading" could include Bible lessons, "hypnosis" could include accepted psychotherapeutic techniques, "magic" might encompass various popular theatrical performances, and the ban on prophesy might apply to some religious services. What if a more carefully worded ordinance, however, were substituted for the badly worded original, one which did not mention "magic" or "spiritual reading" or "hypnotism" or "prophesy," but confined its attention to alleged techniques of foretelling (not scientifically predicting) the future, as for example through crystal balls, tea leaves, palmistry, or similar "occult arts," specifying more exactly what these objectionable practices have in common? Would, or should, that sort of statute pass muster?

The City of Azusa said that its ordinance did not interfere with free speech, since it banned fortunetelling only when done for money, and hence was a valid regulation of commercial activity. But the court had little difficulty showing that speech ("communication of information of any sort") does not lose its protected status when engaged in for profit. "It should be remembered that the pamphlets of Thomas Paine were not distributed free of charge . . . freedom of speech . . . [is] available to all, not merely those who can pay their way."[21] One of those who could not pay her way was the original plaintiff, Fatima Stevens, the duly ordained minister of the Spiritual Psychic Science Church, whose business license, granted originally for the purpose of conducting religious workshops and counseling (for consideration), had been withdrawn by the city when she was discovered to be practicing palm reading for a fee. "Stevens declared she had to charge a fee for telling fortunes because that was the source of her livelihood."[22] It is not revealed whether her customers were contributing to what they took to be a worthy cause in exchange for what they regarded as simple entertainment, or whether they were given serious predictions and advice, made impressive by the prestige of their spiritual leader; nor is it revealed whether they paid token or substantial fees.

The real constitutional issue is not whether speech loses its protection when given for consideration, but rather whether fortunetelling falls into one of the categories of speech not entitled to first amendment protection (e.g. fighting words, obscenity, defamation, incitement). Attorneys for the City of Azusa insisted that fortunetelling does belong in one of these categories, namely fraudulent misrepresentation. Citing another California precedent,[23] they argued further that "The ordinance need not necessarily be limited to cases involving an actual intent to defraud. It is within the police power of the municipality and province of the legislative body to determine that the business of fortunetelling is inherently deceptive and that its regulation or prohibition is required in order to protect the gullible, superstitious and unwary." That fairly sums up the view of the City of Azusa toward commercial fortunetelling. Anyone taken in by an "inherently deceitful" use of language, like a person who believes a lie, is wronged, and if he pays a fee, he is adversely affected, hence harmed.

The trouble with that argument is that no verbal falsehood is "inherently" a lie irrespective of the speaker's actual beliefs and intentions. Justice Mosk cites the California Civil Code's definition of fraudulent deceit (in part) as "The suggestion, as a fact, of what is not true, by one who does not believe it to be true,"[24] and points out that in civil actions, at least, predictions of the future are not actionable unless the speaker *knows* the prediction is unwarranted. So, in criminalizing some honestly believed, good faith prophesies along with the deliberate misrepresentations, the statute is in still another way overbroad. Mosk concedes that many or most actual fortunetellers *are* consciously fraudulent, but he is afraid that statutes like the Azusa ordinance will not only catch *them* in their nets, but also others whose predictions are made in good faith. (Mosk is confused, however, when he likens these supposed well-intentioned oracles to economists, investment counselors, sportswriters, and others who purport to predict events. *Foretelling* by inherently mysterious means a fixed future with all the clarity and certainty of direct perception is quite another thing than *predicting* with admitted fallibility, on the basis of empirical evidence, merely probable outcomes on the race track or in the stock market.)

How then can the public be protected from fraud without suppressing the constitutionally protected free speech of whatever honest fortunetellers there might be? Fortunately, no municipal ordinances against fortunetelling are necessary, Justice Mosk concludes, for statutory protection already exists:

> Penal Code section 332 provides that "any person who by . . . pretensions to fortunetelling, trick, or other means whatever . . . fraudulently obtains from another person money or property of any description, shall be punished as in the case of larceny of property of like value." Such a law prohibits unprotected fraudulent fortunetelling while allowing true believers to practice their art.[25]

Mosk's suggestion that this criminal fraud statute is an adequate remedy is "patently incorrect," however, according to Justice Lucas's partially dissenting opinion, for two reasons. First, the burden would still be on the prosecution to *prove* intent to deceive, a difficult matter to establish beyond a reasonable doubt. Second, and more important, "unlike a prohibition upon the practice itself, the penal laws operate only *after* it [the fortunetelling episode] has occurred and the fraud discovered."[26] By this time the swindler has usually long since vanished with his loot, and in any case the usually elderly victim may be too ignorant of the law, or too embarrassed, to complain to the authorities. When one considers the ruthless manner in which actual fortunetellers prey on the elderly retired citizens of southern California, who are "often the group most easily duped" and least able to afford it, Justice Lucas concludes, Justice Mosk's conception of "the guileless seer accepting money in exchange for bona fide attempts at prognostication,"[27] seems naive.

One solution to the problem posed by the Azusa case then will not do because it is overbroad, restricting the honest as well as the dishonest, and thus violating their free speech, while another offers inadequate protection to the vulnerable. Is there a way to avoid these difficulties? I can, with due modesty, make only a couple of suggestions. An adequate statute should recognize somehow the distinction between amusing or entertaining curious customers on the one hand, and seriously predicting the future and inducing reliance on that prediction in a client with serious hopes and expectations, on the other hand. There can be no legislative litmus test for applying this distinction, but since swindlers can be expected to seek rare gullible victims and charge them high (to them disastrous) fees, while mere entertainers appeal to general masses of people, as for example at carnivals or charitable functions, and charge easily affordable prices, the ordinance might take note of the size of the charged fee, and decree that any price above a certain maximum will be presumed to be evidence of fraudulent intent.

A second suggestion proposes a way to avoid the dilemma between overbroadness on the one hand and judicial "naivete" on the other. A well-worded ordinance would not mention such things as magic, and spiritual reading, but only palmistry, tea leaf reading, crystal ball gazing, and the like, avoiding the temptation to compile an exhaustive list of occult arts. "Fortune-telling" could then be the generic name for the class intended. Then, to give *some* protection to the alleged "guileless seers" who honestly believe they have the power to "see" the future, these activities could be characterized as "presumptively" rather than "inherently" deceptive. As Justice Lucas put it, "We [presumably "we judges"] may take judicial notice of the fact that such devices are routinely, if not uniformly used to bilk or fleece gullible patrons."[28] My proposal would allow legislators to "take notice" of this fact too, in assigning presumptions. The practical effect would be to withdraw the burden of showing intent to deceive from the prosecution and to assign instead the burden of showing good faith and honest belief to the criminal defendant as an affirmative defense.

We must pay attention to one other matter before leaving this topic, the inevitable analogy between fortunetelling and gambling. Justice Lucas claims that "Just as a community can protect its citizens from their own cupidity by passing anti-gambling ordinances, Azusa may protect its citizens from their own gullibility by passing an anti-fortunetelling ordinance."[29] This quotation vaguely suggests that the rationale for both prohibitions might be legal paternalism. In reply, the liberal would have us look carefully at the words "cupidity" and "gullibility." The liberal would leave persons free to wager, provided that they are protected against misunderstandings of the exact nature of the risk they are choosing to take, (see Vol. III, Chap. 20), just as they are free to engage in commercial transactions, providing their agreements are not based on misunderstandings or other voluntariness-defeating factors (e.g. feeble-mindedness). An excellent example of a misunderstood feature of an (otherwise) voluntary agreement is that which Richard Arneson finds in

William Faulkner's novel, *The Hamlet*: "Flem Snopes agrees to lend a dollar in exchange for payment of a nickel per week, for life." Arneson assumes that "the unfortunate buyer knows elementary arithmetic, but fails to utilize his knowledge on this occasion."[30] Similarly, one might know better than to stake a particular unpromising wager but make a foolish mistake about the odds or the like. Anti-gambling ordinances should be designed to protect gamblers from misunderstood risks trickily concealed, to guarantee if possible that all risks, even "unreasonable ones," are voluntarily and knowingly consented to. That would still permit gamblers to decide for themselves whether a given possible gain is worth a given risk of loss. That would appear to be different from "protecting them from their own cupidity."

Gullibility is a different kind of matter. Anti-fortunetelling ordinances protect those who can be persuaded by clever liars to believe what we can presume with near certainty to be false, and to place reliance on the falsehood and pay heavily for it. To protect a person from his "own gullibility" is to protect him from his vulnerability to cheating by others. It is analogous to protecting gamblers from agreeing to wagers whose terms they have failed fully to understand (as Snopes's debtor failed fully to understand the terms of the loan), not to forbidding gamblers from taking great chances in the pursuit of great gains. If a gambler fully understands what he is doing, the liberal state will leave it up to him how recklessly he will act in promotion of "his own cupidity"—at least up to the point at which his recklessness harms the interests of others.

4. Ticket scalping

Chuck and Hank are baseball fans who reside in a city whose team, for the first time in many years, has qualified for the World Series. Like thousands of their fellow citizens, they would like to see one of the games, but they would like even more to be in a position to resell their tickets, if they can make a large enough profit to compensate them for passing up the game. The baseball organization in their city announces that on Monday morning tickets will go on sale on a first-come, first-serve basis, at twice the normal game's price, with a limit of two per customer. Chuck and Hank arise at 4:00 A.M. that morning and an hour later they are near the front of a line that has already begun to form. An hour after the box office opens, at 8:00 A.M., each of them purchases two tickets at $20 each. As game time approaches, excitement mounts in the community, and hundreds of ticketless fans gather outside the stadium on the desperate chance that they will be able to purchase tickets, after all, for the officially sold out game. Chuck and Hank have no problem at all selling their four tickets for $100 apiece to some quite grateful fans. They have worked to achieve a certain advantage over others and then opportunistically "cashed in" on it for a net joint profit of $320.

Who was wronged in these transactions? Was it the owners of the baseball team, the original vendors of the tickets? It is difficult to see how their interests were adversely affected. They sold out their tickets for exactly the fixed price they had freely decided upon and made precisely the same profit they would have made had the "scalpers" never existed. They might have complained with some justice that the scalper's profit was *parasitic* upon their own labors, investments, and wise decisions, a way of making an "unjust gain" that, admittedly, did not cause an unfair loss (to them), but in the absence of such a loss, it is difficult to understand how they could have any grievance against the scalpers. They may have been "exploited" in some sense, but they surely were not victimized.

Perhaps the *purchasers* were wronged by the scalpers, but that seems even more farfetched. They were delighted to have the opportunity to make the purchase even at a greatly inflated price. Just as the scalpers preferred to have that amount of money to having the tickets, so the purchaser preferred having the tickets to having that amount of money. Thus the transaction pleased both parties. It might be replied, however, that the transaction was extortionate (or coercive, or unconscionable), like the owner of a well in the desert charging $100 for a glass of water to a lost hiker in danger of dying of thirst. (See Vol. III, p. 250.) There is, however, one strong disanalogy between these cases. Normal human beings *need* water; they have a vital welfare interest in having access to it; without it they are mortally harmed. Even the most fanatic baseball followers, however, if they are normal human beings, have no welfare interest (see Vol. I, Chap 1, §§1 and 7) in seeing a World Series game. If they are unable to do so, their desires may be frustrated and they may be keenly disappointed, but they will not be harmed. So when a scalper offers them a ticket for an inflated price, he is not threatening them with harm if they do not agree, in the manner of a criminal extortionist. Perhaps that is why some judges have declared that, unlike milk sales (say), which are "vitally affected with the public interest," resales of tickets to popular entertainments—presumably because they do not affect *interests* at all but only wants and desires—do not involve the public interest, and are not therefore subject to the exercise of "the police power."[31]

There are two ways, finally, in which one might argue that the general public, or specific *third parties*, are wronged by ticket scalping. In some circumstances, the resale of tickets to theatrical or sporting events might lead to noisy congregations of buyers and sellers at awkward places, for example directly outside the theatre or stadium on the day of the event, causing a public nuisance. Various town ordinances, therefore, restrict the resale of tickets to specific times and places to better "regulate the use of streets and sidewalks to prevent encroachments upon and obstructions to the streets and to regulate noises in the streets."[32] But that is quite another thing than prohibiting resales unconditionally, and less interesting, since it raises no fundamental problems about the underlying rationale of the law.

The other argument for the contention that ticket scalping wrongs third parties is more subtle. It might be thought that legal ticket scalping would deprive the general public, or those members of the public who are (say) baseball fans, of fair and equal opportunity to obtain admission tickets. Chuck and Hank took two places in line that might otherwise have been filled by Buck and Rick, the two unfortunates who were next up at the ticket window when the supply ran out, hours after Chuck and Hank made their purchases. Buck and Rick, if reasonable persons, might shrug their shoulders and attribute their failure to "the luck of the draw," or to the prompter efforts (no merely arbitrary distinction) of those who got to the ticket line earlier. But when they later learn that Chuck and Hank resold their tickets to two relatively wealthy buyers, who (let us suppose) slept late on the morning of the original sales, they may well become indignant. Being willing to get up earlier and suffer greater inconvenience to get the tickets may indeed seem to them a nonarbitary qualification for preference in the allocation. ("First-come, first-serve" seems an impartial principle of justice that gives most people a fair and equal chance.) But it seems unfair and arbitrary, not at all impartial, to permit rich people the luxury of getting the tickets without submitting to the same rigors as others, to make themselves exceptions to a fair system of allocation, simply because they have more money.

There is some merit, I think, in this complaint, but it would be very difficult consistently to exclude willingness to pay as a relevant qualification in other contexts. Suppose, for example, that the owners of the baseball organization themselves had decided to cash in on the intense public excitement by charging $100 per ticket and printing that as the fixed price on the tickets themselves. In that case, of course, the owners would be taking some risk that their sales would fall, perhaps to the point even of reduced profits, but such are the normal risks of business management. (And scalping too is not without such risks.) If a legislator argued that there should be a criminal ordinance against scalping in the one case, on the "fair and equal opportunity" rationale, he would find it difficult to explain why there should not be a comparable ordinance, in the other case, prohibiting sales for a substantially elevated price, or why wealthier people should not be deprived of the advantages generally bestowed by their wealth in the purchase, say, of luxury goods. It is more plausible to argue that wealth should confer no special privilege in the matter of life necessities like milk or medicine, but sporting and entertainment events are more like the luxuries, I think, than like the essentials.[33]

While there may then be some vague and diffuse wrong done to third parties by Chuck and Hank's type of ticket scalping, it is a kind of unfairness that probably cannot be eliminated if we are to hold on to our basic economic institutions, the kind of minor wrong that cannot consistently be removed from one part of our economic lives without being removed from many others with worrisome consequences. In any event, such "wrong" is not a constituent of a genuine *harm*, because another necessary component of any harm (as we are using that term) is probably missing: no one, with the possible exception of Buck and Rick, who wasted their time and effort, had his interest adversely affected (as opposed to having his desires frustrated).

A final possibility is that while Chuck and Hank's activities are harmless in themselves, they are such that, like those "harmless injustices" that exploit others' honorable forbearance, if everyone who could gain from engaging in them *did* engage in them, the consequences would be generally harmful. Indeed, as we shall see below, insofar as secondary distributors (brokers) begin to rival the primary distributors themselves in the number and size of their businesses, the state may have an interest in licensing and regulating the brokers to prevent fraud and collusion. Until that point is reached, however, the answer to the query, "What if everyone with similar opportunity, desire, and prospect of gain were allowed to do what Chuck and Hank did?" *might* be that things would not be substantially different from what they are now, because there aren't very many people who would think it worth their while to do what Chuck and Hank did. A prohibitive statute then would be unnecessary.

Should the liberal then argue for the legalization of ticket scalping? Some distinctions will have to be made first. The first and most important is between isolated transactions of small magnitude infrequently entered upon, on the one hand, and operating a business, on the other. Prohibitions in the former category (which incidentally would apply to Chuck and Hank's activity) are unlikely to win liberal approval, although that would depend of course on their exact provisions and the nature of the prevailing evils at which they purport to be aimed. Both liberalism and the United States Constitution require that prohibitory legislation be aimed at the proper kind of evil, that there be a reasonable relation between an existing evil and the remedy proposed, and that the remedy not be unduly oppressive. The eligible evils most commonly mentioned by the courts are adverse effects on public health, morals (here liberalism parts company) or safety. It would be very difficult to show how an eligible evil is involved in Chuck and Hank's case, or how a statute aimed at a broader class of genuine evils could find justifiable applica-

tion to them. And yet there are many state anti-scalping statutes[34] and municipal anti-scalping ordinances that forbid "any person" from reselling tickets at
a price in excess of that originally charged, irrespective of "essential differences in modes or in the volume of business transacted."[35] In some cases the
injustice of convicting individual persons for isolated transactions has led
courts to reject the prosecution's interpretation of the governing statute as
conflicting with the conscience of the court and contrary to natural justice.[36]

Sometimes the anti-scalping ordinance forbids resales (*any* resales by "*any*
person") without the prior purchase of a "ticket peddler's license." An old
San Francisco ordinance, for example, stated that "It shall be unlawful for
any person to sell in the city and county of San Francisco any theatre ticket,
or ticket of admission to any place of amusement or entertainment, at any
place other than the office of the management of said theatre . . . [etc.],
without having first . . . obtained a license to be known as a ticket peddler's
license," and further specified that the price of the license should be $300 per
month, and that any one reselling tickets must be prepared to produce the
license upon the demand of any police officer. In the 1920 case, *In Re Application of Dees*,[37] a conviction was overturned by the court which held that as a
police measure the ordinance was an unwarranted interference with liberty,
"not based on any reasonable consideration of the public health, morals, or
safety . . ." Mandatory licensing, then, of inappropriately regulated activity,
can itself be almost as severe a violation of liberty as outright prohibition and,
unless realistically related to an appropriate state purpose, invalid.

San Francisco later amended its ordinance to take account of the court's
complaint that its wording applied too broadly to all modes of selling without
considering essential differences in those modes and in the volume of business
transacted. In a later case,[38] the same person whose conviction had earlier
been overturned was arrested and convicted again, this time under the
amended ordinance. The court refused again on various grounds to uphold
the ordinance but did admit that the amendment had met one of its objections
to the original ordinance, the difference being that "before the change, it
purported to make it unlawful for any person to [re]sell . . . a ticket . . .
without obtaining a ticket peddler's license, and it now purported to make it
unlawful for any person *to engage in the business* of [re]selling tickets . . .
without obtaining a ticket peddler's license."[39] Drawing the line between
occasional "isolated transactions" and business practices, of course, cannot be
done with exactness, but the variables that determine its boundaries are clear,
most cases will be easy to classify, and in close cases a general statute could
give the benefit of the doubt to the scalper. Whether he is engaged in a
business will depend on such factors as the number of tickets he has for sale,
the regularity or frequency of his practice, whether he has a standard head-

quarters or place of sale, whether he holds himself out as a broker or adver-
tises his services, etc. His "business" may not have a name, but it is *de facto* a
business anyway if he sells off blocks of dozens or hundreds of tickets, sells
tickets every day, or even just every weekend, works out of a fixed office, or
passes out flyers or business cards. The essential contrast is between him and
occasional opportunists like Chuck and Hank.

Prohibiting all profitable resales unconditionally, then, is arbitrary and
unreasonable, not justified by the harm principle, and probably contrary to
constitutional requirements. Unconditionally prohibiting all *unlicensed* profitable resales is similarly objectionable. Prohibiting unconditionally all brokerage *businesses* is similarly illegitimate. But requiring the licensing of all brokerage businesses, it is said, is perfectly legitimate. If the license fee is not to be
exorbitant, and hence a covert form of oppressive and discriminatory taxation,
it must be no greater than what is necessary to cover the costs of regulatory
activity, e.g. investigation and enforcement. (Some statutes also require the
posting of bonds to "protect the public".) To be licensed is to be subject to
regulations which attach conditions on how the business may be conducted in
order to protect the public from "rampant abuses" or "predatory practices,"
like deceptive marketing, fraudulent misrepresentation, collusion (with owners), monopolistic powers, discrimination and (it is sometimes said) "extortion," although the latter usually consists in no more than charging whatever
the market will bear, a practice which is not considered abusive in other
commercial contexts, except when a vitally needed commodity is involved.

A liberal might ask at this point how brokerage businesses may be prone to
abuses to which isolated profitable resales are not, especially if "extortionate
pricing" is not in itself to be counted as an abuse. In a 1950 Pennsylvania
case,[40] "The court found it common knowledge that ticket brokers by virtue
of arrangements made with theatre owners ordinarily acquired an absolute
control over the most desirable seats and in some cases all of the seats in
theatres, and thus acquired the 'virtual monopoly' which the statute sought to
remedy."[41] Without regulation, the owner and/or the broker can lie about the
availability of seats, shuffle tickets back and forth to support the deception,
favor cronies, relatives, and special customers, and discriminate among the
public on less innocuous grounds than mere ability to pay, for example race
or sex. Bargaining for a higher price might be a legitimate practice in some
businesses, but accepting bribes (that is what it amounts to) to make a secret
exception to a posted fixed price is an abuse. Brokers may be specially
tempted to engage in these predatory practices by the encouragement of
theatre owners who accept "kickbacks" from brokers in exchange for choice
seats, thus fraudulently concealing from the public the true price of the
tickets. In that case, instead of providing a convenient service, for an addi-

tional fixed price, to enable customers to buy the owner's tickets at *his* announced price, the broker, if he his not strictly regulated, charges a much higher price in part to compensate himself for his secret payments to the collusive owner. If the customer chooses to go back to the owner's ticket office, perhaps at some inconvenience to himself, to purchase tickets at the original posted price, he may then be told that no good tickets, or no tickets at all, are left. The chief source of the wrong in these manipulations is that they are not aboveboard.

The need to prevent fraud and collusion, however, does not warrant the state's fixing upper limits on prices, except when the commodity or service is vitally needed. It does not harm public health, public morals, public safety, or public welfare, if World Series tickets are priced at $100. (Moreover, the public's hostility toward the owners would no doubt be very bad for their business, not to mention sales resistance, which would lead to market readjustments.) Nor would there be such frightful consequences if brokers, taking their own risks, adjusted their prices independently of the owner's original prices. The state might well regulate the manner in which these things are done, requiring, for example, prior notice and public posting, and commitment to a maximum price, once fixed, for a given time interval, but excessive pricing as such is no more a wrongful harm when done by entertainment companies and ticket brokerage firms than when done by private individuals in isolated transactions. Price controls that are not required by the public welfare are, as one court put it,

> arbitrary and unreasonable interference with the rights of the individuals concerned. The business of the broker in theatre tickets is no more immoral or injurious to the public welfare than that of the broker in grain or provisions. If he does not make the price satisfactory to intending purchasers, they are under no compulsion to buy . . . .[42]

In summary, we have concluded that it is illegitimate (1) to prohibit outright isolated instances of individual ticket scalping, and almost equally illegitimate (2) to prohibit all isolated instances of *unlicensed* ticket scalping. (Of course if it were licensed it would not be called "scalping"; it would be called "brokering.") We have concluded further (3) that it is illegitimate to prohibit all ticket brokering whether licensed or not, that is, to refuse to grant ticket brokering licenses and to prohibit outright all profitable resales. On the other hand, we have concluded that it is morally acceptable on liberal grounds (4) to prohibit all unlicensed brokerage *businesses*, that is, to require government regulation of the ticket brokerage business, at least insofar as that appears necessary to protect the public from fraud and other trickery, including underhanded and devious price manipulations.

It is now part of the American tradition of constitutional interpretation, as worked out over the years by the highest appellate courts, that "The right . . . to earn a livelihood in any lawful calling and to pursue any lawful trade or vocation is subject to the government right to require a license where justified under the police power [where for example the calling or trade in question is "affected with a public interest"], especially if the general welfare requires that the public be protected against such dangers as ignorance, incompetence, and fraud in the practice of the particular calling."[43] Thus, gas pumping and barbering do not normally require licensing because neither requires expert knowledge to perform nondangerously, and barbering, at least, causes no significant harm when performed incompetently. General penal statutes are quite sufficient to protect "the public" from dangerous barbers, with no need for further specific rules, like those of a regulatory scheme, defining competent service or reasonable and fair practice. Most American legislatures and courts who have looked at actual ticket brokerage practices have concluded that they are distinguishable from the likes of barbering in these respects and require closer monitoring, not because of the dangers of incompetence but because of the dangers of fraud. If they are right about the facts, then the harm principle firmly supports their licensing requirements.

It is important, however, to qualify this judgment immediately. Legitimate laws are not aimed at commercial opportunism as such, but at advantage-taking only when it is fraudulent, genuinely extortionate, or unconscionable, in which cases it is as clearly harmful as highway robbery, and thus prohibitable, either by criminal statutes or regulatory rules, under the harm principle. While there is an element of exploitative advantage-taking in ticket scalping, it is not clearly the unfair kind (see Chap. 31, §5), and where it may be accompanied by shady business practices, it is implausible to think that no rationale for regulating it can be construed that does not make reference to wrongful gain. Fraud and collusion are the concern of the law because of their tendency to cause wrongful *loss*.

5. The paradox of blackmail

Without closer examination it will seem that blackmail certainly should be a crime, and also that it should be a crime precisely because it severely harms and wrongs its victims. As blackmail is currently defined in our penal codes, however, it is disconcertingly difficult to show that its prohibition satisfies the requirements of the harm principle. It is more clear, at least at first sight, that the criminalization of blackmail does satisfy the exploitation principle and perhaps other forms of legal moralism. (Its many villainous practitioners in Victorian novels are among the sleaziest characters in literature.[44]) In its most egregious instances, blackmail is unfair advantage-taking for great profit. The blackmailer in those cases is an unproductive parasite who sells relief from a danger that would not exist if he had not created it. His opportunistic profiteering may tend to discourage crime and other wrongdoing, (or at least to make the wrongdoer more careful) but only by "threatening to capture its fruits for himself."[45] The blackmailer, in the worst cases, heartlessly exploits the vulnerabilities of his victim and unfairly pockets his loot. It is a free-floating evil, many people would judge, that *he* should make a big gain as a byproduct of someone else's crime or indiscretion, that he should profit unproductively from others' wrongdoing. That his gain is unjust seems clear.

Why is it not equally clear that the party from whom he extracts his gain is wronged as well as adversely affected by his conduct? His choice to pay the blackmailer is considerably less than fully voluntary since it was produced by the blackmailer's coercive threat to disclose information to others that will be at the least severely embarrassing, and at the most damaging to his (the blackmailee's) interests. The question is whether the threats are coercive enough in the circumstances to vitiate the blackmailee's consent, as a threat to kill him, for example, would be, or whether his consent, even though given under coercion, might yet be voluntary enough to provide the threatener with an exculpating defense. (See Vol. III, Chap. 20, *et passim.*) When we compare the blackmailer's threat with threats that *do* invalidate a victim's consent to money demands, we see one striking difference. The blackmailer threatens only to do what he has an independent legal right to do anyway, namely exercise his free speech in truthfully communicating information about his victim to interested third parties. The robber, on the other hand, when he demands money, threatens to commit a criminal act, namely to inflict immediate bodily harm or death (battery or murder) on his victim, something he has neither a moral nor legal right to do, and extortionists (other types of extortionists) threaten bodily harm in the future, or harm to other parties, harm to property, or even harm to reputation through *false* accusations, all of which are independently prohibited by the criminal or civil law. The robber and other extortionists, in short, threaten to do what they have no legal right to do, and then demand money for not doing it, while the blackmailer threatens only to do what he has a legal right to do, and then offers to refrain from doing so for a fee.

The complex fact that both the blackmailer's threatened act and the unconditional threat to perform that act would be legal, yet it would be illegal for him to demand money in exchange for *not* doing it, is now standardly called "the paradox of blackmail."[46] "The heart of the problem," as James Lindgren sees it, "is that two separate acts, each of which is a moral and legal right, can combine to make a moral and legal wrong." For example, "if I threaten to expose a sexual affair unless I am given a job . . . I have committed blackmail. I have a legal right to expose or threaten to expose the . . . affair, and I have a legal right to seek a job or money, but if I combine these rights, it is blackmail." However, "If both a person's ends—seeking a job or money—and his means—threatening to expose—are otherwise legal," Lindgren asks, "why is it illegal to combine them?"[47] The legal moralist who uses the exploitation principle has a ready answer to Lindgren's question. The whole is equal to more than the sum of its independently innocent parts, he may argue, because combining them creates the new element of *wrongful gain*. The "victim" is not wronged any more than he is by any hard commercial bargain which puts an exorbitant price tag on a much desired service (in this case, the service of silence), and his consent, even though subject to coercive pressure, would normally be voluntary enough to defeat the charge that the blackmailer has wronged him. But the chemistry of the combination of innocent parts has produced an unjust gain for the parasitic interloper that the state, so the argument concludes, cannot tolerate. The blackmailer (A), by taking money for not doing what he has a perfect right to do otherwise (reveal the truth about B), seems to be punished for making an unjust gain off of B rather than harming or wronging B.

Thus, the exploitation principle provides a rationale for blackmail laws where the liberal's unsupplemented harm principle finds only a "paradox." If the liberal cannot resolve his paradox by finding a harm principle rationale for blackmail that leaves the criminal law a coherent whole, then either he must grant validity to the exploitation principle, which as a form of legal moralism would be repugnant to his liberalism, or he must abandon the initial assumption of this section, deeply rooted though it seems to be in common sense, that blackmail should be a crime. The best hope of escaping this dilemma is to begin by making some distinctions. It may well be that once we distinguish the various meanings of legal "blackmail," the various mechanisms of blackmailers, the various types of threats and demands, it will turn out that only some types of blackmail are "paradoxical," and that only the nonparadoxical types fit the common-sense expectation of criminalization. In that event the liberal might be able to advocate decriminalization of some types of blackmail without embarrassment while offering a consistent liberal rationale for prohibiting other types. Before attempting to unravel the paradox of blackmail, then, we shall try to locate blackmail's place on the map of coercion.

6. The varieties of blackmail threats: a paradox lost

The terms "blackmail" and "extortion" are often used interchangeably in the law, although they were once the names of quite distinct crimes. Because of this confusion, many recent statutes avoid both terms and speak instead of various types of theft or criminal coercion. In ordinary discourse, however, blackmail has come to be identified with only one type of wrongful coercion, namely the attempt to extract money or advantage by means of a threat to disclose information about the victim, which, since it would embarrass or discredit him, he very much prefers to keep secret. Informational blackmail, as we might call it—blackmail in its commonly understood sense—can be contrasted with the various other kinds of wrongful coercion that have been called "extortion" in the law, those which back up demands with threats of future physical harm to person or property, or with threats to make *false* accusations of criminality—all of which are independently illegal. (In one of the older legal uses, "extortion" was reserved for threats by public officials like policemen or tax collectors made in their official capacities; see Vol. III, Chap. 24, §7.) Characteristically, but not always, the demand that is backed up by a threat in informational blackmail is for "hush money," so we can think of the paradigm of blackmail in the ordinary sense with which we shall be concerned as the demand for money backed up by a threat to disclose embarrassing or damaging information, either to specific third parties or to the general public.

Blackmail is generally classified as a crime against property, in particular, as a form of *theft*. Diagram 32-1 indicates blackmail's place in a classification of types of theft, and its relation to other types of robbery by coercion. Note that theft is the widest genus; that one of its species, robbery, can be by threat or by force; that robbery by threat can employ intimidation or the leverage of "blackmail or extortion" (where the generic terms are used interchangeably); and that blackmail and extortion (*other* extortion) can be distinguished in a number of ways, the most frequent and useful of which reserves the label "blackmail" for what we have called "informational blackmail." I shall follow the latter usage except where otherwise indicated.

Now we can distinguish five categories of informational blackmail corresponding to the types of secrets the blackmailer threatens to reveal.

Category 1. Threats to expose criminal wrongdoing. In the first category are threats to reveal to the police (truly) that the blackmailee has committed a crime and/or to present evidence or testimony in support of that allegation. This is a special case of blackmail, critically different from the threat to reveal merely embarrassing truths, for example, in that the blackmailer does not merely have a "right" to do what he threatens to do; he has a *duty* to do it (i.e., no right *not* to do it) which he would violate if he kept his silence, as he offers to do. Like all of his fellow citizens, he has a duty to cooperate with the police in the enforcement of the law, a duty also owed to all the rest of us insofar as

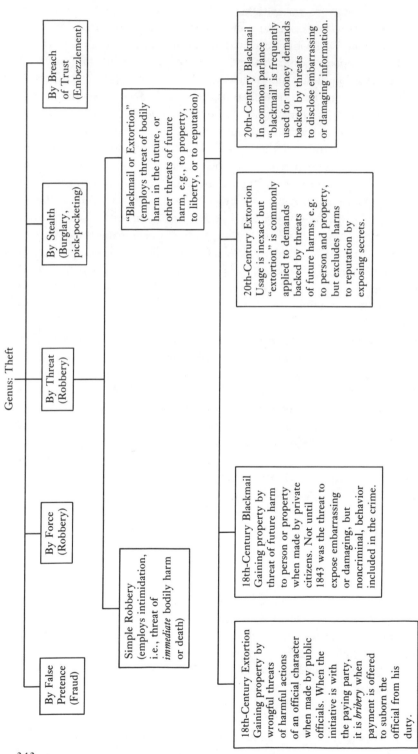

Genus: Theft

By False Pretence (Fraud)

By Force (Robbery)

By Threat (Robbery)

By Stealth (Burglary, pick-pocketing)

By Breach of Trust (Embezzlement)

Simple Robbery (employs intimidation, i.e., threat of *immediate* bodily harm or death)

"Blackmail or Extortion" (employs threat of bodily harm in the future, or other threats of future harm, e.g., to property, to liberty, or to reputation)

18th-Century Extortion Gaining property by wrongful threats of harmful actions of an official character when made by public officials. When the initiative is with the paying party, it is *bribery* when payment is offered to suborn the official from his duty.

18th-Century Blackmail Gaining property by threat of future harm to person or property when made by private citizens. Not until 1843 was the threat to expose embarrassing or damaging, but noncriminal, behavior included in the crime.

20th-Century Extortion Usage is inexact but "extortion" is commonly applied to demands backed by threats of future harms, e.g. to person and property, but excludes harms to reputation by exposing secrets.

20th-Century Blackmail In common parlance "blackmail" is frequently used for money demands backed by threats to disclose embarrassing or damaging information.

Diagram 32-1. The place of blackmail in the classification of crimes.

we are potential victims of the sorts of crime the blackmailee has committed. No citizen can be allowed to barter away his duties for personal advantage, or even offer to do so (the offer in this case being very much like an *attempt* at crime, itself punishable).[48] If the blackmailer has a duty to report the crime, he cannot claim that he is merely proposing an ordinary business deal when he offers to be derelict in that duty in exchange for money. The "paradox of blackmail" does not apply to his crime, because he is not simply charging a fee for "not doing what he has a perfect right to do." Rather he proposes not to do what he has a duty to do; he has no "perfect right" not to do his duty. A "perfect right to do *x*," we might stipulate, is a right to do or not to do *x* as one sees fit.

Furthermore, if the paradox of blackmail does not apply to category 1 blackmail proposals, there is no further difficulty for the liberal defense of their criminal prohibition, for the harm principle provides ample reason for such prohibitions. Category 1 blackmail is a practice that causes public harms (see Chap. 28, §9). Like contempt of court, bribery of policemen, suborna-tion of jurors, obstruction of justice, and deliberate concealment of evidence, it impedes the efficient operation of the criminal justice system in which we all have a stake. The "harm" incidentally caused to the not so innocent "victim"—the money that is periodically extracted from him by extortionate threat—is not the relevant "harm" here. From the public point of view, the category 1 blackmailer benefits his "victim" as much as he harms him, by enabling him to stay free of the police, and their joint agreement is detrimen-tal to the public.

There is admittedly a problem about the precise status of the duty to report crimes to the police. In our own system, it is not clear that this duty is enforced by the criminal law. There was a common law crime called "mis-prision of felony" committed by a person who knows of the commission of a crime and does not disclose it to the proper authorities. Perkins reports a "tendency for misprision of felony to be ignored at the present time,"[49] and quotes a typical judicial dismissal of it: "The common-law offense of mis-prision of felony, being wholly unsuited to American criminal law and proce-dure, was never a substantive crime in this state [Michigan]."[50] Even where misprision of felony is still found in American statutes, according to Perkins, "the words 'whoever. . .conceals' have been held to require something more than a negative failure to report the felony, some affirmative act of conceal-ment."[51] Another common law crime that might be thought to impose a legal duty to report crimes (and not merely not to "conceal" them) was called "compounding crime," which is committed by anyone who accepts money under an agreement not to "prosecute," i.e. bring charges against, a person he knows has committed a crime. Compounding was usually the settling out of court of a claim that was really the state's to make, since it involved criminal, not merely civil, violations. As such, it was not clear whether it could be committed by third parties, but modern statutes now make clear that a crime can be compounded by someone other than its victim.[52] If, however, there is no prior legal duty to report a crime as such, then the category 1 blackmailer who compounds another's crime by accepting money for not reporting it, might invoke the paradox of blackmail, and complain that he is merely taking payment for what he has a legal right to do (no legal duty not to do), namely refrain from reporting a crime.

Partly because of such difficulties, two recent writers of libertarian persuasion, Walter Block and David Gordon, have argued that there is no legal duty, in any sense, to report a crime, and that therefore the law creates an incoherence by criminalizing the blackmailer-compounder. They go too far, however, when they argue not only that the law does not (always) in fact impose duties to report crimes, but that morally speaking the law *cannot* impose such duties: "Just as the law cannot properly compel the individual to be a good samaritan, so can it not compel him to acquaint the legal authorities with the facts concerning crimes he knows to have taken place. Turning in the criminal may be an act over and above the call of duty, but it is not an act of duty itself."[53] In response I should point out, first of all, that even if a given penal code imposes no duty to reveal criminals to the authorities, or no duty to be a good samaritan even when there is no unreasonable risk in being one, it does not follow that there is some inherent difficulty in principle with such provisions. Several American states and most Continental European nations have "bad samaritan" criminal statutes, and misprision statutes are far from unknown. Moreover, the argument that there is something wrong or morally illegitimate in such statutes, that we *ought* not to have legal duties to rescue or to inform on felons, has not been persuasively made. (Indeed, I have argued emphatically in Book I, Chap. 4, on liberal grounds, that there ought to be bad samaritan laws.) Very likely, in fact, misprision of felony statutes have passed into desuetude, not because of moral misgivings, but because of the practical difficulties of enforcement, especially fear of underworld revenge.

In any event, even if there is no *legal* duty to reveal criminals, in the form of criminal statutes that require it or grounds for civil liability for failing to do it, it remains deeply misleading to say that the category 1 blackmailer is merely taking payment for not doing what he has a right not to do anyway. For our political system, itself defined not only by civil and penal codes, but by our constitutional documents and traditions, clearly imposes a *civic duty*, a duty of citizenship,[54] to cooperate with law enforcement, even when that duty is not specifically enforced by the criminal or civil law. It is to assert a false proposition in this democracy to say that a citizen is morally free, with a "perfect right" to cooperate with law enforcement or not, as he sees fit, unless under direct threat of legal punishment. The requirement to report criminals is a civic duty presupposed by our legal system and implicitly recognized by it in many ways, even in some cases by blackmail statutes that forbid accepting pay for doing what the *criminal* law does not explicitly forbid.

Category 2. Threats to reveal that the victim has engaged in, and continues to engage in, perfectly legal but devious trickery or underhanded dealing. Blackmail threats in this second category concern truly discreditable behavior the exposure of which to the general public would quite justly damage the "victim's" reputation. The blackmailee may be a wily womanizer whose reputation is undeservedly good. If he is exposed to the group that contains possible future victims of his harmful but legally innocent exploitation, then his mischief will be more difficult to produce. Or the blackmailee may be a merchant whose underhandedness falls short of outright fraud (which of course is illegal) but misleads unwary customers into purchasing inferior products for inflated prices, or a doctor who strings patients along, collecting high fees for unnecessary office calls, before confessing his inability to provide what the patients seek. The state provides no remedy for these wrongs, relying instead on the marketplace to set things straight. A bad reputation, after all, is bad for business.

Morally, a person who is aware of someone's underhanded dealing may very well have not only the right but a duty of public spiritedness to warn others. Such a duty would be analogous to the civic duty imposed by the political system to report criminals to the police, except that it is *merely* moral, having no quasi-official status or tacit recognition by the law. At the very least, people have the legal *right* to expose noncriminal trickery, the choice to expose or not as they please. A sufficient reason for not imposing a legal *duty* to do so is that it is practically difficult to draw the line between the public-spirited exposer and the gratuitous interloper. Moreover, the act of exposure can be risky even though not as dangerous as informing on genuine criminals. What seems clear, in any event, is that there are cases in which the exposure of perfectly legal wrongdoing would be a socially useful thing and something that ought to be done. If the personal risks in such a case are minimal, then the would-be blackmailer is blameworthy for taking money not to do it.

Despite the lack of moral justification for category 2 blackmail, the attempt to justify its criminalization stumbles over the paradox of blackmail. The difference between category 2 and category 1 in this respect is slight but critical. The legal system tacitly recognizes a civic duty to report criminals even when, for practical reasons, it does not threaten liability for not doing so, whereas the duty to report legally innocent wrongdoing is one that it does not officially endorse. It does, on the contrary, recognize a legal right (liberty) to expose legal trickery or not as one sees fit, provided, of course, that the accusations are true. Therefore, to criminalize category 2 blackmail would indeed be to prohibit the extraction of money by a threat to do what it would be legally permissible to do, namely speak the truth about a wrongdoer. To preserve the coherence of a criminal code, *either* the threatened disclosure should be made independently illegal, that is, illegal in its own right quite antecedent to any blackmail threat, in which case the threat to make that disclosure unless one is paid hush money could be unparadoxically prohibited, *or* the disclosure as such should continue to be independently permissible (a valid exercise of free speech), in which case blackmail could be unparadoxically permitted. In other words, if we make disclosure independently illegal then we can ban blackmail because it uses the threat to do something illegal to extract a gain, and if we legalize the disclosure as such, then we must legalize blackmail too since it only uses a threat to do what is legally permitted, in order to extract a gain. We cannot on liberal grounds independently criminalize category 2 disclosures since they do not wrongfully harm anyone and indeed may indirectly work to prevent harms by putting potential victims on warning. Therefore, we cannot on liberal grounds punish category 2 blackmail either.

It is interesting to notice in passing that if category 2 blackmail were legal, then one form of deterrence of wrongdoing, the warning system, would be weakened, since some tricksters could buy off their exposers, but another form of deterrence would be strengthened, since no one who is tempted to underhanded dealing would want to share his ill-gained profits with a bloodsucking blackmailer. So the rough calculus of indirect social harms and benefits would be indecisive. The main reason for criminalizing, and the only remaining one really, would be provided by the exploitation principle, but even it would not apply with its normal strength since, as we have seen (Chap. 31, §6), "the exploitation of a wicked person's wickedness is not exploitation of the more seriously objectionable kind."

In all the cases summarized in Diagram 32-2, the proposition that *A* makes to *B* can be put either as a conditional threat or a conditional offer. When put as an offer it emphasizes something presumed to be relatively beneficial or advantageous to *B*. The diagram brings out the significant differences between category 1 and category 2 blackmail.

With the possible exception of homosexuality, more people have been blackmailed for marital infidelity than for any other reason. It is very hard to know, at least in our own socially complex age, whether the threat to expose adultery falls in the second category or not. Adultery is no longer a crime in most jurisdictions, and the statutes penalizing it that still exist are no longer

Gunman Case (Criminal Coercion)

1. *A* threatens to shoot *B* unless *B* pays fee to *A*.
2. *A* offers not to shoot *B* if *B* pays fee to *A*.

Thus, *A* demands payment for not doing what he has *no* legal right to do. He threatens to do something illegal. He offers to honor his legal duty not to kill. There is no paradox in prohibiting this kind of conduct.

Protection Racket (Extortion)

1. *A* threatens future damage to *B* unless *B* pays fee to *A* now (and regularly).
2. *A* offers not to inflict future damage on *B* if *B* pays fees to *A* now.

Thus, *A* demands payment for not doing what he has *no* legal right to do. He threatens to do something illegal. He offers to honor his legal duty not to damage another's property. There is no paradox in prohibiting this kind of conduct.

Category 1 Blackmail ("Misprision")

1. *A* threatens to disclose *B*'s crime to the police unless *B* pays fee to *A*.
2. *A* offers not to disclose *B*'s crime to the police if *B* pays fee to *A*.

Thus, *A* demands payment for *not* doing what he has a legal duty to do. He "threatens" to honor his legal duty (or civic duty) of disclosure. *He offers to do something contrary to the law.* There is no paradox in prohibiting this kind of conduct.

Category 2 Blackmail ("Paradoxical")

1. *A* threatens to reveal a damaging truth about *B* to the public unless *B* pays fee to *A*.
2. *A* offers not to reveal a damaging truth about *B* to the public if *B* pays fee to *A*.

Thus, *A* demands payment for not doing what he has a legal right to do. (Legally, he may disclose or not disclose as he sees fit.) Both his threat and his offer are to do something legally permitted. There is an apparent paradox in prohibiting his conduct.

Diagram 32-2. Summary of conclusions about the first two categories of blackmail propositions.

enforced. The threat to disclose an adulterous affair then is certainly not a category 1 threat. It is not always true that exposure of adultery would be socially useful, or that the damage done to the exposed adulterer or to his or her spouse would be justly deserved, and even where that damage would be just and proper, it is often impossible for the exposer to *know* that. To be sure, in most cases adultery is an act of betrayal, of faith-breaking, or "cheating." The ill-used spouses are wronged in these cases even if their ignorance protected them from some of the adverse effects on personal interest such cheating can cause. There is almost always then a *prima facie* wrong done, but so many other subtle and morally relevant factors may be involved that no mere outside observer can know whether the *prima facie* wrong is outbalanced by other morally relevant reasons. So it would be to take high *moral* risks to expose an affair, even when the circumstances seem relatively clear. The threat to expose adultery therefore cannot simply and automatically be placed in the second category, although there must surely be many cases such that if one know enough about the motives and circumstances of the participants, one would so categorize them.

In Victorian and Edwardian England, where blackmail for sexual indiscretions was a major industry,[55] the blackmailer's most potent threat was to publish the embarrassing facts and thus ruin the offender's respectable reputation, especially among his peers, business associates, and others in a position to harm or reject him. Today, at least in the United States, the ideology of respectability is in eclipse, and no one (except perhaps an ambitious politician) is likely to have his career, much less his whole life, ruined because his private sexual life, even his infidelities, are publicized. Indeed, the fact that the respectable classes in Victorian England were so susceptible to disgrace, and disgrace for so many kinds of reasons, explains how blackmail was able to flourish, and blackmail in turn was an ugly symptom of a cultural disorder: an excessive concern, backed by enormous emotional investment, in one's "good name," right down to the most trivial detail. One effective way to weaken blackmail, more economical than criminalization, is to weaken the scope and power of that concern. In our own day, the blackmailer's most potent threat is to reveal marital infidelity, not to the world at large (which is likely to be indifferent) but to the cheated spouse, and the more ashamed the adulterer is, the more potent the threat is likely to be.

Should the blackmail of adulterers be made a crime? I am inclined to think that the benefit of the doubt should go to liberty in this close case. What makes the case close is our doubts about whether a given instance of adultery falls in category 2 or not, a doubt really about the prior distribution of moral rights and duties among the related parties. There is an argument that deserves our respect for the judgment that all adultery-blackmail is immoral since it must necessarily violate someone or other's rights. Either the cheated spouse has a right to know, the argument begins, or he does not. If he does have such a right then a third-party observer has a duty to transmit the unhappy news to him, and it would be wrong to conceal it in exchange for money. If he does not have such a right, the argument continues, then it would be wrong to violate the adulterer's privacy by revealing her secrets spitefully if the blackmail threat fails. If the blackmailer has a duty to the husband (in this example) to inform him, then he does not have a duty to the wife to keep silent, and vice-versa, so once he undertakes the path of blackmail, he is bound to default a duty to one or the other. So the argument goes. But the argument has false premises. The third party observer may *neither* have a duty to inform the spouse *nor* a duty not to. It may be "morally risky" to intervene at all, but whether he does so is up to him. No *law* requiring or forbidding his disclosure would be justified (the analogy with the "samaritan's" duty to rescue is strained). So the blackmailer is within his rights morally, and ought to be within his rights legally, if he informs, and equally within his rights if he does not inform. Surely most of those who advocate criminalization of adultery-blackmail would not also advocate legislation making it an independent crime to inform betrayed spouses; nor would they advocate prior legislation making it a legal *duty* to inform betrayed spouses. They cannot have it both ways. *Either* the blackmailer should have a duty to inform (or a duty not to, as the case may be) in which case it would be consistent to prohibit him from threatening to violate that duty unless paid off, *or* he should have no legal duty one way or the other, in which case it would be incoherent to punish him for threatening to do what is within his legal rights. I conclude that adultery-blackmail (since there is no reliable way of knowing in a given case that it is not in category 2) ought not to be criminalized.

Category 3. Threats to expose some innocent characteristic or activity that is not objectively discreditable but would in fact damage the victim's reputation in some benighted group if it were disclosed. In this third category are various threats to expose matters that the victim should not feel ashamed of, an adult's bed-wetting problem, a southern white's black grandmother, a sensitive or troubled person's continuing psychoanalysis, an ambitious person's humble or "illegitimate" origins, a respectable person's homosexuality. (Some instances of marital infidelity might belong in this category also, but because it is usually impossible for an outsider to know which, moral judgment is hazardous.) The number of traits and activities that could be the basis for category 3 threats was much larger in Victorian times and was itself a symptom, I have suggested, of a cultural disorder—the grotesque overvaluation of respectability.[56]

Neither third parties nor the public in general need to be warned about category 3 activities for their own protection. Otherwise, an informed person might have a duty, morally speaking, to expose them. But exposure would only embarrass or hurt them without "protecting" anyone else (how can it protect *me* to learn that *you* are a bed-wetter?). Whatever basis there may appear to be for some people lowering their esteem for the person with such a "flaw," that basis does not include dangerousness to others or even direct offensiveness to others. There is then no plausible ground for positing a moral duty to disclose the embarrassing information. In fact there is good reason for affirming a moral duty *not* to make the disclosures, which is to say that one does not have a moral right to do so. Thus it would appear, morally speaking at least, that one may not in this way extract money by threatening to do what one has no right to do.

Legally speaking, however, the situation is less clear, and the paradox of blackmail looms menacingly again. A person has no independent duty imposed by the criminal law either to disclose information or not to disclose information of the category 3 kind. One is therefore at liberty, so far as the criminal law is concerned, to disclose or not disclose as one sees fit, and no doubt that is as it should be. Nor is it plausible, in these cases, to posit an implicit "duty as a citizen" either to disclose or not to disclose, analogous to the civic duty to report crime. If there is any duty of citizens at all, then, in respect to these private matters, it must find its source in the private law. After all, the law of torts too can be said to impose duties, though it does not enforce them with criminal sanctions. The law of negligence, for example, imposes a duty—a *legal* duty—of care, and sanctions it by the prospect of civil liability. One does not have "a perfect legal right" to be negligent, or defamatory, or a nuisance. If there is a similar duty to be found in the law of torts to refrain from revealing the intimate secrets of category 3—even secrets that are not truly discreditable—then category 3 blackmail would involve forcing money payments from a victim by threatening to do something one has no legal right to do, and its criminalization would not be paradoxical. Such a duty will not be found in the civil law of defamation because a defamatory statement must be *false* in order to be actionable, and category 3 revelations are perfectly truthful. The most plausible place to look for such a duty, I think, is in the law of tortious *privacy* invasions.

"Violation of privacy" is a general term for at least four quite distinct torts,[57] but the one that is clearly most relevant to our purposes is the public disclosure of private information about the plaintiff, "even though it is true and no action would lie for defamation."[58] The disclosure must be a public disclosure, not merely a private one,[59] and that would leave private disclosures to the spouse of an adulterer within the protection of the law, but the damage of the *clearly* category 3 revelations does consist in the facts getting out to a more general audience. Another requirement of our present law is that the public not have "a legitimate interest in having the information made available,"[60] a requirement that would serve to mark off category 3 from category 2 disclosures. A third requirement is that the disclosed true information "would be highly offensive and objectionable to a reasonable person of ordinary sensibilities."[61] This obscure phrase, I think, refers to a hypothetical plaintiff who is not hypersensitive to what others may know and think of him, and whose upset state of mind on learning of his "exposure" is quite understandable. He may find the information highly embarrassing in its own right, or he may understandably fear that it will damage his standing in some group with power over him, even though it is not truly discreditable (i.e., not such that a reasonable person would think less of him for it).

We can now begin to unravel the paradox of blackmail as applied to category 3 threats. If a certain factual disclosure would lead to civil liability for privacy invasion, then there is a clear sense in which that disclosure is not permitted by law even though it is not subject to criminal sanctions.[62] (That the criminal law is silent about some kind of conduct does not imply that it gives a person some sort of tacit license to do what is elsewhere in the law forbidden.) The category 3 threats in large part *are* threats to invade privacy and therefore to do something prohibited by law. The category 3 blackmailer's threat in support of a money demand is often, therefore, a threat to do something he has no legal right to do, which is to say that he threatens to do what he has a legal duty *not* to do. There is therefore no "paradoxical" incoherence in a law that criminally prohibits category 3 blackmail. Indeed, the criminal law would be incoherent if it *legalized* blackmail threats to invade privacy, for the law in that case might permit a person (A) to demand payment from B for omitting to do something which is such that if he did it, B could legally demand payment (compensation) from *him*.

An advocate of decriminalization, however, might still not be satisfied. He may admit that complete legal permissiveness toward category 3 blackmail would not coherently fit in a legal system that allowed civil damages for privacy invasions. But he may point out that there is a middle way between total permissiveness and criminalization, namely providing a tort remedy for the blackmail itself. He may be driven to this ingenious proposal by a lurking suspicion that it is not yet *fully* coherent to *criminally prohibit* the support of money demands by threats to do what is *criminally permitted*. It would make better sense, he insists, to "civilly prohibit" the supporting of money demands by threats to do what is civilly prohibited.

I agree that this would be a tidier, more symmetrical solution, although I don't agree that it would be more coherent. Let us pause for a moment to imagine how it might work. The blackmail victim would already have the counterthreat of a privacy suit with which to confront his blackmailer, so an additional cause of action, the projected civil blackmail suit, would be redundant, except perhaps for establishing aggravation for punitive damages. The blackmailer A tells B: "I will publicly reveal X unless you pay me $10,000." B then can reply: "I welcome the opportunity to keep X secret by making this payment, but I would much prefer to have my privacy and my money both.

Therefore I refuse to pay you, and I threaten you, in turn, that if you reveal
X I will sue *you* for $10,000 for invading my privacy, and furthermore I will
cite evidence of this blackmail attempt and claim $100,000 more in punitive
damages." One thing B is unlikely to do is to threaten an immediate suit for
damages for an independent blackmail tort even before there is any release of
information, since that would lead to an unnecessary revelation of his secret
during the trial. The privacy suit, on the other hand, would take place only
after the beans have been spilled anyway. An independent tort of blackmail
shares this problem with the remedy of criminal prosecution for blackmail.
The victim would have to initiate the legal action in both cases, and he might
be deterred by fear that his secret will become public during the proceedings.
The civil action would have the advantage in some instances, at least, of
providing him with ample pecuniary compensation for his embarrassment,
although his persecutor may have inadequate funds for this purpose.

Whatever we decide about the desirability of allowing this new civil action,
however, there is no real reason why we should not keep the blackmail threat
a crime, since in theory the victim's rights could be protected by either or
both sanctions. When a blackmailer backs up a money demand with a threat
to do something that is legally prohibited (if only by tort law) his conduct is
legally recognizable as extortive, that is as a coercive use of a threat to do
something that one has no legal right to do as a way of forcing a victim to
relinquish his property. It is therefore an attempt at *theft* (by extortion), and
there is no "paradox" in treating it as a crime.

At this point, the skeptical reader may be inclined to admit that I have
resolved the original paradox in category 3 cases, but only by replacing it
with another paradox quite parallel to it. The traditional paradox of blackmail
consists of the following three propositions and the felt tensions ("inconsisten-
cies" might be too strong a term) between them:

1. S has a legal right to do X.
2. S has a legal right to make an unconditional threat to do X.
3. It would be a crime for S to demand money in exchange for not doing X.

Now, as Tom Senor puts it (in unpublished correspondence), I resolve the
controversy by arguing that in category 3 cases, proposition 1 is false. But
why, he goes on to ask, is the following parallel triad not equally a paradox?

1. S has a right with respect to the criminal law to do X.
2. S has a right with respect to the criminal law to make an unconditional
   threat to do X.
3. It would be a crime for S to demand money in exchange for not doing X.

This is a recasting of the original paradox that appears to survive the point
about tort liability. To be sure, it does not show that the legal system as a

whole contains an incoherence, but only that there is an incoherence restricted more narrowly to one of its branches, the criminal law.

There is no reason, however, why we should restrict our attention so
narrowly. The *prima facie* anomalous status of category 3 blackmail within the
penal code is explained, and thus dissolved, by showing that the criminal law
is only a part of a more comprehensive system of rules and remedies. The
coherence of the larger system is preserved by showing that its different parts
are assigned different but complementary jobs. Senor's second triad appears
paradoxical because its first proposition does not seem to fit with its third
proposition. The criminal law leaves *S* free to invade another's privacy and
then forbids him to threaten to exercise that freedom in support of a request
for money. But the reason the *criminal* law leaves him free to invade privacy is
that his legal duty to refrain from such conduct is backed up by civil not
criminal sanctions. Presumably the reason why this is so is one of practical
convenience in the administration of law. The important point is that "the
law," so far from leaving *S* free in this respect, imposes a duty on him to
refrain, and then as a matter of policy chooses to enforce that duty through
noncriminal mechanisms. There remains a problem in explaining why sanctions of these different kinds are deemed appropriate for their respective
forms of wrongful behavior—why privacy invasion is only a tort whereas
category 3 blackmail is a crime, but absent the striking prima facie inconsistency, is it only a problem not a "paradox."

Whatever appearance of paradox may attach to Senor's second triad van-
ishes when we consider defamation rather than privacy invasion. Consider
the following propositions:

1. *S* has a right with respect to the criminal law to say *false* and damaging
   things about *Y* to others.
2. *S* has a right with respect to the criminal law to make unconditional
   threats to say *false* and damaging things about *Y* to others.
3. It would be a crime for *S* to demand money from *Y* in exchange for not
   saying *false* and damaging things about him to others.

No one would deny that it should be a crime to threaten defamation (defined
as *false* and damaging statements) in support of a money demand (category 5
blackmail) (see below). This conviction might seem anomalous because of
proposition 1, which seems to report an independent legal right to defame.
But such a right is an illusion caused by an inappropriately narrow perusal of
the legal system. In fact there is *no legal right to defame* in our legal system, but
rather a *clear legal duty not to defame* found only in the tort law branch of the
system. The fact that no such duty is included in the criminal codes does not
show that it is included nowhere in the system, or that the criminal law's
silence itself confers on us a special kind of legal license. It shows only that

the mechanism of enforcement of the duty (probably for theoretically uninter-esting practical reasons) is civil rather than criminal.

Category 4. Threats to expose the past mistakes of a currently reformed person. The more common threats in this category include threats to expose past member-ship in a radical political party, or to reveal that a person is an ex-convict, or to disclose that someone bore a child out of wedlock as a teenager and gave it up for adoption. These examples are much like those in category 3 in an important respect. The revelations can not only embarrass a person but also damage her reputation in certain benighted circles in a way that could be harmful to her interests. Given that the person has outgrown her youthful errors and is now genuinely reformed, she does not deserve to have her past held against her; she has paid her bill and her slate is clean. Still, the threat of exposure may force her to pay a blackmailer to be silent. The blackmailer in these cases can truthfully argue that he threatens nothing illegal. He does seem to have a legal right to make the disclosures if he chooses. He would certainly not incur *criminal* liability if he did. Nor would he incur civil liability for defamation since what he says is true. Nor would a civil action for invasion of privacy be possible since what he reports is part of the public record (you could look it up), and so, in a relevant sense, consists of public rather than private facts. It is open to the liberal, however, to argue that there *ought* to be a civil remedy for such moral wrongs, so that he can argue for criminalization of category 4 blackmail without being thwarted by the para-dox of blackmail. To avoid that paradox a person must argue that either category 4 blackmail should be legalized (since the blackmailer threatens to do only what it is legal to do), or else the threatened disclosure should be made independently contrary to law, in this case to the law of torts. The liberal who advocates preserving the criminal status of category 4 blackmail then has a strong motive to make a case, if he can, for imposing an independent duty through tort law to refrain from malicious disclosures (relevations serving no proper public purpose).

The introduction of such a tort is by no means a new idea. Various commentators, over the years, have considered modifying the truth defense to defamation charges in such a way as to protect reformed persons, among others, from maliciously motivated harmful revelations. In an earlier article I favorably summarized the case for a new "malicious truth" remedy with rather more optimism than was justified by subsequent events:

> In the large majority of American jurisdictions, truth is a "complete defense" which will relieve the defendant of liability even when he published his defama-tion merely out of spite, in the absence of any reasonable social purpose. One wonders why this should be. Is the public interest in "the truth" so great that it

should always override a private person's interest in his own reputation? An affirmative answer, I should think, would require considerable argument.

Most of the historical rationales for the truth defense worked out in the courts and in legal treatises will not stand scrutiny. They all founder, I think, on the following kind of case. A New York girl supports her drug addiction by working as a prostitute in a seedy environment of crime and corruption. After a brief jail sentence, she decides to reform, and travels to the far West to begin her life anew. She marries a respectable young man, becomes a leader in civic and church affairs, and raises a large and happy family. Then twenty years after her arrival in town, her neurotically jealous neighbor learns of her past, and publishes a lurid but accurate account of it for the eyes of the whole community. As a consequence, her "friends" and associates snub her; she is asked to resign her post as church leader; gossipmongers prattle ceaselessly about her; and obscene inscriptions appear on her property and in her mail. She dare not sue her neighbor for defamation since the defamatory report is wholly true. She has been wronged, but she has no legal remedy.

Applied to this case the leading rationales for the truth defense are altogether unconvincing. One argument claims that the true gravamen of the wrong in defamation is the deception practiced on the public in misrepresenting the truth, so that where there is no misrepresentation there is no injury—as if the injury to the reformed sinner is of no account. A variant of this argument holds the reformed sinner to be deserving of exposure on the ground that he (or she) in covering up his past deceives the public, thereby compounding the earlier delinquency. If this sort of "deception" is morally blameworthy, then so is every form of "covering up the truth," from cosmetics to window blinds! Others have argued that a delinquent plaintiff should not be allowed any standing in court because of his established bad character. A related contention is that "a person is in no position to complain of a reputation which is consistent with his actual character and behavior."[63] Both of these rationales apply well enough to the unrepentant sinner, but work nothing but injustice and suffering on the reformed person, on the plaintiff defamed in some way that does not reflect upon his character, or on the person whose "immoralities" have been wholly private and scrupulously kept from the public eye. It does not follow from the fact that a person's reputation is consistent with the truth that it is "deserved."

The most plausible kind of argument for the truth defense is that it serves some kind of overriding public interest. Some have argued that fear of eventual exposure can serve as effectively as the threat of punishment to deter wrongdoing. This argument justifies a kind of endless social penalty and is therefore more cruel than a system of criminal law, which usually permits a wrongdoer to wipe his slate clean. Others have claimed that exposure of character flaws and past sins protects the community by warning it of dangerous or untrustworthy persons. That argument is well put (but without endorsement) by Harper and James when they refer to ". . .the social desirability as a general matter, of leaving individuals free to warn the public of antisocial members of the community, provided only that the person furnishing the information take the risk of its being false."[64] (Blackstone went so far as to assert that the defendant who can show the truth of his defamatory remarks has rendered a public service in exposing the plaintiff and deserves the public's gratitude.)[65] This line of argu-

ment is convincing enough when restricted to public-spirited defamers and socially dangerous plaintiffs; but it lacks all plausibility when applied to the malicious and useless exposure of past misdeeds, or to nonmoral failings and "moral"
flaws of a wholly private and well-concealed kind.

How precious a thing, after all, is this thing denoted by the glittering abstract
noun, the "Truth"? The truth in general is a great and noble cause, a kind of
public treasury more important than any particular person's feelings; but the
truth about a particular person may be of no great value at all except to that
person. When the personal interest in reputation outweighs the dilute public
interest in truth (and there is no doubt that this is sometimes the case) then it
must be protected even at some cost to our general knowledge of the truth. The
truth, like any other commodity, is not so valuable that it is a bargain at any cost.
A growing number of American states have now modified the truth defense so
that it applies only when the defamatory statement has been published with
good motives, or is necessary for some reasonable public purpose, or (in some
cases) both. The change is welcome.[66]

The welcome I expressed in this passage was premature, and for practical
reasons the changes I described might be difficult to implement, but from the
moral point of view I still think they would be desirable. Were they made, the
category 4 blackmailer could no longer say in his own defense that he is
threatening to do only what he has a perfect legal right to do, since the new laws
would impose a legal duty on him, civilly sanctioned, to refrain from malicious
or spiteful revelations. If his threatened revelation had as its sole purpose to
extract money from the reluctant victim, that alone would argue for its malice;
if the harmful truths were actually revealed because of the victim's refusal to
pay, that would argue quite conclusively for their spitefulness.

*Category 5. Threats in any of the other categories to make accusations that are known
to be false.* It would surely be criminal blackmail without paradox for *A* to
demand money from *B* under threat of denouncing him as a Communist, and
making the threat credible by showing or implying the existence of fabricated
and perjured evidence. Lest this seem farfetched, the reader should consult
the history of blackmail prosecutions, from which he may learn that category
5 is prominently represented in the record and may even be the most common species. At one stage in the development of English criminal law, robbery, a capital offense, was defined as the taking of property by threat of
actual violence to the person. Since this was thought to leave loopholes, in the
eighteenth century the list of threats was expanded, case by case, to include
the threat to destroy the victim's home by mob violence, and the threat to
accuse the victim, truly or falsely, of sodomy. The latter was the first threat
to "character" (reputation) to be recognized as an instrument of theft, and the
only kind of threat (such was its terror) to be punishable by death when used
to extract money. In the Victorian period, the heyday of blackmail, one of

the most common forms of the crime (which had by then changed its name to blackmail, or "demanding money with menaces") involved the *false* accusation of "sodomitical practice" supported by trumped up evidence and fraudulent manipulation. The following example of the racket is typical:

> On 7 May 1895 at Marlborough Street police court in London a hairdresser recalled that he went into a lavatory in Oxford Market, London, and coming out was accosted by a youth of about 17. The following series of incidents were then unfolded to readers of "The Times":
>
> The Youth—"Can you give me a drink please Sir?"
>
> The Hairdresser—"A drink boy! Why should I treat you? Where do you come from?"
>
> The Youth—"I am out of work and hard up."
>
> The hairdresser said he then attempted to get away from the boy, but two men came and caught him by the arms. They stated they were detectives and were going to take him to the station. He replied "I will come, but for what I don't know," to which they responded ominously: "For some Oscar Wilde business." Turning then to the boy the detectives asked, "What has he been doing with you in the lavatory?" The boy started to cry and said "I will give you five shillings to let me go." Eventually he agreed that the hairdresser had "something to do with him" in the lavatory. At this point one of the detectives expressed his reluctance to arrest the hairdresser: "You are a man of position and I should not like to mix you up in this sort of thing." As they walked along, one man on either side of the hairdresser holding him by the arms, he was asked "What are you going to do to settle it?" A law-abiding man, the hairdresser replied that he did not want any settlement at all but would go to the police station with them. They then said "We will make it pretty thick for you, my Lord. You had better settle it."
>
> At that moment the victim realized his captors were not policemen, called two passers-by to his aid and the would-be blackmailers disappeared. They were later arrested and jointly charged with demanding money with menaces.[67]

This typical blackmail scheme involved more than the threat to publish information. It also had elements of false accusation, perjury, fraud, and impersonation of police officers. It was in fact an elaborate confidence swindle. Not a trace of "paradox" remains in cases of this sort. Even without the more egregious manipulation involved in the example, category 5 blackmail is unproblematic and unparadoxical. A person has no legal right to falsely accuse another of a crime. To do so is itself to commit a crime. Nor is there a legal right to publish false and defamatory allegations of legally innocent conduct or of disreputatble characteristics, no right at least that will protect one from civil liability. It follows that the criminalization of category 5 blackmail does not mean that one is prohibited from taking money by threatening to do what the law considers an innocent exercise of free speech. Hence, there is no paradox in the prohibition, and since the prohibited conduct is of a kind that violates the rights and sets back the interests of its victims, its criminal prohibition is, on liberal grounds, morally legitimate.

In summary, I have argued in this section that only category 2 blackmail involving threats to warn the public of legally innocent underhanded dealing need be legalized to preserve the overall coherence of a legal system. Coherence could be preserved otherwise only by the independent criminalization of disclosures of the category 2 type (or independent creation of a duty to make that kind of disclosure), and the harm principle, not to mention the first amendment, would not warrant that. The other four categories, however, are instances of attempts to force payments by threats that are legally extortive, since they threaten to do what is contrary either to the criminal law or to the civil law, or to what *ought* to be forbidden by a legal rule of one kind or another. Admittedly, the five categories are not finely drawn, and there are many cases that will be hard to classify without further refinements. So the fivefold classification is not a practical model for legislative draftsmanship, but it does reveal, in a rough way, how in principle one can resolve the paradox of blackmail without being committed either to the exploitation principle and its legitimization of the punishment of wrongful gain as such, or to the complete decriminalization of informational blackmail.

7. The varieties of blackmail demands: justified blackmail

So far, we have considered only informational blackmail in support of hush-money demands, and there are good reasons, in this limited space, to restrict ourselves to that class of criminal extortions as our major concern. But it would be highly misleading to leave our discussion of blackmail without a quick survey of the various types of *threats* in addition to threats to reveal information; of the various types of *demands* in addition to demands for money or property; and of the various types of *means* employed in addition to single-shot random opportunism. To neglect these further distinctions would leave readers with a distorted impression of simplicity, and, in particular, blind them to the many modes of justification that may be invoked by accused individuals for using modes of coercive leverage which in more standard circumstances should be condemned.

The question to which this book is devoted is: What crimes would it be morally legitimate for a legislature to create?, not: What crimes, all things considered, ought a legislature to create? And the answer I have been trying to defend is: Only conduct that causes harm or offense to others *and* whose prohibition would not create an incoherence in an otherwise liberal penal code (e.g., would not stumble over the paradox of blackmail). Surveying the moral complexities in actual blackmail transactions may convince us either that an adequate statute would recognize an elaborate set of justificatory defenses, or that listing and refining all the acceptable justifications would not be worth the trouble since it would make the law too cumbersome to enforce, while excessive reliance on judicial or jury discretion as an alternative would make the law too vague and unpredictable. In that case, a legislature might be justified on balance in legalizing large categories of blackmail, even though their criminalization, if only it were not impracticable, would be morally legitimate on liberal principles.

Non-informational blackmail may employ threats of an endless variety of kinds, some of them to do things that are clearly contrary to law, some not. There should be no legal prohibition of typical demands that are backed by threats to demote, fire, or flunk, such as "Come to work on time or I'll fire you," or "Do better on your next exam or I shall have to flunk you." The demand, the threat, and the action threatened are all separately legal, and their combination is clearly acceptable. On the other hand, "Sleep with me or I'll demote you," and "Pay me $100 or I'll flunk you," are clearly abuses of authority that should be forbidden. But in these cases it is not what is threatened that makes the act extortive and violates the victim's rights, so much as what is demanded, though the demand would be permissible if not backed up by a threat, or even if supported by a minor threat, as in "Sleep with me or I'll stop bringing your coffee" or "I won't like you any more." Clearly then, whether a coercive threat is severe enough, and wrongful enough, to be extortive is a function both of the nature and degree of the threat and of the nature and degree of the demand, and not just of the one considered in abstraction from the other.

In some paradigmatic cases, however, namely those involving abuse of power or authority, the threat itself in support of *any* personal demand, is condemnable. Certain types of negotiating are simply not open to the office-holder or authority; he may not use his public powers for *any* merely private gain without violating trust. The labor leader who threatens to call a strike unless the employer makes him an under-the-table personal payment violates not only the right of the employer (his "victim"), but even more the rights of the union members he represents and whose trust he betrays in a way that may defraud them of their rightful gains. In Lindgren's words, "The blackmailer is negotiating for his own gain with some one else's leverage or bargaining chips."[68]

Let us now turn our attention away from threats to misuse authority, passing by those philosophically less difficult threats that the law has always considered extortive, such as threats to use violence against persons or property, and consider only threats to reveal information. In that way we can hold the threat-variable constant while we survey the morally bewildering variety of *demands* that can be backed up by the threat of exposure. One distinction that will cut across all the others we make among types of demand is that between independently warranted and independently unwarranted demands. For example the "demand" (it could be a mere request if considered independently of any threat that might be used to support it) for money, or for a job, or for a favor, or for return of what is due one, are all independently warranted, so the full demand-threat proposal of which they are parts will itself be morally permissible provided the *threat* is not unwarranted (like the threat of violence). On the other hand, the demand (request) for military secrets is *not* warranted, even if supported by legitimate threats or by no threats at all but only enticing offers of reward, as in bribery. Blackmail demands, and the contexts in which they occur, vary in many other ways, but perhaps the following rough classification will be useful.

A. *Demands for property or other pecuniary or personal advantage.* The demands in this category are independently warranted, but the back-up threats, as we have seen in §6, may be either warranted or unwarranted, legal or illegal. Several subclasses can be distinguished.

   1. *Hush money.* "Unless you pay me $1,000, I will reveal your secrets." This is the paradigmatic example of criminal blackmail and, with the exception of category 2 threats, it is rightly prohibited.

   2. *Other pecuniary advantage.* "Make me a legal partner in the firm or I will tell the world we spent last night together."

   3. *Improved status or power.* "Promote me to office manager, or I'll tell. . ."

   4. *Third party advantage.* "Promote my nephew or else. . ."

B. *Demands for independently unwarranted behavior.* Some actions tend to be wrong in whatever circumstances they occur, morally mitigated if done under severe threat, perhaps even excused if the threat is extreme enough, but when considered independently of the threats that prompted them, are always "unwarranted." Most of the actions in this category are illegal as well.

   1. *Demands that one do what is independently criminal.* This subclass includes demands backed by blackmail threats that one kill, maim, beat, rape, or rob, and (much more typically), that one betray secrets, including military secrets to be transmitted to the agents of foreign governments.

   2. *Demands that one default on a duty owed to another.* The blackmailee might be in a position of trust in which he has a duty as an agent to a principal, a leader to those he represents, or a civil servant to the state

he serves. If his blackmailer demands that he do something inconsistent with that duty, he demands an act that is "independently unwarranted." This is the mirror image of the self-serving labor leader example, in which the union leader, as the representative of his workers, threatens (offers) to do something inconsistent with his official duty to negotiate honestly in their behalves. In contrast, the situation I envisage now is one in which the employer blackmails the union leader by demanding that he betray the interests of his members by agreeing to disadvantageous terms or else the employer will release compromising sexual photographs to the press. A similar example would be a criminal defendant's demand that a witness refrain from testifying against him at his trial or suffer the exposure of his secrets. The latter example invites comparison with the case in which the defendant makes the same demand (though without a threat, it would be called a mere "request") and offers $10,000 as an inducement. Why isn't the one (bribery) as wrongful as the other (blackmail-extortion)? One difference between the two is that in successful bribery both parties are equally guilty, one for offering a bribe, the other for accepting it and acting on it. But in the blackmail case, the blackmailed wrongdoer is guilty of less than his blackmailer, since he acted under coercion, and coercion tends to mitigate. The poor coercee is guilty of less than the bribee also, since the enticement of reward has no tendency to mitigate, and (morally speaking) may even aggravate the offense. Finally, when we come to compare the briber in the one example with the blackmailer in the other, we must find them guilty of equally serious crimes, although the blackmailer may seem slightly more blameworthy since he resorts to a kind of force (extortion) and thus takes advantage of his direct victim in a stronger sense than does the briber.

3. *Demands for undeserved honors or privileges.* A blackmailing student's demand that his teacher give him a better grade than he deserves, a blackmailing worker's demand that an employer give him a job he is not qualified for, any blackmailer's demand that his victim tell a helpful lie about him are all demands for independently unwarranted behavior likely to be unfair, if not harmful, to the interests of third parties. Even if the threat to reveal information that backs them up is a minor one (as such threats go), the whole blackmail proposal will be unjustified. (Whether it would in principle be criminalizable depends on which category the blackmail threat falls in, but we must remember that the harm principle is mediated by the maxim "*De minimis non curat lex*," "The law does not concern itself with trifles" (see Vol. I,

pp. 189–190). It is important to notice at this juncture that a teacher can be blackmailed into giving a student the grade he truly deserves instead of the lower one his biased teacher would otherwise give him, or that an employer can be blackmailed into giving a worker the job he is truly most qualified for instead of giving it to a less qualified favorite, or that anyone can be blackmailed into telling the truth about a person instead of the lies he would otherwise be disposed to tell. Since the demands in these cases are all just and in no way unwarranted, any threat in their support that falls short of what is independently forbidden by law would be justifiable. It would surely *not* be justifiable to murder the teacher's family, say, to support one's warranted demand. But it might be justifiable to threaten a truthful revelation that would be prohibited at most by the law of torts (category 3 and 4 threats) in these circumstances, since the self-defensive motive would cancel out the malice required for civil liability.

C. *Plausibly justified blackmail demands.* There are still other circumstances in which it is morally justified to back up a demand with an informational disclosure threat. In many or most of these circumstances it is also legally justified to make the demand-threat even though it would otherwise satisfy the defining conditions of a crime of blackmail-extortion. Plausible examples follow.

    1. *Minor demands.* "I will reveal your secret unless you take me to dinner" or "unless you help me improve my essay," or "unless you be civil to me," or "unless you do me a favor," or "unless you run a simple errand for me." All these demands are independently warranted and not *very* demanding. If they are backed up by correspondingly minor disclosure threats ("I'll tell your mother that you were drunk last Saturday") they can hardly be regarded as unreasonably coercive. If they are backed up by a threat to report a crime to the police, however, they will not be justified, not because they are necessarily unfair to their direct victim, but because they default on a civic duty to the community. "Be civil to me or else I will tell your boss you are a homosexual," appears to exceed the limits of moral propriety for a different reason. The demand is undemanding as demands go, but the threat is not unthreatening as threats go. Moral justifiability then appears to be a function not only of (a) the independent degree of warrantedness of the demand, (b) the independent degree of warrantedness of the threat, but also of (c) the degree of demandingness of the demand and (d) the degree of threateningness of the threat. When the demand is relatively undemanding (minor), the "blackmail demand," if not morally justified, is at least an insufficient wrong to be

the concern of the law. And in some circumstances, where for example the victim *B* has been frequently and regularly unpleasant to the
demander, *A*, it is only right that *A* exercise some leverage in his own
behalf; if that produces some minor anxiety in *B*, it is no more than he
has coming.

2. *Demand for reform. A* says to *B:* "I know about your history of philan-
dering and debauchery on business trips, and your wife, I am sure,
would have nothing more to do with you if *she* knew. As it is, she
trusts you completely, poor thing, and you could easily take advantage of her. So unless you desist from this shameful behavior in the
future, I will tell her." *A* is not necesssarily an officious intermeddler.
He may be a good friend of *B*'s spouse who is also respectful of *B*'s
privacy, and reluctant to cause unnecessary trouble. He is willing to
leave past secrets untold unless necessary to prevent future wrongs.
He demands nothing for himself but only what will protect an innocent party. It is at least plausible to judge that his behavior is morally
justified, and it is more than merely "plausible" to judge that convicting him of some crime would be an abomination.

When we supplement this example of protecting others with a similar example of a threat to expose adultery from the self-defense category (see number 6 below), the verdict of moral justification is even
more convincing. In a hypothetical example invented by the Oregon
Supreme Court, *A* threatens to *B:* "If you don't quit making love to
my wife, I'll tell your wife."[69]

3. *Demands for fair compensation for considerate offers not to publish.* These
examples are perhaps less compelling, and it might tax legislative
ingenuity to acknowledge them in the wording of a justification defense in a blackmail statute. But it is often clear that what is technically blackmail in cases like these is morally justified, indeed even
commendably benevolent to its "victim." Jeffrie Murphy gives one
example:

> I own, publish, and edit a scandal magazine. Compromising pictures of
> you come to my desk. I am set to have them published, but then it occurs
> to me that you might be willing to pay me more for them than I would get
> from increased revenue from circulation. So I go to you and make the
> following offer: "I will sell you these pictures for $500." Let us suppose
> that you are wealthy and that a loss of $500, though a sacrifice, is no grave
> hardship—that, indeed, as you assess the situation (exposure or loss of
> $500) you are *glad* to have the chance to buy them for this price.[70]

Another example is from James Lindgren, making a different but related point: "Consider . . . the biographer or memoirist who seeks

money to refrain from publishing a book that will damage someone's reputation. Publishing would further the writer's lawful business, but seeking money to refrain from ruining someone's reputation or business is blackmail."[71] To embellish Lindgren's example, we can imagine that the biographer has already invested months of labor in research and on writing the one damaging chapter, and then he experiences genuinely moral misgivings and pangs of sympathy for the figure who will be damaged by that chapter. He thoughtfully contacts that person and suggests a fair price that would compensate him for what he has already invested in the project and for settling for a book that is less satisfactory and less profitable than it otherwise would be. If his considerate conduct is morally wrong, it is impossible to find a "victim" of it.

Suppose the initiatives are reversed, and B comes to A, the publisher, and says: "I know you have this information and intend to publish it, as is your right. But it would be damaging to my marriage and my family if you did, and I am filled with remorse anyway. Please let me pay $500, or whatever you think would be fair compensation for your losses, to buy this morally incriminating evidence from you." This offer is not legally a "bribe," because A is not a public official and the voluntary transaction which it might produce could not rightly lead to criminal liability on any other ground for either A or B. One wonders why the legal consequences should be different when the same transaction is initiated through A's generosity rather than B's guilty anxiety.

4. *Demands as claims of right.* A frustrated creditor (A) may finally lose his patience with his dilatory debtor (B) and tell him: "If you don't repay the debt within the next month, I shall reveal your secret to interested parties." On the surface this looks like the standard case of informational blackmail for hush money. The threat is to disclose information and the demand is for money. The difference, of course, is that the money that is demanded is only that which is due the blackmailer anyway. He simply wants back what is rightfully his, having no intention opportunistically to extort additional profit or maliciously to expose for exposure's sake. Some threats, of course, must still be forbidden, even in support of so rightful a demand. One cannot point a gun and demand back one's due, or threaten arson or abduction, under claim of right. The money is one's own, but it does not follow that one can use "whatever means are necessary" to recover it. Threats of truthful disclosures, on the other hand, seem to be fully justified by so righteous a purpose. A category 2 threat, I have argued in §6, ought to be legally permitted even when personal profit is its sole motive.

But even category 3 and 4 threats, which are normally malicious and properly prohibited as reenforcers of profitable money demands, should be legally justified when used only to recover rightful debts.

Some American states do have blackmail statutes with clauses excepting "claims of right." These clauses allow the threatener an affirmative defense "that he genuinely believed the property sought was due him." Many other jurisdictions, however, allow no such defense.[72] The Model Penal Code, in its "theft by extortion" section, does allow as an affirmative defense that the property obtained by threat of accusation was honestly claimed as restitution or indemnification *for harm done in the circumstances to which such accusation [or] exposure. . . relates*, or as compensation for property or lawful services."[73] The Model Penal Code, in virtue of the italicized wording, has provided a narrower defense than many statutes do, because the threatened truthful accusation must relate to the very conduct that wronged the accuser. Thus, the blackmailer cannot threaten "Pay your debt or I will reveal that you are an adulterer (or a homosexual)," but he can threaten "Pay your debt or I will reveal that you are a deadbeat, thus ruining your reputation and your credit." I think there are circumstances, however, in which stronger disclosure threats, irrelevant to the accuser's own wrong, would be at least morally justified in support of a rightful claim for restitution, e.g. "Pay me what you owe me or I'll give tapes to your employer in which you express contempt toward him."

Another section of the Model Penal Code defines a distinct crime that is similar to "theft by extortion" but is aimed not at demands for money but rather at demands, backed by threats, for types of action (and inaction) other than money payments or property transfers. That crime is called "criminal coercion," and it is defined in part as the support of a nonpecuniary demand by threat to "(a) commit any criminal offense, or (b) accuse anyone of a criminal offense, or (c) expose any secret tending to subject any person to hatred, contempt or ridicule, or impair his credit . . ." But the provision then states that "It is an affirmative defense to prosecution based on . . .(b) or (c) . . . that the actor believed the accusation or secret to be true . . . and that *his purpose was limited to compelling the other to behave in a way reasonably related to the circumstances which were the subject of the accusation* . . . as by desisting from further misbehavior, making good a wrong done, refraining from taking any action or responsibility for which the actor believes the other disqualified" (italics added).[74] The affirmative defense is broad enough to exculpate "Stop sleeping with my wife or I will tell your wife," but in virtue of the italicized clause it is not wide enough to exculpate "Keep your promise to help me do a job or I will reveal your adultery to your wife," a category 2 threat that probably should not be criminalized in the first place, but even when criminalized, is at least mitigated by the rightful nature of the demand. Neither would the Model Penal Code affirmative defense exculpate "Stop sleeping with my wife or I will tell your boss that you have been borrowing from his funds." Again, it seems to me that it is arguable that the rightful character of the demand justifies even a threat to disclose matters unrelated to it. At least, a jury should be given the opportunity to make such judgments having heard the defendant's case for justification. The Model Penal Code rule, on the other hand, would rule out any justification for threats unrelated in content to the subject of the demand. That seems too restrictive.

5. *Other benevolent, just, or public-spirited demands not designed to promote the demander's personal profit.* An abundance of examples in this category are provided by a libertarian advocate of the decriminalization of blackmail, Professor Eric Mack.[75] Though Mack would not agree that informational blackmail is ever rightly prohibited, I am sure he would agree that where it *is* criminally proscribed, the prohibitory statutes should contain broad and flexible exceptive clauses allowing an affirmative defense for the kind of cases his examples envisage. Mack's examples have us imagine that we can avert some terribly harmful and/or wicked acts that happen to be legally permissible only by threatening to expose the secrets of the would-be actor: "Imagine that you can only deter a factory owner from (safely) burning his plant to the ground (and thus thoroughly eliminating many employment opportunities) for the sake of destructive glee, by threatening to reveal his secrets." In this example, as in similar examples invented by Mack, it seems to make little difference whether the blackmail is done by a public-spirited third party or one of the threatened workers. In the latter case the justification would be similar to self-defense; in the former case it would be similar to defense of others. In neither case would the blackmailer's purpose be to make an opportunistic profit (net gain) for himself.

Mack's hypothetical case is a good example of morally justified blackmail, and he has other persuasive examples too.[76] But we can go too quickly down this road. There is another "paradox" lying in wait if we propose to give *legal* justification, in the form of exceptive clauses to criminal blackmail statutes, to morally justified blackmail of the sort Mack has us imagine. The law would permit the factory owner's irresponsible egotism on the one hand, but also permit a normally prohibited use of blackmail to prevent it on the other hand. Legal justifications for other types of prohibited extortion do not work that way. The law prohibits me from demanding something I desire from you under threat of shooting your wife, or burning your car, or abducting your grandchild. But I am legally justified in *threatening* to do these things to support my demand that you refrain from shooting *my* wife, or burning *my* car, or abducting *my* grandchild, or performing any other *criminal* act of comparable gravity.[77] I am not justified in making such threats to prevent you from doing something that is legally permitted. That "justification" would seem to be incoherent, for it would put the law in the awkward position of taking very lightly and tolerantly an untoward action (say the factory owner's destruction of his plant) for one purpose (criminalization) and very seriously and intolerantly for another (defending resorting to criminal conduct to prevent that action).

The solution to the paradox must be found in the notion of moral proportionality. Morally speaking, extortion, like all wrongful coercion, tends to be wrong because it artificially restricts a victim's choices to two that both seem harmful to his interest. Even if he chooses the lesser evil he is likely to be harmed. If a given instance of *prima facie* wrongful coercion is nevertheless justified on balance, it must be because its purpose is to avert an even greater evil that would otherwise be imposed on others by the coercee. Its wrongness in that case is outweighed by other moral considerations. Threats of violence to a person's or (other people's) property are justified, morally and legally, only to prevent comparable violence from the other party. Violence is too grave a wrong to be outbalanced by its prevention of other behavior whose harmfulness is not sufficiently serious even to be criminalized in its own right. Revealing secrets, however, since it is much less serious than violence and even legally permissible in most cases, can be a justifiable thing to threaten in order to prevent wrongs that are of equal or greater moral seriousness, and these may include wrongs that are not independently criminalizable. I may be justified in threatening to reveal your homosexuality to prevent you from killing your neighbor but not to prevent you from being impolite to your neighbor. It may well be that when weighed on sensitive moral scales your plan to demolish your factory, even though the harm will be to *your* factory and not preventable by the criminal law, is more like the intention to kill one's neighbor than like the intention of being impolite to him even though it is not independently criminal. Perhaps jurors should at least have a right to decide that question.

The threat to reveal a person's secret in order to force him to contribute to Cambodian Relief and thus help rescue thousands of people from misery and death (another Mack example of justified blackmail) is even trickier. One could not employ *other* forms of extortion (like the threat of violence) even for so worthy an end. Should one be legally justified then in threatening serious but lesser harms than violence, like damaging revelations, in order to prevent even greater harms like mass starvation? The danger in this approach is that it might tempt us to solve moral problems by adding up numbers, sacrificing the interests of one innocent victim to save larger numbers of endangered people, who are threatened by independent causes, not by the person whose interests we are tempted to sacrifice. The moral justifiability of blackmail in the charity case is surely not so clear that a jury of ordinary reasonable persons could unanimously endorse it. When the blackmail threat is designed to prevent proportionate or greater harms *intended by the very party being blackmailed*, however, the case is significantly different, even though it would not have been independently criminal to produce those harms.

6. *Counterblackmail*. Here there is an analogy with threats of violence to person or property, and other criminal threats used in robbery and extortion. Suppose A, in support of a demand against B, has threatened to inflict injury on C—B's child or spouse. B then responds firmly by threatening: Do not harm C (a warranted demand if ever there was one) or I shall retaliate against D (A's spouse or child). The threat in B's warning is to commit a crime against D, but B is within his rights in *threatening* it even though he would not be justified in actually doing it. The threat is a rightful attempt to deter wrongdoing in defense of one's own or another party's interest. The actual violence after the threat has failed would be an unwarranted (though understandable) act of pointless retaliation. The informational blackmail analogue to this example is the case in which B threatens his threatener (A): If you release X about me, I will release Y about you," a threat which may look extortive but one which is certainly worthy of legal justification. The analogy fails, however, in one interesting respect. If B's counterthreat fails to deter A from releasing the embarrassing or damaging information about B, then B is legally justified in retaliating by doing what he threatened in self-defense to do, namely, release his embarrassing or damaging information about A.

That concludes our survey of the various kinds of demands that are backed up by informational blackmail threats and can tend to give moral or legal justification to those threats. Now we can conclude this section by mentioning a couple of types of informational-disclosure *threats* that may also have this effect, and a pair of distinctions among types of blackmail *technique* that may also be relevant to the degree of justification or moral gravity of informational blackmail threats.

A. *Threats to reveal information about unrelated third parties.* I should think that it would be clearly unjustified, at least from the legal point of view, for *A* to demand, in violation of a validly enacted blackmail statute, that *B* pay hush money in exchange for *A*'s not revealing damaging information about *B*'s son. On the other hand, it would be morally justified, and plausibly ought to be legally justified, even though otherwise in violation of a validly enacted statute, for *A* to demand that *B* pay hush money for *A*'s not revealing damaging information about George Washington. (*A* may be a research historian and *B* a rich layman with a worshipful admiration for Washington.) As so often happens in the law, a problem arises in drawing a line between these relatively clear cases. How close must the third party be for *B* to be *coerced* or *extorted* in a legally effective sense by a mere threat to reveal embarrassing information about him? The solution of the problem probably requires the use of an "objective standard" of coercion, an appeal to what would force a typical "reasonable person" to choose to pay in *B*'s circumstances. (See Vol. III, pp. 210-12). All we can say with confidence here is that the more remote the relation between *B* and the third party, the more justified (or the less culpable) is the blackmail threat to expose the third party. Those unfortunately vulnerable persons with abnormal sensitivities here as elsewhere must provide their own protection, and sometimes the best way to do that is to toughen up.

It is interesting to note that the historian (*A*) who discovers that Washington may have been cruel and unfaithful to Martha may sadly refrain from publishing his disillusioning evidence entirely out of consideration for *B*'s sensitive feelings, and that would not be a crime. If he takes money from *B* his tenderness is put in doubt, since his primary motives are seen to be mercenary. The only other difference between the two cases is that *A* profits personally in the blackmail case, and does not in the voluntary withdrawal case. In every other way the consequences for everybody—*A*, *B*, Washington's reputation, and the historical record—are the same. So criminalization, if it were to be justified at all in the blackmail case, would have to be justified by its prevention of wrongful gain. But that seems a slight foundation for so momentous a thing as punishment of the opportunistic historian. The only clear *victims* of *A*'s action are historians and other third parties who have a stake in the accuracy of the historical record, but that interest, while worth protecting on liberal grounds, may be too dilute to counter the personal and social costs of criminalization.

B. *Threats to withhold favorable information.* "Genealogists, for example, may sometimes threaten to withhold favorable information from prospective clients while bargaining over its price."[78] *A*, the enterprising genealogist, may have discovered evidence that one of *B*'s ancestors came over on the Mayflower. If disclosed, this information would greatly enhance *B*'s stature in a group of snobbish bluebloods to which he aspires. *A* knows this means much to *B*, and, like a shrewd businessperson, inflates his price accordingly. If *A* overprices the information, however, it will do *him* no good, since the information can benefit only one person; if that person refuses to pay, there is no other market, no other customers, for it. Thus, *B* has some self-protective leverage of his own to use in negotiating the price, and the demand made by the genealogist is not strictly coercive, as the demand for $100 for a glass of water extracted from a lost traveler in the desert would be. In fact, to the ordinary "reasonable person" invoked in legal standards, the loss of the desired status might be a failure to benefit rather than a suffered harm to any vital interest.

Other favorable information can not be rightly or even legally withheld, for its concealment would seriously harm the person it concerns, who could even sue for a legal injunction to disclose it. For example, *A* might have evidence that *B* could not have committed the crime of which he has been charged, or convicted. In that case, *A* would be threatening to do something that is illegal, namely obstruct justice, so he may not legally do what he threatens to do (withhold the exculpatory evidence). That would be more than merely "withholding favorable information"; it would be to harm another severely by omission. (See Vol. I, pp. 171–81.)

In a more difficult example, *A* has evidence that *B* did all the original work for which *C* was awarded the Nobel Prize. In this example, *A*'s demand for money from *B* as a condition for releasing the information would probably not satisfy the definition of informational blackmail or "theft by extortion"[79] of most prohibitory statutes, but it would *not* be morally justified. It is therefore the mirror image analogue of cases we have considered of technically illegal blackmail demands that *are* morally justified. But to say in this case that the morally unjustified but legally innocent behavior ought to be *legally unjustified* too, says no more than that criminal statutes ought to prohibit it. At the very least, there should be civil actions to enjoin release, if not tort actions for damages from concealment. It is doubtful, however, that the harm principle can legitimate the criminal punishment of a person who inflicts no harm himself on another's reputation, but fails to release information (perhaps only his personal testimony as an eyewitness) that would give the other party the credit he deserves. Perhaps the failure to rectify this wrong is part of the price we pay for keeping the door closed to legal moralism in our zeal to protect individual liberty; perhaps failures to benefit, like other "merely moral" offenses like discourtesy, are not sufficiently significant for legal intervention; perhaps these examples require us to enlarge our conception of "harm" to include some nonbenefitting.

The best liberal approach to the problem, I think, is to distinguish sharply between withholding benefits *simpliciter*, and withholding "benefits," like "credit" that one has *already earned*, and classifying the latter with the harms, offenses, and "exploitational injustices" from which a person can claim legal protection. The person who does not get the credit he deserves is, morally speaking, akin to the person whose property (what is rightfully his) has been taken by theft or fraud, or, more exactly, like the person whose properly earned profit has been fraudulently withheld—in either case, like someone who has been deprived of what is his due. If one's reputation is a kind of "property," then in principle it too can be protected against the withholding of earned improvements, under the harm principle. Withholding evidence that supports a rightful reputational claim is not the sort of wrong that has no victim, or the sort of evil that "floats free."

In principle then it is morally legitimate to criminalize threats to withhold favorable information as blackmail. But there is no real need to go so far if adequate civil remedies are provided. Court orders to produce the evidence are surely a more economical intrusion on private liberty. In any case, the moral legitimacy of a criminal statute would not be undermined by the "paradox of blackmail." A is not merely threatening to do what he has (or ought to have) a perfect legal right to do, if it is true (as I believe) that there is (or ought to be) a provision of the civil law which (in the manner of the civil law) "forbids" nonrevelation. In demanding money by threatening not to do what he can be legally compelled to do, the "reverse blackmailer" tries to extort money by a threat to do what is independently unlawful, though not criminal. I do not advocate the inclusion of his sort of racket in the criminal extortion statutes, only because I think it would be impractical and unnecessary, not because I think it would be illegitimate.

C. *Opportunistic vs. entrepreneurial blackmail.* "On February 4, 1930, a laborer at work on a ladder caught sight of a clergyman in a 'compromising position' in an adjoining building and 'immediately seized upon it to turn it to commercial purposes,' " . . . threatening that unless money payments were made he would expose the unseemly behavior to another clergyman, "and failing him the bishop, and then they would know what sort of villain the victim had been."[80] That paradigmatic example of merely opportunistic black-

mail was clearly the work of an amateur, and in the historical case, a blunder-
ing one. But despite his plea that he had acted "more like a fool than a
criminal" and was a hard-working man with no criminal record, he was
sentenced to ten years' penal servitude. (It is not revealed what became of the
clergyman.) Arguably, this was an example of a category 2 threat which I
have suggested (*supra*, §6) ought not to have been criminal in the first place.

In contrast, Hepworth distinguishes what he calls "entrepreneurial blackmail" and what I would prefer to classify as two of its species, "commercial
research" and "participant blackmail."[81] The entrepreneurial blackmailer
blackmails for a living. His work typically requires planning, searching systematically for vulnerable parties, acquiring information through extralegal
violations of privacy (keyhole-peeping, breaking and entering, telephone tap-
ping, electronic bugging, etc.), or else elements of fraud, deception, and
manipulation, even elaborate trap-setting. Victims are often lured into their
wrongdoing (a technique that even policemen seeking out genuine criminals
may not use) and then trapped and "punished" by coercive threats of exposure and demands for hush money. "Probably the most familiar version is the
celebrated "badger game,' where an unsuspecting man is lured into a sexual
relationship and "suddenly discovered' by an extorting accomplice in the
guise of a disconcerted husband."[82] Entrepreneurial blackmailers are confidence game swindlers. They either arrange the very behavior they later
threaten to expose, or they discover it by methods that are independently
criminal or actionable in civil suits. Their conduct is clearly criminalizable on
harm principle grounds, and that criminalization does not stumble over the
paradox of blackmail insofar as the prohibited behavior uses fraudulent entrapment and/or illegal methods of information acquisition.

D. *Single-shot versus repetitive blackmail.* The single-shot blackmailer offers
his victim a way out of his dilemma once and for all. He sells the damaging
information for a single cash payment and then is heard from no more. If he
has photographs, he sells the negatives and all prints; if he has tapes, he sells
the originals and keeps no copies; if he has letters, he sells originals and all
duplicates. But sometimes he sells only his silence about what is in publicly
accessible records, and sometimes, of course, he keeps secret copies of other
documents and is lying when he says he has destroyed all duplicates. In
either case, he does not relinquish his power over his victim and may come
back again and again with further demands. The victim who was lied to once
by his blackmailer knows after the second demand that he is now permanently at the other's mercy. Famous victims of repetitive blackmail in literature and life have thus been faced with a difficult dilemma. They may
continue to pay over and over until ruined; they may call the blackmailer's
bluff and tell him in the words of the Duke of Wellington when his mistress

threatened to publish her diary and his letters, "Publish and be damned!"; or they may eliminate their tormentors by murder.

The only acceptable choice, of course, is to emulate the Duke of Wellington. One of the reasons for criminalizing repetitive blackmail in cases in which single-shot blackmail might be properly permitted, or for making it an aggravation where single-shot blackmail is properly forbidden, is that it would give victims of repetitive blackmail some counter-leverage of their own. The victim can say "publish and be damned" and then point out that once the revelation is published, the blackmailer has killed the goose that laid the golden egg. He has no more leverage to produce further payments from the victim, having spitefully given away his valuable secret, and, moreover, he is now more vulnerable himself to exposure as a blackmailer, since his victim no longer has anything to lose by bringing him to public justice.

Another reason for more severe penalties for repetitive blackmailers is that they are liars, false promisers, faith-breakers and cheaters, not keeping (and never intending to keep) their side of a bargain, even when the bargain itself seemed legitimate. If A has agreed to sell his permanent silence for B's $500, and then, contrary to his promise, comes back later to demand another $500, he has in effect upped the price from the one agreed upon to $1,000—a fee B may not have accepted in the first place. B then does not get what he paid for, knowing now that he will never have security from A, and it is too late to get his money back. He has been swindled as surely as if he had prepaid for merchandise that was never delivered. He has no real choice now but to follow the Duke of Wellington's example and give up hopes of recovering his initial payment.

Still another reason that can be given for treating the repetitive blackmailer more severely is less likely to survive scrutiny. If we severely criminalize repetitive blackmail, then—assuming that the threatened punishment actually deters some blackmailers from repeating their demands—the number of victims with a incentive for murder will be decreased, and the homicide rate will decline. Quite apart from its dubious factual claims, however, this argument appears to share a difficulty with all criminal statutes that penalize one party's activities (e.g. his exercise of free speech) on the grounds that it might lead *others*, voluntarily enough, to commit crimes, e.g. through imitation (see Vol. I, pp. 232–42), or provocation of retaliatory violence against the speaker, or fortuitous causation of voluntary behavior of others against third parties (see Vol. II, p. 155). If there were already enough wrong with a specific type of blackmail proposition to warrant its criminalization, then this further tendency to lead to harm, even harm to the wrongdoer himself, might be a reason to institute more severe penalties. But if the blackmail transaction would be morally unobjectionable and harmless but for its repetitive character, then this further fact about its tendency to cause retaliatory harm would not be a good reason all by itself either for criminalization or aggravation, for those legal responses would be like punishing an otherwise innocent use of speech on the ground that it might lead others voluntarily to cause harm to the speaker. The best grounds for more severe treatment of repetitive blackmail are its fraudulent techniques and the greater counter-leverage that severe penalties give to threatened victims.

8. Summary

There is a class of crimes that seems to create a special kind of problem for liberalism. These are actions whose criminalization, at first sight at least, seems to be called for by common sense, even though they do not, at first sight, appear to have harmed victims, that is they do not damage others' interests in a way that violates their rights. It is characteristic of some of the conduct in this class that it yields an unjust gain for those who engage in it even when it is not *unfair to* any particular victims, since those whose interests are set back by it, if any, have freely consented to it in advance. It would seem, then, that either these actions are not properly criminalizable or that their moral legitimation must come from the exploitation principle, which is a form of legal moralism, and thus inconsistent with liberalism.

There are several options open to the liberal when confronted with the crimes in this problem class. (1) He can claim that some of them do cause right-violating harm after all, which can be seen if only one looks in the right place for it. For example, we have argued that insider trading causes a subtle kind of public harm, threatening to undermine general confidence in an essential financial institution, and that next of kin organ sales make medical practice more expensive, hence less effective in treating harmful maladies of many prospective patients. (2) He can bite the bullet and urge decriminalization of what *seemed*, before careful examination, to be a kind of conduct whose prohibition would be supported by common sense. Usually this approach requires some deft surgery on existing statutes, decriminalizing some but not all of the forms of conduct currently under blanket interdiction. Thus, we have argued that fortunetelling for purposes of entertainment, at a nominal price which is posted in advance, should be permitted, whereas making inherently deceptive claims of foretelling the future at an individually negotiated high price may properly be proscribed as a kind of theft by fraud. Similarly, ticket scalping in isolated transactions should be permitted, but as a business practice it may be regulated by a scheme of licensure designed to protect the public from fraud and collusion. Many current statutes forbidding fortunetelling and ticket scalping are overbroad, prohibiting harmless as well as genuinely harmful forms of an activity for which there is one common name.

(3) The liberal could also, of course, abandon his liberalism by endorsing the exploitation principle as a ground for criminalizing conduct in the problem class when options (1) and (2) both seem unacceptable. The crime for which this approach seems most plausible, at first sight, is blackmail, which makes it a crime to threaten to do what one has a legal right to do anyway unless some demand, which one also has an independent legal right to make, is granted by the victim. If the victim would not be sufficiently wronged by the threatened action (truthful disclosure of information) for it to be criminal in a liberal code, how can he be sufficiently wronged by the blackmailer's conditional threat to perform that legal action unless the "victim" does something for him that is also permitted by a liberal-based criminal code? The proponent of the exploitation principle has the simplest explanation. The basis of the prohibition, he claims, is not the prevention of any wrongful loss on the part of a "victim," but rather the prevention of a morally inappropriate "wrongful gain," a kind of unjust cashing in or unproductive parasitic profit by the blackmailer that remains a free-floating evil even if it is unfair to no person in particular.

I have tried to find a liberal alternative to the legal moralist's account of blackmail, by combining approaches (1) and (2). The most radical thing in our discussion of blackmail is its advocacy of the decriminalization of informational blackmail of our "second category"—legally permissible demands backed by threats to reveal that the victim has engaged in, and continues to engage in, perfectly legal but devious trickery or underhanded dealing. I came to this radical conclusion only because I take the argument of the "paradox of blackmail" very seriously. I don't see how a coherent criminal code based on liberal principles (and therefore excluding the exploitation principle) can prohibit people from offering, in exchange for consideration, not to do what they have an independent legal right (but no legal duty) to do. The radical impact of my proposal, however, is quickly mitigated by arguments to maintain the criminalization of informational blackmail in each of the other four categories of disclosure-threat. I support this predominantly conservative proposal by arguing that these categories involve threats to do what is contrary either to the criminal law or to the civil law, or to do what *ought* (on liberal grounds) to be independently forbidden by legal rules of one kind or another. Moreover, all forms of informational blackmail that involve fraudulent misrepresentation, manipulative entrapment, forbidden methods of acquiring information, entrepreneurial practices, and repetitive demands—the criminal rackets that are the most lurid and scurrilous specimens of the blackmail genus—can be banned on harm-principle grounds, even when they involve disclosure threats of the second category. What can remain criminal then on liberal grounds are precisely those actions that common sense most insistently demands should be criminal.

Blackmail is so morally complex a matter, however, that we should not be surprised if an adequate criminal code not only prohibits some but not all of its forms, but also recognizes an elaborate set of acceptable justifications for it even in the cases where it it otherwise strictly forbidden. Even blackmail for money is morally (and should be legally) justified when the threat and demand are not morally disproportionate, and the demand is a rightful claim for repayment of a debt. The "claim of right" defense can be recognized without causing entanglement in the paradox of blackmail, for the disclosure threat supports a legally proper demand, and (unless it is in category 1—a threat to expose criminality) it is in itself neither a violation of criminal nor civil law, nor ought it to be a wrong under tort law, for its motive is not at all malicious or spiteful. In other special cases, a jury should be entitled to consider a claim of justification for *offering* not to publish what one could properly publish in the normal course of events, in exchange for a reasonable compensatory fee. Cases in which the demand is not for money are likely to suggest more diverse candidates for legal justification. Morally proportionate minor demands, demands for reform under proportionate threat of exposure, demands that the victim forgo planned actions or omissions that would cause even greater harms to the threatener or to others, and demands that the other desist from blackmailing the threatener (counterblackmail) are all plausible candidates for legal justifications of disclosure-threats that would otherwise be considered extortive even in a liberal code. But the standard case of informational disclosure-threats in support of hush money demands, and arranged by rings of professionals employing timeworn techniques of fraudulent entrapment or privacy invasion, could be treated as severely by a liberal code as by any other.

33

Legal Perfectionism and the Benefit Principles

1. The concept of character

According to the liberty-limiting principle we shall call "legal perfectionism," it is a proper aim of the criminal law to perfect the character and elevate the taste of the citizens who are subject to it. Perfectionists claim, therefore, that it is always a good and relevant reason in support of a criminal prohibition that it will make citizens better people.

The more general political doctrine that it is a proper job, and indeed the principal task, of the state to inculcate and strengthen the virtues has an ancient and impressive pedigree, going back to Plato and Aristotle.[1] This general political doctrine, one of many bearing the confusing label "conservatism," remains popular today, as is shown by the large number of writers who put at the very center of politics such goals as "republican virtue," "traditions of manners and civility," and "quality of life." In his review of George Will's *The Pursuit of Happiness and Other Sobering Thoughts*, Ronald Dworkin paraphrases the doctrine felicitously: "The essence of conservatism, on Will's view, is this: it is the job of government to define, achieve, and protect a society and public virtue, that is a society which shares a strong and accurate sense of what is valuable in life and history, and what is not."[2] Will himself puts it this way:

> Men and women are biological facts. Ladies and gentlemen—*citizens*—are social artifacts, works of political art. They carry the culture that is sustained by wise laws, and traditions of civility. At the end of the day we are right to judge a

society by the character of the people it produces. That is why statecraft is, inevitably, soulcraft . . .³

I think a liberal can condede that, other things being equal, some forms of human life—those manifesting excellence of character—are intrinsically superior to others.⁴ It also seems undeniable that the state may properly attempt to promote public virtue and raise the level of excellence throughout society by such methods as moral and cultural education in the public schools, subsidies to the arts and sciences, and awards and prizes to virtuous exemplars. What is distinctive about legal perfectionism, however, is the reliance it places on the mechanisms of criminal law for this end, a means that seems to the liberal both inappropriate and inefficient as a tool for making people good.

What exactly should we mean by human *character* and what are the distinctively human *virtues?* I think it will be most useful if we take a broad conception of a person's character, which, while it includes his "morals" and his "manners," takes in more than that. Even in that wide sense, one's character is to be contrasted with one's physique and health, so that muscular strength and running speed, for example, are no part of it. We can also exclude acquired skills and certain aptitudes and talents, like carpentry, or the ability to paint pictures or prove theorems. Then we can use "character" as a comprehensive term for a set of dispositions to act or feel in certain ways, so that when a given disposition is by and large commendable, we call it a virtue or excellence (I will use these terms interchangeably), and when it is on the whole subject to disapproval we call it a flaw or defect of character. (I will *not* use the word "vice.") When we refer to a person's character, it is to the whole set of these praise- or blameworthy dispositions. No one has an entirely praiseworthy character, but we call a character good insofar as its virtues predominate over its flaws.

Virtues and flaws of character can be classified in many ways. One of the simplest and (despite its simplicity) most useful is that of David Hume, who divided virtues into four classes: qualities useful (helpful) to others, qualities useful to ourselves, qualities immediately agreeable (pleasing) to others, and qualities immediately agreeable to ourselves.⁵ Defects of character could be divided into four corresponding classes: dispositions to behave or have feelings that are harmful or offensive (displeasing) to self or to others. The main problems with Hume's classification, as with all others, is that many virtues fall into more than one of his categories. Still, it will be useful to employ Hume's scheme to illustrate the abundance of distinctively human excellences and failings, and their many subtle differences and shadings. Among the other points that will emerge are that a substantial portion of the English vocabulary, numbering thousands of words, consists of the names of virtues and flaws of character; that many of these terms are such that they can apply only to a special class of people (women only, or warriors only, or medical personnel only) or people in special circumstances (merchants, sick people, or people with authority over others); that only some of these terms refer to virtues and flaws that are *moral* excellences and failings in a familiar narrow sense of "moral"; and that there are probably far more defects than excellences, since, as Aristotle noted, there are many ways of missing a target but only one way of hitting it.

Consider, then, examples of qualities (dispositions) *helpful to others:* trustworthiness, honesty, dutifulness, conscientiousness, truthfulness, integrity, probity, judiciousness, fairness, cooperativeness, caringness, lovingness, warmheartedness, benevolence, generosity, sensitivity, courage, steadfastness. Dispositions that are *pleasing to others* include refinement, wit, sense of humor, cheerfulness, interest in others, style, grace, subtlety, sensitivity, charm, spontaneity, tact, and tolerance. (Hume also included "politeness," "modesty," and "decency.") Among the qualities *useful to oneself* are self-control, self-knowledge, prudence, industriousness, courage, wisdom, and decisiveness. Examples of qualities that are *pleasing to self* will include many already mentioned under other headings, but most distinctively and importantly, cleanliness (it is unpleasant to be dirty, smelly, itchy, and the like), temperance, self-confidence, self-control, and cheerfulness. Various classes of virtues have an element of intrinsic worthiness that makes them difficult to classify in a simple utilitarian system like Hume's. Two families in particular come to mind, the one that includes judgment, taste, discernment, discrimination, and perceptiveness, virtues that could fit in any or all of the four classes, and would be virtues anyway, even if they fit in none, and the family that includes qualities that are more admirable than "agreeable," such as magnanimity, high-mindedness, a sense of honor, "proper pride," and personal dignity.

On the negative side, dispositions that are *harmful to others* can include cowardice, unreliability, deceitfulness, mendacity, dishonesty (relating to property), untrustworthiness, prejudice, indifference to others' suffering, malevolence, cruelty, selfishness, savagery, barbarity, ruthlessness, unscrupulousness, mean-spiritedness, and spitefulness. Hundreds of flaws are included in the *offensive to others* category, of which the following perhaps are typical: crudity, uncouthness, dirty-mindedness, unctuousness, obsequiousness, intense seriousness, self-centeredness, censoriousness, gloominess, tactlessness, prejudice, coldness, priggishness, hypocrisy, sanctimoniousness, prudery, selfrighteousness, pedantry, officiousness, envy, jealousy, pushiness, sentimentality, snideness, loudness, shrillness, slobbishness, snobbery, and discourtesy. Examples of dispositions *harmful to onself* include impulsiveness, rashness, imprudence, diffidence, abjectness (the tendency to let others use one as a doormat), some self-deception, spitefulness, gullibility, gluttony, sloth, recklessness, carelessness, and a tendency to have knee-jerk emotional responses. Finally, those defects of character that are *disagreeable to oneself* (as well as to others) include envy, jealousy, obsessive resentfulness, implacable unforgivingness, uncleanliness, squeamishness, fearfulness, diffidence, and irascibility. More difficult to classify are some intrinsically unworthy flaws like lack of self-respect, lack of integrity, lack of discrimination, unperceptiveness, poor taste, and erratic judgment.

Given this conception of human character, it will be very difficult to make precise comparative evaluations of the characters of two or more people. There will be a great deal of incommensurability, so that only limited comparisons are possible. If Doe and Roe compare equally in all their relevant dispositions but one, and Doe ranks higher in that one, then Doe has a better character on the whole. But no easy comparison is possible if Doe and Roe are equal in most of their qualities, but Doe is higher in six and Roe is higher in another six, or if Doe is systematically higher in one category or subcategory and Roe is another. The only judgment that may be possible in that case is that Doe has a better character in some respects than Roe, and Roe has a better character in other respects, and that they are quite different sorts of persons. Which we rank higher, if we must rank them, may depend on the purposes for which we evaluate them: Do we want to find someone to rent our house, or do we wish to invite someone to a cocktail party? Do we want someone to like, or to admire, or to trust? Some traits, of course, are to be given more weight in comparisons than others, which helps limit the incommensurability. Doe will rank higher, that is qualify as a better person on the whole, than Roe, even though Doe is dour, moody, and irascible, if he is also honorable and trustworthy, and Roe, though charming, witty, and loving with his family, is also ruthless, unscrupulous, and savage in his treatment of rivals. There is a sense in which the bare minimal negative virtues— dispositions not to cheat, not to beat, not to kill—are the most important— since anyone who lacks even them is a monster indeed, no matter how cheerful, witty, clean, temperate, and self-disciplined he might be. But as we shall see in §2 below, these essential but minimal virtues do not give a person a very admirable character on the whole if he is cold, unperceptive, unloving, and disinclined to perform positive services beyond these minimal duties.

There is a final point about this conception of character that should be made in passing. We should note the emptiness of individual perfection, on a single model, as a *social* ideal. A functional society with a complex economy that requires a specialization of labor needs some diversification even in its distribution of virtues. If we all aspired to a single model of individual perfection, many of the critical tasks of our complex civilization would not be as well done. St. Francis of Assisi is a most fitting model for a person in some walks of life, and some Franciscan kindness would serve us all well, but Francis himself would have made a poor combat infantry officer or slaughter-house worker. General Patton was an inspired military leader who may have been less effective had he had a richer complement of the softer virtues. In fact, some socially indispensable virtues—those of specialized merchants, surgeons, generals, and the like—may be causally linked to character flaws, "the other side of their coin." What produces the social virtues tends to produce the individual flaw as a byproduct. A merchant's officiousness makes him useful to the customers whose business he makes his own and yet would make him a painfully boring friend or acquaintance. A cold-blooded, rigidly controlled surgeon may save many lives through his technical skill but be a failure as a husband, parent, or friend because the same rigid self-discipline that makes him a good surgeon might preclude warmth and sponta-neity. An obsessively devoted scientist thoroughly immersed in his research may make immense contributions to the public weal, but he may not "have time" to be genuinely interested in other people's problems. A kind of self-centered singlemindedness may be linked in his case with his devotion to his calling. And who would find Aristotle's usefully magnanimous man "agree-able"? In general, some private vices (to speak in the language of eighteenth century moralists) may indeed be public virtues. If a single conception of human perfection were satisfied or approached closely by *everyone*, we might have less helpful merchants, less skilled surgeons, less devoted scientists, and less effective generals. What we want in a friend is not always what we commend in a specialized professional.

We have now said enough about character to suggest the complexity of the concept and the subtleties involved in trying to improve others' characters. We must now ask what role force and threats of punishment can play in the process.

2. Coercion to virtue

Thoughtful legal perfectionists do not advocate legal coercion as a technique for producing character virtues of all kinds. It would be manifestly absurd to threaten people with punishment in order to give them wisdom, style, integ-rity, or a better sense of humor. Very likely then they have in mind only those dispositions of character that are *moral* virtues in a familiar stricter sense, but not all of *them* either. Genuine generosity, concern, magnanimity, and courage are not readily produced by a policeman's billy club or threats of imprisonment, and integrity (fidelity to one's principles and ideals—see Vol.

III, pp. 40, 45–46) has frequently led highly moral persons into defiance of the criminal law. Since virtues often consist not merely of conditioned inhibitions but rather of tendencies to act or feel in the right way for the right reasons,[6] it would be ludicrous to attempt to inculcate these virtues by intimidation: "Really care about another or else . . . ," "Be truly courageous or else I'll bully you into it." The only virtue clearly produced by such methods, namely simple obedience, may not in its own right be a moral virtue at all.

The subclass of moral virtues that it is most plausible to think could be produced by legal coercion are the socially indispensable but bare minimal negative virtues we have already mentioned: dispositions *not* to kill, maim, beat, rape, steal, or cheat that a person might have because he is *not* cruel (but not necessarily kind), and honest (but not necessarily conscientious). It is, of course, extremely important that the criminal law keep people from being violent and grossly deceitful to one another, but a person who *merely* was not cruel and was honestly rule-abiding might yet have so poor a character—even so poor a *moral* character—that a perfectionist like George Will would treat him with utter disdain and bemoan the loss of public civility his example illustrates.

The enforcible "negative part" of morality with its corresponding "minimal virtues" is well described by J.S. Mill (where he discusses corrupted forms, as he regards them, of Christian ethics):

> Its deal is negative rather than positive; passive rather than active; innocence rather than nobleness; abstinence from evil rather than energetic pursuit of good; in its precepts (as has been well said) "thou shalt not" predominates unduly over "thou shalt." In its horror of sensuality, it made an idol of asceticism which has been gradually compromised away into one of legality. It holds out the hope of heaven and the threat of hell as the appointed and appropriate motives to a virtuous life: in this falling far below the best of the ancients, and doing what lies in it to give to human morality an essentially selfish character, by disconnecting each man's feeling of duty from the interests of his fellow creatures, except so far as self-interested inducement is offered to him for consulting them. It is essentially a doctrine of passive obedience . . .[7]

The merely passive abstemious innocent who satisfies the negative conception of morality is hardly a model of human perfection, and, unless he has a fair complement of the unenforcible virtues, he could hardly be proud of his own character. If he says in his own defense, "At least I am not a murderer" (with obvious pride), he would be laughable if he were not pathetic.[8]

D.H. Lawrence's novel *Sons and Lovers* is in part about the effects on human relations of the sordid conditions of a British coal mining town. One of the characters, Mr. Morel, a miner, and a most inept and uncaring husband, survives his long-suffering wife. Bernard Mayo, in his ethics text, quotes from Lawrence's description of the funeral preparations what he rightly takes to be a comment on "the man who tries to persuade himself that the morality of [negative] duty is the whole of morality":

> [He] sat in the kitchen with Mrs. Morel's relatives, "superior" people, and wept, and said what a good lass she'd been, and how he'd tried to do everything he could for her—everything. He'd striven all his life to do what he could for her, and he'd nothing to reproach himself with. She was gone, but he'd done his best for her. He wiped his eyes with his white handkerchief. He'd nothing to reproach himself for, he repeated. All his life he'd done his best for her.
>
> And that was how he tried to dismiss her. He never thought of her personally. Everything deep in him he denied.[9]

Morel had committed no crime, nor had he acted in any way that plausibly should have been a crime. He didn't kill or beat his wife, or cheat or steal from her. So in his self-deceptive blindness "he had nothing to reproach himself for." If the criminal law is responsible for his "virtues," it doesn't have much to boast about.

Perhaps unviolent, minimally uncruel, and "honest" people like Moral are the best the criminal law, all by itself, can produce. But can it be expected to do even that much? How does the criminal law inculcate even those minimal and mostly negative "virtues" (can we really call them *excellences* without irony?) that correspond to the law-abiding citizen's unwillingness to kill, beat, cheat, and rob? At this point I must refer to the experience of the one moral agent I know best and examine some autobiographical data. I suspect that *I* have an implacable inhibition against killing human beings that would prevent me from killing even a person I hated in circumstances I judged to be justifying. (Perhaps I share this inhibition with many other "overcivilized" moderns. A study of American infantrymen in the Korean War, as I recall, claimed that 50% of those who had had enemy soldiers in the sights of their weapons had been unable to pull the trigger even though it was their acknowledged military duty to do so.) *A fortiori*, I am unlikely ever to commit murder for gain, revenge, ideological zeal or any other standard forbidden motive (with the possible exception of mercy). I have a similarly inflexible inhibition against hitting a woman—any woman, in any circumstances. But before the reader nominates me for some medal, I must confess that I had no choice in acquiring these restraints. They were obviously instilled in me by the earliest influences—parents, family, friends—reenforcing perhaps some native dispositions and an imaginative capacity to put myself in the other person's shoes. The criminal law might have had something to do with it, but one can overstate its *deterrent* role. After all, I don't usually park illegally either, but I must confess that my reluctance to disobey traffic laws is almost entirely derived from my fear of penalties, mild as they may be. I have no prior "implacable inhibition" against illegal parking. (Maybe I'd be a better man if I did.) One thing, however, is clear: I do not refrain from murder and rape simply out of fear of punishment.

Nonetheless, the "majesty of the law" may have helped implant my inhibition and then helped to strengthen it. Very early I learned how seriously society takes the prohibition against these worst forms of violence. I sensed the aura that surrounds the originally legal term "murder" and gives it an unrivalled emotive force. I have observed the hush of silence and the shared horror when that crime is reported, or when its perpetrator is accused or convicted, and I have witnessed (through books, movies, television programs) the distinctive ceremony of the courtroom—the solemn condemnations, the symbols of ignominy, and the sentence to the supreme punishment. Perhaps that helped accomplish the internalization of the authorities—political, religious, and especially parental—that were responsible in the first place for my inhibition. That of course is quite another thing than refraining from murder simply from fear of punishment. I never thought of the criminal law as making personal *threats* to me. But once more I must modestly decline a medal for my moral virtue. There is much more to moral character than finding oneself with implacable inhibitions. The more subtle virtues are not simply implanted; they are taught through precept and example, functions that would seem to exceed the capacities of the criminal law. (But see §4 below on the law as an instrument of moral education.)

If we allow that the criminal law does have a role, at least, in implanting the "minimal negative virtues," like restraint from murder and rape, but not the more difficult (subtle or complex) virtues of civility and beneficence then the most plausible version of legal perfectionism would have the criminal law enforce *only* the rules corresponding to the virtues it *can* help implant and strengthen. It would enforce the mostly negative duties of restraining from violence and dishonesty, not in order to protect victims from harm, but to inculcate the minimal adult requirement of social virtue as an end in itself. In its actual proscriptions and injunctions it would coincide almost exactly with the unsupplemented harm principle, ignoring the higher flights of morality and concentrating on the flagrant mistreatment of one person by another. It would also—incidentally, as it were—prohibit various forms of *public* harm not in order to protect the public interest (as the liberal would have it) but to develop the virtues of public-spiritedness and fair play in the citizens. Since the effectiveness of the criminal law's punitive and condemnatory apparatus for implanting these public virtues is doubtful, the legal perfectionist might not have a reason for criminalizing publicly harmful behavior, unless of course he *also* endorses the harm principle. The harm principle then would legitimate the criminalization of some behavior that perfectionism (all by itself) would not, but there would seem to be no behavior, on the other hand, whose criminalization would be legitimated by perfectionism but not by the unsupplemented harm principle, unless *mirabile dictu*, the criminal law can all by itself *teach* a person how to be genuinely excellent in a more full-blooded way, making the blind see and the uncaring care. Failing that, the principle of legal perfectionism in its practical legislative prescriptions adds nothing to the harm principle, and may even have to borrow here and there from the harm principle if it is to give moral warrant to criminal prohibitions of which we all approve.

In respect to the acts of violence and fraud whose criminalization both legal perfectionism and the harm principle would warrant, does it matter whether we say that their prohibition is for the sake of making people more virtuous or for protecting other people from harm? It could make a great difference, I think. In the first place, the perfectionist reason, in this context, implicates moralistic paternalism in its most extreme form. (See "Definitions of Liberty-limiting Principles," *supra*, p. xx.) The form of perfectionism invoked by such a reason is the principle that it is always a good reason in support of a proposed prohibition that it will improve the character of the very person whose liberty is limited. Unlike the more usual physical and economic forms of paternalism that justify restricting a person's liberty by the need to prevent him from being harmed (i.e. from having his interest set back), this moralistic form of the principle legitimates restrictions on his liberty by the need to confer on him a "benefit" (whether he sees it as such or not), namely, the benefit of an improved character. The state does not tell him that he must be restrained to protect others, nor that he must be protected from himself, but rather "for his own good." If it would be an invasion of his autonomy to restrict his liberty to protect his own interest (as I argued in Vol. III), then it demeans his autonomy all the more to coerce him to increase what we take to be his own benefit. Moreover, since we found reason to doubt (Vol. I, Chap. 2, §1) that a bad moral character necessarily is a harm, one would expect there to be equal reason at least to doubt that an improved moral character is necessarily a benefit.

There is no logical reason, however, why the legal perfectionist cannot *also* endorse the harm principle, so that he would have a double reason for criminalizing violent and fraudulent behavior. In that event, he would have his ideal legislator tell the citizen that he is not at liberty to act in those antisocial ways because doing so would tarnish his virtue and would *also* cause harm to others. And instead of saying that the prohibition is motivated only by the former reason, he might now say that it is motivated equally by both reasons, the harm-preventing reason as well as the perfectionist reason. But if either reason alone is thought to be sufficient, why not abandon the reason that impugns autonomy? That way we can restrict a person's liberty while at the same time showing respect for his autonomy and personal dignity. How the state justifies its restraints then makes a great difference indeed.

In the second place, the criminal law, if its aim is only to make people good, could well be counterproductive, producing the wrong virtue in them, or at least an incomplete virtue in them, for there is a great difference, morally speaking, between acting (or refraining) out of obedience, respect for law, or fear merely, and doing so because one really cares about other people and respects their rights. Heavy emphasis on the importance of personal virtue, if it were educationally effective, could make citizens into conscientious virtue-hoarders, proud of their own excellence, but devoid of warmth and concern for others. That would be self-defeating, of course, because citizens of that description would not be truly virtuous at all. Genuine excellence, I should think, consists in acting or forbearing with genuine understanding of the ground for reasonable restrictions on one's conduct, and a commendable motive for it, not just out of prudent fear of sanctions or the desire for respectability.

The most extreme example of the dissociation of virtue and harm prevention was that of the ancient Stoics. The Stoics valued personal virtue above all other goods. Indeed, to the Stoic sage there was no other good, nothing else worth pursuing as an end, nothing else worth caring about. External events were not totally within his power; if he invested desire and effort in any particular outcome, he could be frustrated and disappointed. The only thing that was totally within his power was trying his best to do his duty, which is precisely what he thought personal virtue consisted in. Stoics, therefore, were not virtuous in order to do good (or prevent harm); rather they did good in order to be virtuous. They did their duty for the sake of moral excellence, but excellence itself they sought for its own sake. Thus, if a Stoic husband had a fatally sick wife, he would conscientiously and tirelessly do his duty as a husband to the very end, treating her pain, comforting her, consoling her. He would do these admirable things not because he cared emotionally what happened to her one way or the other[10]; *all* he cared about was his *own* personal excellence. Bertrand Russell thus parodied the whole Stoic ethic in a nutshell: "Certain things are vulgarly considered goods, but this is a mistake; what *is* good is a will directed toward securing these false goods for other people."[11]

The Stoics' basic mistake, I think, was not over-estimating the importance of personal excellence, but their duty-centered conception of what excellence is. It makes no sense to suppose that a person could truly be morally excellent if nothing mattered to him except his own moral excellence. Yet the Stoic's counterfeit of genuine virtue might lead him into precisely the same conduct as the genuinely excellent person who does care about matters other than his own virtue. The difference is that the Stoic is play-acting, whereas the feeling person cares deeply that the outcomes at which his virtuous actions are aimed come about. And the Stoic cannot satisfactorily explain *why* it should be his duty, say, to treat his ailing wife, if her health or sickness, suffering or peace, life or death, are all matters of indifferent value.

The legal perfectionist does not go so far as to say that nothing has value apart from virtue (or apart from his *own* virtue) and that prevention of harm to others is a matter of indifferent value. But his theory does seem to ground our legal duties on their conducibility to the virtue of the actors rather than on their protection of the interests of those they affect, and it offers no convincing explanation of why these particular acts and abstentions should *be* our duties in the first place. One can paraphrase Russell: "Harm prevention is vulgarly considered to be a good, but this is a mistake; what *is* good (excellent) is a will directed toward securing this false good for other people, and for that reason alone we should legally coerce people to prevent harm to others." That paraphrase would not be quite fair to the legal perfectionist, since he can reply that harm prevention *is* a genuine good but that personal excellence is another genuine good—and in fact the good which provides the reason for our legal duties. That is not as paradoxical a theory as Stoicism, but it does seem to tell the citizen that the *really important* good in the eyes of the state is personal virtue, not prevention of harm to others, since *it* is the good that provides the rationale for restrictions on liberty. If people really believed that, I should think, it would make fewer rather than more excellent persons, since it is not exellent to regard one's own excellence as more important than the rights of others. It is not consistent with the highest virtue to care only (or mainly) about one's own virtue. On the other hand, if the harm principle is *also* endorsed by the legal perfectionist, so that there are now two extensionally equivalent reasons for the criminalization of violence and fraud, then the perfectionist's reason becomes a mere redundancy, or epiphenomenon. If preventing harm is the grounds for a prohibition, and virtue consists in observing the duty to avoid harming others, then of course promoting virtue will also be a reason for the prohibition, but a derivative one. We need to know what conduct causes wrongful harm *before* we can know either what conduct to forbid, or what conduct it is virtuous to avoid. The harm principle shows the way; both criminal law and personal virtue follow behind.

3. Automatic goodness: Skinner versus Mill

In contrast to the ancient Stoics who taught that *only* personal excellence had any value at all, the eminent psychologist B.F. Skinner appears to hold that

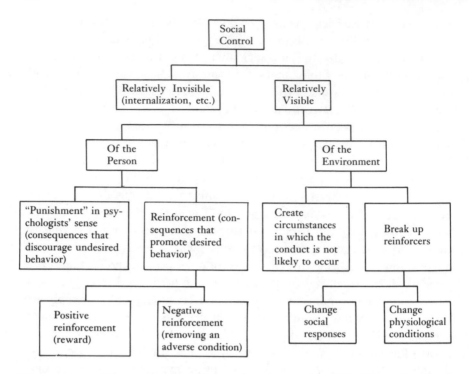

Diagram 33–1. The modes of social control as discussed by B.F. Skinner in *Beyond Freedom and Dignity*.

personal goodness has hardly any importance. The problem for public policy, he writes, is "to induce people not to be good but to behave well,"[13] and it is to his credit that he fully understands the difference between the two. (How well one behaves is determined in large part by the effects of one's behavior on the interests of others; one's goodness is determined by the quality of one's motives and the fullness of one's understanding. An automaton could "behave well" but it could not have a good character.) J.S. Mill, on the other hand, seems right in the middle of the spectrum that runs from Stoicism to Skinnerian behaviorism, paying goodness of character its due, while remaining steadfastly liberal in the limits he assigns to the criminal law. "It really is of importance," he writes in one of his more famous lines, "not only what men do, but what manner of men they are that do it."[14] Mill is a good example, indeed the best example, of how good character can matter to a liberal. Perfecting character is not the criminal law's job, Mill insists, but he won't settle for "automatic goodness" without its necessary internal accompaniment, either. Before examining his views in more detail it will be helpful to establish their essential contrast with Skinner's. (The other essential contrast, with Stoicism, has already been sketched in §2.)

In respect to human behavior, at least, Skinner, like most psychologists, is a determinist. All human behavior, he believes, is in principle explainable by laws of psychology linking certain sorts of responses to certain sorts of stimuli. It follows that human behavior is subject to modification and control by anyone who knows the laws and can control the stimuli. This is not an implausible view to begin with. Indeed it is a presupposition of much scientific work, a view that understandably seems to most social scientists to be beyond questioning. These investigators spend so much of their energies sorting out how much of human behavior is to be attributed to nature (heredity) and how much to nurture (environment) that it hardly occurs to them that there could be qualities that come from neither, but whose source is the "autonomous person" causally independent from both nature and nurture. To the scientific psychologist looking for the causal determinants of behavior, indeterminism is a thoroughly mysterious doctrine.

All human behavior to Skinner, then, is in a sense "controlled," either naturally and, from the human standpoint, "randomly," or else socially. Social control can be indirect and inconspicuous, as when the authority of parents, teachers, or even of "the law" is internalized in the form of a person's own conscience or "superego." The authority, in a sense, still "controls," but his commands are no longer external; they are now a thoroughly absorbed and integral part of the person's own self. Skinner, I think, would say that the conscientious person is not really free, since he cannot act against his conscience, which is, in turn, the voice of outsiders who are still "controlling" him. But if a person's conscience has become an essential part of his own nature, however it was acquired, I think it makes no sense to say that that person is *compelled* by his own nature to act as he chooses. This kind of "moral compulsion" is indistinguishable from genuine self-determination, even though the determining self is originally the product of the external factors that shaped it. Genuine compulsion can only be inflicted by forces independent of the true self, by "outside" rather than "inside causes." The person whose own moral convictions dictate his actions, and who therefore can say, like Martin Luther, "Here I stand; I can do no other,"[15] is probably as close as we can come to an applicable conception of a free person, even given the assumption of determinism.

Social control is more typically direct and relatively conspicuous. This more visible control can work either directly on the person to be controlled or on his environment. When it works on the person, it can be directly forceful, or it can manipulate his motives, as in coercion, persuasion, and inducement. These latter techniques employ either "negative reinforcement" of motives, which consists in making credible "aversive threats," like the threat of punishment, or "positive reinforcement," which consists in making credible offers of "rewards." In time the person learns to associate the threatened aversive response with the antisocial behavior being discouraged, or the promised desired response with the socially acceptable behavior being encouraged, or both. Then, whether through conscious intimidation (or inducement) or from strengthened "force of habit," he becomes more disposed to behave well. Criminalization is a system of social control using only "negative reinforcement." Skinner has very little good to say about the criminal process, which he seems to regard as inefficient, unreliable, and even cruel. He has a more favorable attitude in general toward positive reinforcement, but he says little about it as an alternative to criminal punishment, probably because he thinks it is impractical as a social cure, but not because he shares the contempt of the ancients (particularly the Platonists and Stoics) for those who must be paid to be good.

Skinner prefers techniques of social control that work directly on the environment rather than on the motives of the person. (Despite his materialistic behaviorism, Skinner in some places seems to use the word "environment" in a very broad sense to include even a person's body or brain which are, after all, nearby parts of the world surrounding his choosing self.) Some of these techniques work on the wider environment by creating circumstances in which the unwanted behavior is not likely to occur. These techniques, in effect, reduce or destroy *opportunity*. Thus, Prohibition was an effort to control drunkenness by removing alcohol altogether from the environment. Solitary confinement is imposed on otherwise uncontrollably aggressive prisoners. (They cannot attack people if there are no people to attack.) Theft is minimized by schemes such as that of many municipal bus companies, which have required passengers to pay in exact change on public buses so that bus drivers no longer carry money and attract holdup men. The coins are paid directly into a strongbox, which the drivers are unable to unlock. Almost overnight, bus robberies ceased once and for all, and the need for deterrent punishment vanished. These are examples of "engineering the environment" to destroy the occasions for criminal conduct, at the cost (obviously minor) of closing options to choose antisocial conduct and depriving good people of credit and bad people of blame. If all occasions for crime could thus be eliminated, the elaborate ritual complex of sin, punishment, and remorse would vanish as well, a consequence which, given the unreliability and the suffering associated with the old system, Skinner would not regret.

Another method of engineering the environment in the interest of social control is to "break up the contingencies under which [undesired] . . . behavior is reinforced."[16] If a child is subject to temper tantrums, for example, we can desist from either quarreling or sympathizing with him, and simply ignore him, a strategy that may reduce the incidence of tantrums in the future

by withdrawing social responses that function as reinforcers. More positively, sublimation and displacement activities can be provided, and then our
positive responses to these activities can reinforce them. Thus organized
sport sublimates aggressive tendencies, and our responses to an athletic
achievement can reinforce the motivation for it, thus making antisocial aggres-
siveness less likely. These techniques reduce the inner *need* to behave badly
(or redirect it), rather than the opportunity to do so.

Then in the extreme case in which all the above techniques fail, the social
control could remove the *ability* (rather than the psychological need or the
environmental opportunity) to behave in the undesired way by "changing
physiological conditions." Hormones could be used in "therapy" for sex
offenders; psychosurgery could render the otherwise incorrigibly violent
more docile; appetite depressants could control overeating, and so on. These
methods sometimes must be abandoned because of unforeseen side effects,
and similar practical difficulties have bedeviled some of the other techniques
for reducing antisocial behavior by engineering the environment. "These
problems are in essence soluble, however, and it should be possible to design
a world in which behavior likely to be punished seldom or never occurs. We
try to design such a world for those who cannot solve the problem of punishment [by nature or by man] for themselves, such as babies, retardates, or
psychotics, and if it could be done for everyone, much time and energy
would be saved."[17] In particular, we would no longer have to try to bully or
terrorize difficult people by making aversive threats, or have to back up those
threats by keeping other difficult people under lock and key, while the worst
are hanged, gassed, shot, or electrocuted.

The great drawback of Skinner's imagined world, and the one that he
claims his enemies, "the partisans of freedom and dignity," cite as decisive, is
that it leads only to "automatic goodness." When a person has no choice but
to do the approved thing, then he deserves no credit for doing it. If there are
no people for him to attack then he gets no credit for not attacking them; if
alcohol is removed from his environment, he gets no credit for staying sober;
if bus drivers carry no money, he gets no credit for not robbing bus drivers; if
he is deprived of responsive audiences, he gets no credit for not playing up to
audiences; if female sex hormones reduce his sex drive, or appetite depressants his hunger, then he gets no credit for abstaining from sex crimes or from
overeating. His goodness in these respects is purely automatic, hence not
genuine goodness of character at all. And if one never deserved credit or
blame for what he did, because he had no choice but to do it, this would not
only reflect his lack of freedom; it would also impugn his personal dignity.

Freedom and dignity, however, are overrated values, Skinner insists, and
sacrificing them is a reasonable price to pay for the greater goods of security

from attack and injury, and the cessation of inhumane retaliatory punishments. In this stand, he draws support from the nineteenth century scientist-
philosopher, T.H. Huxley, who made his preference for "automatic goodness" clear: "If some great power would agree to make me always think what
is true and do what is right on condition of being some sort of a clock and
wound up every morning before I got out of bed, I should close instantly
with the offer."[18] Skinner would also accept the offer (though he might prefer
to be the one to *make* the offer!) but perhaps with a tad less enthusiasm than
Huxley. It is not a *fatal flaw* in his engineered world, he insists, that it is a
system (as T.S. Eliot put it) "so perfect that no one will need to be good."[19]
But it is *a* flaw. Skinner readily concedes that "There are, of course, valid
reasons for thinking less of a person who is only automatically good, for he is
a lesser person."[20] In a world freed of dangers, he will not need, nor will he
have bravery. In a world in which hard labor is no longer needed, he will no
longer need to be industrious. In a world in which "medical science has
alleviated pain," he will no longer need fortitude. Many distinctive forms of
personal excellence will disappear because they no longer have a function,
and many of the virtues that remain will be merely automatic, hence
inauthentic. The world will be diminished in one way, but it will also be
freed of a "permanently punitive environment," and of most violence and
cheating. And some of the more agreeable virtues might still remain in a
perfectly genuine form.

There is an implicit assumption in Skinner's argument that criminal punishment is at least partially consistent with the "freedom and dignity" approach
that he rejects. He makes this assumption, if my interpretation is correct,
only for the sake of the argument against his opponents. His own hard
deterministic theory implies, as he freely admits, that we are *never* free of
external controls of one kind or another, that therefore we never deserve
credit or blame for what we do, and that therefore all personal "dignity" is
illusory. Nevertheless, he addresses his opponents by saying, in effect: Let us
assume for the sake of the argument that the person who acts under the threat
of punishment *does* have a choice in the matter. On this assumption, even
though the law which makes the aversive threat is coercive, it does give a
person *some* choice for which he can receive *some* credit if he acts as directed,
since unlike direct physical constraint, it allows him to choose whether to
obey and thus avoid the threatened aversive consequence, or to disobey and
risk being punished. Skinner's enemies, he tells us, do make that assumption,
and for that reason strongly prefer a regime of punishments under law to
Skinner's recommended alternative. But Skinner's response is to affirm that if
freedom and dignity are possible only if we continue to threaten and punish
our antisocial problem-cases, then so much the worse for freedom and dig-

nity. They aren't worth it. In short, Skinner rejects legal perfectionism lock, stock, and barrel. The virtue of character produced by a system of criminal punishments does not itself have enough value to provide, all by itself, the rationale for legitimate criminalization, with its self-righteous cruelties, ineffective threats, and losses produced by undeterred crime. And, of course, if freedom of choice permits law abiders to deserve credit and dignity, by the same token it qualifies lawbreakers for blame, permits the further degeneration of *their* moral characters, and subjects their victims to harm and suffering. To the question, "Which criminal prohibitions are morally legitimate?", Skinner would reply, "none."

Unlike Skinner, John Stuart Mill could not accept merely automatic goodness. It really did matter to him not only what people do but what manner of people they are who do it. Mill's argument, as we might reconstruct it, begins by rejecting the "tacit assumption" I have attributed to Skinner. Since criminal law with its aversive threats really is coercive, and often quite effectively coercive, it is simply not true that it leaves us with a choice to obey or not. The assumption that Skinner makes for the sake of the argument is little more plausible than saying that the gunman's threat "Your money or your life" leaves you with a free choice. The only real difference is that the gunman is already within shooting range; his aversive threat (if he is not bluffing) is more inescapable. Statutory threats of legal punishment therefore must be classified with, not contrasted with, what Skinner calls environmental controls. They do not always make it impossible to choose the forbidden behavior, but they come much closer to making that behavior impossible for most of us than they do to leaving us entirely at liberty to choose. Insofar as we choose socially acceptable behavior under legal coercion, no real credit is due us, for we had no choice about it, and our goodness is merely "automatic." If that acceptable behavior is what we would have chosen anyway if we had been allowed a fully voluntary choice, then it would have reflected our own internalized norms and governing ideals, manifesting thereby a goodness that is more than automatic. Therefore, as far as acquiring good character, manifesting virtue, and deserving credit are concerned, there is no productive role for punitively sanctioned criminal prohibitions to play. In fact, they can be counterproductive, producing only automatic conformity to rules rather than the reasoned choice of conduct that is right, and the sympathetic concern, social cooperativeness, and respect for the rights of others in which genuine virtue in large part consists.

It does not follow that Mill, like Skinner but for opposite reasons, would do away with the criminal law system altogether. He would maintain all statutory prohibitions whose restrictions on liberty can be justified by the need to prevent serious private or public harm. What does follow is that Mill, like

Skinner but for opposite reasons, rejects legal perfectionism. Unlike Skinner, Mill does attribute a great deal of value—indeed a central importance—to the perfection of human character. But that can hardly be a reason for *restricting* the liberty that is absolutely required if human virtue is to unfold and flourish. The perfection of human character is simply not the work of the criminal law. From its perspective, the criminal law is an evil, not a good, but an evil that is sometimes necessary as a means of preventing harm to others when that harm would be grave enough to counterbalance the evil of liberty restriction.

The restrictions on liberty produced by Skinner's favorite methods vary in their severity, and thus put different weights on the measuring scales. When they are less severe deprivations, but equally effective as criminal prohibitions, there is no reason why Mill would not join Skinner in preferring them. Sometimes, as in the municipal bus system's removal of the opportunity for robbery, they complement rather than replace criminal punishments, while minimizing the occasions for their use. Sometimes, as in involuntary psychosurgery, they are flagrant violations of personal autonomy, more extreme than criminal punishment. But even these "alterations of physiological conditions" could be legitimate on liberal grounds, if they were done with the fully voluntary informed consent of the offender. (See the discussion of behavior control, Vol. III, Chap. 19, pp. 66–68.)

It is not that Mill thinks less of human excellence, but rather that he thinks more of human liberty. That is why he rejects legal perfectionism on grounds so different from Skinner's. And if one were able to ask Mill *why* personal liberty is so important, he would not reply that it is a value at once superior to and unrelated to personal virtue. Rather liberty is an essential prerequisite for personal virtue. Without liberty, the most we can hope for from human beings is that they will be effectively conditioned conforming robots, unable to comprehend the grounds of their duties, incapable of subtle discriminations, devoid of human sympathies and respect for rights. If they can escape this "automatic goodness" even now, it is despite the necessary evil of punishment, not because of it. Human excellence comes not from moral intimidation, which by itself can produce only rigid obedience, but from moral education, a job that the criminal law, by itself, is not fit to perform.

4. The educative function of law

Some legal perfectionists have argued, contrary to the above, that the criminal law can, by itself, perform the kind of pedagogic function that is required if citizens are to have virtues beyond mere automatic conformity, unexamined inhibitions, rigid obedience, and the like.[20] All of us would agree that the criminal law can teach people what is in fact permitted and forbidden if, amazing to tell, they had somehow forgotten or failed ever to learn these things, and that the symbolic trappings of legal punishment can express the condemnation of the community in a way that dramatically impresses it on the criminal and "rubs it in." Moreover, judges during sentencing often take advantage of the opportunity to address morally didactic homilies to the hapless convict. Imaginative judges, when they have discretion, may circumvent the prison system to impose especially fitting penalties that give the prisoner a "taste" of what he had done to his victims. A number of years ago, for example, a New England judge faced some teenagers who had been convicted of throwing stones at a passing train, breaking the windows and causing severe eye injuries to some of the passengers. He sentenced them to spend two weeks in an eye injury ward of a hospital with their eyes completely bandaged, and then at the end of their "term" to write an essay on "what it must be like to be blind." This experience presumably helped produce remorse, and in one respect at least, made the prisoners better people than they were before. Even those convicted persons who are sentenced to prison terms may have occasion to be interviewed and counseled by moral "straighteners" during their incarceration, but in their case, the punishment (incarceration) is one thing and the "education" quite another thing, the latter being a supplementary technique for improving the prisoner while he is being punished, not a part of the punishment itself. (This is a point that will be expanded below, pp. 301–305.) In any case, it is a notorious commonplace that moral counseling in the punitive setting of prisons hardly ever works, and that the great majority of prisoners emerge either unchanged morally or worse than before. Apart from such occasional effects of the criminal system as those just surveyed, there seems to be no tendency of that system to produce the improvements in character that Mill so treasured, and which the legal perfectionists accept as a reason for criminalization.

To make someone into a morally better person in a full sense, I should think, would inclue at least the following pedagogic achievements: (1) getting him to *see the point* in right action, (2) getting him *to care* about, not be indifferent to, both the interests and the rights of other people, and to respect their autonomy as he wishes them to respect his, (3) getting him *to be sensitive*, not blind, to the needs and wishes of others, (4) getting him to acquire the habit of *thinking for himself*, and thus avoiding mere conventionality or robot-like goodness, and (5) getting him to acquire certain intellectual virtues that are essential to moral virtue, like the knack of discerning similarities among differences and differences among similarities, and skill at predicting remote causal outcomes, not to mention the more subtle skills involved in Aristotle's notion of practical sagacity (phronesis). How can the criminal law do all, or even *any*, of that? How can it ever be a reason in support of a proposed new criminal prohibition that it will make people morally better, with all that entails, if the obedient majority of them are simply made subject to the threat of punishment, and thus abstain from the prohibited conduct, and the disobedient minority are punished?

To better understand the legal perfectionist's program, we should look at the criminal prohibitions he is most likely to defend on perfectionist grounds, in particular, statutes to which *other* liberty-limiting principles (as he may acknowledge), give no support. We should look for examples where legal perfectionism and the harm to others principle seem to diverge, or are thought to diverge, at any rate, by the legal perfectionist, who nevertheless enforces criminalization in those instances on *exclusively* perfectionist grounds. Two quite different kinds of example come to mind. The first is advocacy of the criminalization of failures to rescue, assist, or protect others. These examples would require people to involve themselves more positively in the affairs of others and exhibit social virtues beyond the merely negative ones of minding one's own business and refraining from inflicting injury. The other kind of example is strikingly different. It involves advocacy of criminal statues designed to protect pure-minded innocents from being corrupted and suffering a kind of "moral harm"[22] that makes them worse people than they would otherwise be, even if it has no deleterious effects on their interests. This second kind of example is a rather negative one. Advocacy of criminalization in these cases is not supported by the prospect of making people better, but rather by the need to "protect" them from getting worse. (Technically, the latter is not a "perfectionist" consideration at all, but stems from "moralistic paternalism." See "Definitions of Liberty-limiting Principles," *supra*, pp. xix–xx.)

A bold and ingenious recent paper in a law journal provides an example of the first kind. Its author, Keith Burgess-Jackson, states his thesis as follows: "Specifically [this paper] argues that a particular type of criminal statute—a bad samaritan statute under which citizens are required to render assistance in time of need (on pain of punishment)—is *justified solely on the basis of its beneficial pedagogical effects on the citizenry*" (italics added).[23] People would be morally better, I don't doubt, if they were more willing to inconvenience or even endanger themselves for the sake of others in need. If their moral improvement were the *only* reason for criminalization of failures to assist, then a liberal would have no grounds for endorsing bad samaritan statutes. I was relieved, therefore, when in my detailed discussion of the bad samaritan problem (Vol. I, Chap. 4), I discovered that the harm principle does give support to such legislation. I argued there that there is a moral right to be rescued if it can be done without undue risk, that such assistance prevents harm to the imperiled party's interest rather than merely conferring a windfall benefit on him, and that the omission to offer assitance can itself be a cause of the harm that ensues. Bad samaritan legislation therefore is for the sake of the imperiled parties, not (or not only) for the moral good of their samaritan rescuers.

But how can threats of punishment improve people's moral characters? There would seem to be a paradox in addressing would-be rescuers as follows: "Learn to have greater concern for the safety of others and less for your own selfish interest or else the law will set back your personal interest by punishing you." Such a law appeals directly to the interest of the party it constrains, a strange way of making him less exclusively concerned with his own interest. It would seem then that if a bad samaritan statute is to be an effective instrument of moral pedagogy, it must be in virtue of some supplementary message attached to it, some demonstration that helping endangered parties is indeed a moral duty and that greater willingness to do so is indeed a moral virtue. In our individualistic society, people may not have fully realized those truths, and the message may come as news to them. Perhaps some sort of preamble in the statute itself could set out in a clear and convincing way the reasons for the new legal duties it imposes. Even if the moral lesson in the statute were convincingly laid out, however, there would be a practical problem in seeing to it that the public has access to it, studies and discusses it, and takes it seriously. Burgess-Jackson admits that "a statute cannot educate unless citizens are made aware of it," and he therefore suggests that "citizens should be provided with a copy of the statute at public expense and tested on it regularly as a condition of obtaining some public privilege, say, a driver's license. Those citizens who fail to understand the reasoning behind the statute, as well as its basic terms, will be denied the privilege in question."[24] (He doesn't tell us whether the test should require essays or mere true or false or multiple choice questions, or whether there is any injustice in depriving people who are untalented at moral philosophy of their driver's licenses.)

Even if the moral reasoning in the statute is comprehensible, convincing, and effectively disseminated, however, there remains a kind of tension between the parts of the statute meant to persuade and the parts that categorically prohibit and threaten penalties for disobedience. One part says: "We are sure that if you are reasonable you will see the need and the rational ground for this new requirement, and that your rational acquiescence will make you a morally better person and influence your conduct accordingly." But then the second part adds: "But just in case we are too sanguine about that, we must warn you that we are prepared to confine you in prison at hard labor for six months if you disobey our command." Strictly speaking, there is no paradox or contradiction between these two parts, but psychologically they might get in each other's way. The nice guy–tough guy alternation might suggest to the skeptical reader that the argument as a whole rests ultimately on the arbitrary threat of force: "Behave in the required way because we will beat you if you don't." I should think it would be preferable to separate functions altogether and create a state office of moral education that is independent of the system of criminal legislation and enforcement. The point to emphasize is that prohibitions backed by sanctions are one thing and didactic essays written in their justification are quite another. The latter, of course, *can* be assigned an educative function (though one might doubt the capacity of government bureaucrats to morally transform the citizenry merely by publishing government documents), but the threat of punishment in itself does not educate. You do not make a citizen a morally better person by frightening him into his duty, though that might be worth doing anyway if it will prevent harm to others.

There are still other difficulties for the perfectionist reconstruction of the rationale for bad samaritan statutes. If the whole point of the statutes is to make people better morally, why not require genuinely heroic self-sacrifices instead of merely helpful conduct done without "unreasonable risk"? After all, the more saintly or heroic a person is, the more moral credit he deserves. There would be obvious *practical* difficulties in such legislation, including problems of individual motivation and social coordination, but on perfectionist grounds, such a statute would be legitimate in principle, practical difficulties aside, since it is always a relevant legitimizing reason for criminal legislation that it aims to improve moral character, and what could be more praiseworthy than self-sacrificing heroism, beyond the call even of moral duty?

The legal perfectionist could protest at this point, following Aristotle,[25] that there is a lot more to *being* courageous than merely acting in an incidentally courageous way from some unrelated motive. In general, Aristotle taught, acts that are incidentally virtuous must be distinguished from those that flow from an already virtuous character, or at least from those that resemble the acts of an already virtuous person in their motivational structure, differing only in strength of habit. Legal intimidation can cause a person to accept grave risks to his own safety to assist another party in peril, but if he acts only because of the intimidation, he does not act in the manner of the truly heroic person who acts "knowingly, of choice, and from an already virtuous disposition." Force alone cannot make him heroic; it can only lead him to pick the less dangerous of two alternatives—the risk of a rescue attempt or the risk of severe punishment. This reply, I think, is perfectly cogent, but it should not be resorted to by the perfectionist only in the extreme case of self-endangering heroism. It applies equally well to the cases normally included in a bad samaritan statute. The selfish person who can't be bothered to throw a life preserver to a drowning swimmer, at no risk to himself, is not likely to be forced into a virtuous character in the full-blown Aristotelian sense, by threats of fine and imprisonment.

The strongest reason against accepting the perfectionist rationale for bad samaritan statutes is that it is *paternalistic* in the most extreme degree. Ordinary moralistic paternalism is bad enough. It argues that a morally worsened character is a kind of harm to its possessor—a "moral harm"—and that the state therefore, on paternalistic grounds, may intervene to prevent people from harming themselves even by their voluntary actions. Legal perfectionism of the sort apparently espoused by Burgess-Jackson goes farther than that. It would justify paternalistic interference not merely to prevent a person from harming himself, but also to force him (or teach him), whatever his own wishes in the matter, to *benefit* himself. In other words, a coercive statute may not only prevent the worsening of the actor's character (Moralistic Harm-Preventing Legal Parternalism), it may also enforce the improvement of the actor's character (Moralistic Benefit-Conferring Legal Paternalism). If restricting a person's liberty to prevent him from being physically harmed is an indefensible violation of his personal autonomy, as I have argued (Vol. III, Chaps. 19 and 20), then all the more so is legal coercion designed to prevent him from inflicting moral harm (which is not genuine harm, in itself, to his interests) on himself. But if legal coercion designed to prevent self-inflicted moral harm is an indefensible violation of personal sovereignty, then *all the more so still* is legal coercion to promote the actor's own moral *good*. If a person is genuinely autonomous it cannot be morally legitimate to address coercive threats at him to force him to improve his character when nobody else's interest would be protected thereby.

The legal perfectionist might rightly reply, of course, that other people's interests *are* protected by bad samaritan legislation, in effect conceding a harm principle rationale for the legislation he recommends. If he has two rationales, however, one provided by the harm principle and the other by legal perfectionism, one of which respects personal autonomy while the other impugns it, then he might have everything a theorist should want if he keeps the one and drops the other. If the statute works, then he will have diminished harm and improved conduct. Improved character requires proper motivation, which cannot be guaranteed by criminal prohibitions, but insofar as that too comes about in time through habit and changed expectations, that would be a fringe benefit.

The more common employment of perfectionist arguments in support of criminal statutes, however, is of the second kind, prohibitions of pornography being the most typical example. The perfectionist argument for the legitimacy of the prohibition in this case would be very difficult to present in a "pedagogic example" or widely distributed "educational" pamphlet. In the bad samaritan example, the argument was to establish a duty to others from which a personal virtue of an other-regarding kind is derived, from thence to derive the conclusion that the reader would be a better person if he had this other-regarding virtue, and finally to assert that to produce that moral benefit is the reason for enforcing the other-regarding duty. But in the pornography case the argument would have to be wholly self-regarding, since it aims to establish the inherent depravity of lascivious states of mind, even when totally private and unproductive of harmful conduct. "You can not read such and such because it would be bad for your character. Trust us; we *know*."

In fact, a habit of reading pornography, like that of reading other stereo-typed pseudo-literature, probably does reenforce stock responses. It is not what one would expect of a person of refinement, cultivation, insight, sub-tlety, and the like. But merely banning the unnutritious experience will not contribute to the greater nutrition of the mind, if it is not followed automatically by genuinely enlightening and stimulating fare. It is much easier to ban literature that does not contribute to virtues of mind and sensibility (like pornography) than it is to require literature that does indeed elevate, in main part because the state cannot force a person to be benefitted by that which he cannot appreciate. By passing bad samaritan statutes the state can force better behavior (whatever its effect on character), but by banning pornography, the state produces neither better conduct[26] nor improved character. Pornography-assisted "wicked" fantasies will be easily replaced by wholly unassisted but equally "wicked" fantasies. And how can the pornography user possibly be persuaded by a didactic essay accompanying the prohibition that it is for his own (moral) good that he be deprived of his favorite reading, when he is initially disposed not to believe that? The most tempting "argument" would merely beg the question, assuming at the start what needs to be shown, that salacious states of mind are inherent evils, unworthy of a truly excellent person. Other arguments might link mistaken beliefs about sex induced by unrealistic pornography to unsatisfactory sexual experiences and "performances" in real life, but a positive antidote like sex-education or good (realistic) literature with sexual themes would be both a more effective and a more economical way of preventing these subtle harms to self than punitive threats.

5. A note on the moral education theory of punishment

There have been few detailed recent discussions, apart from Burgess-Jackson's useful essay, of whether the mere fact of criminalization—in particular its component element of deterrent aversive threat—can have a tendency to improve the moral character of those subject to the threat. But the theory that actual punishment (as opposed to effectively threatened punishment) is justified chiefly by its role as an instrument of moral education is a hardy perennial, not without its current able defenders. Perhaps its most accessible sources in twentieth century philosophy are papers or chapters by J.E. McTaggart,[27] Herbert Morris,[28] Robert Nozick,[29] and Jean Hampton,[30] but I shall restrict my discussion here to the paper of Professor Hampton. In her view, punishment is "a moral message aimed at educating both the wrong-doer and the rest of society about the immorality of the offense. . ."[31] That is not *all* that punishment is, she readily acknowledges, but the pedagogic lesson is a central feature of punishments and one that is essential to their justifications (when they are justified). "Punishments," she adds, "are [also] like electrified fences," staking off forbidden territory:

> Consider the kind of lesson an animal learns when, in an effort to leave a pasture, it runs up against an electrified fence. It experiences pain, and is conditioned, after a series of encounters with the fence, to stay away from it, and thus remain in the pasture. A human being in the same pasture will get the same message and learn the same lesson—"if you want to avoid pain, don't try to transgress the boundary marked by this fence." But, unlike the animal in the pasture, a human being will also be able to reflect on the reasons for that fence being there, to theorize about *why* there is this barrier on his freedom.[32]

This example makes Hampton's commendable motivation clear. Like He-gel,[33] she wishes to locate the element in the punishment of human beings that distinguishes it from the way we treat (say) dogs when we attempt to condition them. In that way she can justify the practice of punishment (at least in part) by showing that it is a way of changing antisocial behavior that is consistent with freedom and dignity.

Hampton's theory of punishment implies no particular theory of the moral limits of the criminal law and is therefore quite consistent with the liberal's rejection of perfectionism as a liberty-limiting principle. Her theory tells us why we are justified in using punishment (understood as Skinner's aversive conditioning plus a "moral message" directed to the prisoner's rational nature and free will) to back up our prohibitions, not what the content of those prohibitions may legitimately be. The question of this book, in contrast, is not (or not only) why Hampton's fence should be electrified, but why it should be located where it is. Understandably then, Hampton takes great pains to distinguish her theory both from what I have called legal perfection-ism and from what she calls "state paternalism." Opponents of paternalism (as a liberty-limiting principle) "have rejected the state's passing any law which would restrict what an individual can do *to himself* (as opposed to what he can do to another). They have not objected to the idea that when the state justifiably interferes in someone's life *after* he has broken a law (which prohibited harm to another), it should intend good rather than evil toward the criminal."[34] The questions "What ought to be made law?" or "What is the appropriate area for legislation?," Hampton tells us, are questions "to which the moral education theory can give no answer, for while the theory maintains that punishment of a certain sort should follow the transgression of a law, it is no part of the theory to say *what* ethical reasons warrant the imposition of a law."[35] It follows, of course, that legal perfectionism, despite its superficial resemblances to Hampton's theory, is an answer to a logically independent question, and that liberalism, which rejects perfectionism, is not a rival to Hampton's theory.

In fact, there is an argument that suggests that the moral education theory of punishment presupposes the *denial* of legal perfectionism, or at least the denial of the view that legal perfectionism can provide a reason, all by itself, even when the harm principle is not implicated, for criminalization. When the human being, in Hampton's pastoral metaphor, learns that the fence is electrified, he can, unlike the animal, "reflect on the reason for that fence's being there, . . . theorize about *why* there is this barrier to his freedom." But suppose that the only answer forthcoming is that "the fence is there in order to make you a better person; that's why." And suppose the prisoner is told that there is no *further* reason why the territory marked off by the fence is forbidden and no further lesson explaining why entering that territory is incompatible with being a good person, except that in the eyes of the state the ideal of a virtuous person includes an unwillingness to walk in that area. If walking on the forbidden ground would *harm* other people and violate their rights, then the state could accept the pedagogical challenge, and reply: "You may not enter because doing so would make you a worse person, and the reason why it would make you a worse person is that it would cause harm to others, and it is part of the state's ideal of a virtuous person that he does not knowingly cause harm to others." Then the moral lesson could be all about the evil of suffering harm and the importance of respecting rights, with the matter of personal virtue left derivative and secondary. But if the forbidden act is not of the sort that causes harm to others, then it would appear empty and groundless to condemn it as a corruptor of the actor's virtue. Even if the act *is* of the sort that would cause harm to others, if *that* is not the reason given for criminalization, the only reason allowed to count being an act's inconsistency with personal virtue, then the state would fall into the stoic make-believe lampooned by Russell. "Certain states," it would seem to say, "like freedom from harm, are vulgarly thought to be goods, but that is a mistake. Only moral virtue is a true and properly enforcible good, and it consists in providing these false goods for others." Hampton's theory of punishment then, at the very least, is consistent with our rejection of legal perfectionism, and may even be thought to presuppose that rejection, at least in perfectionism's strong sense, in which it can be a reason all by itself rather than a reason derived from the harm principle when it also applies.

Even though the moral education theory of punishment is no rival to liberalism, however, there is reason to examine it carefully here on its own terms, if only because legal perfectionists often slip subtly into it. They do so by arguing that a legitimate criminal prohibition is morally beneficial to those who obey it, since by their noninfringement they become morally better people, and, *anyway*, those who don't obey thereby qualify for the moral benefit of legal punishment, if they are willing to accept it. The latter thesis, which seems to suggest the moral education analysis of punishment, remains obscure to me, however. The argument seems to be that punishment can benefit a person by conveying to him not only that the action he performed is prohibited ("The pain says 'Don't!' "[35]), but also "an educative message"[36] to the effect that his action was immoral and for *that* reason prohibited. If he is willing to consider and take to heart this lesson, then his character will be improved, and that will be in itself a benefit to him, whatever the effect on his interests. The moral message that can have such useful effects is simply "implicit in the punishment."[37]

What puzzles me most in this account is what it can mean for a morally educative lesson to be "implicit in the punishment." Clearly the ritual acts constitutive of legal punishment do convey by an implicit symbolism *some* messages. I have myself argued that punishment is a conventional device for expressing the reprobation and condemnation of the community.[38] But it is not clear to me how a solemn condemnation can itself be genuinely educative, how it can make the prisoner realize, what he did not before, that his act was not only disobedient but immoral, and exactly why it was immoral apart from its being disobedient. Insofar as punishment involves compulsory confinement, of course, moral counselors can have the opportunity to instruct and attempt to persuade by rational methods (as opposed to the mere conditioning that Hampton, like Hegel and Mill, detests). But, once again, it is important to distinguish punishment in a strict and proper sense from supplementary techniques used during punishment or contingent consequences of the punishment in its circumstances. In the strict sense, the punishment is the pain and/or deprivation inflicted on the criminal as an authoritative response to his crime, and the reprobation conventionally expressed by it. If one accepts a narrow definition of that sort of "punishment," then the problem for Hampton is to explain just how the authoritative and denunciatory infliction of pain or deprivation of liberty in itself can impart a moral education.

There is, moreover, much to be said for such narrow definitions of "punishment." J.D. Mabbott made the case best in his famous 1939 paper, "Punishment." He argued there that both deterrence and reform were "external to the matter," not being essential parts of punishment or of its justification.

> The truth is that while punishing a man and punishing him justly, it is possible to deter others, and also to attempt to reform him, and if these additional goods are achieved the total state of affairs is better than it would be with the just punishment alone. But reform and deterrence are not modifications of the punishment, still less reasons for it . . . Prison authorities may make it possible that a convict may become physically or morally better. They cannot ensure either result, and the punishment would still be just if the criminal took no advantage of their arrangements and their efforts failed. Some moralists see this and exclude these "extra" arrangements for deterrence and reform. They say that it must be the punishment *itself* which reforms and deters. But it is just my point that the punishment *itself* seldom reforms the criminal and never deters. [Only the publicity deters.] It is only "extra" arrangements that have a chance of achieving either result. . . [39]

If Mabbott is right, then Hampton faces an unenviable dilemma: she must either defend a broad conception of "punishment" that incorporates what Mabbott calls "extraneous" elements, or else explain more successfully than she has how punishment in the more familiar, narrow sense can by itself improve a person's character by methods other than aversive conditioning or supplementary counseling.

Hampton seems to prefer the latter course, as when she compares legal punishment to a mother's punishment of her daughter, which is meant not simply to add the incentive of avoiding pain to the child's future decisions how to act but "to deter her *by convincing her* . . . to renounce the action because it is wrong."[40] Perhaps a mere parental spanking as such can impart a moral lesson to a small child in virtue of the child's prior identification of the parent as the source of moral authority. ("It must be wrong if Mommy feels so strongly about it.") Yet adult citizens can hardly be expected to have a similar attitude towards the state, at least in a democracy, so when the moral education theorist speaks of criminal imprisonment as a way of "convincing" the criminal of the immorality of his act, the reader must suspect irony. In underworld cant, a gun is a "persuader"; in like mode one might speak of a spanking as a "convincer" or "educator."

Punishment in the narrow sense can be indispensably useful to the wrongdoer who is already convinced of the heinousness of his crime and is conscience-stricken over it. His remorse may be genuine when he enters prison, but it may be psychologically essential to him that he undergo punishment as a means of expiation, purification, and reconciliation. In these considerations there may be the germ of a moral reform theory of punishment as applied to those who seek penitence. But many other criminals are not predisposed to repentance, being either dedicated zealots or revolutionaries, calculating amoral risk-takers paying the price, without regret, for their losing gamble, sullen prisoners of the class war (in their own eyes), or sociopathic personalities.[41] Inflicting pain on these individuals by depriving them of their liberty may be socially necessary to protect others, but its most likely effects on the prisoners themselves will be to confirm their cynicism and hatred, or convince them to take greater precautions against discovery next time around—hardly "moral messages."

6. A red herring across the trail: ethical relativism

Some forms of ethical relativism are more plausible than others, but by and large the theory has not found much favor with moral philosophers. Yet the liberal case against legal moralism in some of its expressions may seem to presuppose relativism, and some critics have counted that as a reason against the liberal argument. I have in mind familiar situations in which unsophisticated liberals, arguing against legal moralism, add at a certain point in exasperation—"and who's to say what is morally right, or what is moral virtue, anyway? One group says one thing; one group says another." The liberal however, had better beware of ethical relativism—or at least of a *sweeping* ethical relativism, for his own theory is committed to a kind of absolutism about *his* favorite values. If his arguments conveniently presuppose ethical relativism in some places yet presuppose its denial elsewhere, he is in danger of being hoist with his own petard. Michael Sandel, himself no friend of liberalism, portrays the danger vividly:

> Relativism usually appears less as a claim than as a question. ("Who is to judge?") But it is a question that can also be asked of the values that liberals defend. Toleration and freedom and fairness are values too, and they can hardly be defended by the claim that no values can be defended. So it is a mistake to affirm liberal values by arguing that all values are merely subjective. The relativist defense of liberalism is no defense at all.[42]

The liberal would do well to take Sandel's advice and be cautious in handling the relativistic double-edged sword. Still, the liberal who tends to be relativistic about some of the conflicting "moralities" he would protect need not fear inconsistency if he interprets the basic principles of his liberal political morality as objective truths. Sandel takes ethical relativism to be a thesis about "values." As such, it can be a thesis about some, most, or all values, depending on how sweeping it is. The value category, after all, is quite a miscellany. "Values" include ideals, virtues, duties, preferences, self and other-regarding varieties of all of these, duties imposed by a society's "moral minimum" of rules and others imposed by its "moral residuum" (see *supra*, Chap. 29, §2), or by rules in the residuum's "central core" or rules at its periphery (also Chap. 29, §2), virtues whose basis is in immediate appeal to self or others and virtues whose basis is helpfulness or protection from harm (see *supra*, §1), personal and external preferences (see *supra*, Chap. 29, §4), moral as well as aesthetic and other nonmoral values, and so on. So there is no obvious contradiction in being relativistic about some but not others. And there is even a *prima facie* plausibility in being absolutistic about the duties of the moral minimum and their derivative virtues and flaws of character, while remaining relativistic about the duties and virtues of the moral residuum. There does indeed seem to be a virtually universal cross-cultural consensus about the wrongness of cruelty, mendacity, deceit, and the necessity of prohibiting murder, mayhem, fraud, and theft; whereas mores are diverse and conflicting concerning food and drink taboos, sexual conduct, and a variety of other "values" classified sometimes under "morality." Diversity of opinion, of course, does not imply diversity of truth, and even some of the controversial values (that is, those not associated with the essential moral minimum) may be objective too. But there is no immediate and obvious inconsistency in holding that some values are objective and others merely traditional and customary.

At first appearance then, liberalism is quite compatible with, though it does not require, the view that some of the contending group "moralities," with their conflicting ideals and principles, are closer to objective truth than others. *Even so* (and this is the second part of the liberal reply to the quotation from Sandel), there should be no state interference to enforce the "truer" beliefs and practices. The liberal case for non-interference itself follows directly from the more general moral absolutes of liberal political morality: "tolerance, freedom, and fairness." So objective correctness (which in a given case the liberal can but needn't acknowledge) does not entail enforceability—at least not without further support from the harm principle.

Is it true that (apart from the incautious rhetoric of some of its advocates) liberalism in some of its essential doctrines and arguments "presupposes" ethical relativism? It will be useful, before examining this question directly, to ask what exactly ethical relativism is. It purports to be a theory about "all morality," and since "morality" is a word for a miscellany of norms of conduct and character, one would expect that most ethical relativists would be relativistic about some but absolutistic about others. If we define relativism as a balanced and partial claim of this sort, however, that will seem to make *it* the moderate view. Ethical absolutism, its logical contradictory, will seem to be the extreme position, for if relativism says that *some* moral norms are relativistic, then absolutism will say that *all* moral norms are absolutistic. Perhaps the best approach is to stipulate that a theory of morality (or some part of morality)is relativistic *to the extent that* it interprets norms relativistically and absolutist to the extent that it interprets norms absolutistically. He can proceed from there to suggest that an interpretation of a norm is relativistic to the extent that it models its understanding of that norm and its associated virtue on the rules of etiquette and positive law, and absolutistic to the extent that it uses culturally invariant models like the laws of nature or the laws of mathematics.

In some cultures it is good manners to belch loudly after a meal; in most it is not. In some countries it is illegal to have an abortion, or to gamble in a casino, or to drive on the right side of the road; in others it is not. While we may argue rationally over which customs and laws are wiser, more useful, better or worse than others, we don't say that the better customs of etiquette, simply by virtue of being better customs of etiquette, really apply everywhere, that it is truly bad manners in Ruritania to belch after dinner whatever the local customs are. Nor do we say that it is truly illegal to drive on the left in England despite the local laws. On the contrary, if the rule permitting or requiring belching is established in a given group then it is truly good manners to belch *in that group.* And if the left-side rule has been enacted in a given country, that rule is the law *in that country,* for better or worse. One must specify the group or the country when one states that a practice is good manners or legal, otherwise one's statement is elliptical, waiting to be filled in for full sense. "Good manners," we might ask, "according to whom?," or "relative to which norms?," or "legal in which political jurisdiction?" The ethical relativist is likely to claim that the same is true of moral rules (or *some* moral rules). They are not, he insists, like the laws of nature that science seeks to discover, true everywhere equally, quite independently of what groups of people happen to think of the matter. The particular decisions, practices, and enactments of people, even of highly qualified people like scientists, are not what make statements of natural laws true. Laws of nature are not made true by any set of accepted beliefs, but are true whatever those beliefs might happen to be. The law of gravity cannot apply in one place but not in another. So any community which unanimously held that bodies attract one another with a force directly proportional to their masses and inversely proportional to the *cube* of the distances between them would simply be dead wrong.

According to the ethical relativist, moral rules (or most, or some of them) are just like the rules of etiquette and enacted law, not at all like the laws of nature. If one tribe holds that it is virtuous to go wild with drink periodically or to dispatch one's elderly grandparents, then those things are morally right *in that tribe,* though they may be wrong elsewhere. The absolutistic view, on the other hand, is that these things are morally wrong everywhere, regardless of local beliefs, though we may moderate or withdraw our blame when it is pointed out to us that a given wrongdoer was merely doing what was widely believed to be morally right in his community.

I cannot argue here against an extreme ethical relativism, though it seems to me to be clearly mistaken about moral rules that condemn the arbitrary mistreatment of other people, the invasion of their most vital interests, and various cruel, mendacious, and deceitful practices. What I wish to argue for here is that one can reject this implausible relativism and still be a consistent liberal. When we go beyond the moral minimum of rules, and the mostly negative and minimal virtues associated with them, and consider the more positive virtues, and duties of group membership like cooperativeness and fair play, relativism is mistaken, I think, even about many of *them*, though some, for example religious duties and the associated virtue of piety, do fit the relativistic account, and a liberal need have no embarrassment, nor incur any vulnerability in saying so.[43]

What then is the argument of traditional liberalism that may suggest relativism? When Mill is discussing questions of harmfulness, and particularly harm to bodily health or economic interest, he permits himself to use what appears to be objectivist language. In arguing against paternalistic interventions that purport to be justified by empirical judgments linking dangerous behavior to self-harms of a physical, psychological, or economic kind, Mill writes that ". . . the strongest of all the arguments against the interference of the public with purely personal conduct is that when it does interfere, the odds are that it interferes wrongly and in the wrong place."[44] On the other hand, Mill admits that public opinion is more often right than wrong in its judgments about the likelihood that actions of certain kinds will have injurious effects on the interests of *others*. That is because each person, as a member of the public who can be affected by the actions in question, is asked only to judge his own interests and how certain actions of others would be likely to affect them. When asked to judge the effects of self-regarding conduct, however, he must give his opinion "of what is good or bad for other people," a matter much more difficult to judge. That is hard enough for questions of physical or psychological or even economic harm, but much more difficult still for "harm to character," where there is less agreement presupposed on what constitutes ("moral") harm and the judgments are more often required to go beyond the empirical questions of cause and effect.

In respect to "harm to character" then, the impatient liberal is likely to jettison Mill's objective language and substitute the relativist's question: "And anyway, who's to say what is *morally* beneficial or *morally* harmful to other individuals? Who is to say, harm to our interests aside, what is virtuous conduct productive of good character and what is morally flawed conduct productive of bad character? It is difficult enough to judge what is physically or psychologically harmful to the other party when the facts are hard to come by and the danger of error is great; but it is more difficult still (so the relativistic liberal concludes) to judge what is morally elevating or corrupting where the facts (if any) are *impossible* to come by, when one must judge, for example, the comparative merits of sectarian and liberal life-styles, or of Moslem and Christian dietary practices. We can say that eating pork is wrong (as well as bad manners) in Moslem communities but not in Christian ones, but that neither community practice is wrong absolutely, that is, wrong in all communities regardless of their own rules and traditions. When we ask "Who's to say which practice is truly right?" we mean "No one *can* say that either is truly right, that is, right in every social group, local customs notwithstanding." On the other hand, when we compare two communities, one in which physical violence is countenanced and cruelty deemed a virtue, and the other in which violence is condemned and cruelty is deemed a serious moral failing, the liberal can join the absolutists and argue that cruelty is immoral everywhere whatever local traditions may say. So whether "morality" is relative or absolute may depend on what we mean by morality, whether we are referring to its inner core transcultural principles or to those local rules that define and distinguish particular communities. What leads to the association of liberalism with relativism in the public mind is that the controversies that divide liberals from legal perfectionists and other legal moralists tend invariably to be over proposed legal enforcement of local sectarian "moralities" for which the relativistic analysis is plausible.

In respect to these controversies over legally enforcing subcommunity norms, however, the ethical relativism issue is a red herring. Liberals need not argue that the norms are merely relative to group practices in the manner of rules of etiquette or traffic ordinances to support their stand against legal enforcement. They need only insist on the *fact* of ethical disagreement for the arguments of J.S. Mill to apply. They do not need to make the fallacious inference from factual diversity to ethical diversity (diversity of ethical truth), as some of the more naive relativists do. The point they should insist on is that reasonable persons can and do differ in their genuine convictions about the correctness of various sectarian norms, that these disagreements, whether or not they might be resolvable in principle, can be, and often are, intractable. That fact does not *show* that neither side (or both sides) is right, as the relativist holds, although it is consistent with that position. Nor does it *show* that there is no "fact of the matter," no reasons that might be telling for the one position but not the other. But it does show the wisdom and the justice of refraining from force, even legal force, as the expression of the greater power of a political majority, to settle the matter. When we give moral license to state enforcement of the majority will, overruling individual autonomy even in matters that do not violate the rights of others, that is unfair in itself; moreover (and this is the point which Mill emphasized), there is no telling what values will be enforced in the name of universal truth; sometimes, at least, objectively mistaken values will be enshrined, while dissenters who recognize this will be imprisoned for that reason. And, what is perhaps not quite so bad, sometimes the state will enforce a merely "relative truth" as if it were an absolute one. The absolutistic political morality of liberalism insists that it is objectively wrong, in either kind of case, to impose constraint on dissenters. One example of each follows below.

Legal perfectionists sometimes argue against legalized voluntary euthanasia that there is a virtue in suffering bravely, and that to take the easy way out prevents the development of that virtue and of ennobled character. Fortitude is indeed a virtue, and in many of life's difficult situations an indispensable one. But the legal perfectionist, in the argument I have ascribed to him, has used a mistaken analysis of that virtue. There is no virtue in pointlessly suffering for no purpose other than to strengthen one's moral muscles to endure further pointless suffering. In this example, coercing someone to be virtuous is a way of enshrining an objectively mistaken value at great cost in suffering to the coercee.

For an example of coercion to virtue that might enforce a merely relative virtue as if it were an absolute (transcultural) one, I turn to the history of the European colonization of Africa, in which a culturally distinct minority imposed hardships on the majority, justifying them by the "moral improvement" (according to the alien standards of the enforcers) that they would produce. The Europeans made supreme virtues of self-advancement, diligence, and thrift. The natives they imposed upon, on the other hand, had evolved a system of collective responsibility, well adapted to their circumstances, guaranteeing survival for them all in an insecure preindustrial rural economy. The ordinary Africans, according to Basil Davidson,

> . . . had no zeal for accumulation. It was to be one of the great complaints of European settlers in Africa that the "savages" were immune to the offer of monetary award—that their objection to earning money lay not only in their unfamiliarity with it and what could be done with it but also and above all in their unwillingness to work beyond the mere point of providing for themselves and their families. Schooled in a sterner tradition, these settlers saw in such "stubborn idleness" a main proof of damnation . . .
>
> Both Protestants and Catholics saw matters in this way but the Puritans said it most clearly. "The standing pool is prone to putrefaction," said Richard Steele in *The Tradesman's Calling*, published in 1684, "and it were better to beat down the body and keep it in subjection by a laborious calling, than through luxury to become a castaway." Such ideas would serve later on as a moral veneer for methods of coercion. Speaking on his Glen Grey Act of 1894—a measure which imposed an annual money tax on Africans in South Africa so as to force them to leave their villages and go to work for European-paid wages—Cecil Rhodes

uttered a comment which may stand as typical. "You will," he told the Legislative Assembly of the Cape Province, "remove [the Africans] from that life of sloth and laziness: you will teach them the dignity of labour and make them contribute to the prosperity of the State: and make them give some return for our wise and good government." Across a crazy paving of such ideas as these the clumsy steamroller of subjection and "trusteeship" has gone testily through the years; and only of late have men begun to question its right of way.[45]

Legal perfectionism would not necessarily lead, of course, in every case, to such abuses. But there is a high probability that the policy of self-righteous coercion to virtues, beyond the coercion justified by the harm and offense principles, in the long run would produce many such outrages. That likelihood further weakens perfectionism's claim to legitimacy, a claim that is weak enough to begin with.

7. Harm and nonbenefit again

Legal perfectionism, in the narrow sense my definition has assigned it, is a benefit theory. Limitations on liberty are legitimized by the positive benefits the coercees or third parties receive in the form of improved character. The theory comes in two primary forms, one a moralistic counterpart of extreme paternalism, the other a moralistic counterpart of the harm principle. The paternalistic version in effect tells the citizen that the state may use legal coercion against him not only to prevent (moral) harm to him but for his own positive (moral) good. The benefit principle that is a moralistic analogue of the harm-to-others principle—the moral benefit to others principle—claims that legally coercing A can be legitimate if, morally or otherwise, it benefits others, either specific third parties like B or C, or the public generally. Except indirectly (Vol. I, Chap. 4), we have not discussed benefit theories generally. Such theories are not widely held when the benefits in question are the more familiar physical, psychological, and economic kinds, or where the benefits consist in the promotion of ordinary welfare interests to advanced transminimal levels or the realization of more specialized focal aims, but they deserve some discussion here, partly for the sake of completeness, and partly because they lead quickly into deep questions of political theory where we cannot follow them.

Benefit-conferring legal paternalism (Table of definitions, p. xx, #9) is in a clear sense a more *extreme* version of ordinary harm-preventing legal paternalism (Table of definitions, p. xix, #4). If our arguments in Volume three against legal paternalism are convincing, then all the more so would extreme paternalism be vulnerable to them. That is to say that if it is not morally legitimate to constrain a person even to prevent harm (set-back interest) to him, then all the more so must it be illegitimate to constrain him for the sake of conferring a benefit on him. But we cannot avoid, on similar grounds, discussing the general benefit-to-others principle, since we have *not* already rejected its weaker analogue, the harm-to-others principle. It *is* a good reason for coercion, we have conceded, that it will prevent harm to others; maybe, for all we can know in advance, it is also a good reason for coercion that it will positively benefit others, that is bring them to a condition beyond the baseline of their normal state or the condition we initially find them in. Perhaps we should be made to confer on others not only "benefits" whose absence would be harmful to them (which they *need*), but also some further benefits (in a proper sense) whose absence would not be harmful to them (which they do not *need*). That is the possibility we will consider briefly in this section.

The natural examples that come to mind of windfall benefit-conferrals seem to be mostly pecuniary, and the idea that *they* could be moral duties, much less proper legal duties, seems absurd. If I randomly walk up to some well-dressed stranger on the street and "confer a benefit" upon him (what could that be but money or something worth money?), say by giving him $100, my action would seem to make no sense. My beneficiary is not a creditor of mine, so I had no obligation to pay him and he had no entitlement to be paid by me. He is not a member of "the deserving poor," therefore my donation is not an act of charity and could not satisfy any general "duty of charity" I might have. Neither is my beneficiary a member of "the undeserving poor," so my act cannot count as an act of mercy or simple humanity. Instead it seems a purely gratuitous act, a random gift from my perspective, and a pure windfall gain from his. If it seems absurb for me to do this voluntarily, a law compelling me to do so would be absurdity on stilts.

And yet a powerful traditional argument for the exclusivity of the liberal's commitment to the harm and offense principles is that it does not legitimize some enforced acts of benefitting, that is some bestowals of advantage that are more than mere nonharms. Governmental subsidies for high-powered telescopes are strictly needed only by that small minority of citizens who are impelled by powerful cosmic curiosity, yet are paid for, often ungrudgingly but still necessarily, by all of us. Similar remarks could be made about requiring everyone to pay for subsidies to opera companies, symphony orchestras, the arts and humanities generally, and even the more abstruse and "impractical" sciences. Such requirements are less obviously fair than making us all pay (say) for police forces that protect people, including us, from harm.

James Fitzjames Stephen argued in this fashion against Mill in 1873. Speaking of such examples as those I have given of enforced support of government subsidies, he wrote,

> None of these can in the common use of language be described as cases of . . . the prevention of harm to persons other than those coerced. Each is a case of coercion for the sake of what the persons who exercise coercive power regard as the attainment of a good object, and each is accordingly condemned . . . by Mr. Mill's principle. Indeed, as he states it, the principle would . . . condemn . . . all taxation to which the taxed party did not consent, unless . . . [their purposes could be described as protective of others from harm] . . . To force an unwilling person to contribute to the support of the British Museum is as distinct a violation of Mr. Mill's principle as religious persecution. He does not, however, notice or insist on this point, and I shall say no more of it . . .[46]

The problem raised by Stephen, of course, is not just that of justifying forced support of the British Museum, but of justifying mandatory taxation in general. The problem of this book, on the other hand, is to justify legislative proposals of another liberty-limiting kind, namely those that create criminal offenses. The only *crime* resulting from the taxation process is tax-evasion (in a sense wide enough to include tax fraud). *That* crime is legitimately created on harm-principle grounds. If there were no crime of tax evasion, then there would be no efficient way of raising revenue for public expenditures, at least some of which are needed by everyone (courts, police, defense forces, some social insurance schemes), and all of which (even telescopes) are needed by someone or other. So there is no insurmountable problem in legitimizing the crime of tax evasion. Stephen's more general problem about taxation gets us into areas of political theory where we have not yet ventured, and we cannot pursue them far in that direction. In general, that problem is how to legitimize particular legislative proposals of projects and causes to be supported by public revenue, as well as other proposals of how these programs are to be financed—in particular, who is to be taxed and how. Such questions are much more complex than questions calling for us to decide what conduct is to be prohibited and by threat of what penalties, and we would have even less expectation that some "single simple principle" could offer an answer.

Tax-supported bills of the sort thought by Stephen to be a problem for Mill often create patterns of benefits that put most citizens in one of four categories: (a) those whose interests would otherwise be adversely affected, (b) those who would be benefitted by what is proposed but would not otherwise be harmed, (c) those "indifferents" whose interests would not be directly affected one way or another, and possibly (d) those whose interests would be directly harmed by the proposed legislation (presumably there are many in this fourth category). Since all four groups would, in their capacities as taxpayers, suffer some damage to their pecuniary interests if the bill passed, all those in category (c) as well as (d) would be net losers. Some of those in category (b) might be net losers too, if the degree of benefit promised by the proposed legislation would be less than the degree of pecuniary harm represented by the tax levy. Other members of (b) might find that the expected advantage to them outweighs the cost, so they would be net gainers. All members of category (a)—usually a small class—would be net gainers since in being provided with what they need they would be protected from a harm, and the cost of that protection would be shared by everyone else, thus diluting their own pecuniary harm to the point where it will seem a reasonable price to pay.

An important point overlooked by Stephen is that there almost always are some people in category (a). *Some* people would suffer setbacks to their interests if the British Museum were not supported, though perhaps most of those who are forced to pay taxes in its support would not be harmed on balance even if the British Museum were to disappear entirely. But for scholars who depend directly on the Museum's resources, withdrawing those resources would be a serious setback to some of their most important personal interests. That fact by itself does not automatically justify taxing the others, but it shows that the bill of legislation supporting the British Museum can be classified as taxing some people to *prevent harm* to others, as well as taxing some people to provide a mere benefit to others (those in category b).

It is also important to note that some of those whose interests would not be harmed by the impoverishment of the British Museum would be harmed by the withdrawal of some other governmental subsidy—the weakening of support for the visual arts, or the theoretical sciences, or the loss of the tax exemption for churches (an indirect subsidy). This suggests that there may be a justification for the whole system of which these particular enactments are the products. When the system works fairly, it may make it seem tolerable to the citizens it represents that sometimes they should be net losers, provided they have a fair opportunity to be net winners other times. Almost everyone may have reason to prefer such a system of fluctuating benefits to its more cumbersome alternatives in which, for example, unanimity is always required for appropriations.

When it comes to political institutions, there is much to be said, I think, for the view that what is the primary subject of justification is the full institutional complex of rules and practices, not each small component or byproduct of it, in isolation from the rest. Part of that complex consists of a democratically elected legislature, using majority rule to govern its procedures, making laws of which some confer powers, others prohibit and regulate conduct directly, others raise revenue, and still others set up programs to be paid for out of the revenues that were raised by virtue of the techniques and powers created by other rules. The system is meant to represent the interests and wishes of ordinary citizens and groups. Thus, if a given citizen is in the minority on one issue of how to spend money from a pool to which he has been forced to contribute, he will have a fair chance to be in the majority on another such issue. Different programs will create different patterns of protectees, beneficiaries, and indifferents, and each represented citizen will (it is hoped) "win some and lose some," never feeling as a consequence that he is completely overlooked and impotent. Individual tax-supported programs win their moral legitimacy (though in specific instances they may not be ideally wise, fair, or useful), and are in that sense justified (legitimized), by virtue of being the end product of a legitimate procedure, a complex institutional practice without which, in turn, everyone would be a net loser. That is the sort of justification for legally compelling people to pay for particular programs, like the British Museum, which they do not want, and from which they may not benefit. Citizens pay their money and take their chances, knowing that they will not win all the time, but also that they may be protected from harm to some of their own vulnerable ulterior interests which are not widely shared.

It is not an essential part of the rationale for coercion, as Stephen suggests, that it permits some people to be gratuitously benefitted at the expense of others. The benefit-to-others principle is a silly principle. When it seems to be the only principle that can legitimize an obviously unsilly use of political coercion, that is because a more subtle and complex set of reasons is doing the work behind the scenes. These reasons show the overall fairness and utility of an institutional practice which in some circumstances permits taxing some for the "benefit" of others. It is not the "benefit-to-others" principle, however, that legitimizes criminalizing tax evasion, for if evading taxes were not a crime, this highly beneficial and protective system would not work, and that would be a public harm of major magnitude. It is no accident that the crime is defined in terms of failing to pay one's assigned share to the general tax funds; there is no separate crime of failing to pay one's share of support for the British Museum, a crime supposedly legitimized by the benefit-to-others principle!

Providing an accurate description and actual justification of the political system that works so well it can tolerate instances in which the unbenefitted are required to pay for the protection and/or benefit of others is well beyond the scope of the present work. But I have attempted to sketch one form such justification might take. Supplementary modes of justification might employ the new techniques of the theory of collective action.[47] If those who were unwilling to pay their share of the cost of a particular piece of legislation were exempted, the per capita costs to the remainder would go up, making many of them unwilling to pay, further elevating the costs, and so on. Many citizens would discover that what is in their individual interests is that they pay provided others also *pay in numbers sufficient to make the unit costs reasonable*. But without any assurance of forthcoming cooperation, enough of them might drop out so that the final costs would be prohibitive for the remainder. In that case the legislation might fail, which would deprive some otherwise willing taxpayers of mere unneeded benefits (windfall advantages) but would inflict real setbacks to the interests of those who were in genuine need. Even if the costs should reach an expensive equilibrium acceptable to a majority, there may be no way of excluding nonpayers from sharing the benefits,[48] so that free-riders, after having raised the costs to others, can share the benefits that come free to them. These familiar difficulties and many other similar complications create a powerful case that it is to everyone's initial advantage to have a kind of coercive voting rule, permitting a majority in given instances to spend money from a central pool to which the constituents of the dissenting minority have contributed.

8. Conditional acceptance of a coercive rule: a brief note on collective goods

There are many situations in which it is in the interest of each member of a group to agree to behave in a certain way which *prime facie* may seem self-sacrificial, on condition that many or all the other members similarly agree. In the simplest cases a coordinating uniformity is itself the collective good in question. It is in no one's interest to lack a governing convention about which side of the road to drive on, and each person can agree to drive on the right side assuming the others do too. Any rule would be better than none at all. It would be (indeed it was) entirely legitimate for a legislature to impose a coordination rule backed by criminal sanctions, on the assumption that each person would voluntarily agree to be subject to such a rule if he could be assured (as the enactment of the rule in fact assures him) that the others would agree also. The rationale for the rule will appeal to the harm principle, though obviously that principle is applied to coordination problems in a somewhat less direct way than to other problems, for the chief harm averted is the chaotic condition of having no rule, not some condition (like broken bones) that is harmful independently.

In another kind of case where a major part of the rationale of a coercive rule is the assurance it gives each person that the others will conform, the harm averted has a source other than simple lack of coordination. Let me take an example not of a criminal statute but a rule of a private organization, an International Olympic Committee, or the rule-making body of some other international athletic federation concerned with sports requiring physical strength, like javelin throwing, wrestling, or weight lifting. At issue is whether the use of anabolic steroids to build muscular strength should be prohibited. Each athlete might reason as follows. I have two strong interests at stake: (1) my competitive interest in having a fair opportunity to win (say) a medal, and (2) my health. (An authority writes: "The American College of Sports Medicine as well as other medical groups warn against serious side effects. These are believed to include, at least at high levels of dosage, liver damage, atherosclerosis, hypertension, and a lowered sperm count in males.")[49] If all competitors use steroids, then I have the option of endangering my health or losing my fair opportunity to win my competition. Thus, I will be harmed one way or the other. A compulsory rule would prevent that harm and thus be manifestly in my interest as well as in the interest of my competitors, for now we all can protect our health interest without fear of putting ourselves at a competitive disadvantage. Since it prevents harm to everybody who is subject to it, a prohibitory rule is justified by the harm principle, and the behavior it requires, which would seem self-sacrificial but for the assurance it gives that my competitors comply too, is now in my best interest. Both my competitors and I are better off with such a rule, and if we understand its function and trust the techniques for its enforcement, we will happily consent to it.

After the coercive rule is adopted and becomes established, new expressions of consent are no longer required to renew and maintain it. It simply "remains on the books." New athletes become subject to it without having formally consented to its authority. Nobody, however, will take that to undermine the rule's legitimacy. The consent we attribute to the athletes is not (or not merely) hypothetical rational consent, the consent they would give if they were rational (see Vol. III, pp. 184–86), but the actual consent we presume they would give if asked, since we assume that they are reasonable people. The rule then is not paternalistic in the sense that it imposes duties of prudence on people without their voluntary consent, but rather it finds its legitimization in the harm it prevents each from suffering grudgingly in order to avoid a competitive disadvantage caused, with equal reluctance, by the others. No new nonliberal legitimizing principle is implicated in this reasoning. What is involved in the reconstructed rationale for the coercive rule is a more complicated way of applying the harm principle. Without a coercive rule the situation is tragically tangled. Like residents of Hobbes's state of nature, each athlete finds himself coerced by all the others into behaving in a way dangerous to his health, and thereby, also out of self-defense, coercing all the others into endangering *their* health. Everyone is a reluctant coercer of everyone else. A prohibitory rule against steroids, backed up by sanctions, would liberate all who become subject to it. The rule is justified by its *prevention of the harm* that each party is forced in self-defense to inflict on all the others. The mode of justification is liberal, neither paternalistic nor moralistic.

Conclusion

1. Making the strongest case for liberalism

A book as long as this one deserves a short conclusion. It would not be wise to attempt to summarize the conclusions and their supporting arguments regarding the myriad of subtopics discussed in this four-volume work. The book as a whole provides strategic groupings of problems within its general organizational structure, and there are so many of them that there is no point in repeating, even in abbreviated form, its various analyses and theses, for example about "moral harm," death as a harm, "wrongful life" suits, bad samaritan statutes, environmental harms, imitative crimes, offensive nuisances, mistreatment of dead bodies, organ transplant policies, the "bare knowledge" problem, "Skokie-type" free speech cases, pornography, "fighting words," obscene language on radio programs, autonomy and paternalism, reasonable risks, dangerous drugs, mandatory protective helmets, neurosis, coercion, fraud, voluntariness and drunkenness, voluntariness and depression, voluntary euthanasia, living wills, collective harms, cultural change, linguistic and evolutionary models for cultural change, community, tradition, alienation, the concept of a morality, retributive punishment, exploitation, ticket scalping, blackmail, the concept of character, ethical relativism, and many others. I hope that all of these subtheses can easily be found by a curious reader, that they can be understood and evaluated independently of the book as a whole, and that some of them, at least, are correct. I intend this work, however, to be more than a loose collection of interrelated essays.

Throughout, the overriding concern has been the tenability of liberalism as an account of the moral limits of the criminal law.

Detailed as it has been, however, the discussion up to this point has not been able to generate a clear answer to the question of whether or not liberalism, as here understood, is correct. I have tried to put the doctrine in the best possible light, modifying it or qualifying it where necessary, defending it against facile "refutations," supplying it with normative content, positing mediating maxims for its application, stipulating new definitions for its constitutive terms, acknowledging apparent exceptions, twisting it to accommodate apparently unassimilable examples, exercising as much dialectical dexterity as a I can in its behalf. Through four volumes the argument has taken a zigzag course, making unanticipated changes of direction to avoid unforeseen obstacles, jettisoning unnecessary cargo, taking new compass readings to get back on course after windblown detours. The weary liberal reader, aware that his initial liberalism may not have survived altogether unscathed, must feel something like Voltaire's Candide after repeated encounters with Turkish pirates and similar hazards. The author shares that feeling.

There are some undoubted soft spots in the case for liberalism, and in virtue of these it is impossible for me to claim that I have shown liberalism to be true, or—what comes to the same thing—that I have shown legal paternalism and legal moralism to be false. Instead, what I have tried to do is to give shape to the doctrine that is closest to traditional liberalism from among those that are plausible, or alternatively, to develop the most plausible doctrine from among those that can be called liberal. The theory that emerges, loose strings, soft spots and all, is not the "one very simple principle" that Mill affirmed in *On Liberty*, but a much more complicated construction. This should not surprise us, since the rival liberty-limiting principles are not absurd on their face and have been defended by wise and decent persons. While arguing against them, I have tried to be alert to the possibility that each might contain a kernel of truth, or the germ of some significant difficulty for a theory that employs the harm and offense principles alone. Where I have been forced to make concessions to them and subsequent amendments to my liberalism, I have tried to do this in a way that departs as little as possible from the original formulation, and without my primary concern being whether the modified theory still qualifies for the liberal label. (In the end, the definition of liberalism itself will have to change if the resultant theory is still to be called "liberalism"; see §2 below.)

Frequently the form these efforts have taken in the preceding pages has been to bolster liberalism by adding supplementary provisions meant to obviate otherwise formidable objections to it. For example, the interpretation of *de jure* individual autonomy as a kind of absolute personal sovereignty was necessary, I argued, to defend liberalism from the otherwise potent arguments of legal paternalists that mere "liberty" is a value that can sometimes be "outweighed" by reasonable estimates of the actor's own good. Without so strong a concept, liberalism, I fear, is a sitting duck. *That* conclusion can be considered one of the central theses of this book. How does it bear then on the question of whether liberalism is a true doctrine? It obviously doesn't answer that question. What it asserts is that any version of liberalism that lacks such a theory of autonomy will be inadequate, and that therefore a version of liberalism that does employ so strong a conception of autonomy has a better chance of being adequate, *ceteris paribus*, than one which does not.

Another way to put this point is to say that I have tried in this work to inform the would-be liberal what some of the "costs" of his theory are in terms of other positions to which a defensible liberalism seems to commit him. If the interpretation of autonomy as sovereignty seems independently unappetizing to him, he may wish to evade any commitment to it, in which case he will have to abandon some ground to the paternalist. Similarly, I have argued (*supra*, pp. 55–62) that "when two persons each have interests in how one of them leads his life, the interests of the one whose life it is are the more important," partly on the grounds that this is the judgment most consonant with personal sovereignty, but also partly on the grounds that liberalism will be an easy mark for "the impure moral conservative" without this supplementary criterion of "importance." My strong thesis again is not that liberalism has been shown to be true, but that without this supplementary feature liberalism will be fatally vulnerable, that it will condone illiberal laws on ultimately liberal grounds. Once again, liberals who are not attracted to the recommended judgment of the relative importance of conflicting harms on its own merits will have to decide whether its "cost" to their belief systems generally is too great to justify the protection it provides against an otherwise lethal objection. If the cost is excessive, then liberalism as we understand it in ordinary life may have to be abandoned, and the community prohibition of otherwise "harmless private activities" must be conceded in certain circumstances to be legitimate. On the other hand, if the cost is not excessive, then the proposed criterion of importance becomes part of the most plausible doctrine that can still be called, "with linguistic and historic propriety" (see Vol. III, p. 3) "liberal."

2. Belated redefinitions

One final change of course is necessary before the task of fashioning the "most plausible liberalism" is completed. As things now stand, liberalism as strictly defined in this work is not only not plausible, it is quite clearly not true! The remedy for this embarrassment is not to seek further arguments to show that the patently false is really plausible, but rather to readjust the system of definitions so that liberalism as plausibly redefined can be seen to be seriously eligible for belief. Whether the view I find most compelling is properly called "liberalism" is not a very interesting question. "Liberalism," after all, is just a name. Moreover, no matter how much precision we try to give to it, it will have still a wide margin of ineradicable vagueness simply in virtue of the kind of name it is. "Liberalism," I wrote in Volume one, "requires commitment to the presumption in favor of liberty." (p. 14) But how strong must that presumption be? It "could be thought of at one extreme as powerful enough to be always decisive, and at the other as weak enough to be overridden by any of a large variety of liberty-limiting principles, even when minimally applicable." Liberalism then, however it is further specified, is a matter of degree, depending on how great a surcharge the liberal would impose on the reasons that can outweigh liberty. How much weight does liberty put on the decisional scales, and how much weight therefore does another kind of reason have to exert in order to override it? Any liberal will say that liberty has "substantial weight" compared to other kinds of considerations, but there is room for much disagreement among liberals about exactly how much weight that is, and more precise quantitative measures are not readily available. So "liberalism" remains vague, representing the upper segment of a scale of degrees of valuing liberty. Everyone (almost) "believes in" liberty, but how strongly must one believe in it, how much must one love it compared to other things, in order to be a liberal?

I did not hesitate long in answering that question in the Introduction (pp. 14–15) in Volume one. To be a liberal one must value liberty far more than one objects to voluntarily risked injuries or "harmless immoralities": "We can define liberalism in respect to the subject matter of this work as the view that the harm and offense principles, duly clarified and qualified, between them exhaust the class of morally relevant reasons for criminal prohibitions. Paternalistic and moralistic considerations, when introduced as support for penal legislation, have no weight at all." By Volume four, it had become apparent that this definition defined a position that was liberty-loving enough to be called "liberal," but too extreme to be called "plausible." I had wisely avoided the language of necessary and sufficient conditions in defining the various liberty-limiting principles, speaking instead of "always relevant reasons." Liberalism then, as I defined it, entails that the prevention of certain obvious evils (voluntarily risked injuries and free-floating evils like harmless immoralities and unjust gains), insofar as those evils do not ground grievances and are therefore "harmless" in our technical sense, are always and necessarily *irrele-*

vant and hence *utterly without weight* as reasons for criminal prohibitions. That position, however, is obviously too extreme. The need to prevent evils of any description is at least *some* kind of reason, putting at least *some* amount of weight, however slight, on the decisional scales. It is wrong to say that it is neither here nor there, having no bearing at all, as a person's eye color, for example, would have no bearing. To be sure, this concession is a trivial one, correcting an inadequate definition merely, with no obvious implications for any substantive matter. But it does turn our attention immediately to the important question: Which types of evils are those the prevention of which is a *good* reason for criminal prohibitions? In response to this question the liberal will want to hold his ground stubbornly.

In formulating definitions of liberty-limiting principles in terms of reasons, we may choose among a half dozen variables. First there are the modal or temporal qualifiers: always, never, and sometimes. Second, there are the variables designating degrees of cogency: relevant (at least minimal weight), good (substantial weight), and good enough (decisive weight). All of the major coercion-legitimizing principles (the harm and offense principles, legal paternalism, legal moralism) and subprinciples (e.g. moral conservatism, strict moralism, the exploitation principle, legal perfectionism) state reasons that are at least sometimes relevant. I would now go so far as to say that they all state reasons that are *always* relevant, though usually of very slight weight.

The argument against paternalism might seem to provide an exception to this generalization. Since we have given personal sovereignty absolute weight (trumping effect) within the self-regarding domain, there is a sense in which the interest in avoiding personal injury even when voluntarily risked has "as if no weight" at all when it is in the opposite balancing pan of the scale. The best way to put this point, I think, is to say that personal sovereignty is not just another interest, subject to balancing tests when in conflict with another interest. Sovereignty cannot be put on the interest-balancing scales at all. Personal sovereignty places an absolute duty on lawmakers not to cross its boundaries. To "weigh" such a duty against mere interests brings to mind Laurent Frantz's remark in a similar context: "One's need for a new car can be balanced against the other uses to which the same money might be put but not against 'Thou shalt not steal'. "[1] Still, voluntarily risked injuries, deaths, broken backs, and broken hearts, are evils of *some* kind, even though not violations of rights or grounds for grievance, and the prevention of any evil is a relevant reason for any action. That should not be denied. The point is rather that this reason is "trumped" by personal sovereignty on the other side, and therefore is "as if naught" when compared with the absolute principle governing the self-regarding realm. If not taken too seriously, a mathematical analogy might help. A moderate or even large finite number is as if naught when compared with an infinite one.

The need to prevent an evil then is always a relevant reason in support of a criminal prohibition. But very little is being said for a reason when it is allowed to be relevant, unless it is also acknowledged to be cogent or compelling, a "good reason" with more than mere minimal weight. The need to prevent harm to others is always a *good* reason for criminal prohibitions. So much is a central tenet of liberalism, indeed of "moral common sense." When the harm to be prevented is great enough, and the various mediating maxims are satisfied, and the costs of enforcement reasonable, preventing harm to others will be not just a good reason but a decisive one. We can say of the harm and offense principles then that they always state relevant reasons, always state good reasons, and frequently state decisive reasons for criminalization. When one considers that interference with people's liberty is always a good reason *against* legal coercion (so says the presumption in favor of liberty), one can appreciate how very good a reason in general the prevention of harm to others is, in the liberal view. Preventing likely setback to the actor's own interest, on the other hand, while always a relevant reason in the sense explained above, never becomes a good reason for interfering with fully voluntary conduct, because in the latter case it crosses the boundaries of the actor's self-regarding domain and violates her autonomy, not just her liberty.

Finally, those "non-grievance evils" that wrong no one and/or set back no interests, since they *are* evils (in some sense) are such that their prevention is always a relevant reason for prohibition. But such evils, particularly the free-floating ones, never—well, hardly ever—are good reasons, and perhaps never are decisive ones. The qualifying words "hardly ever" and "perhaps never" reflect the conscientious liberal's inevitable wavering in the face of the legal moralist's strongest counterexamples, mentioned in sections 3 and 4 below. For the present, however, we can define liberalism cautiously as the view that as a class, harm and offense prevention are far and away the best reasons that can be produced in support of criminal prohibitions, and the only ones that frequently outweigh the case for liberty. They are, in short, the only considerations that are *always good reasons* for criminalization. The other principles state considerations that are at most sometimes (but rarely) good reasons, depending for example on exactly what the non-grievance evil is whose prevention is supposed to support criminalization. Indeed there are some extraordinary, and up to now only hypothetical examples of non-grievance evils (neither harms nor offenses, nor right-violations of any kind) that are so serious that even the liberal (if he is sensitive and honest) will concede that their prevention would be a *good* reason for criminalization, and in the most compelling examples of all, perhaps even a *good enough* reason, on balance, for criminalization. Note, however, that liberalism as cautiously redefined above can make this concession without inconsistency.

A further gain in consistency could be achieved if we redefined legal moralism in such a way that it shared the same form as the other liberty-limiting principles. The other definitions, as formulated in the earlier volumes of this work, all begin "It is always a good reason in support of a criminal prohibition that . . ." whereas the definitions of legal moralism in both the broad and narrow senses begin "It can be morally legitimate for the state to prohibit conduct on the ground that . . ." Given these definitions, the "cautious liberal" who is prepared to admit that in certain extraordinary circumstances some types of moralistic considerations (citing harmless immoralities) *can* be good reasons for criminal prohibitions does not qualify as a liberal at all, for it would be contradictory to claim that *some* moralistic considerations can be good reasons (which is all that the old definition of legal moralism affirmed) and also that only the harm and offense principles *ever* are good reasons (which is what the definition of liberalism affirmed). If we reformulate the definition of legal moralism, however, so that it parallels the definitions of the other liberty-limiting principles, the inconsistency disappears. Now legal moralism is defined as the principle that *it is always a good reason* in support of criminalization that it prevents non-grievance evils or harmless immoralities. The cautious liberal who concedes that the prevention of non-grievance evils may sometimes (though rarely) be a good reason for criminalization might now still reject legal moralism in its redefined stronger sense, while maintaining his liberalism, for he can still insist that only harm and offense principle considerations are *always good reasons* for criminalization.[2]

We can now distinguish between *cautious liberalism* and *bold liberalism*, the former holding that only the harm and offense principles state reasons that are always good and frequently decisive for criminalization, while conceding that legal moralism states reasons that are sometimes (but rarely) good. Bold liberalism, on the other hand, asserts that the harm and offense principle reasons are not only always good and frequently decisive, but also that they are the only kinds of reasons that are *ever* good or decisive (though other kinds of reasons might be always relevant). (This distinction is not the same as that made earlier between *extreme liberalism*, which endorses only the harm principle, and *moderate liberalism*, which endorses the harm and offense principles.) Bold liberalism is the doctrine I set out to defend, or at least make the strongest case for, at the start of this work. Cautious liberalism is the fallback position to which we must retreat if some of the legal moralist's counter-examples prove too difficult to handle satisfactorily.

3. Stubborn counterexamples (A):
Parfit's misconceived baby

Throughout this work I have been jousting over hypothetical examples, both those meant to support the liberalism I had set out to defend and those meant to refute it. In Volume two the examples were mine, and through them I attempted to show that the harm principle is not sufficient to explain all the criminal legislation that it would be legitimate to enact, and that it therefore needs to be supplemented by the offense principle. In Volumes three and four, however, having endorsed as many liberty-limiting principles as liberalism seemed to permit, I was put on the defensive, and took on counterexamples from liberalism's opponents. I have grappled with all the main types of these counterexamples, attempting to explain away any need to resort to nonliberal principles in response to them. They included those meant to demonstrate the need to criminalize behavior dangerous only to the actor as well as those purporting to show the legitimacy of enforcing the non-grievance sector of morality, of using the criminal law to help preserve traditional ways of life from spontaneous change, of criminalizing unjust gains even without wronged victims, or prohibiting modes of conduct that hinder the development of good taste and good character in other adults.

The counterexamples that gave me the most trouble were in the category of "welfare-connected non-grievance evils," both the deaths and physical injuries that follow from voluntarily incurred personal risks (Vol. III), and the residual injuries produced by conduct that makes its "victims" better off than they would otherwise have been, and which therefore neither adversely affect their interest on balance nor wrong them (Chap. 28, §8). For the most part, it was easier to resist the counterexamples based on the other species of non-grievance evils, namely the free-floating ones, though there were several examples in which the harmless evil cited seemed to be a sufficiently "bloated mouse" (*supra*, p. 67) for its prevention to be a good reason for criminal prohibition, but even in these cases I expressed skepticism that the good reason could ever be *good enough* to warrant restricting liberty.

The most difficult counterexample in the class of welfare-connected non-grievance evils was posed by "the Parfit baby problem" (*supra*, pp. 27–33). In the most dramatic version of Parfit's hypothetical story, a couple deliberately conceive a child, knowing that it will be born with a serious and permanent impairment—though not one that is so serious that the child would prefer even nonexistence to it—when if only they had taken prescribed medication and waited to conceive for one month they might have produced a normal child. The child is born in a harmful (impaired) condition, but his parents have not harmed him since if they had acted otherwise (as morality required), he would not have been born at all, and he rationally prefers existence, even with his impairment, to nonexistence. Neither have they violated his rights since he would not have been better off if they had acted otherwise. Therefore, he has no grievance against them. The parents "must be blamed for wantonly introducing a certain evil into the world, not for harming, or violating the rights of, a person" (p. 28). And yet when he is old enough to understand what happened, the child seethes with understandable resentment.

The Parfit baby problem leaves the liberal with only three options. First, he might enlarge his conception of a grievance so that it covers the case in which a person (a "victim"?) experiences warranted and understandable resentment against a malicious incidental benefactor, even though he has not, on balance, been harmed or personally wronged by that evil person. I did in fact argue (p. 31) that the child's disapproval of his parents would be warranted and understandable, and that there would indeed be something "personal" in it by virtue of which it could properly be called "resentment." But while the sense of self-related resentment and the sense of personal grievance may be easy to confuse in one's own consciousness, they are in fact conceptually separable, and the Parfit child could not convince an impartial outsider that he had been harmed, wronged, or taken advantage of by behavior that left him better off than he otherwise would have been. If, therefore, "malicious conception" were to be made criminal, it would have to be on grounds other than the harm principle, presumably on the moralistic ground that wanton wrongdoing of a certain kind can legitimately be made criminal even when it has no proper victim.

The liberal's second option is boldly to stand his ground. If he takes this line, he will admit that the harm principle can give no support to criminalization of "malicious (or reckless) conception," but he will add—"Very well then, I will remain true to the liberal principles that have served me so well in other contexts, and conclude that criminalization in this case, since it would prohibit mere immorality without on-balance harm, would be illegitimate." This kind of stonewalling would have been the simplest and easiest tack to take, but I could not do it with a clear conscience. I share the "intuitions" of the large majority of those with whom I have discussed the matter that it would be perfectly legitimate to criminalize conduct that wantonly introduces a certain amount of avoidable human suffering into the world. (There might be no present need for such legislation and a preponderance of practical reasons against it even if there *were* a problem to be dealt with, but these are other matters.)

The third option for the liberal is the one I chose, in fact, and that is to allow the Parfit baby case to carve out a clear categorical exception to one's liberalism. Malicious or reckless conceptions like that in the Parfit example *can* in principle be legitimately proscribed by the criminal law even though they harm no one in the sense required by the harm principle. Liberalism might still apply exceptionlessly to the postnatal world, but for actions and omissions that lead to the existence of new human beings, and perhaps for these actions only, penal legislation based solely on a form of legal moralism would be legitimate.

This is an untidy solution, but the one that appears to fit most smoothly without our spontaneous convictions. Making so singular an exception to liberal principle might strike some as suspiciously *ad hoc*, departing from principle for the sake of mere convenience, without logically relevant ground. Revising a generalization to cover a recalcitrant special case, however, is only sometimes objectionably *ad hoc*. Consider a clearer example of an illicit *ad hoc* revision. Scientists in Melbourne conclude from an experiment that under circumstances *C*, electrons behave in a certain way, *X*. The experiment is repeated in Bundoora and fails to yield the same result. Undaunted, the scientists amend their theory to say that electrons behave in way *X* under circumstances *C, except in Bundoora*. This is unsatisfactory, of course, because of the well-founded expectation that if electrons don't do *X* in Bundoora, then they do not do it elsewhere either. That is, we assume that there is nothing special about Bundoora that would uniquely affect the behavior of electrons there, and we judge that the errant physicists have not indicated what any such unique feature of Bundoora might be. There is, however, something very special about "harmful conception" that might lead us to expect that its peculiarities will not be repeated elsewhere. It is the only example we can have of a person's being put in a harmful condition by the very act that brings him into existence, and the only example where determinations of harm require comparison of a given condition with no existence at all. No wonder it seems to call for special treatment![3]

I concluded my discussion of the Parfit baby problem in Chapter 28 by remarking that I was reluctantly departing from the letter of liberalism but not from its spirit. That remark needs a little more explanation here. It is distinctive of the liberal harm principle that it is a humane principle. Adverse effects on human interests are apt to constitute or cause impediments to human fulfillment; setbacks to welfare interests, in particular, may lead to suffering and misery as well. No one should be at liberty to inflict such dire injuries on one's fellows. Nor should one be permitted seriously to injure oneself, unless of course it is through the voluntary exercise of one's own autonomy. Liberalism as a legislative policy toward state coercion must per-force blind itself toward some human suffering insofar as it rejects paternalistic interventions, though liberalism in a broader sense will warrant humane extralegal efforts to ameliorate the sufferings even of those who suffer as a consequence of their own voluntary choices. But where autonomy is not at issue, the humane component in the animating spirit of liberalism can come to the fore. And in the case of wrongly conceived infants, the infants' autonomy is *not* at issue. The infants did not decide to bring themselves into existence. They did not consent to the risks in their being born (as the infants in Samuel Butler's *Erewhon* do). They just come into existence and suffer. The letter of liberalism will not permit a law that would impose criminal responsibility on their parents for the parents' (admittedly) wrongful behavior. But the spirit of liberalism, whose concern for humanity is limited only by its respect for autonomy, is not violated by the criminal prohibition of behavior that brings a human being and its unhappiness-engendering impairment into existence at one stroke. This is not a case of suffering whose tolerance by the law is necessitated only by a respect for autonomy. It is rather a case of suffering whose tolerance by the law is necessitated by nothing at all.

4. Stubborn counterexamples (B): Kristol's gladiatorial contest

The counterexample that gave me the most trouble in the category of free-floating evils (non-grievance evils that are not welfare-connected) was the gladiatorial contest story proposed by Irving Kristol (*supra*, pp. 128–133). In Chapter 30, where I considered this proposed counterexample, I wavered in my response between cautious and bold liberalism. There is especially strong incentive to affirm the bold position in the face of arguments that purely free-floating evils should be criminalized, and it is a tribute to the ingenuity of this example that it caused me to waver at all. A *pure* free-floating evil, after all, is nothing that anyone needs protection from in any sense. It neither violates any one's rights nor causes any setback to interests the risk of which had not already been voluntarily accepted by the interest-holder. If the "evil" in question, nevertheless, truly is an evil, then its occurrence is regrettable and the universe as a whole would be a better place without it, but it is nothing that anyone has a right to make a personal complaint (or feel personally aggrieved) about. *I* don't have a right, for example, that *you* think only pure thoughts. That is your business, no one else's. I am not harmed either with or without my consent by your thoughts, and neither are you (necessarily) harmed either. It is better, perhaps, that you not have such thoughts, and regrettable that you do, but no one is made worse off by them, so why bring the law into it at all (one might naturally ask)?

Kristol's example, however, is impure. There is a sense in which the voluntarily produced and witnessed contest *is* a free-floating evil. It is objectively regrettable (to put it mildly) that several hundred thousand adults should derive great pleasure from gory bloodshed, human suffering, and the sight of savage cruelty. When we isolate that grossly inappropriate mass response we find it *very* regrettable indeed and morally revolting even to think about. But who would need protection from it, given that no children are exposed to it and there are no unwilling participants or spectators? To us disapproving outsiders the spectators might all say "It is none of your business." If the isolated free-floating evil (the morally inappropriate response of the audience) were all there was to consider in the example, the slightly fazed liberal might maintain some of his boldness. He might concede that the free-floating evil has some weight on the scales, if only because the moral responses of so many people are so extremely distorted, but he might still deny that preventing the evil has substantial weight, given that it is freely chosen and harmless to the disapproving "others." He can boldly insist, therefore, that the law be kept from interfering, and thereby reject the force of the story as a counterexample.

The free-floating evil in the example, however, is not so easily isolable. The story is drenched in ominous danger. The imagery in the reader's mind includes excited, savage mobs thirsting after the blood of those who have been paid to take extreme risks, but how easily contained or limited is their bloodlust to those who consent? One tries to think of the sorts of people who would enjoy such an experience, and it is hard to bring into focus the image of a "fan" whom one would be prepared to trust outside the arena. The sensitive reader then feels threatened in his imagination as well as repelled, and reasons of the harm principle type are on his mind when he judges that "there ought to be a law against it." If one argued against him that for the enthusiastic spectators the contest is a mere healthy catharsis leaving them less prone to violence in ordinary life, he will probably reply not that the contest should be prohibited despite its innocuous character, but rather that the prohibition should hold because he doesn't believe for a minute that it is "innocuous."

Kristol's example is also impure in another way. It not only brings in harm principle considerations, it also naturally implicates legal paternalism and incites the paternalist to defend his favored sorts of reasons. The evils in the story include not only free-floating moral evils in the response of the spectators and the enrichment of the pandering promoter, but also welfare-connected non-grievance evils in the injuries to the gladiators themselves. Taken as an argument in favor of paternalism the example has more initial force. Its form is quite the same as the argument from voluntary slavery in

Volume three (pp. 71–81) and the bold liberal will respond in similar ways. The gladiators in principle have a right to risk their lives if they truly wish to do so, but the humane element in the liberal spirit rises to the fore when the liberal thinks about it, and he is moved to ask: "Do they really know what they are doing?" In the end, he will find nonpaternalistic grounds—doubts about voluntariness and appeals to the prevention of public dangers—for refusing permission to the promoter.

Think of how a legalized fight to the death before paying spectators would work. The state would insist on a licensing procedure to confirm voluntariness and protect innocents from indirect dangers. In the beginning, the criminal law need not be involved at all. It would be reserved as a back-up sanction to enforce the prohibition of unlicensed promotions. The explicit aim of the contest in the promoter's application for a license would not be the vindication of the combatants' honor, as in a duel; nor would it be to put one of them out of his misery, as in legalized euthanasia. Rather the aim of the combat would be to establish the dominance of one of the combatants, to establish once and for all which of them is the more formidable gladiator, and incidentally to give thrills of the most basic animal kind to the audience. If the combat is to achieve these aims, if it is to be a *contest* at all (as opposed, for example, to a public mugging), it must be governed by fair rules impartially administered. Both wary gladiators would want to insist on that in advance, and most spectators would agree. Without such rules the spectacle might be a mere homicide committed with impunity by a cheater. It might also occur to the contracting contestants, and certainly to the state licensors, that there would be just as much excitement of the primordial thrilling kind if the rule-governed contest were permitted to last only until one party has clearly established his superiority. At that point it could be stopped by an impartial referee appointed by the licensing commission. This would surely make the deal more attractive to the gladiators, and because it would be no less exciting to the spectators, it would be no less remunerative to the promoter and the participants. It might even be *more* attractive to the audience because it is less gruesome, shocking, and heart-breaking. And the appeal of the contest would be not just primitive thrills but also the spectacle of skill and technique, and even strategy and tactics. It would be no less thrilling but much more interesting than a mutual bashing with clubs. In fact, its appeal would be more effective if the weapons that could be used were restricted. The contest would also last longer that way. Just as a pornographic show will be more exciting if more subtle, the performers teasing their audiences along rather than being unrestrained and fully naked from the start, so the fighting match will be more thrilling if the battlers are less destructive.

Given the greater reasonableness all around of the sublimated type of contest, and especially its lesser risks to the pugilists themselves, it would bring into question how truly voluntary the participants' insistence on combat to the death with lethal weapons would be. Unreasonableness is not the same thing as involuntariness, of course, but extreme unreasonableness creates a strong presumption of nonvoluntariness that would be difficult to rebut, and the state might even be justified in making the presumption conclusive for practical reasons. (Compare Vol. III, pp. 79–80 on the slavery example.) The sublimated form of contest would also be less likely to cause harm to others by leading to a general coarsening of sympathies and a sharpening of lethal impulses in real life. In short, the arrangement most appealing to promoter, participants, audience, and the state in its role as protector of the public, would resemble our own boxing, wrestling, and fencing matches, not the barbarous killings in Kristol's example, and a liberal state would have many reasons for refusing to license the latter. Liberalism might remain bold in the face of the Kristol example, even though the liberal concedes some weight to preventing the evil of exploitation by pandering and the evil of inappropriate thrills at the sight of injuries being inflicted on a human being.

5. Confusions about what is to count as a counterexample

Not just any logically possible world can produce relevant counterexamples to the liberal thesis (or to any other thesis designed to answer the same question as that addressed by liberalism). In that respect liberalism differs from the more familiar philosophical model. It is thought to be a counterexample to a philosophical analysis (definition) of knowledge, for example, that there is a logically possible world in which the definition is satisfied by something that is clearly not knowledge, or that a clear case of knowledge in that world fails to satisfy the definition. It doesn't matter that the nonconforming world is not actual, or not physically possible, or that it requires weird science-fiction assumptions in its very description; if it fails to confirm the proposed definition and is not logically inconsistent, that is sufficient. Thus some philosophical disputants might attack the view I have labeled "liberalism" by having us imagine a world in which human nature is very different from human nature here and now in our actual world, a bizarre universe where humans love pain or are genetically programmed for martial self-sacrifice, where they are all purely angelic or else purely diabolical, where they are naturally solitary animals like earthworms or bears, who come together only to mate or to care for temporarily helpless offspring, or they are all mere cells in social organisms, like ants or bees. How counterintuitive liberalism would be in such worlds!

We could hold human nature constant and seek our counterexamples in exotic human cultures that are quite unlike those that currently exist in most of the world, where a ruler is worshipped as a god and thought to be as indispensable as a queen bee is to the hive, or where the bravest warriors and comeliest maidens are regularly sacrificed to propitiate insatiable deities, or where filial piety imposes an iron obligation not to depart in the slightest from the life-style of one's parents and ancestors. Alternatively, we could restrict the range of argument to our actual human nature in the various prevalent types of cultural organization, but permit the search for counterexamples in unusual circumstances like famines, insurrections, sieges, and the like, or to a general situation in which human populations are extremely dense and necessary resources very scarce, or to circumstances once common but now disappearing, such as a world of small, independent farming villages interspersed among forests, offering an abundance of opportunities to new settlers. Surely liberalism would be less plausible in those Arcadian circumstances. If a nonconformist in a religiously homogeneous community in such a world were to protest against very illiberal laws enforcing community traditions, he could be told to leave if he didn't like it and to join another village more to his liking, which he could realistically hope to do without great material or psychological cost. (Life in seventeenth century colonial America may have actually approximated this description. See Chap. 29A, pp. 117–118.)

The question of what counts as a counterexample to the liberal thesis has no one uniform and general answer. It all depends on exactly what question the liberal writer intends his liberal principle to answer. The more alternative natures, cultures, and circumstances he intends it to cover, the more ambitious it is, and the more ambitious it is, the more vulnerable it becomes to counterexamples. It seems to me, moveover, that the more vulnerable liberalism is, the less plausible it becomes, and since my aim is to defend liberalism by selecting the most plausible view that can be called "liberal," I had better restrict liberalism to a relatively narrow scope, by proposing it as an answer to a relatively narrow question. The basic question addressed by this book is: What criminal legislation would be morally legitimate (justified in principle) for a democratic parliament to enact in a world populated by people like us (where "us" includes virtually *all* of us, including Third World countries) in circumstances like those that prevail in our modern period. The book then seeks general principles to determine the moral acceptability of penal legislation as considered by such actual and hypothetical legislators, and opts for a refined kind of liberalism. That principle would be wildly implausible both in a world that resembled Hobbes's state of nature and in an Arcadian paradise. And there is no point in even asking whether it would be plausible in a logically possible world in which people had four heads and tails and made their babies in factories. The only hypothetical worlds that can produce relevant counterexamples are those within the proposed scope of this book's modest purpose, which is to formulate principles for worlds like ours, for earthlings with our human nature, with at least potential access to our technology, in our world's various prevalent circumstances including general affluence and general poverty, and our worldwide cultural diversity.

6. Liberalism and dogmatism

Liberalism would be more obviously plausible and easier to defend if it were meant to apply only to pluralistic secular societies like the United States and most of the other "First World" countries. Even without such a restriction, counterexamples that are situated in such societies would be the most telling since they would strike against liberalism in its home terrain where it could be presumed to be least vulnerable. A liberalism restricted to such societies, however, would be too modest. A more ambitious and significant liberalism would also include within its scope traditional homogeneous societies, both small (like Amish villages, and ethnic neighborhoods), and large (ethnically and racially homogeneous nations like Sweden and Japan and religiously uniform ones like Ireland and Iran). To attempt to subject such societies to the requirements of liberalism is definitely to swim against the current, for most of these societies have used their criminal law (or would use it if they could), often with popular support, to protect their traditional ways of life against individual nonconformity. And yet we must attempt to justify the imposition of liberalism even in these cases if our arguments are to achieve coherence, and if we are to avoid ending up with a doctrine which is plausible within a shrunken domain, but which in its diminished form would become an anemic, parochial, and ultimately trivial ideology.

Those who would confine liberalism to the pluralist societies of modern industrial nations, however, often justify this restriction of liberalism on liberal or liberal-like grounds. Three types of arguments are characteristically used by these modest liberals: the argument from liberal tolerance, the closely related condemnation of "cultural imperialism," and an application to *societies* of Mill's famous celebration of individual diversity. Let us take these in order. Tolerance of cultural differences is of course characteristic of liberalism historically. As we have seen (Chap. 33, pp. 305–311), the liberal need not extend his tolerance to the point of skeptical relativism, the denial that there are any rational grounds for affirming some cultural practices' superiority to others, though in respect to some aspects of culture, such relativism might be justified. The liberal need only insist that while some transcultural comparative judgments are possible in principle they are very difficult to make in fact, and so he puts forward "the useful warning that because our moral knowledge is tenuous we ought to be very careful about imposing our moral beliefs on others."[4] Just as we expect Third World zealots to acknowledge the rationality *for us* of permitting a wide variety of modes of dress for men and women, foods of all kinds, and religious observances in diverse churches as well as religious laxity and indifference, so in all consistency we should acknowledge the rationality of *their* enforcement of sartorial uniformity (especially for women), and religious dietary laws, and universal daily public prayer. We liberals liberate "our" women; they cover up and isolate theirs. Just as we have a right to our liberal indulgences so they have a right to their unmixed traditions. They don't presume to judge us; we should show a similar respect for them. So the liberal-appearing argument goes.

Often the modest liberal supplements his plea for mutual respect and tolerance with the charge that the dogmatic liberal's critique of the legal enforcement of tradition in some Third World countries is just another form of Western cultural imperialism, like exporting television programs, perfumed soaps and luxury cars, and rock and roll, or sending missionaries to "convert the natives" to Christianity. These impositions are an illicit use of our superior economic muscle and show no respect for local cultural forms.

Finally, some "tolerant liberals" might even invoke John Stuart Mill's impressive arguments for "experiments in living"—with a twist—to support a worldwide diversity not only of religion and culture, but of political and economic regimes. Mill's original arguments[5], of course, supported the experiments of groups of nonconforming individuals within a nation-state, not the political nonconformity of political state themselves. He argued in three ways for the tolerance of such experiments as utopian socialist communes, Eastern mystic settlements, religious villages, nudist camps, and so on. First of all, by allowing each individual to experiment among a great variety of alternatives in his efforts to discover what kind of life is good for him, we increase the likelihood of each discovering the life that best fits his own aptitudes and ideals, that is, which best fulfills his nature. Second, by putting alternative forms of group organization to the test, the experiments show the rest of us how these systems succeed or fail—valuable lessons for us all. Third, these experiments create a rich and harmonious diversity which is good in itself and pleasant to behold, but also, from our social point of view, prudent in the manner of a balanced portfolio of investments, or a diverse gene pool in protecting the species from epidemics. If tolerance of many living styles and forms of social organization produces these advantages within a state, why should it not be equally valuable when applied to the worldwide collection of nation-states themselves? If liberalism works for individuals within one nation, why should it not work equally for nations within one world? Tolerant liberalism would allow each nation to seek its own collective good in its own way, thus putting the different ways to the test to the benefit of us all, maximizing the likelihood of national self-fulfillment, creating a pleasing diversity to counter what would otherwise be a deadening uniformity, and ensuring that the world community—"the human race"—does not put all its eggs in one basket, thus risking universal disaster. John Stuart Mill, if he reasoned in this way, would prefer a world in which some nations were organized according to Mill's own liberal principles while others followed the teachings of Lenin, Mussolini, Mao Tse-tung, and Khomeini, to a world in which all nations followed the principles of Mill. In short, he would want even liberalism "put to the test" of competition.

How should we reply to these arguments from our fellow liberals? The doctrine of personal sovereignty which we found in Volume two to be essential to liberalism would not permit liberalism to be "put to the test" at the expense of sovereign individuals who can no more properly be the objects of political experiments than they can properly be the objects of medical experiments without their consent. The more dogmatic liberalism endorsed in this book absolutely requires a doctrine of human rights to act as a moral restraint on what governments may do to individuals whether by law (our subject) or by arbitrary action. If all of us Americans are blessed (or cursed) with personal sovereignty—the natural right of self-determination—how could it be that individual Iranians are not similarly endowed? Are we Americans (and British, French, German, Japanese, etc.) God's chosen peoples? On the contrary, the derivation of *de jure* autonomy in Volume three (pp. 47–71) absolutely commits us to the view that all individual human beings have these basic rights, and any state that suppresses its minorities by means of illiberal criminal laws and refuses to permit nonconforming conduct even when it is directly victimless and discreet, violates those rights, whatever its own political and legal traditions may be. One must be free to be an atheist even in Ireland, to eat pork even in Israel, and to go unveiled even in Iran. In a way, the smaller and more unprotected the minority, the greater the injustice of the legal repression of autonomy. The rare dissenter bucks overwhelming social pressures even without legal coercion. When the state adds its powers to an already unequal contest, it becomes mere bully.

To the claim that the Western human-rights activists are the true bullies in virtue of their transmission of the liberal message along with their rock and roll music and television soap operas, the liberal has a ready reply. Not one jot less respect is shown for a nation's cultural traditions, its folkways and music, its religious faith, its family organization, its wedding and burial customs, and its traditional festivals and holidays, when the liberal shows

equal respect for its sovereign individuals and condemns its political repression. One cannot rejoice in a hundred blooming flowers in the nations of the
world when some of the "flowers" are liberal governments, and other are
tools for terrorizing and subduing individuals, even when those political
instruments are ancient and traditional in the country in question. Quite
apart from this point, the dogmatic liberal might find that it is his more
tolerant cousin who has the patronizing "imperial" attitude toward (say) the
Third World theocracies. He too readily assumes that human rights have a
place in our political culture but not in theirs. Thomas Scanlon takes up the
charge from there:

> . . . this argument rests on the attribution to "them" of a unanimity that does not
> in fact exist. "They" are said to be different from us and to live by different
> rules. Such stereotypes are seldom accurate, and the attribution of unanimity is
> particularly implausible in the case of human rights violations. These [govern-
> mental] actions have victims who generally resent what is done to them and who
> would rarely concede that, because such behavior is common in their country,
> their tormentors are acting quite properly.[6]

Cultural and political traditions may vary greatly among the peoples of the
world, and that is a good thing, but it does not follow that anyone enjoys
repression, or should tolerate being prevented forcibly by his government
from doing what he wants to do.

The argument, purportedly derived from Mill, from the advantages of
diversity misconstrues the sorts of diversity a liberal ideology must treasure.
Some kinds of cultural diversity might well be unlimited in their variety, the
liberal maintains, but the diversity of kinds of *political* institutions must be
limited by the very reasons that count against limits of other kinds. Even if
limits to acceptable forms of political authority are adopted, there will still
remain different languages and literature, different religions, different economic and political structures, different characteristic cultural styles. James
Nickel's way of making the point is just right:

> Cultural diversity is an important value, I think, but it is not absolute nor does it
> rule out many of the changes involved in complying with human rights. One
> may see the value of preserving, say, the cultural and religious traditions of India
> without concluding that the Indian caste system should have been preserved.
> Cultures and value systems typically have many parts, and it is sometimes
> possible to preserve the best and most distinctive features while jettisoning the
> most repugnant—particularly when making the changes required for compliance
> with human rights. These rights have the behavior of governments as their
> central focus, and government practices are seldom central to the identity and
> persistance of a culture.[7]

The most comprehensive liberal ideal envisions a world community that is
not only diverse in the kinds of countries that make it up but also diverse

within each of these parts. But the pleasing character of that double diversity (diversity within parts and diversity between parts) is not further enhanced by a certain diversity of prevailing political moralities. A world in which socialist and capitalist nations coexist is benignly diverse. Even a world in which there is a division between poor-simple (pastoral, elemental) peoples and rich-complicated (industrial, neurotic) peoples has something to be said for it. But a world in which some parts permit diversity and others forbid it does not achieve the kind of overall diversity that Mill had in mind. A world that is half slave and half free is not thereby "pleasingly diverse."

Even in the most homogeneous cultures there will be some natural diversity, some of it derived from differences in basic temperament. In our own large and multiform land, there are many other forms of diversity with many more origins. But it is a serious mistake to insist that human beings acquire human rights only by membership in a political community of the relatively mixed-up kind. If anything, human beings need the protection of human rights more in the smaller and simpler homogeneous kinds of community. Year ago Ruth Benedict, in a study of four relatively simple "primitive civilizations," pointed out that because of the malleability of their natures most human beings can and do assume the behavior dictated by the prevailing norms of their society. This is not because the institutions of that society "reflect an ultimate and universal sanity," but only because people are, for the most part, "plastic to the moulding force of the society into which they are born." "They do not all, however, find it equally congenial, and those are favored and fortunate whose potentialities most nearly coincide with the type of behavior selected by their society."[8] The unfortunate ones whose natural proclivities are not favored by the prevalent expectations are then labeled "misfits" (or worse), even though their characters conform to other cultural patterns that prevail in other cultural groups. In a large pluralistic country every type of person can find subcommunities in which his own kind of character can find respect and dignity. But where diverse subcommunities have been abolished and only one prevalent character type is permitted by the state, then the acknowledgment of the human rights of endangered minorities becomes most urgent. From Ayatollah Khomeini's point of view, the inevitable nonconformists are gangrenous appendages on the body politic that must be surgically removed.[9] But from the liberal's point of view each misfit is a real flesh and blood human being, harmlessly seeking his or her own fulfillment; not a gangrenous infection or a cancerous growth, rather a beauty mark.

Anyway, diversity keeps breaking out, Benedict's point about natural differences aside. The economy generates classes; overall size produces regional differences; more efficient transport mixes things up. Foreign influences get harder and harder to keep out. Some come from trade, some from television, some from new communications media. People do tend to become different unless ruthlessly kept the same. Efforts to join them all into one mold are a constant struggle against the odds. There is no danger, as the confused "tolerant liberal" fears, that restrictions on the political power to accomplish this homogenization will somehow diminish the world's overall diversity.

My conclusion is that if there is personal sovereignty anywhere, then it exists everywhere, in traditional societies as well as in modern pluralistic ones. Liberalism has long been associated with tolerance and caution, but about this point it must be brave enough to be dogmatic.

Notes

28. Legal Moralism and Non-grievance Evils

1. See, for example, Ronald Dworkin, "Lord Devlin and the Enforcement of Morals," *Yale Law Journal*, vol. LXXV (1966), reprinted as Chapter 10 in Dworkin's *Taking Rights Seriously* (Cambridge, Mass: Harvard University Press, 1971), and H.L.A. Hart, "Immorality and Treason," *The Listener* (July 30, 1959), reprinted in R.A. Wasserstrom (ed.), *Morality and the Law* (Belmont, Calif.: Wadsworth, 1971), pp. 49–54.

2. On the first interpretation of the self- and other-regarding distinction, it is the other-regarding category that is clear, and the self-regarding category is merely defined in contrast to it. Whatever is not other-regarding is self-regarding, and the distinction is exhaustive. The self-regarding category then is a miscellany that includes *everything* that is harmless to others, including both harms (dangers) to self and impersonal harmless evils. On the second interpretation, it is the self-regarding category that is clear, and the other-regarding is defined only in the sense that it is not self-regarding, and the distinction is exhaustive. Other-regarding acts on this interpretation include those that affect the interests of others *and* the miscellany of "impersonal evils" if any. On the first interpretation, harmless evils since they are not other-regarding must be self-regarding. On the second interpretation, harmless evils since they are not self-regarding must be other-regarding. On the first interpretation, harmless evils *are* shielded by the actor's personal sovereignty; on the second interpretation, they are not so shielded.

3. I shall use this phrase to refer to states of affairs that are evil in themselves quite apart from—even in the absence of—any further relation they might have to human interests or to offended mental states. For a more precise account, see n. 6 below.

4. J.S. Mill, *On Liberty*, chap. IV, para. 18.

5. A less extreme and more plausible version of the "social rights" theory eludes Mill's attack. It ascribes a right to some people (often a majority) in some circumstances to live in a certain kind of community. These people have invested so much desire, hope, and effort in creating that kind of community for themselves that they have a genuine interest that it be achieved and maintained, and when noncomformists behave even in private in a manner inconsistent with the community's desired character, they therefore *harm* the majority by setting back their interest. In virtue of that harm to their interests the right of the majority has been violated. Eugene Schlossberger presents a sophisticated version of a similar argument in his forthcoming "Liberalism and the Enforcement of Morality." I discuss arguments of this kind in more detail in Chap. 29, §4.

6. Cf. Anthony D. Woozley, "Law and the Legislation of Morality," *Ethics in Hard Times*, ed. Arthur L. Caplan and Daniel Callahan (New York: Plenum, 1981), p. 158.

7. Neil MacCormick, *Legal Right and Social Democracy* (Oxford: Clarendon Press, 1982), p. 29.

8. Ernest Nagel, "The Enforcement of Morals," *The Humanist* (May/June, 1968), pp. 19–27.

9. *Ibid.*, p. 22.

10. MacCormick, *op. cit.* (see n. 6), p. 30.

11. *Ibid.*, p. 212. The words quoted are MacCormick's paraphrase of the position he is rejecting.

12. *Ibid.*, p. 34.

13. Nagel, *op. cit.* (see n. 7), p. 26.

14. H.L.A. Hart, *Law, Liberty, and Morality* (Stanford, Calif.: Stanford University Press, 1963), p. 41.

15. Patrick Devlin, *The Enforcement of Morals* (London: Oxford University Press, 1965), p. 138.

16. Nagel, *op. cit.* (see n. 7), p. 26. Emphasis added.

17. *Loc. cit.*

18. Hart, *op. cit.* (see n. 13), p. 32.

19. Devlin, *op. cit.* (see n. 14), pp. 135–36.

20. *Ibid.*, p. 136.

21. Bernard Gert, *The Moral Rules* (New York: Harper & Row, 1973), p. 55ff.

22. If it were not so cumbersome, a better label for this subclass of evils would be "adversely welfare-connected non-grievance evils." That would explicitly rule out of the class a type of non-grievance evil that does not belong in it, namely *wrongful gain*, or unjust benefit, accruing to an exploiter, even when the exploitee suffers no wrongful loss. See below, Chap. 31, pp. 321–87.

23. I discuss both prenatal harmings and the causal overdetermination of harms in much greater detail in my "Wrongful Life and the Counterfactual Element in Harming," *Social Philosophy and Policy*, vol. 4, no. 1 (1986), pp. 145–78.

24. The paragraphs that follow in this section are drawn with only minor changes from my article "Legal Moralism and Free-floating Evils," *Pacific Philosophical Quarterly*, vol. 61, nos. 1, 2 (1980), pp. 129–133.

25. Jerome Neu, "What is Wrong with Incest?", *Inquiry*, vol. 19 (1975), p. 32.

26. Graham Hughes, *The Conscience of the Courts: Law and Morals in American Life* (Garden City, N.Y.: Anchor Press/Doubleday, 1975), p. 29.

27. *Abelard's Ethics*, trans. J. Ramsay McCallum (Oxford: Basil Blackwell, 1935), chapter III.

28. *Ibid.*

29. For a development of this point, see, among others, A. M. MacIver, "Ethics and the Beetle," *Analysis*, vol. 8 (1948). Reprinted in *Ethics*, ed. Judith J. Thomson and Gerald Dworkin (New York: Harper & Row, 1968).

30. See my "Human Duties and Animal Rights," in *On the Fifth Day*, ed. R.K. Morris and M.W. Fox (Washington, D.C.: Acropolis Books, Ltd., 1978), pp. 67–68. Reprinted in my *Rights, Justice, and the Bounds of Liberty* (Princeton, N.J.: Princeton University Press, 1980), pp. 204–5.

31. I regret that this usage deviates somewhat from that proposed in Vol. I, Chap. 1, p. 49.

32. A special sense of "victim" goes along with that sense, namely that in which *B* is a victim of *A* when and only when *A* has harmed him in that full sense.

33. I suggest several strategies for dealing with these cases in the context of tort liability in my "Wrongful Life and the Counterfactual Element in Harming," *op. cit.* (see n. 22).

34. Derek Parfit, "On Doing the Best for Our Children," in M.D. Bayles, ed., *Ethics and Population* (Cambridge, Mass.: Schenkman, 1976).

35. I consider in more detail how we can decide what is rationally preferable when one of the alternatives is nonexistence in my "Wrongful Life and the Counterfactual Element in Harming," *op. cit.* (see n. 22).

36. See his very important review essay, "Collective Evils, Harms, and the Law," *Ethics*, vol. 97 (1987), pp. 414–40.

37. *Ibid*, pp. 425–26. The quotation is slightly paraphrased.

38. *Ibid.*, p. 423.

39. *Ibid.*, p. 424.

40. *Ibid.*, p. 435.

41. There is *only* an "analogy" between collective harms and vicarious harms as the latter term is defined in Vol. I, Chap. 2, §2. There are also important differences. You harm me in my collective interest when you damage some *impersonal thing* in which I, as a community member, have a stake which I share in an interdependent way with others. Part of the source of my personal harm, however, is the like harm suffered by the others with whom I have solidarity. You harm me vicariously, on the other hand, by directly harming the interests of another *person* in whose well-being I have a stake.

42. Gerald Postema, *op. cit.* (see n. 35), p. 435. The parallel holds here to other vicarious harms. The mother cannot voice a grievance especially or exclusively on her own behalf when her child is wrongfully injured by another party. (If the child is killed, however, the parent may sue for compensation of her *own* loss and her own "pain and suffering").

43. *Ibid.*, p. 433n.

29. *Moral Conservatism: Preserving A Way of Life*

1. There are many writers, however, who are "morally conservative" in some respects but who oppose victimless crimes and thus are "liberal" in the sense used in this work. See, for example, Thomas Aquinas, *Summa Theologica*, "Whether It

Belongs to Human Law to Repress All Vices?" (New York: Random House, 1945), vol. II, ed. A.C. Pegis, pp. 793–95, and Michael Oakshott, "On Being Conservative," in *Rationalism in Politics and Other Essays* (London: Methuen & Co., 1962), pp. 168–96.

2. The following excerpts are from the interview between Khomeini and the Italian journalist Oriana Fallaci, published in the *New York Times Magazine*, 1979:

> K: . . . The people fought for Islam. And Islam means everything, also those things that in your world are called freedom, democracy. Yes, Islam contains everything. Islam includes everything. Islam is everything.

> F: . . . The people who are still being shot today for adultery or prostitution or homosexuality. Is it right to shoot the poor prostitute or a woman who is unfaithful to her husband, or a man who loves another man?

> K: If your finger suffers from gangrene, what do you do? Do you let the whole hand, and then the body, become filled with gangrene, or do you cut the finger off? What brings corruption to an entire country and its people must be pulled up like weeds that infest a field of wheat. I know there are societies where women are permitted to give themselves to satisfy the desire of men who are not their husbands, and where men are permitted to give themselves to satisfy other men's desires. But the society that we want . . . does not permit such things . . .

> F: . . . the fact that women can't study at a university with men, or work with men, for example, or go to the beach or to a swimming pool with men. They have to take a dip apart in their chadors. By the way, how do you swim in a chador?

> K: This is none of your business. Our customs are none of your business. If you do not like Islamic dress you are not obliged to wear it . . .

3. The quoted words are from Walter Barnett's excellent "Corruption of Morals: The Underlying Issue of the Pornography Commission Report," *Arizona State University Law Journal*, vol. 19, no. 2 (1971), p. 212. In my opinion Barnett's article is one of the best in the extensive journal literature on legal moralism. See also his *Sexual Freedom and the Constitution* (Albuquerque: University of New Mexico Press, 1973).

4. Basil Mitchell, *Law, Morality, and Religion in a Secular Society* (London: Oxford University Press, 1970), pp. 34–35.

5. See Joseph R. Gusfield, "On Legislating Morals: The Symbolic Process of Designating Deviance," *California Law Review*, vol. lvi (1968), p. 69.

6. H.L.A. Hart, "Social Solidarity and the Enforcement of Morality," *University of Chicago Law Review*, vol. 35 (1967), p. 2.

7. James Fitzjames Stephen, *Liberty, Equality, and Fraternity* (Cambridge: Cambridge University Press, 1967), p. 162.

8. H.L.A. Hart, *op. cit.* (see n. 6), p. 9.

9. *Ibid.*, p. 10.

10. *Loc. cit.*

11. Walter Berns, "The Case for Censorship," *The Public Interest*, vol. 22 (1971), pp. 3–24.

12. Alexander Bickell, "Dissenting and Concurring Opinions," *The Public Interest*, vol. 22 (1971), pp. 25–44.
13. Joseph R. Gusfield, *op. cit.* (see n. 5), pp. 59, 61–65, 66.
14. *Ibid.*, p. 69.
15. *Loc. cit.*
16. Ronald Dworkin, "Lord Devlin and the Enforcement of Morals," in *Taking Rights Seriously* (Cambridge, Mass.: Harvard University Press, 1977), p. 242.
17. *Ibid.*, p. 255.
18. Berns, *op. cit.* (see n. 11), pp. 19–20.
19. R. Dworkin, *op. cit.* (see n. 16), p. 257. Dworkin is here paraphrasing Devlin, not expressing his own views.
20. Raymond D. Gastil, "The Moral Right of the Majority to Restrict Obscenity and Pornography Through Law," *Ethics*, vol. 86 (1976), p. 237.
21. Walter Barnett, *op. cit.* (see n. 3), p. 215.
22. *Ibid.*, p. 216.
23. *Loc. cit.*
24. Raymond Gastil, *op. cit.* (see n. 20), p. 232.
25. C. J. Ducasse, *Art, the Critics, and You* (New York: Hafner, 1948), p. 143. See also I. A. Richards on "stock responses" in "Badness in Poetry," chap. 25 of his *Principles of Literary Criticism*, 3rd ed. (New York: Harcourt, Brace, 1949), pp. 201–206.
26. J.S. Mill, *On Liberty*, chap. IV, para. 12.
27. Vol. I, Chap. 1.
28. Vol. I, Chap. 2, §2.
29. The following nine paragraphs are drawn with only minor changes from my "Harm to Others—A Rejoinder" in *Criminal Justice Ethics*, Vol. 5 (1986).
30. Thomas Jefferson, *Notes on the State of Virginia*, ed. William Peden (New York: W. W. Norton, 1955), p. 159.
31. Vol. I, Chap. 5, §6, pp. 202–206.
32. Ronald Dworkin makes a similar but by no means identical distinction between personal and external preferences in *Taking Rights Seriously*, *op. cit.* (see n. 16), pp. 234–38.
33. Unfortunately, we are threatened here with a certain amount of terminological confusion. I have earlier used the term "personal interest" as a relatively generic label whose species are "self-regarding" and "other-regarding." Up to now when I have contrasted "personal interest" with anything, it has been with public, national, corporate, and collective interests.

   "Self-regarding interests" include both selfish and unselfish interests, that is those that are and those that are not unreasonably at the expense of other people. Under each of these headings we can distinguish self-centered relational interests like the interest in being well-liked by others, and self-confined interests which a person could have (in C.D. Broad's words) "if he were the only person that had ever existed," like the interest in being a self of a certain kind, or in having self-respect, or in maximizing one's own pleasure. See Broad's "Egoism as a Theory of Human Motives," in his *Ethics and the History of Philosophy* (London: Routledge & Kegan Paul, 1952), p. 220. Some interests tend to straddle the line between wholly self- and wholly other-regarding, e.g., the vicarious interest in the well-being of *my* child, which involves essential reference to me (I can substitute my proper name) as the person whose relation of fatherhood to the other person creates the interest, even though the interest is directed to the good of a party (selected out by her relation to me) as an end in itself, not merely a means to my good.

There is more terminological confusion in the other-regarding category. If we mean by "other-regarding" simply "not self-regarding," then the distinction between self- and other-regarding is exhaustive. But if we mean by "other-regarding" "other person-regarding," then we must add another generic category to our chart, namely "interests in the coming about or continuance in existence of relatively impersonal states of affairs." I propose that we *do* mean by other-regarding "not self-regarding." In that case the other-regarding category divides into two: "other person-regarding" and "impersonal states of affairs regarding." As we have seen in the text, the "other person-regarding" species divides into "vicarious" and "external" subspecies, and we could if we wished divide the vicarious subspecies further into benevolent and malevolent categories.

The "relatively impersonal states of affairs" category introduces new complexities, since examples in this genre are seldom pure. I might have an interest in the extension of scientific knowledge as an end in itself, though typically such an interest would be mixed with a self-regarding interest that I contribute *my* share to the impersonal good. Similarly, Truview's interest in the bare existence of a sanctified society (that such a society exist) is probably mixed with a personal interest that *he* be a part of it, and, what creates further problems, that interest entails that all individuals in the community, including Fairjoy, live sanctified lives. The latter interest, however, even though derivative from an "impersonal" one, is in itself, an external one. The distinctions in this note are summarized in the diagram below:

In the rough distinction introduced in the text between "personal" and "external," the personal interests include the unselfish self-centered ones, the unselfish self-confined ones, and the (benevolently) vicarious ones. The external interests are those other person-regarding interests in the external category.

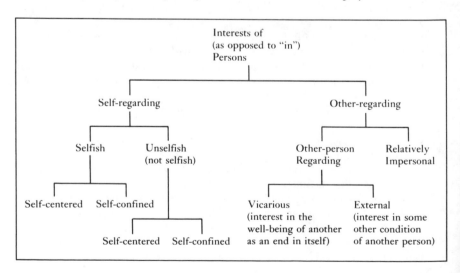

34. J.S. Mill, *On Liberty*, chap. IV, para. 12.
35. The personal external test for the importance of an interest developed in the text has an uncertain status. It could be a fourth criterion of importance on an equal footing with the other three, or it could be a tie-breaker to be used only if the other three fail to yield a decisive judgment comparing the importance of a given set of conflicting interests. (The *ceteris paribus* formulation would seem to suggest the latter.) Tom Senor suggests a third and more plausible alternative. He argues that the personal-external criterion is actually *prior* to the others, so that a personal interest of low vitality, for example, might still be more important, more worth protecting, than a highly vital external interest of another person that conflicts with it. I think Senor's suggestion better preserves the liberal's natural preferences than its alternatives. We can imagine, for example, that Fairjoy does not have a very vital interest in beer-drinking (if his want amounts to an *interest* at all), whereas the town elders each have a highly vital interest in living in a non-beer-drinking society. The liberal's desire to protect Fairjoy in this conflict cannot be guaranteed justification if the personal-external criterion can be used only as a tie-breaker for conflicts between equally vital interests, or if it is only one of four coordinate criteria of equal weight.
36. In a still unpublished paper, "Liberalism and the Enforcement of Morality." The quotations that follow from Schlossberger will not be separately footnoted. They are all from that essay.
37. J.S. Mill, *On Liberty*, chap. IV, para. 12.
38. The reader of Volume one of this book, *Harm to Others*, may be reminded of another consideration that can serve in an argument against the moral conservative who argues that social change would harm one of his interests. His desire to preserve the old ways, if it truly generates an authentic interest, will probably produce what in Volume one I called an "ulterior interest" or "focal aim." I claimed in Chap. 1, §7 that: "Our more ulterior interests, which since they include our highest aspirations, are in a sense the most important elements of our well-being, are for the most part *not* protectable by the law. If I have an interest in making an important scientific discovery, creating valuable works of art, or other personal achievements [to which list one might also add "impersonal achievements"], the law will protect that interest by guarding my welfare interests that are essential to it. But given that I have my life, health, economic adequacy, liberty, and security, there is nothing more that the law . . . can do for me; the rest is entirely up to me."
39. As quoted by Graham Hughes, *The Conscience of the Courts: Law and Morals in American Life* (Garden City, N.Y.: Anchor Press/Doubleday, 1975), pp. 46–47.
40. Ernest van den Haag, in *The New York Times*, Sunday, November 21, 1976, sect. 2, p. 26.
41. Even in relatively trivial matters there is a deep social inertia inhibiting change. Often resentment to new trends and fads manifests itself in overt hostility and even violence. A recent magazine article (Julie Raskin and Carolyn Males, 'Some Joggers Run a Gauntlet of Fear," *Parade*, July 15, 1979) gives graphic accounts of the widespread harassment of joggers in the period during which that new practice was establishing itself as a widespread and prominent feature of American life. Joggers reported that their attackers were "out to get them solely because they were runners": "While injuries as severe as [one] David Gottlieb's are rare,

other runners throughout the country have reported being punched, shouted at, thrown at (bottles, cans, cherry bombs, rotten apples, eggs, milkshakes, coat hangers), or having drivers deliberately intimidate them with their cars." The motivations for these attacks were probably mixed, but there seems little doubt that some expressed a natural resentment against fancied exclusiveness, cultish trendiness, and the like, taking it somehow to be threatening to the attacker's own self-confidence or self-esteem. To many people, anything new is *eo ipso* something alien, menacing, and contemptible. This mindless conservative inertia is a social tendency equal and opposite to bandwagon-jumping, and faddishness, which are, of course, equally mindless. In less injurious forms, it has a valuable function of regulating social change, quickly deflating fads, and providing a test that new practices must pass if they are to become entrenched (as jogging apparently has) in our way of life. It is in the nature of mere trendy fads to come and then (partly under conservative pressure) to go. Those that have some useful basis (like jogging), and perhaps only these, catch hold in some firm and permanent fashion.

42. See the discussion of the "magnitude of offense standard" in Vol. II, Chap. 8, §1.

43. The situation is different when uncontrolled hordes of immigrants are permitted to enter a country and become citizens before the country is prepared to absorb them in a "natural" assimilative way. Changes in custom, in tradition, religion, and language may be too extreme, too sudden, and too disruptive, and those reasons, which invoke shared harms and offenses, may support procedures that moderate and control the flow.

44. David Gill has reminded me that cultural change is often a complicated mixed evil. Given instances of cultural change, he points out, can be located on a spectrum anchored at one end by sudden and totally involuntary extinctions, and at the other extreme by those gradual evolutions that are at most free-floating evils. In between are changes that may be more or less extreme, more or less continuous and smooth, or sudden and disruptive, more or less voluntary or nonvoluntary, more or less welcome or distressful. Insofar as these changes are not forced or coerced, they do not constitute grievance evils for anyone, but Gill suggests that the relatively abrupt and extreme changes may cause various nongrievance welfare-connected evils. For expository economy I have restricted discussion in the text to the conceptually accessible ideal extremes of sudden extinction and gradual evolution.

45. Scholars, of course, might have regrets, but it can be pointed out to them that had not the linguistic evolution occurred, our culture might have been far more impoverished, and various tongues that evolved from the ancient ones might never have come into being. Moreover, the scholarly interest, as such, would be fully satisfied if more detailed *records* of the ancient languages and their literatures had survived, just as paleontologists are satisfied to find fossil skeletons and have no further regrets that *Eohippus* is not still grazing the African savannahs.

46. H.A. Gleason, *An Introduction to Descriptive Linguistics* (New York: Henry Holt, 1955), p. 6.

47. Albert C. Baugh, *History of the English Language* (New York: Appleton-Century-Crofts, 1935), p. 322.

48. Defoe, as quoted by Baugh, *ibid.*, p. 328.

49. Those of us who tend to get righteously indignant over such newly coined words or uses as "finalize," "hopefully," "uptight," and "laid back," might well ponder

the expressions that George Harris and Thomas Campbell in the eighteenth century condemned as outrageous coinages. The list includes "handling a subject," "driving a bargain," "bolstering up an argument," "encroach," "inculcate," "purport," "subject matter," and such French imports as "brunette," "canteen," "cartoon," "coquette," "dentist," and "routine." (Baugh, pp. 356–357).

50. John Boswell, *Christianity, Social Tolerance, and Homosexuality* (Chicago: University of Chicago Press, 1980), p. 8.

51. *Ibid.*, p. 59. Boswell's reviewer in *Newsweek*, Sept. 29, 1980, writes: "He begins with Rome in the first two centuries A.D., observing that urban societies, which tolerate religious diversity and are organized along political lines, have accepted a great deal of sexual variation without much fuss. Gay literature flourished in early imperial Rome, and non-gay writers treated homosexuality with candor and moral indifference. The Emperor Nero married two men in succession, and Suetonious reports people joking that if Nero's father had married that sort of wife the world would have been a happier place."

52. My argument has been that we needn't lament the disappearance of our evolutionary ancestors since the drastic changes in their characteristics that led them to "disappear" were the very changes which, over a period of time, turned them into us. For biologically sophisticated readers, however, two qualifications must be made. First, biological evolution is *not* constant and gradual. Rather there are some long periods of almost changeless stability, then stresses occur, and then there is relatively rapid change. These changes are "rapid" at least in terms of geologic time, though not overnight. They usually take place over a reasonably extended period of *human* generations. Second, it is a merely contingent fact that when species *B* evolves out of species *A*, species *A* then "becomes extinct" or disappears. Sometimes that does not happen, and instead species *A* divides into two groups: those that stay *A*s and those that change into *B*s. Then *A*s and *B*s can be contemporaries. Perhaps that did not happen when *Homo sapiens* evolved from its most immediate ancestors, in part because we ourselves helped destroy our less well-adapted cousins. For clear and up to date discussions of Darwinian mechanisms with application to human evolution, see Stephen Jay Gould, *Ever Since Darwin* (New York: W. W. Norton, 1977), esp. pt. 2.

53. Russell Baker, "Miss America and Life After Death," *New York Times*, September 2, 1980.

54. "Protections We Don't Need," *The Arizona Daily Star*, editorial, Sunday, May 2, 1982.

29A. Autonomy and Community

1. George Santayana, for example, defines "piety" in this sense as "man's reverent attachment to the sources of his being and the steadying of his life by that attachment. . .This consciousness that the human spirit is derived and responsible, that all its functions are heritages and trusts, involves a sentiment of gratitude and duty which we may call piety." George Santayana, *The Life of Reason* (New York: Charles Scribner's & Sons, 1954), p. 258. Santayana's piety is a form of "fraternity" with generations of ancestors and decendants, reminiscent of Burke's conception of society as a bond between the present, the past, and the future.

2. Honorable people, Stephen wrote, do not welcome love that they do not or

cannot return. His response to Rousseau's avowal of love for mankind is to say "Keep your love to yourself, and do not daub me or mine with it." "It is not love that one wants from the great mass of mankind," he adds, "but respect and justice." J.F. Stephen, *Liberty, Equality, and Fraternity* (Cambridge: Cambridge University Press, 1967), p. 221.

3. Alasdair MacIntyre, *After Virtue* (Notre Dame, Indiana: University of Notre Dame Press, 1981), esp. chap. 15.

4. Ludwig Wittgenstein, *Philosophical Investigations*, pt. I.

5. Ian Hacking, "Wittgenstein the Psychologist," *New York Review of Books*, April 1, 1982, p. 42. The most extreme departure from what might be called "linguistic individualism" is Wittgenstein's famous argument against a private language. As Hacking summarizes it (*op. cit.*, p. 43): "There cannot be a language that is in principle inaccessible to anyone else. There can, for example, be no language with names for just *my* sensations. A word like "pain" does not get its use by first naming something that we feel, and then telling others about it. Instead it is necessarily embedded in various kinds of things we do in connection with being hurt . . . The idea of stoically concealed pain is nested in and parasitic upon more public ways of talking about pain—evincing it, wincing, trying to comfort the victim or relieve the suffering."

6. Compare T.H. Green on national communities, *Prolegomena to Ethics*, ed. A.C. Bradley (Oxford: Clarendon Press, 1980), p. 193: "The saying that 'a nation is merely an aggregate of individuals' is indeed fallacious, but mainly on account of the introduction of the emphatic 'merely.' The fallacy lies in the implication that the individuals could be what they are, could have their moral and spiritual qualities, independently of their existence in a nation. . .But it is nonetheless true that the life of a nation has no real existence except as the life of the individuals composing the nation . . ."

It should be noted, incidentally, that the communitarian can use the emphatic "merely" in an equal and opposite mistake. S.I. Benn and G.F. Gaus, for example, attribute to the communitarian the view that "society is a single whole of which individual persons are merely constituents, each being nothing more than terms in various social relations." "The Liberal Conception of the Public and Private" in *Public and Private in Social Life* (New York: St. Martin's Press, 1983), p. 61. But surely the communitarian can consistently say that society is composed of flesh and blood persons in various social relations. It is not true that such persons are "nothing but terms," or "merely constituents," that is, just logical abstractions.

7. Cf. Benn and Gaus: "What would it mean, for instance, for an individual to value consciousness of his membership in an *aggregation?*" (emphasis added). *Op. cit.* (see n. 6), p. 48.

8. Michael J. Sandel, *Liberalism and the Limits of Justice* (Cambridge: Cambridge University Press, 1982), p. 179.

9. *Loc. cit.*

10. Michael J. Sandel,"Morality and the Liberal Ideal," *The New Republic*, May 7, 1984, p. 16. This essay, a clear summary of Sandel's views, also was published in substantially unaltered form as the Introduction to *Liberalism and its Critics*, ed. M.J. Sandel (New York: New York University Press, 1984).

11. *Loc. cit.*

12. *Ibid.*, p. 17.
13. Amy Gutman, "Communitarian Critics of Liberalism," *Philosophy and Public Affairs*, vol. 14 (1985), p. 311n.
14. Brian Barry, review of Sandel, *Ethics*, vol. 94 (1984), p. 525.
15. Compare the liberal hero John Dewey writing in 1930 in rejection of an "old individualism" in favor of an equally liberal new individualism: ". . . the mental and moral structure of individuals, the pattern of their desires and purposes, change with every great change in social constitution. Individuals who are not bound together in associations, whether domestic, economic, religious, political, artistic, or educational, are monstrosities. It is absurd to suppose that the ties which hold them together are merely external and do not react into mentality and character, producing the framework of personal disposition." *Individualism Old and New* (New York: Minton, Balch, and Company, 1930), pp. 81–82.

    Dewey apparently means the same thing by "internal ties"—those that imprint the "framework of personal disposition"—that Sandel and other writers mean by one's essential "personal identity"—a constituent of one's true self. An interesting consequence of this common notion expressed differently is, I think, that what is part of my "identity" (disposition framework), that is, what is truly me, is something that can be constrained, compelled, or coerced (by "outside" force), but it cannot be a constrainer of itself; it can be the object of outside compulsion but not an internal source of compulsion. (Other psychological traits, less central and therefore inessential to one's "identity," can count as "outside causes" and therefore as constraining.) We could not say "I was forced by my essential identity to do x." "Escaping" from a group affiliation then, in some cases, makes no more sense than "escaping" from (part of) one's own true self.
16. Robert N. Bellah, Richard Madsen, William M. Sullivan, Ann Swidler, and Steven M. Tipton, *Habits of the Heart: Individualism and Commitment in American Life* (Berkeley: University of California Press, 1985), p. 153.
17. *Loc. cit.*
18. *Loc. cit.*
19. *Ibid.*, p. 154.
20. *Loc. cit.*
21. Traditions must be distinguished from group *customs* within a community of memory. For example, one might write that it is the tradition at our college to begin the commencement exercises with a prayer, and also that a (lamentable) custom has grown up in recent years for the graduates to pop open champagne bottles. The distinction is a vague one, especially since many traditions begin as mere customs (social habits) and in time are sanctified by sentiment and thus transformed into genuine traditions. The distinction, I think, is primarily one of degree of acceptance and approval, especially by those whose acceptance and approval is most important, leaders, spokesmen, office-holders, and the like.
22. Robert N. Bellah *et al.*, *op. cit.* (see n. 16), p. 303.
23. Alasdair MacIntyre, *op. cit.* (see n. 3). I regret that I cannot do justice in this short space to the richness and subtlety of MacIntyre's analysis.
24. *Ibid.*, p. 192.
25. *Loc. cit.*
26. *Ibid.*, p. 200.
27. Cf. Epictetus, *The Enchiridion*, XVII: "Remember that you are an actor in a

drama of such sort as the Author chooses—if short, then in a short one; if long, then in a long one. If it be his pleasure that you should enact a poor man, or a cripple, or a ruler, or a private citizen, see that you act it well. For this is your business—to act well the given part, but to choose it belongs to another."

28. MacIntyre, *op. cit.* (see n. 3), p. 199.

29. *Ibid.*, pp. 204–05.

30. For a subtle development of the metaphor and a discussion of its implications, see Alan Ryan's suggestive article "Private Selves and Public Parts," in *Public and Private in Social Life*, ed. S.I. Benn and G.F. Gaus (New York: St. Martin's Press, 1983), pp. 135–54. He is especially good on the limits of role-playing. "Played too rigorously," he says, "the whole thing would become impossible." He points out too that our modern notion of privacy functions to protect us from the rigors of role-playing: "Although a family *can* be "the public" before which we enact our roles as fathers and sons or whatever, it is also true that at least in our sort of society, the family is private, a sort of backstage area where one can wipe off the greasepaint, complain about the audience, worry about one's performance, and so on. In their company we can engage in repairs and rehabilitation, chew over performances, and think how to improve them, and even rethink the whole play in which we are engaged. . ." (pp. 151–52).

31. Alan Ryan, *ibid.*, p. 137.

32. *Loc. cit.*

33. The term is Robert A. Nisbett's. See his *Community and Power* (New York: Oxford University Press, 1962), pp. 70–74 *et passim.*

34. MacIntyre, *op. cit.* (see n. 3), p. 117.

35. On this point see Gutman, *op. cit.* (see n. 13), p. 316.

36. MacIntyre, *op. cit.* (see n. 3), p. 205.

37. My only quibble with MacIntyre here is over his *apparent* suggestion that the difficulty is logical or conceptual. I think that effectively disowning one's national identity and its heritage of moral debts is only a practical difficulty, but an exceedingly great one, more like the difficulty of highjumping eight feet than the "difficulty" of lifting oneself by one's bootstraps.

38. MacIntyre, *op. cit.* (see n. 3), p. 206.

39. See my essay "Collective Responsibility" in *Doing and Deserving* (Princeton, N.J.: Princeton University Press, 1970), pp. 222–51.

40. MacIntyre, *op. cit.* (see n.3), p. 205.

41. *Ibid.*, p.206.

42. John Stuart Mill, *On Liberty*, chap. 2, para. 19–36, chap. 3, para. 17–19, *et passim.*

43. See George Lichtheim, "Alienation," *International Encyclopedia of the Social Sciences* (New York: Macmillan and The Free Press, 1968), vol. I, p. 264.

44. Karl Marx, *Economic and Philosophic Manuscripts of 1844* (New York: International Publishers, 1964), p. 108.

45. Tony Honoré, "The Human Community and the Principles of Majority Rule," in *Community as a Social Ideal*, ed. Eugene Kamenka (New York: St. Martin's Press, 1982), p. 159. Honoré continues: "But domesticity is relative. A man is at home in varying degrees with his family, his fellow townsmen, his fellow country-men, his trade union. The groups to which he belongs present themselves to him among other aspects as guarantors of the vicarious autonomy which he enjoys as a member of a group in which he is at home and which draws a firm line between

members and non-members: those who do not belong to the family, the town, the union, or the country in question. The strength of nationalism in this century, contrary to the expectations of nineteenth century theorists, shows how important it is psychologically for people to have a sense of relative domesticity even in relation to a very large group. . ."

46. "Suicide varies inversely with the degree of integration in society. Hence as Durkheim pointed out in studies which have been confirmed by the researches of many others, there is a higher rate of suicide among [individualistic] Protestants, among urban dwellers, among industrial workers, among the unmarried, among in short, all those whose lives are characterized by relative tenuousness of social ties. When the individual is thrown back upon his own inner resources, when he loses the sense of moral and social involvement with others, he becomes prey to sensations of anxiety and guilt. Self-destruction is frequently his only way out." Robert A. Nisbet, *Community and Power* (New York: Oxford University Press, 1962), pp. 14–15.

47. Alexis de Tocqueville, *Democracy in America*, trans. George Lawrence (New York: Doubleday Anchor Books, 1945), vol. 2, esp. p. 318.

48. Nisbet, *op. cit.* (see n. 45), pp. 204–05.

49. *Ibid.*, p. 268.

50. *Ibid.*, p. 265.

51. *Loc. cit.*

52. Sandel, *op. cit.* (see n. 10), p. 17.

53. Bellah, *et al.*, *op. cit.* (see n. 16), p. 333.

43. *Ibid.*, p. 335.

55. *Ibid.*, p. 179.

56. Aristotle, *Politics*, 1260b–1264b. Aristotle actually makes the very uncommunitarian observation at 1261b that "if self-sufficiency is to be desired, the lesser degree of unity is more desirable than the greater."

57. Carl J. Friedrich, "The Concept of Community in the History of Political and Legal Philosophy," in *Nomos* II, *Community* (New York: The Liberal Arts Press, 1959), p. 5.

58. "The United States," Bellah *et al.* tell us, "is a nation of joiners." *Op. cit.* (see n. 16), p. 167. In this respect Americans have not changed much since the time of Tocqueville who wrote in 1830: "Americans of all ages, all stations in life, and all types of disposition are forever forming associations. These are not only commerical and industrial associations in which all take part, but others of a thousand different types—religious, moral, serious, futile, very general and very limited, immensely large and very minute. . .In every case, at the head of any new undertaking, where in France you would find the government or in England some territorial magnate, in the United States you are sure to find an association." De Tocqueville, *op. cit.* (see n. 47), p. 523. Quoted by Bellah *et al.*, p. 167.

59. Cf. Bellah, *et al.*: "The public realm is an enduring association of the different." Quoted without citation by Naomi Bliven in her review of *Habits of the Heart*, *The New Yorker*, April 21, 1986, p. 120.

60. Note the way John Rawls now defends his version of the liberal ideology: "The essential point is this: as a practical political matter no general moral conception can provide a publicly recognized basis for a conception of justice in a modern

democratic state. The social and historical conditions of such a state have their origins in the Wars of Religion following the Reformation and the subsequent development of the principle of toleration, and in the growth of constitutional government and the institutions of large industrial market economies. These conditions profoundly affect the requirements of a workable conception of political justice: such a conception must allow for a diversity of doctrines and the plurality of conflicting, and indeed incommensurable, conceptions of the good affirmed by the members of existing democratic societies." John Rawls, "Justice as Fairness: Political Not Metaphysical," *Philosophy and Public Affairs*, vol. 14 (1985), p. 225.

61. Octavio Paz, *On Earth, Four or Five Worlds: Reflections on Contemporary History*, trans. Helen R. Lane (New York: Harcourt, Brace, Jovanovich, 1985). These notes will refer to that book only as quoted in the review essay of Naomi Bliven in *The New Yorker*, February 3, 1986, pp. 134–38.

62. *Ibid.*, p. 137.

63. *Loc. cit.* Italics added.

64. For a summary of factors to be weighed by courts in cases of the attempted community enforcement of aesthetic standards, and a fascinating fictitious case illustrating how they apply, see F. Patrick Hubbard, "Taking Persons Seriously: A Jurisprudential Perspective on Social Disptues in a Changing Neighborhood," *University of Cincinnati Law Review*, vol. 48 (1979), pp. 15–41.

65. Roger Scruton, *The Meaning of Conservatism* (Harmondsworth, England, Penguin Books, 1980), p. 74.

66. Gutman, *op. cit.* (see n. 13), p. 318.

67. J. Anthony Lukas, "Community and Equality in Conflict," *The New York Times*, September 8, 1985. All the quotations from Lukas are from this source and will not be further footnoted. His book-length study of Charlestown has now been published, *Common Ground: A Turbulent Decade in the Lives of Three American Families* (New York: Random House, 1986).

68. Gerald Postema, "Collective Evils, Harms, and the Law," *Ethics*, vol. 97 (1987), pp. 419–29.

30. Strict Moralism: Enforcing True Morality

1. Anthony D. Woozley, "Law and the Legislation of Morality," *Ethics in Hard Times*, ed. Arthur L. Caplan and Daniel Callahan (New York: Plenum, 1981), p. 158.

2. *Loc. cit.*

3. Bertrand Russell, *Skeptical Essays* (London: George Allen & Unwin, Ltd., 1935), pp. 121–22.

4. William F. Buckley, Jr., "Death for Gilmore?," *New York Post Magazine*, December 7, 1976, p. 32.

5. *The New York Times*, editorial, March 10, 1971.

6. Gurdip S. Sidhu, M.D., letter to the editor, *New York Times*, March 17, 1971.

7. Irving Kristol, "Pornography, Obscenity, and the Case for Censorship," *The New York Times Magazine*, March 28, 1971.

8. Repellent as the farfetched example of the gladiatorial contest is, it seems no worse, and indeed in some respects better, than the sanguinary excesses of new

forms of commerically organized brawling actually existent in the United States. See *Newsweek*, April 6, 1981, on "The Tough-Guy Bars," and *The New York Times* editorial, "Macho Mayhem," December 26, 1980, quoted here in its entirety:

> The newest rage in spectator entertainment is a kind of gladiatorial combat known as The Tough Guy (or Toughman) contest. Promoters descend on a community and advertise for the toughest, meanest bar brawlers and street fighters in need of work and arrange for a bloody brawl in which, usually, anything goes.
>
> The profitable attraction is gore. This is not the sham struggle of professional wrestling or the legally restrained fisticuffs of boxing. Tough Guy sells raw violence by ill-trained men (and women, in the Tough Gal division) who beat each other bloody, even senseless. Most matches are one-sided, with the young thrashing the old, the heavy demolishing the light, and the muscular mauling the flabby. One contestant is said to have suffered brain damage.
>
> The idea of callous promoters making a fast buck out of base passion—and of pathetic brawlers selling their macho fantasies for, at best, $1,000—is appalling. The spectacle is even worse when blacks are pitted against whites to stir racial antagonisms in the crowd. The spectators pay $6 to $20 for this mayhem, and occasionally follow the scheduled entertainment with their own fist fights. In one such battle, a security guard had his head split open. The spectators in Rome's Colosseum could occasionally demand that a valiant but outpointed gladiator be spared. Tough Guy contests apparently don't go in for mercy.

 9. *Webster's New Collegiate Dictionary* (Springfield, Mass.: G. C. Merriam Co., 1977).
10. Patrick Devlin, "The Enforcement of Morals," republished in 1965 as "Morals and the Criminal Law," chap. I of *The Enforcement of Morals* (London: Oxford University Press, 1965), pp. 1–25.
11. *The Wolfenden Report* (New York: Stein and Day, 1963), p. 143.
12. Devlin, *op. cit.* (see n. 10), preface, p. vi.
13. *The Wolfenden Report*, *op. cit.* (see n. 11), para. 224.
14. Devlin, *op. cit.* (see n. 10), p. 4.
15. *Ibid.*, p. 69.
16. *Ibid.*, p. 7.
17. *Ibid.*, p. 10.
18. *Ibid.*, p. 8.
19. *Ibid.*, p. 11.
20. *Loc. cit.*
21. *Ibid.*, p. 13.
22. *Ibid.*, pp. 13–14.
23. *Ibid.*, p. 15.
24. *Ibid.*, p. 17.
25. *Loc. cit.*
26. *Ibid.*, p. 8.
27. H.L.A. Hart, "Immortality and Treason," *The Listener*, July 30, 1959. Reprinted in Richard A. Wasserstrom, ed., *Morality and the Law* (Belmont, Calif.: Wadsworth, 1971). The quoted passage is from Wasserstrom, p. 54.

28. *Ibid.*, pp. 52–53.
29. Hart characterizes Devlin's conception of popular morality as "a single seamless web." *Law, Liberty, and Morality* (Stanford, Calif.: Stanford University Press, 1963), p. 51. Devlin (*op. cit.*, n. 10, p. 115) replies that "Seamlessness presses the simile rather hard but, apart from that, I should say that for most people morality is a web of beliefs rather than a number of unconnected ones."
30. Ronald Dworkin, "Lord Devlin and the Enforcement of Morals," *The Yale Law Journal*, vol. 75 (1968). Reprinted in Dworkin's *Taking Rights Seriously* (Cambridge, Mass.: Harvard University Press, 1977). The quoted passage is from the latter source, p. 248.
31. H.L.A. Hart, *Law, Liberty, and Morality, op. cit.* (see n. 29).
32. James Fitzjames Stephen, *Liberty, Equality, Fraternity* (Cambridge: Cambridge University Press, 1967), pp. 152ff.
33. Hart, *op. cit.* (see n. 29), p. 36.
34. Stephen, *op. cit.* (see n. 32), p. 152.
35. Hart, *op. cit.* (see n. 29), p. 37.
36. *Loc. cit.*
37. Patrick Devlin, *The Enforcement of Morals; op. cit.* (see n. 10), p. 130.
38. *Ibid.*, p. 131.
39. H.L.A. Hart, "Prolegomenon to the Principles of Punishment" in his *Punishment and Responsibility* (New York and Oxford: Oxford University Press, 1968), esp. pp. 2–3 and 8–11.
40. Aristotle includes among the "moral virtues" both cheerfulness and a sense of humor. (These are translated by Ross as "good temper" and "ready wit"). See *Nichomachean Ethics*, Book IV, Chaps. 5 and 8.
41. J.L. Austin wrote that we might admit that an act, *A*, was not a good thing to have done, but go on "to argue that it is not quite fair or correct to say *baldly*, "*X* did *A*." He explains: "We might say it isn't fair just to say *X* [with emphasis] did it; perhaps he was under somebody's influence or was nudged. Or, it isn't fair to say baldly he *did* it; it may have been partly accidental, or an unintentional slip. Or it isn't fair to say he did simply *A*—he was really doing something quite different, and *A* was only incidental, or he was looking at the whole thing quite differently. . ." J.L. Austin, "A Plea for Excuses" in his *Philosophical Papers* (Oxford: Clarendon Press, 1961), p. 124.
42. See my "The Expressive Function of Punishment" in my *Doing and Deserving* (Princeton, N.J.: Princeton University Press, 1970), pp. 95–118. The point is also given emphasis by Neil MacCormick in his *Legal Right and Social Democracy* (Oxford: Clarendon Press, 1982), pp. 30–34. MacCormick invokes the stigmatizing nature of punishment, however, to make a point at first sight opposite to mine, namely that "any principle whatever which allows that the state may resort to punishment necessarily allows state enforcement of some moral values." (p. 33).
43. A more thorough account of procedural justice would have to make many more distinctions, and say more about the interplay between formal (Aristotelian) justice and what is often called "material justice." The requirements of procedural justice are not exhausted by the simple Aristotelian formula. What if we treated relevantly similar cases in similar ways but then used an inverted rank order: lowest scores ranked at the top, and highest scores disqualified! Also the

formal principle could be satisfied by a procedure that is too severe, one that flunked, say, the lowest 99%.

44. See *supra*, Chap. 28, §3.

45. I should mention again the possible exception to this generalization constituted by involuntarily suffered or risked evils of the sort I called "welfare-connected non-grievance evils" in Chap. 28,§6. These are virtually confined to those harmful states permitted or caused by wrongful acts and omissions leading to the party's conception or birth in a harmful condition, but where nonexistence would not be preferred.

46. A more extreme example might be more convincing. Imagine a statute then that makes "negligent jaywalking" while in a lascivious daydream more punishable than "negligent jaywalking" while absorbed in thought about the ontological argument.

47. Stephen, *op. cit.* (see n. 32), p. 151.

48. *Loc. cit.*

49. *Loc. cit.*

50. *Loc. cit.* Stephen is too delicate to say so here, but he is obviously referring to such "unnatural" sex crimes as sodomy, bestiality, and incest.

51. *Loc. cit.*

52. Stephen's most famous example (*op. cit.*, p. 153) is as follows:

> A judge has before him two criminals, one of whom appears from the circumstances of the case to be ignorant and depraved, and to have given away to a very strong temptation under the influence of the other, who is a man of rank and education, and who committed the offense of which both are convicted under comparatively slight temptation. I will venture to say that if he made any difference between them at all, every judge on the English bench would give the first a lighter sentence than the second."

Stephen's intention is to show that any philosophers who makes deterrence the primary and overriding determinant of individual sentences should make the existence of widespread temptation an aggravating circumstance; whereas a philosopher who makes either the degree of hatefulness or the degree of moral blameworthiness the paramount determinant will *not* consider the temptation to be an aggravating circumstance. But Stephen proceeds to assume more than what is required by his argument when he claims that the vengeance-blameworthiness philosopher considers temptation to be not merely *not aggravating*, but positively *mitigating*. Thus, a person who commits a criminal act that he is only moderately tempted to do is more blameworthy than a criminal who performs the same act (in Stephens' own example as a partner) having "given way to very strong temptation." Not only is the claim not required by Stephens' argument; it is far from being intuitively compelling. If Stephens' example makes it seem plausible, that is perhaps because it introduces extraneous elements, in particular influence, ignorance, education, and rank. The moderately tempted party in Stephens' example is also the party who should have known better.

52. Punishment may *also* be deterrent according to this view, and it is a good thing that it be so, but deterrence *alone* can never justify a particular instance of punishment. On the other hand, punishment is justified in those cases in which it is retributive whether it is deterrent in those cases or not. Note also that in the

weakest sense of "retributive," that term may refer only to the requirements of procedural fairness that all punishment theorists must recognize, that there be no punishment without legal guilt, that the degree of punishment be proportionate to the degree of blameworthiness and discounted in proportion to the degree of nonresponsibility, and so on. In this sense of "retributive," we are (almost) all retributivists. Whatever the criminal law is *for*, it must be administered fairly. Most of the theories to which the label "retributivism" has adhered, however, assert that giving wrongdoers their due is precisely what the system of criminal law *is* for (as well as reducing the amount of wrongdoing by the intimidation of example). In short, retributivism makes retribution part of the justifying aim of criminal law and not merely a requirement derivative from procedural fairness.

53. *Webster's New Collegiate Dictionary.*

54. A.C. Ewing, *The Morality of Punishment* (London: Kegan Paul, 1929), p. 13.

55. For a sophisticated development of a retributive theory of this sort, see Herbert Morris, "Persons and Punishment," *The Monist*, vol. 52 (1968).

56. H.L.A. Hart, "Law, Liberty, and Morality," *op. cit.* (see n. 29), p. 60.

57. *Loc. cit.*

58. Tradition shows Lucifer, as a mere functionary, usurping the role and symbolic trappings of his superior. Marlowe characterized Lucifer's sin as "aspiring pride and insolence" (the insolence adds something to the pride). According to some church fathers, Lucifer's original sin was "refusal to bow before the Great White Throne," but according to others, he actually tried to seize the throne itself or simply to seat himself on it. In certain medieval mysteries, Lucifer sits next to God by night, but when God leaves his throne for a moment, Lucifer, "swelling with pride, sits down on the throne of heaven" (the greatest wickedness open to him) and that is when "the Archangel Michael, indignant, takes up arms against him, and finally succeeds in driving him [out of heaven]." See Maximilian Rudwin, *The Devil in Legend and Literature* (Chicago: Open Court Publishing Co., 1931), chap. 1.

59. The classic source, I think, in Christian theology for the doctrine that sin (presumably even otherwise "victimless sin") wrongs God, is St. Anselm's *Cur Deus Homo?* As I understand Anselm, all sins in effect steal something from God that rightfully belongs to Him, or alternatively default on a debt one has to God, and in that way deprive Him of His due. To sin, by definition, is "nothing else than not to render to God his due." That debt, in turn, consists in maintaining a justness or uprightness of heart. "This is the sole and complete debt of honor which we owe to God and which God requires of us. . .He who does not render this honor which is due to God robs God of his own and dishonors him; and this is sin." *Saint Anselm, Basic Writings*, trans. S.N. Deane (La Salle, Ill.: Open Court Publishing Co., 1962), chap. XI, "What it is to Sin, and to Make Satisfaction for Sin," p. 202. See also St. Thomas Aquinas, *Summa Theologica* (London: Burnes, Oates & Washbourne, Ltd.), 2d ed., 3rd pt., QXII, art. 3 QXIII, art. 1–3, pp. 205–33. I am indebted to Jacob Adler for all these references.

60. Georg Wilhelm Friedrich Hegel, *The Philosophy of Right*, trans. T.M. Knox (Oxford: Oxford University Press, 1942), sects. 99, 100.

61. G.E. Moore, *Principia Ethica* (Cambridge: Cambridge University Press, 1903), chap. 1, D.

62. A.C. Ewing, *Ethics* (New York: Macmillan, 1953), pp. 169–70.

63. It is not clear whether this kind of retributive theory is consistent with a general consequentialism in ethics. According to it, punishment *is* justified by some of its results, namely those which alter the moral relations between events one of which (the original wrongdoing) was in the past. According to this kind of retributivism, the "consequence" of punishment that justifies it is a "backward-looking consequence," a result that somehow alters the past. Punishment is justified if, as one of its results, a stretch of time beginning at a given point in the past and ending with *it*, an event in the present, is better as a whole than it would otherwise be.

64. "It is not a defense," Devlin writes, "to any form of assault that the victim thought his punishment well deserved and submitted to it." (*The Enforcement of Morals*, p. 8). Devlin may be confusing assault with battery here. Graham Hughes corrects the record: "The position in fact appears to be that in the general crime of assault at common law the consent of the victim will be a defense provided that no serious bodily harm was caused." "Morals and the Criminal Law," *Yale Law Journal*, vol. 71 (1962), p. 670. Battery is defined as "the unlawful application of force to the person of another," whereas assault is "either (1) an attempt to commit a battery, or (2) an unlawful act which places another in reasonable apprehension of receiving an immediate battery," e.g. by threatening with an unloaded gun. One does not normally commit battery without also committing assault, but people frequently make an assault without inflicting a battery. A private scuffle is normally innocent if both parties have consented to the assault of the other and no *serious* battery results. See Rollin M. Perkins, *Criminal Law* (Brooklyn: The Foundation Press, 1957), pp. 80, 86.

65. Perkins, *ibid.*, p. 131.

66. *Ibid.*, p. 134.

67. See Graham Hughes, *op. cit.* (see n. 63), pp. 669ff.

68. Perkins, *op. cit.* (see n. 63), p. 142.

69. *Ibid.*, p. 143. Perkins cites the authority of Blackstone for these words, *Commentaries*, 205.

70. 1 Coke on Littleton 194 (127a, 127b); 1 Hale PC 412. See John Kleinig, "Consent as a Defense in Criminal Law," *Archives for Philosophy of Law and Social Philosophy* (ARSP), (Wiesbaden: Franz Steiner Verlag GMBH, 1979), vol. LXV, no. 3, pp. 335ff.

71. Jesse Dukeminier, "Supplying Organs for Transplantation," *Michigan Law Review*, vol. 81 (1968).

72. Sir William Blackstone, *Commentaries on the Laws of England*, book 4, 145.

31. Exploitation With and Without Harm

1. This point was first called to my attention by Bruce Landesman in his written but unpublished comments on my paper, "Noncoercive Exploitation," presented at the Liberty Fund Conference on Paternalism in Lutsen, Minnesota, in September, 1980. When two distinctions cut across one another, they necessarily yield four distinguishable classes, in this case (1) pejorative exploitation of persons, (2) nonpejorative exploitation of persons, (3) pejorative exploitation of traits and circumstances, (4) nonpejorative exploitation of traits and circumstances. But in this case one of the distinguished classes is empty. There is no such thing as (2),

nonpejorative exploitation of persons. It is at least *prima facie* wrong, always, to exploit persons.

2. Landesman, *ibid.*

3. When *A* takes advantage of desperate circumstances of *B* that were deliberately created by *C* (another party), by making an offer *B* cannot, in the circumstances, refuse, the opportunistic offer is (a) exploitative, and (b) coercive in effect, but (c) not employing typically coercive methods (not deliberately closing options by forceful intervention). Because of (b), I have classified these cases as coercive exploitation, but because of (c), David Zimmerman calls them "noncoercive exploitation." (See Vol. 2, Chap. 24, §§3 and 4.) Be that as it may, my intention in this chapter is to discuss cases of exploitation that are clearly and noncontroversially noncoercive, both in method and effect.

4. For fuller and more accurate accounts, see Richard J. Arneson, "What's Wrong with Exploitation?," *Ethics*, vol. 91 (1981), pp. 202–227; Allen E. Buchanan, *Marx and Justice* (Totowa, N.J.: Rowman and Littlefield, 1982), chap. 3; and G.A. Cohen, "Karl Marx and the Withering Away of Social Science," *Philosophy and Public Affairs*, vol. 1 (1972), pp. 182–203.

5. Summarizing Marx's theory of exploitation, Arneson writes: "Without force or coercion there is no exploitation." *Op. cit.* (see n. 2), p. 225.

6. John Kleinig, "The Ethics of Consent," *Canadian Journal of Philosophy*, vol. XI (1981).

7. The facts in this hypothetical case are very close to those in the actual case of *R. v. Wright*, 1 Coke on Littleton 194 (127a, 127b); 1 Hale PC 412. See *supra*, Chap. 23, §6.

8. *Parade Magazine*, June 29, 1980.

9. The point is well illustrated in the 1973 movie *The Sting*, which tells the story of a large profit made by some swindlers by turning the greed of a ruthless gangster to their own advantage. The comeuppance of the gangster was so "just right"—so much what "he had coming"—that even though his fleecing was thoroughly fraudulent, we would not naturally use the pejorative "exploitation" to describe it.

   A more recent illustration of the general point is suggested by the widely quoted moral judgment of the Roman Catholic Cardinal of Manila during the Phillipine election campaign of 1986. During a period when it was well known that agents of the incumbent president Ferdinand Marcos were spending millions "buying votes," the Cardinal was quoted as saying "It is not wrong to take a bribe to vote so long as one votes as one's conscience dictates." Apparently the cardinal's purpose was to assure those voters who had already accepted Marcos's money that they were still morally free to vote, if they genuinely preferred to do so, for his rival. But another interpretation is possible. One might have held that taking advantage of (exploiting) Marcos's evil disposition for one's own gain at the briber's expense is morally permissible. At the very least one might maintain that no one (certainly not Marcos!) would have a moral grievance against one if one did.

10. As quoted in an Associated Press dispatch, London, December 24, 1980.

11. Jack Kroll, review of "The Class of 1984" in *Newsweek*, August 30, 1982, p. 61.

12. *Time Magazine*, June 20, 1977, p. 54.

13. *Loc. cit.*

14. Patrick Devlin, *The Enforcement of Morals* (London: Oxford University Press, 1965), p. 12.

15. *The Wolfenden Report: Report of The Committee on Homosexual Offenses and Prostitution* (New York: Stein and Day, 1963), p. 163.

16. Louis B. Schwartz, "Morals Offenses and the Model Penal Code," *Columbia Law Review*, vol. 63 (1963), as reprinted in Richard A. Wasserstrom, ed., *Morality and the Law* (Belmont, Calif.: Wadsworth, 1971), p. 96.

17. *Ibid.*, p. 97.

18. 383 U.S. 463 (1966).

19. *Ibid.*, at 467, quoting *Roth v. United States*, 354 U.S. 476, 495–96 (1957) (Warren, C.J. concurring).

20. This interpretation of coercive offers is expanded with considerable ingenuity by Harry Frankfurt, "Coercion and Moral Responsibility," in *Essays on Freedom of Action*, ed. Ted Honderich (London: Routledge and Kegan Paul, 1973).

21. Norman Mailer, *The Executioner's Song* (Boston: Little, Brown, 1979).

22. Diane Johnson, "Death for Sale," *New York Review of Books*, vol. XXVI, December 6, 1979, p. 4. Johnson's reaction strikes me as excessive. Mailer depicts Schiller as someone troubled by his reputation as a "carrion bird," very sensitive to the interests of those he is "exploiting," worried in his conscience, and very determined to be as "professional" as possible. Still, Mailer's attitudes toward Schiller seem ambivalent, and the facts are never altogether clear to the reader, so we can treat the episode as interpreted by Johnson at least as a "hypothetical example" of great philosophical interest, even if not altogether accurate historically. Whether Schiller was an exploiter or not, there is no doubt that those who sold tickets to the execution, the wax museums who bid for Gilmore's clothes, the sellers of Gilmore T-shirts, and many others were.

23. The public in the United States has traditionally attached a kind of stigma to life-insurance salesmen and undertakers but not to physicians. Viviana A. Rotman Zelizer explains why: "The occupational stigma of selling insurance cannot . . . be explained away by an unqualified statement of its relation to death in general. It is the specific nature of that involvement which built its ill-repute. To life insurance salesmen, as to undertakers, death is a moneymaking business. As "businessmen" of death they are differentiated from the "professionals" of death, physicians and clergymen, whose connection to death is made legitimate by their service orientation . . . Regardless of the individual motivations of the practitioners—their greed or beneficence—professions institutionalize altruism while business institutionalizes self-interest. To save and to heal is holier than to sell." *Morals and Markets: The Development of Life Insurance in the United States* (New York: Columbia University Press, 1979), p. 135. This book is an enlightening sociological study of the shifting attitudes of the American public.

24. The $50,000 paid to Gilmore for "exclusive rights" and $25,000 to his disturbed girlfriend dribble through their hands almost entirely before the book's story is even finished.

25. Buchanan made this suggestion in his remarks at the Liberty Fund Conference, Lutsen, Minnesota, September 1980.

26. *Newsweek*, April 19, 1982.

27. Morris raised this question at the Liberty Fund Conference, Lutsen, Minnesota, September 1980.

28. American Law Institute, *Restatement of the Law of Restitution* (1937), chap. 1, §2.

29. *Ibid.*, chap. 1, §1, comment I.

30. Dan Dobbs, *Law of Remedies* (1973), p. 224.

31. *Ibid.*, p. 223.

32. *Ibid.*, p. 224.

33. Bruce Landesman, *op. cit.* (see n. 1.)

34. Kant makes similar distinctions but in quite distinct, even contrary, terminology. He uses a hypothetical case similar to my typist example to illustrate a distinction between what he calls "justice" and "equity." *A* makes an agreement to pay *B* a specified amount for a year's work, but suppose that by the end of that time, the currency has inflated significantly. Justice (in Kant's sense) does not require that *A* give *B* a compensatory dividend, but equity does. If *A*'s failure to make the extra payment truly exploits *B*, then this shows that not all exploitation is the doing of an injustice in Kant's sense, and if inequity is a species of unfairness, that not all unfairness is injustice in Kant's sense. (I owe these points to Allen Buchanan.) See Immanuel Kant, *The Metaphysical Elements of Justice* (Part I of *The Metaphysics of Morals*), trans. John Ladd (Indianapolis: Bobbs-Merrill, 1965), para. 234, pp. 39–40. Kant's distinction seems virtually identical to the one I make in quite different terminology. I use "Injustice" as a genus, and divide it into two species: *unfairness* (involving victims, grievances, violated rights), and "other injustice." Kant uses "Unfairness" as the genus and divides it into the same two species, which he calls "injustice" (corresponding to my "unfairness") and "inequity" (corresponding to at least part of my "other injustice").

35. The point applies unless the avoidable loss of dignity is a "harm" even when the deformed person does not care about his dignity. Harmful or not, the loss of dignity is an *evil*, and drawing profit from an evil is what offends in this kind of exploitation.

36. In Volume one, *Harm to Others*, Chap. 1, §1, I distinguished between the ordinary sense of "harm," in which it means roughly "setback to interest," and the sense of the term it must bear in the harm principle if that liberty-limiting principle is to be remotely plausible. The latter sense, which I have used throughout this work, is roughly "setback to interest which is also a violation of a right." So "harm" in this second, technical sense, stands for a harm in the ordinary sense *that is also a wrong* to the harmed party.

32. The Exploitation Principle: Preventing Wrongful Gain

1. For the distinction between justice as a virtue of actors and justice as the effects of actions on the rights of "the other party," see Josef Pieper, *Justice* (London: Faber and Faber, 1957), pp. 13ff.

2. John Kleinig, "Consent as a Defense in Criminal Law," *Archives for Philosophy of Law and Social Philosophy* (Wiesbaden: Franz Steiner Verlag GMBH, 1979), vol. 65, no. 3, p. 340.

3. *Loc. cit.*

4. *Ibid.*, p. 344.

5. *Loc. cit.*

6. R.M. Hare, *Freedom and Reason* (Oxford: Clarendon Press, 1963), p. 147.

7. *Loc. cit.*

8. *Loc. cit.*

9. Thomas C. Grey, ed., *The Legal Enforcement of Morality* (New York: Alfred A. Knopf, 1983), p. 141.

10. John Fedders, as quoted in Julie Kosterlitz, "The Thomas Reed Affair," *Common Cause*, January, 1983, p. 21.

11. According to Kosterlitz (see n. 10), this is the view of the Securities and Exchange Commission, whose 1981 Chairman, John Fedders, she quotes as saying, "Anyone who engages in insider trading is clearly a thief." *Loc. cit.*

12. Kosterlitz, *loc. cit.* (quoting an unnamed Wall Street securities attorney).

13. The example is fleshed out as follows: *A*, an impatient driver in a traffic jam, moves his car to the forbidden emergency lane on the right side of the highway and then accelerates by a long line of stalled, law-abiding motorists, including *B*. The indignant *B*, let us suppose, will get to his destination no later because of *A*'s cheating (since *A*, after driving at high speed for several miles, will turn right on to a different road rather than reentering the traffic on the original road at a place well ahead of *B*), so *B* cannot claim that his interests were *harmed*, even though he was unfairly taken advantage of, in the sense that *A*'s gain was made possible only because he and the other motorists in his lane were too honorable to do the same thing themselves.

14. Kosterlitz, *op. cit.* (see n. 10), p. 21.

15. Jesse Dukeminier, "Supplying Organs for Transplantation," *Michigan Law Review*, vol. 68 (1970), p. 811. Reprinted in Thomas C. Grey, ed., *The Legal Enforcement of Morality* (New York: Alfred A. Knopf, 1983), pp. 141–144. All references here are to the Grey volume.

16. *Ibid.*, p. 143.

17. Grey, *op. cit.* (see n. 15), p. 141.

18. Dukeminier, *op. cit.* (see n. 15), pp. 143–44.

19. Azusa Municipal Code, Azusa, California, sec. 8.52.060.

20. *Spiritual Psychic Science Church of Truth, Inc. et al. v. City of Azusa*, 217 Cal. Rptr. 225 (Cal. 1985).

21. *Ibid.*, quoted by Judge Mosk from *Murdock v. Pennsylvania*, (1943) 319 U.S. 105, 111, 63, S. Ct. 870, 874, 87 L. Ed. 1292.

22. *Spiritual Psychic Science Church of Truth, Inc. v. Azusa, op. cit.* (see n. 20), p. 227.

23. *In re Bartha*, 63 Cal. App. 3d 584, 591, 135 Cal. Rptr. 39. The quotation in the text is from this case.

24. California Civil Code, sec. 1710.

25. *Spiritual Psychic Science Church of Truth, Inc. v. Azusa, op. cit.* (see n. 20), p. 235.

26. *Ibid.*, p. 237.

27. *Loc. cit.*

28. *Ibid.*, p. 236.

29. *Ibid.*, p. 237.

30. Richard J. Arneson, "Mill versus Paternalism," *Ethics*, vol. 90 (1980), p. 486, n. 25.

31. *Estell v. Birmingham*, 291 Ala 680, 286 So 2d 872, 81 ALR 3d 650. There are various other leading cases, however, from other states, that differ from this Alabama Supreme Court decision.

32. Lynn C. Cobb, "Annotation: Validity of State or Local Regulation Dealing with Resale of Tickets to Theatrical or Sporting Events," American Law Reports, 3d, *Cases and Annotations*, vol. 81 (1977), p. 672. The court upheld such an ordinance

in *People ex rel. Lange v. Palmitter* (1911) 71 Misc. 158, 128 NYS 426, aff'd. 144 App Div 894, 128 NYS 1140, aff'd 202 NY 608, 96 NE 1126. For a contrary opinion in a factually similar case, see *People v. Van Wong* (1958) 165 Cal App 2d Supp 821, 332 P2d 872.

33. There has been widespread disagreement among courts both about this point and about the obscure but related question of which resales are and which are not "affected with a public interest." In *People v. Johnson* (1967) 52 Misc 2d 1087, 278 NYS 2d 80, the court said that a statute regulating resale of theatre tickets had as its whole purpose "to preserve the public welfare, to advance the enlargement of the arts and theatre, so that many could enjoy those fine facets of life, and not merely let them be saved for the favored few," and that that purpose gave it constitutional vindication.

34. For examples, see West's Ann. Calif. Codes (Penal Code, 1986 Supp.), 346, and Minn. Stat. Ann. (1964 and 1986 Supp.), 609.805. Various other states, including Arizona, Michigan, New York, Texas, and Washington, have no anti-scalping statutes.

35. Lynn C. Cobb, *op. cit.* (see n. 32), p. 680.

36. Cobb (*ibid.*, p. 678) describes such a case:

> In *People v. Johnson* (1967) 52 Misc 2d 1087, 278 NYS 2d 80, in which the defendant . . . was charged with a violation of a statute designed to regulate the resale of theatre tickets, in that she did sell two tickets to an opera for $40 each, which tickets were originally priced at $20 each, the court found the defendant not guilty. It appeared that the defendant had purchased the tickets for $20 each in hopes of making them the key to a reunion with her estranged husband. When her husband refused to accompany her, she decided not to attend the opera, and placed an ad in a local newspaper inviting offers to purchase the tickets. In response to the ad a city police inspector telephoned the defendant. He and a policewoman went to the defendant's apartment, agreed upon a price of $40 per ticket, and after the exchange was made, the officers disclosed their identity and placed the defendant under arrest, charged with the resale of tickets of admission . . . The court could not believe that it was the legislative intent to embrace a case such as the one at bar within the ambit of the statute . . . Rather, the court said, the statute was designed to apply to those engaged in the *business* of reselling tickets, and the court observed that "business" has been described as a word of large import, rather than a mere isolated transaction . . . The court found that the prosecution's contention that any sale, even to a relative or friend, of a ticket . . . with or without profit, constituted a violation of the law, was unacceptable, and a *reductio ad absurdum* [of the prosecution's case].

37. *In Re Application of Dees* (1920) 46 Cal App, 656, 189, p. 1050.

38. *In Re Application of Dees* (1920) 50 Cal App, 11, 194, p. 717.

39. *Loc. cit.*

40. *Brody v. Marshall* (1950) 72 Pa D&C 197.

41. Cobb, *op. cit.* (see n. 32), p. 677.

42. *People v. Steele*, 231 Ill. 340, 83 N.E. 239.

43. Cobb, *op. cit.* (see n. 32), p. 659. Cobb here cites 51 Am Jur 2d, Licenses and Permits, 14.

44. See for example, Charles Dickens's *Bleak House*, George Eliot's *Middlemarch*, and Anthony Trollope's *The Eustace Diamonds*.

45. Walter Block and David Gordon, "Blackmail, Extortion and Free Speech: A Reply to Posner, Epstein, Nozick, and Lindgren," *Loyola of Los Angeles Law Review*, vol. 19 (1985), p. 40. Robert Nozick emphasizes the unproductive and parasitical character of blackmail in *Anarchy, State, and Utopia* (New York: Basic Books, 1974), pp. 85–86. Even though James Lindgren gives central importance to protecting the rights of third parties in his reconstructed rationale of blackmail, his major emphasis, I think, is on the unjust gain of the blackmailer: ". . . when a blackmailer threatens to expose damaging but noncriminal behavior unless paid money, he is . . . turning third party leverage to his own benefit. What makes his conduct [properly prohibitable] blackmail is that he interposes himself parasitically in an actual or potential dispute in which he lacks a sufficiently direct interest. What right has he to make money by settling other people's claims?" James Lindgren, "Unraveling the Paradox of Blackmail," *Columbia Law Review*, vol. 84 (1984), p. 702.

46. The phrase was originally coined by Glanville Williams in his "Blackmail," *The Criminal Law Review* (1954), pp. 79–92, 162–72, 240–46. The paradox, according to Williams, is that "two things that taken separately are moral and legal whites together make a moral and legal black" (p. 163).

47. Lindgren, *op. cit.* (see n. 45), p. 671.

48. Lord Mansfield, speaking of the similar crime of bribery, declared: "Whatever it is a crime to take, it is a crime to give: They are reciprocal. And . . . the attempt is a crime: it is complete on the side who offers it." (*Rex v. Vaughan*, 4 Burr. 2494, 2500, 98 Eng. Rep. 308, 311, 1769.) If the agreement of the secret criminal blackmailee to buy his accuser's silence had been his own original proposal, then it could be called a bribe in the layman's everyday sense, since it would be an effort to persuade a person to violate a trust, though in many jurisdictions it would not be called a bribe in the legal sense, because a private citizen is not a public official, like a judge or tax collector, as is required by many statutes. He does have duties to report, or at least not conceal, evidence of crimes, however, and he can commit a crime bearing another name, like "compounding a felony" for failure to discharge that duty. In that event, the secret criminal who bribes him, would be guilty of his crime as an instigator.

49. Rollin M. Perkins, *Criminal Law* (Brooklyn: The Foundation Press, Inc., 1957), p. 563.

50. *People v. Lefkovitz*, 294 Mich. 263, 293 N.W. 642 (1940).

51. Perkins, *op. cit.* (see n. 49), p. 563n. Perkins cites *Neal v. United States*, 102 F.2d 643 (8th Cir. 1939).

52. Cf. West's Ann. Cal. Pen. Code, 153: "Every person who, having knowledge of the actual commission of a crime, takes money . . . upon any agreement to abstain from prosecution thereof, or *withhold any evidence of* . . ." (emphasis added).

53. Block and Gordon, *op. cit.* (see n. 45), p. 40, n.9.

54. Like all other classes of moral duty, a duty of citizenship can be cast in the language of "my duty as a ———." My duty as a citizen to report a criminal to the police may, of course, conflict with "my duty as a father or husband," or "my duty as a Christian" or "my duty as a patriot." It is a moral commonplace that there are tragic situations in which it is very difficult to know which of two

conflicting duties is the stronger. Sometimes, it seems safe to say, one's duty as a citizen can be overridden by a more stringent moral duty of another kind. Sophocles' *Antigone* thought so.

55. See Mike Hepworth, *Blackmail: Publicity and Secrecy in Everyday Life* (London: Routledge & Kegan Paul, 1975), esp. chap. 4.

56. Cf. Hepworth, *ibid*, p. 70, where he argues that the vulnerability of government employees to blackmail by foreign espionage agents was in large part the consequence of this cultural disorder: ". . . in some situations the betrayal of state secrets proves more acceptable to the victim than the anticipated revelation of otherwise harmless preferences to a specific audience of fellow patriots."

57. W. Page Keeton, Dan B. Dobbs, Robert E. Keeton, and David G. Owen, eds., *Prosser and Keeton on the Law of Torts*, 5th ed. (St. Paul, Minn.: West Publishing Co., 1984), p. 581.

58. *Ibid.*, p. 856.

59. *Santiesteban v. Goodyear Tire and Rubber Co.*, 5th Cir., 1962, 306 F.2d 9.

60. Keeton and Prosser, *loc. cit.* (see n. 57), 857.

61. *Ibid.*

62. To those readers who think it is incorrect to speak of tort law as "not permitting," "prohibiting," "requiring," and the like, I can only repeat what I have written elsewhere:

> Our civil law does not [characteristically] tell us that we *may* inflict harmful or offensive bodily contacts on our neighbor, falsely defame him, eavesdrop on him, or collide into his vehicle, provided only that we are willing to pay just compensation to him afterwards. I think it is closer to the truth to say that the law of torts, no less than the criminal law, *prohibits* such harmful and annoying behavior. After all, we do speak of "civil *sanctions*" as well as criminal ones for enforcing legal requirements. And the law of torts holds us to certain *standards*, even—in the case of inadvertent torts—to standards of due care. All legal commentators speak of the law of torts as imposing *duties* on citizens and cite the defendant's "breach of duty" to the plaintiff as one of the conditions of civil liability. Moreover, the traditional tort procedure issues judgments of *fault*, and requires determination of which party was *to blame* for a harm. The damages paid by the defendant to the plaintiff are not just the price he pays for an already consumed benefit . . . it is thought also to be a *penalty* paid by a *law violator*, even though paid to the victim of his wrongdoing rather than to an independent authority representing the state. To interpret the law of torts as "permissive" would be almost as inaccurate as the interpretation of criminal penalties as [retroactive] licensing fees meant to discourage behavior without actually prohibiting it. The proper reply in both cases is that legal rules, in H.L.A. Hart's phrase, "are meant to be taken seriously as . . . standards of behavior" (*The Concept of Law*, Oxford, 1961, p. 39). They are more than mere price lists for various modes of permitted harmful acts. A tortfeasor may not be as stigmatized as a criminal, but he is a wrongdoer, after all, and not a mere customer.

> "Harm to Others: A Rejoinder," *Criminal Justice Ethics*, vol. 5, 1986, p. 20.

63. Fowler V. Harper and Fleming James, Jr., *The Law of Torts* (Boston: Little Brown and Co., 1956), vol. I, p. 416. The authors do not endorse this view.

64. *Loc. cit.*
65. William Blackstone, *Commentaries on the Laws of England*, vol. III, 1765 reprint (Boston: Beacon Press, 1962), p. 125.
66. This long quotation is from my "Limits to the Free Expression of Opinion" in J. Feinberg and H. Gross, eds., *Philosophy of Law* (Belmont, Calif.: Wadsworth Publishing Co., 1975). In the third edition of Feinberg and Gross (1986), the quoted passage appears on pp. 220–21.
67. Hepworth, *op. cit.* (see n. 55), p. 37. His reference is to *The Times of London*, May 8, 1895.
68. Lindgren, *op. cit.* (see n. 45), p. 702. Lindgren stretches his good point to cover all cases of informational blackmail, and thereby weakens it, I think. "Playing with someone else's chips" is what is common to, and what is wrong with all blackmail, he claims. Clearly his theory does not fit categories 3 and 4 of informational blackmail, but perhaps Lindgren would not criminalize *them*. On the other hand, his theory makes a better fit with category 2 which I would not criminalize but perhaps he would. In all cases, though, his theory overlooks the direct and primary wrong done to blackmailees while emphasizing the derivative and remote harms done to third parties (like blissfully ignorant cheated spouses). The closer the case is to the extortive labor leader example the more plausible his theory is, but many cases of informational blackmail are quite dissimilar to that model, and even in the labor leader case, one should not *completely* overlook the wrong done the blackmailee (the employer), though it is less conspicuous in that example than the wrong done to third parties (union members).
69. The Oregon coercion statute (Or. Rev. Stat. 163, 275, 1953) prohibited attempts to force another to act by "a threat to expose a crime or a secret." It allowed a narrow "claim of right" defense, permitting some disclosure threats only when used to force payment of a legitimate debt. The Oregon Supreme Court, in *State v. Robertson* (649 P.2d 569, 1953) declared the statute unconstitutional because it would prohibit such innocent threats as the hypothetical one quoted in the text. See Lindgren, *op. cit.* (see n. 45), pp. 678–79.
70. Jeffrie G. Murphy, "Blackmail: A Preliminary Inquiry," *The Monist*, vol. 63 (1980), pp. 24–25.
71. Lindgren, *op. cit.* (see n. 45), p. 683.
72. Lindgren cites an Alabama statute (Ala. Code 13-a-6-25 commentary, 1978) that is remarkable in two respects, (1) in contemplating a justification for category 1 threats, and (2) relying on prosecutorial discretion instead of guaranteed exemption for claim of right: "No explicit exemption from liability is provided for a threat to charge another with a crime where there is an honest belief that the threatened charge is true and defendant's sole purpose is to induce reasonable action to correct the believed wrong; such instances may be left to prosecutorial discretion." Lindgren, *ibid*, pp. 671–72n.
73. *Model Penal Code*, 223.4 (Official Draft and Revised Comments, 1980).
74. *Ibid.*, 212.5.
75. The quotes from Mack that follow will not be separately footnoted. They are all from an unpublished paper which he presented to an American Philosophical Association symposium on blackmail in 1980.
76. "Or imagine a case in which one party, by legally permissible trickery . . . acquired what another party truly deserves. Wouldn't it be perfectly moral for

the morally deserving party to blackmail the first party into transferring that valued good—*especially* if [but presumably not "only if"] what was threatened was precisely the revelation of the trickery. . . ?"

77. I could be legally justified in making these normally extortive threats (in self-defense or defense of others) but not legally justified in actually doing what I justifiably threatened to do. I may not shoot your wife even if you have already shot mine. That would be vengeful retaliation, not defense of self or others.

78. Lindgren, *op. cit.* (see n. 45), p. 688.

79. The closest the Model Penal Code comes to capturing the "withholding favorable information" case in its definition of theft by extortion is its paragraph (6): "[Demanding money by threatening to] testify or provide information or *withhold testimony or information* with respect to another's legal claim or defense" (italics added). But the claim to have deserved the Nobel Prize is not a *legal* claim.

80. Hepworth, *op. cit.* (see n. 55), p. 67.

81. *Ibid.*, pp. 74–77. "Commercial research" is the name for modes of finding people, e.g., by searching through data banks, whose records suggest that they may already be vulnerable to blackmail for past behavior. "Participant blackmail" is distinguished by arising out of a pre-existing relationship between the blakmailer and his victim.

82. One can imagine, however, a professional blackmailer working without accomplices, who seduces his victims without a trace of force or fraud, thus exploiting their weaknesses in the same way a prostitute or a pornographer might, and then threatening exposure unless paid off. This comes close to the line of liberal acceptability but probably falls short because the concealed initial intention to "kiss and tell . . . or else. . . ," itself was a form of duplicity, rendering the customer's uninformed consent sufficiently nonvoluntary to support a claim that he was wronged.

33. Legal Perfectionism and the Benefit Principles

1. The primary sources are Plato's *Republic* and *Laws,* and Aristotle's *Nicomachean Ethics* and *Politics.*

2. Ronald Dworkin, "Soulcraft," *New York Review of Books,* October 12, 1978, p. 18. Dworkin points out, further, that Will's theory "values civilization and amenity—what he calls in a generous conception of the word, "manners"—for their own sake, rather than as conditions under which human beings may most easily and fairly lead lives *they* find successful. It puts at the center of politics, not the rights and independence of human beings that liberals emphasize, but their duties and responsibilities."

3. George F. Will, *The Pursuit of Happiness and Other Sobering Thoughts* (New York: Harper & Row, 1978), from the Introduction, as quoted by Dworkin, *loc. cit.*

4. That this proposition is compatible with a rights-based liberalism is one of the theses of Vinit Haksar's *Liberty and Perfectionism* (New York: Oxford University Press, 1979).

5. David Hume, *An Enquiry Concerning the Principles of Morals,* originally published in 1777.

6. Aristotle, *Nic. Eth., op. cit.* (see n. 1), book II, chaps. 4 and 6.

7. John Stuart Mill, *On Liberty,* chap. II, para. 34.

8. The 1986 film *About Last Night*, based on the play *Sexual Perversity in Chicago*, by David Mamet, is about two unmarried lovers who decide to live together, an experience neither has had before. In time their quarrels become more frequent, and finally they agree to separate after an abusive exchange of grievances. The man, especially, has been selfishly unwilling to make many modifications in his former lifestyle and has been self-centered, uncooperative, and insensitive. But he leaps at the chance to make one cheap debater's point. "I haven't had sex with another woman once since we've been living together," he says with great pride. "Well, give the man a medal!," she responds derisively. Obviously, mere innocence of that kind is not *much* of a virtue, essential as it may be.

9. Quoted by Bernard Mayo in his *Ethics and the Moral Life* (London: Macmillan & Co., 1958), p. 208.

10. He might shed some tears anyway, because this sort of play-acting is part of his *role*, therefore one of his duties, as a husband. But Epictetus warns us to "Take heed, however, not to groan inwardly too." (*Enchiridion*, XVI).

11. Bertrand Russell, *A History of Western Philosophy* (New York: Simon & Schuster, 1945), p. 244.

12. He can only point out that these actions are part of the "job description" that defines what it is to occupy the role of "husband," but he cannot explain why it should be a matter of importance or binding obligation that one discharge those duties when nothing of value depends on it.

13. B.F. Skinner, *Beyond Freedom and Dignity* (Harmondsworth, Middlesex: Penguin Books, 1974), p. 70.

14. J.S. Mill *op. cit.* (see n. 7), chap. III, para. 4.

15. Martin Luther, Speech at the Diet of Worms, April 18, 1521. "Hier steh'ich, ich kann nichtanders" is inscribed on Luther's monument at Worms.

16. Skinner, *op. cit.* (see n. 13), p. 68.

17. *Ibid.*, pp. 68–69.

18. T.H. Huxley, *Methods and Results* (New York: Macmillan, 1893), Chap. 4.

19. Skinner, *op. cit.* (see n. 13), p. 69. There is no citation for the words quoted from Eliot.

20. See, for example, Keith Burgess-Jackson, "Bad Samaritanism and the Pedagogical Function of Law," *Criminal Justice Journal*, vol. 8 (1985). Burgess-Jackson there quotes other writers who ascribe a pedagogical role to criminal statutes: Aristotle in the *Nicomachaen Ethics* wrote that "Legislators make the citizens good by forming habits in them, and this is the wish of every educator, and those who do not effect it miss their mark . . ." (Ross trans., rev. ed., 1980, p. 29). In Aristotle's *Politics*, according to its translator, Ernest Barker (in *The Politics of Aristotle*, p. 367), he holds that "The purpose of [laws'] sovereignty is a moral purpose; they are 'intended to make men good and righteous.' " Waller in his contribution to *The Good Samaritan and the Law*, ed. J. Ratcliffe (University of Chicago Press, 1966, p. 141) writes: "There is general agreement today [!] that the criminal law has a strong didactic purpose. It serves to teach, in its own terrible fashion, the canons of right and wrong to the community." (To be sure judges are prone to say to the hapless criminals they have just sentenced, "I hope this teaches you a lesson," but the lesson likely to be taught is that crime does not pay, and punishment hurts, not the kind of lesson that elevates character and teaches people that in which goodness consists.) In the same book, A.N. Honoré

writes: "Rules of law which mirror moral duties have among other things, an educative function. They formulate, in a way which, though not infallible, is yet in a sense authoritative, the content of the shared morality" (p. 240).

21. See my "The Expressive Function of Punishment" in *Doing and Deserving* (Princeton, N.J.: Princeton University Press, 1970), pp. 95–118.

22. I have rejected the very concept of "moral harm" in Vol. 1, Chap. 2, §1. See also Vol. 2, Chap. 12, for arguments against moralistic paternalism.

23. Burgess-Jackson, *op. cit.* (see n. 20), pp. 3–4. In using the word "solely," though, Burgess-Jackson may have overstated his own view which in many places seems to be that moral improvement supplements quite ample harm-prevention reasons in support of bad samaritan sanctions, and elsewhere (pp. 14–19) he accepts even benefit-to-others reasons.

24. *Ibid.*, p. 10, note 21.

25. See especially *Nicomachean Ethics*, book II, chaps. 1–4, *et passim*.

26. Unless, of course, there are significant causal connections between reading or watching pornography and such violent behavior as rape, an empirical question that should be left open at the present time, with the burden of evidence-acquisition on the party claiming such a connection. See Vol. II, Chap. 11, §§7–9.

27. J.E. McTaggart, "Hegel's Theory of Punishment," *International Journal of Ethics* [now simply *Ethics*], vol. 6 (1896), pp. 482–99, reprinted in J. Feinberg and H. Gross, *Philosophy of Law* (Belmont, Calif.: Wadsworth, 1986), 3rd ed., pp. 612–21.

28. Herbert Morris, "A Paternalistic Theory of Punishment," *American Philosophical Quarterly*, vol. 18 (1981).

29. Robert Nozick, *Philosophical Explanations* (Cambridge: Harvard University Press, 1981), pp. 363–97.

30. Jean Hampton, "The Moral Education Theory of Punishment," *Philosophy & Public Affairs*, vol. 13 (1984), pp. 208–38.

31. *Ibid.*, p. 216.

32. *Ibid.*, pp. 211–12.

33. Hampton cites Georg W.F. Hegel, *Philosophy of Right*, trans. T. Knox (Oxford: Clarendon Press, 1952), para. 99, p. 246.

34. Hampton, *op. cit.* (see n. 30), p. 219.

35. *Ibid.*, p. 212.

36. *Loc. cit.*

37. *Loc. cit.*

38. "The Expressive Function of Punishment," in my *Doing and Deserving* (Princeton, N.J.: Princeton University Press, 1970), pp. 38–54.

39. J.D. Mabbott, "Punishment," *Mind*, vol. 48 (1939), p. 153. Mabbott also offers there an explanatory analogy: "A parallel may be found in the case of tact and truth. If you have to tell a friend an unpleasant truth you may do all you can to put him at his ease and spare his feelings as much as possible, while still making sure that he understands your meaning. In such a case no one would say that your offer of a cigarette beforehand or your apology afterwards are modifications of the truth, still less reasons for telling it. You do not tell the truth in order to spare his feelings, but having to tell the truth you also spare his feelings."

40. Hampton, *op. cit.* (see n. 30), p. 218.

41. See the essay "Crime, Clutchability, and Individuated Treatment" in my *Doing and Deserving, op. cit.* (see n. 38), esp. pp. 260–62.

42. Michael J. Sandel, ed., *Liberalism and its Critics* (New York: New York University Press, 1984), Introduction, p. 1.
43. Even so ardent a defender of state enforcement of religious custom as the Ayatollah Khomeini seems to endorse a relativistic account of the very practices he enforces. See note 29, Chap. 29, p. 343.
44. J.S. Mill, *On Liberty*, chap. 4, para. 12.
45. Basil Davidson, *The African Slave Trade: Precolonial History 1450–1850* (Boston/ Toronto: Little, Brown, and Co., Atlantic Monthly Press ed., 1961), p. 110. Davidson further characterizes the African system in which "stubborn idleness" (by European standards) was a virtue, and cooperation, not competition and possessiveness, was a way of life:

> Most Africans found such notions [as Cecil Rhodes's] whenever they came across them or were forced to take account of them, absurd or inexplicable. The majority of peasants and stock breeders lived in communities where the idea of private property had scarcely appeared, let alone the more objectionable notion of private enterprise. "All the land occupied by the tribe," writes Schapera of the Bantu-speaking peoples of southern Africa . . . , "is vested in the Chief, and administered by him as head of the tribe . . . the land is not his personal possession . . . The natural resources of the land—earth, water, wood, grass, clay, edible plants, and fruits—are all common property, never reserved for the use of any particular persons. It is only in regard to land for residence and cultivation that private rights are universally recognized . . ." (pp. 110–11).

How arrogant, and how mistaken it was, to call the Bantu's disposition to share a "character failing," not just by the standards of European practice, but by some transcultural, objectively true standard! The very opposite judgment would perhaps have greater plausibility.
46. James Fitzjames Stephen, *Liberty, Equality, and Fraternity* (Cambridge: Cambridge University Press, 1967), p. 61.
47. See Russell Hardin, *Collective Action* (Baltimore: Johns Hopkins University Press, 1982), esp. chaps. 1–4.
48. The situation I have in mind resembles the economists' conception of a "public good." Allen Buchanan defines such a good as "Any desired state of affairs that satisfies these conditions: (i) efforts of all or some members of a group are required to achieve the good; (ii) each member of the group regards his contributions as involving a cost; (iii) if the good is achieved, it will be produced in such a way as to be available to all members of the group, including noncontributors (jointness of supply); and (iv) if the good is produced it will be impossible or unfeasible to exclude noncontributors from partaking of it." Allen Buchanan, *Ethics, Efficiency, and the Market* (Totowa, N.J.: Rowman & Allanheld, 1985), p. 125.
49. Robert L. Simon, *Sports and Social Values* (Englewood Cliffs, N.J.: Prentice-Hall, 1985), p. 65.

Conclusion

1. Laurent B. Frantz, "The First Amendment in the Balance," *Yale Law Journal*, vol. lxxi (1962), p. 1440.

2. I have benefitted from various suggestions for this section from Tom Senor, but he is not to be blamed for the remaining confusions.

3. Most of the preceding paragraph is taken from my "Wrongful Life and the Counterfactual Element in Harming," *Social Philosophy & Policy*, vol. 4, no. 1 (1986), pp. 145–78.

4. James W. Nickel, *Making Sense of Human Rights* (Berkeley: University of California Press, 1987), p. 70.

5. John Stuart Mill, *On Liberty*, chap. III.

6. Thomas M. Scanlon, "Human Rights as a Neutral Concern," in Peter G. Brown and Douglas MacLean, eds., *Human Rights and U.S. Foreign Policy* (Lexington, Mass.: D.C. Heath, 1979), p. 88. As quoted by James W. Nickel, *Making Sense of Human Rights, op. cit.* (see n. 4), p.72.

7. Nickel, *op. cit.* (see n. 4), p. 79.

8. Ruth Benedict, *Patterns of Culture* (New York: Mentor Books, 1946), p. 235.

9. *Supra*, Chap. 29, note 2.

Index

Joel Feinberg

HARMLESS WRONG-DOING

THE MORAL LIMITS OF THE CRIMINAL LAW

Harmless Wrongdoing is the final volume of *The Moral Limits of the Criminal Law*, a four-volume work that addresses the question: what kinds of conduct may a legislature make criminal without infringing upon the moral autonomy of individual citizens? In Volume I, *Harm to Others*, Joel Feinberg illuminated the moral implications of the "harm principle" and demonstrated how it must be interpreted if it is to be a plausible guide for legislation. The second volume, *Offense to Others*, focused on the "offense principle," the principle stating that prevention of shock, disgust, or revulsion is always a morally relevant reason for legal prohibitions. Volume III, *Harm to Self*, looked at the questions associated with the coercion-legitimizing principle of "Legal Paternalism," evaluated the principle that it can be right to impose coercion on people "for their own good," whatever their own wishes in the matter, and discussed the